Lecture Notes in Computer Science   6264

Commenced Publication in 1973
Founding and Former Series Editors:
Gerhard Goos, Juris Hartmanis, and

Sokratis Katsikas   Javier Lopez
Miguel Soriano (Eds.)

Trust, Privacy and Security in Digital Business

7th International Conference, TrustBus 2010
Bilbao, Spain, August 30-31, 2010
Proceedings

 Springer

Volume Editors

Sokratis Katsikas
University of Piraeus
Digital Systems
Piraeus 18534, Greece
E-mail: ska@unipi.gr

Javier Lopez
University of Malaga
Computer Science Department
29071 Malaga, Spain
E-mail: jlm@lcc.uma.es

Miguel Soriano
Technical University of Catalonia
Department of Telematics Engineering
08034 Barcelona, Spain
E-mail: soriano@entel.upc.edu

Library of Congress Control Number: 2010932039

CR Subject Classification (1998): C.2, K.6.5, D.4.6, E.3, H.4, J.1

LNCS Sublibrary: SL 4 – Security and Cryptology

ISSN   0302-9743
ISBN-10   3-642-15151-5 Springer Berlin Heidelberg New York
ISBN-13   978-3-642-15151-4 Springer Berlin Heidelberg New York

springer.com

© Springer-Verlag Berlin Heidelberg 2010
Printed in Germany

Typesetting: Camera-ready by author, data conversion by Scientific Publishing Services, Chennai, India
Printed on acid-free paper   06/3180

Preface

This book presents the proceedings of the 7th International Conference on Trust, Privacy and Security in Digital Business (TrustBus 2010), held in Bilbao, Spain during August 30–31, 2010. The conference continued from previous events held in Zaragoza (2004), Copenhagen (2005), Krakow (2006), Regensburg (2007), Turin (2008) and Linz (2009).

The recent advances in information and communication technologies (ICT) have raised new opportunities for the implementation of novel applications and the provision of high-quality services over global networks. The aim is to utilize this 'information society era' for improving the quality of life for all citizens, disseminating knowledge, strengthening social cohesion, generating earnings and finally ensuring that organizations and public bodies remain competitive in the global electronic marketplace. Unfortunately, such a rapid technological evolution cannot be problem-free. Concerns are raised regarding the 'lack of trust' in electronic procedures and the extent to which 'information security' and 'user privacy' can be ensured.

TrustBus 2010 brought together academic researchers and industry developers, who discussed the state of the art in technology for establishing trust, privacy and security in digital business. We thank the attendees for coming to Bilbao to participate and debate the new emerging advances in this area.

The conference program included one keynote presentation and six technical paper sessions. The keynote talk, "Trust, Risk and Usage Control," was delivered by Fabio Martinelli from CNR (Italy). The reviewed paper sessions covered a broad range of topics, from access control models to security and prevention systems, and from privacy to trust and security measurements. The conference attracted many high-quality submissions, each of which was assigned to at least three referees for review, and the final acceptance rate was 37%.

We would like to express our thanks to the various people who assisted us in organizing the event and formulating the program. We are very grateful to the Program Committee members and the external reviewers, for their timely and rigorous reviews of the papers. We would also like to thank our Publication Chair, Carmen Fernandez-Gago, and Publicity Chair, Isaac Agudo. Thanks are also due to the DEXA Organizing Committee for supporting our event, and in particular to Gabriela Wagner for her help with the administrative aspects.

Finally, we would like to thank all of the authors that submitted papers for the event, and contributed to an interesting set of conference proceedings.

August 2010   Sokratis Katsikas
                                                                                      Javier Lopez
                                                                                   Miguel Soriano

Organization

Program Committee Co-chairs

Sokratis Katsikas   University of Piraeus (Greece)
Javier Lopez   University of Malaga (Spain)

General Chair

Miguel Soriano   UPC (Spain)

Publication Chair

Carmen Fernandez Gago   University of Malaga (Spain)

Publicity Chair

Isaac Agudo   University of Malaga (Spain)

Program Committee Members

Alessandro Acquisti	Carnegie Mellon University (USA)
Cristina Alcaraz	University of Malaga (Spain)
Vijay Atluri	Rutgers University (US)
Marco Casassa Mont	HP Labs Bristol (UK)
David Chadwick	University of Kent (UK)
Nathan Clarke	University of Plymouth (UK)
Frederic Cuppens	ENST Bretagne (France)
Ernesto Damiani	Università degli Studi di Milano (Italy)
Sabrina De Capitani di Vimercati	University of Milan (Italy)
Josep Domingo-Ferrer	University Rovira i Virgili (Spain)
Eduardo Fernandez	University of Castilla la Mancha (Spain)
Eduardo B. Fernandez	Florida Atlantic University (USA)
Josep L. Ferrer	University Islas Baleares (Spain)
Simone Fischer-Huebner	Karlstad University (Sweden)
Sara Foresti	University of Milan (Italy)
Jordi Forne	UPC (Spain)
Steven Furnell	University of Plymouth (UK)
Juergen Fuss	University of Applied Science in Hagenberg (Austria)

External Reviewers

Jorge Bernal Bernabé
Katrin Borcea-Pfitzmann
Katja Böttcher
Mohamed Bourimi
Bastian Braun
Christian Broser
Sebastian Clauß
Rafael Deitos
Jaromir Dobias
Stelios Dritsas
Ludwig Fuchs
Manuel Gil Pérez
Andre Groll
Stephan Heim
Jan Holle
Benjamin Kellermann
Stefan Köpsell
Tracy Ann Kosa
Ioannis Krontiris
Juan Manuel Marín Pérez

Michael Netter
Christoforos Ntantogian
Vinh Pham
Henrich C. Pöhls
Denis Royer
Rainer Schick
Agusti Solanas
Boyeon Song
Yannis Soupionis
Mark Stegelmann
Andriy Stetsko
Petr Svenda
Dionysia Triantafyllopoulou
Rolando Trujillo
Bill Tsoumas
Pavel Tucek
Alexandre Viejo
Benedikt Westermann
Lei Zhang

Table of Contents

Access Control

Security and Trust Concepts

Security for Dynamic Collaborations

Usage Control, Risk and Trust*

Leanid Krautsevich[1,2], Aliaksandr Lazouski[1,2], Fabio Martinelli[2],
Paolo Mori[2], and Artsiom Yautsiukhin[2]

[1] Department of Computer Science
University of Pisa
[2] Istituto di Informatica e Telematica
Consiglio Nazionale delle Ricerche

Abstract. In this paper we describe our general framework for usage control (UCON) enforcement on GRID systems. It allows both GRID services level enforcement of UCON as well as fine-grained one at the level of local GRID node resources. In addition, next to the classical checks for usage control: checks of conditions, authorizations, and obligations, the framework also includes trust and risk management functionalities. Indeed, we show how trust and risk issues naturally arise when considering usage control in GRID systems and services and how our architecture is flexible enough to accommodate both notions in a pretty uniform way.

1   Introduction

Usage control (UCON) is a conceptual model, developed by Park and Sandhu (e.g. see [25]), which is able to embody and encompass most of existing access control models. The main features are attribute mutability that allows a flexible management of policies and continuity of the usage decision process, i.e. the resource access has a duration and the specific authorization factors must continuously hold. This enhanced flexibility w.r.t. the usual access control frameworks, where, for instance, authorizations are checked once before the access, induces several opportunities as well as new challenges.

Usage control seems a particularly suitable model for managing resources in GRID systems. Those systems often consist of federations of resource providers and users, with many long-lived executions and several conditions and factors to be considered during the usage decision process. For instance, it is common to have GRID computations lasting for hours/days. During the access it is possible that conditions that were satisfied when the access to the computational resources was requested, change by demanding a revocation of access to the resource itself.

GRID systems allow for remote execution of code, where the user that submitted the code is often a priori unknown. This feature demands for both coarse grained usage control, managing the access to the GRID services (also taking

---

* This work has been partially supported by the EU FP7 project *Context-aware Data-centric Information Sharing* (CONSEQUENCE).

S. Katsikas, J. Lopez, and M. Soriano (Eds.): TrustBus 2010, LNCS 6264, pp. 1–12, 2010.

into account the service workflow), and fine grained control on the interactions of the code with the resources of the GRID node.

Managing resources offered by several providers to several users demands also for mechanisms to represent trust relationships, and monitor their evolutions during the system computations. Indeed, it is possible to apply stricter policies depending on the trust level of certain users as well as to reduce the trust level of users that do not respect security policies as initially declared.

Also risk naturally arises when dealing with access and usage control in GRID services in several dimensions. For instance, a wrong access decision may have a negative impact on the resources of GRID providers as well as a wrong access revocation on GRID users. While the model defines a continuous monitoring of decision factors (authorizations, conditions and obligations), in order to ensure that these factors are satisfied even when the access is in progress, from a practical perspective this control often must be implemented by a sequence of discrete events, by introducing the possibility that the decisions are not precise enough.

The paper is organized as follows. Section 2 shows a possible scenario where the notions of usage control, trust and risk naturally arise in a GRID framework. Section 3 illustrates the application of usage control to GRID systems. Section 4 shows how our architecture considers also trust management languages. Section 5 shows potential areas where risk plays a central role and how we embedded it in our framework. Finally, Section 6 concludes the paper and recalls some related work.

2   A Possible Scenario

Consider an Italian university (ItUni) which is involved in a huge GRID project. There are several servers which apart of some internal jobs provide their computational resources (i.e., CPU cycles, memory, disk space) for heavy computations of other Italian universities belonging to the same GRID. Sometimes other research organisations, which are also the subjects of the Italian Ministry of Education, ask for access to the resources. Thus, the first challenge for ItUni is to map unknown subjects to the roles defined in its domain using trust chains defining indirect relationships between those subjects and ItUni.

ItUni allows usage of its resources only to the users and computational jobs which can be considered not very risky. This risk can be connected with a number of possible threats, e.g., normal operation of the servers can be stopped; more resources than asked can be consumed; important data stored or processed by internal jobs can be stolen or destroyed, etc. On the other hand, ItUni is paid for allowing other jobs to run on its servers. Moreover, in order to use the GRID resources for its own purpose the organisation has to allow certain amount of jobs to be processed by its servers (and get some amount of points).

There are two ways of checking the riskiness of granting access to a specific subject: use trust/reputation and/or risk analysis. Trust and Reputation management helps ItUni to allow access only to the subjects which do not usually abuse granted privileges according to the past experience of GRID nodes. Risk analysis, next to taking into account past behaviour of subjects, also considers possible losses and benefits of every access. Since sometimes GRID jobs last for several days it is not enough to check reputation or risk ones before granting the access. This decision must be constantly re-evaluated during the whole session and the access should be revoked if further operation becomes too risky.

3   Usage Control in GRID

GRID technology enables resources sharing within a heterogeneous, dynamic, and distributed computational environment through Virtual Organization (VO) [9,11]. The Open GRID Service Architecture (OGSA) [13], defined a standard for sharing resources on the GRID that is based on the concept of GRID services. GRID services are designed to broadcast, provide and compose the available resources to the VO's members. The Globus Toolkit 4 (GT4) [10] is the reference implementation of GRID middleware according to the OGSA standard. The GRID Security Infrastructure (GSI) [23] implemented in GT4 provides a set of mechanisms and tools to manage accesses to GRID services. However, this support is not adequate for the kind of resource sharing defined by the GRID. For example, the default authorization in GT4 implies that an access decision is evaluated only once before starting the service, and no further controls are executed while the access is in progress. However, the usage of a services in GRID could be long-lived, lasting hours or even days. Let us suppose that the access to a service is granted if the requestor's reputation is above a given threshold. During the service execution, the reputation can be lowered as the result of other activities of the requestor. Meanwhile, one-time authorization does not affect granted rights and can not revoke the service execution because of the lowered reputation of the requestor. Hence, the security framework should allow the resource provider to specify that some factors should be reevaluated continuously during the service execution.

In [21,20,4], we advocated the adoption of the UCON model for continuous control of services usage in GRID. The Usage Control (UCON) model is a new model that encompasses and extends the existing access control models [25,30]. Its main novelty is the continuous enforcement of the security policy during the access time, because besides classical attributes, UCON also defines *mutable* attributes, whose value is updated as a consequence of accesses performed by subjects on objects. Moreover, besides the classical authorizations, UCON also introduces two new decision factors that are evaluated in the decision process: conditions and obligations. A more detailed description of usage control can be found in [17].

In our framework [21,20,4], we applied the usage control model at two levels: over GRID applications formed by a workflow of GRID services invocations, and over computational GRID services. The usage control over GRID applications monitors the workflow of services invocations, i.e., the invocation to GRID services performed by the GRID users, and the security policy defines the allowed pattern of invocations along with conditions and obligation that should

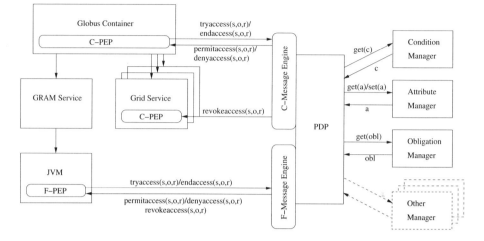

Fig. 1. Architecture of authorization framework

be satisfied before and/or during the service execution. The monitoring of GRID computational service, instead, concerns the applications that are run by remote GRID users on the local GRID node, and checks the usage of the underlying resources allocated for the service instance by the resource provider. Hence, at first the workflow level determines whether the GRID user has the right to access the service and monitors that this right is still valid while the service is running. The computational service, that in Globus is implemented by the GRAM service, is protected by a further level of control, the fine-grained one, that checks that the job submitted for execution satisfies the usage control policy while running.

The architecture we defined for the GRID service usage control is integrated in the Globus one, as shown in Figure 1, and consists of two main components: a Policy Decision Point (PDP), and a set of Policy Enforcement Point (PEP).

The PDP is the component that performs the decision process, by evaluating the security policy for each access request coming from a PEP. The PDP loads the security policy from a repository and every time an access decision is taken, updates the current state of the policy. The PDP is invoked by PEPs through the $tryaccess(s, o, r)$ control action every time a subject s requests to perform an operation r on an object o, and every time an access terminates, sending the $endaccess(s, o, r)$ control action. Moreover, the PDP continuously evaluates ongoing authorizations, conditions, and obligations according to the security policy. Indeed, the PDP invokes the proper PEP to terminate the service through the $revokeaccess(s, o, r)$ control action when an ongoing factor of the policy does not hold any more,

To process an access request, the PDP needs to evaluate various factors, and some of these factors are not directly managed by the PDP, but by some other components of the architecture. Hence, the PDP can be viewed as an orchestrator of various policy managers. Every time when a policy requires the evaluation of a factor that is not managed by the PDP, the PDP issues a request to the proper manager. Moreover, the PDP could also send some feedbacks to the managers, to affect their internal status. In the architecture shown in Figure 1, the PDP interacts with the Condition Manager, the Attribute Manager, and the Obligation Manager. However, other managers could be integrated in the architecture. For instance, Section 4 describes the integration of the RTML manager, that deals with user Trust and Reputation, and Section 5 presents the integration of a Risk manager.

The Condition Manager is invoked by the PDP every time a security policy requires the evaluation of environmental conditions. The Condition Manager interacts with the underlying system to get environmental information. As an example, the Condition Manager could retrieve the current time, workload, free memory, and so on. The Attribute Manager is in charge of retrieving fresh values of attributes. When PDP needs a value of subject's or object's attribute, it invokes the Attribute Manager. The PDP also exploits the Attribute Manager to update values of attributes. The Obligation Manager monitors the execution of obligations. If an obligation is controllable, the Obligation Manager can ask the subject to perform it. Instead, if an obligation is observable only, the Obligation Manager simply checks it. The Obligation Manager returns true to the PDP if the obligation is satisfied, or false otherwise.

The PEP components are integrated in the Globus architecture components to intercept invocations of security-relevant operations, send the $tryaccess(s, o, r)$ control action to the PDP, and suspend the operation waiting for the decision of the PDP. Each PEP enforces the decisions received by the PDP by executing or skipping the required security-relevant operation. Moreover, each PEP is also able to detect when a security-relevant operation terminates, to issue the $endaccess(s, o, r)$ control action to the PDP, and to force the termination of the operation while it is still in progress to enforce the $revokeaccess(s, o, r)$ control action. The PEPs designed to intercept service invocations are different from the ones that controls applications executed by GRID computational services. These PEPs manage distinct sets of actions on distinct objects, and they are integrated in different components of the architecture. The PEP that intercepts all requests for GRID services done by remote GRID users (C-PEP), consists of two parts. The first part is embedded in the Globus container and enforces PDP decisions done before starting the service. The second part is active during the usage and is responsible for continuous policy enforcement, and revokes access if usage conditions are not satisfied. In our architecture, a fine-grained PEP (F-PEP) is designed to monitor the execution of Java computational jobs. The F-PEP is integrated into Java Virtual Machine (JVM) that executes Java jobs submitted by GRID users, and intercept the operations that applications try to perform on the resources of the underlying machine. The interactions among PEPs and PDP are executed according to a message exchange protocol, and are implemented through two messages dispatchers, C-Message and F-Message engine, for the two levels.

4   Trust and Reputation Management with Usage Control for GRID

Besides the need of monitoring the usage of the shared resources after the access right has been granted to GRID users, security management in GRID environment also requires to establish secure relationships between GRID resource providers and users. As a matter of fact, direct trust relationships among GRID users may not exist a priori, because during the VO formation phase, no trust relationships are required to be in place among the parties that are joining the organization. Hence, the security support should be able to evaluate whether an unknown VO member that requires to access the local resources is reliable enough to grant him the access. Moreover, the access should be granted even if the user didn't subscribe to the GRID node before. The standard authorization system provided by the Globus Toolkit is static, because the identity of each authorized user is statically mapped on a local account that is exploited to execute remote jobs on behalf of the user. Hence, given a GRID resource R, only the users that have been previously registered on R can access the services provided by R. This feature is a limitation in an open and distributed environment such as GRID.

In [6,5], we proposed to exploit Trust and Reputation management to enhance the GRID security support. In particular, in [6] we proposed the integration of an extended version of the RTML framework in the Globus authorization infrastructure to grant access rights taking into account the trust relationships that each VO member collects as a consequence of his interactions with other GRID resources. The Role-based Trust Management framework (RTML) [18], [27] combines the strength of Trust-Management (TM) and Role-Based Access Control (RBAC), providing policy language, semantics, deduction engine, and concrete tools to manage access control and authorization in large-scale and decentralized systems. The trust relationships are expressed in form of credentials, issued by the GRID sites, that define the roles that a given user holds in those domains. Each role is paired with a set of privileges on the resources of the domain, and it is enforced by creating new local accounts with the corresponding set of rights. The set of credentials is dynamic, because new credentials could be added by other GRID sites and some of the existing ones could be expired. When an unknown user asks to access the GRID services provided by a given domain, he submits the credentials that grant him some roles in some (other) domains. The RTML authorization system computes the roles that the user holds in the local domain by combining the credential submitted by the user with the local access rules, that represent the trust relationships that the local domain has with other organizations. If at least one of the roles found by the RTML system grants the right to access the requested service, than the access is allowed, otherwise is denied.

Example 1. Figure 4 shows an example of RTML user's credentials and provider's access rules. In this case, the user Alice has the role *GRIDAdmin* in the domain *CNR*, and the role *user* in the domain *ERCIM*. Alice exploits these credentials

1. *CNR.GRIDAdmin(mat='12345', firstname='alice', lastname='rossi')* ← *Alice*
2. *ERCIM.user(number='IS137', firstname='alice', lastname='rossi')* ← *Alice*

User's credentials

1. *ItUni.GRIDGuest* ← *CNR.GRIDAdmin(mat=?,firstname=ref_{first},lastname= ref_{last}) ∩ ERCIM.user(number=?, firstname=ref_{first}, lastname=ref_{last})*

Provider's access rules

Fig. 2. Example of user's credentials and provider's access rules in RTML

to access the services of domain *ItUni*, because the access rules of this domain grants the role *GRIDGuest* to those users that have the roles *GRIDAdmin* in *CNR*, and *user* in *ERCIM*.

In [5], we enhanced the previous approach by extending the RTML framework to deal with a quantitative notion of reputation, and by integrating the resulting framework within a preliminary prototype of fine-grained usage control system for GRID. Hence, the resulting architecture has the capabilities of: *i)* allowing the access to GRID computational resources to unknown users on the basis of the reputation paired to them as a result of their previous interactions with other (trusted) GRID nodes, *ii)* monitoring the operations executed by the user's applications on the local resources once the access right has been granted according to the Usage Control model and also exploiting Trust and Reputation as decision factors collected by the PDP to perform the decision process, and *iii)* providing feedbacks on the behaviour of the user that define the new reputation of the user according to this GRID provider. These feedbacks (represented as credentials) will be exploited by other GRID nodes to decide whether to grant or not some access rights to the user in their domains.

From the architectural point of view, the extended version of the RTML framework has been interfaced with the PDP like the managers of other decision factors, and it is invoked by the PDP, when the security policy requires the evaluation of the roles held by a specific user or of his Reputation. The RTML framework exploits both the credentials submitted by the user and the ones stored in the local repository of the GRID node to infer the roles held by the GRID user and his Reputation. The result is returned to the PDP that combines it with the other factors expressed in the policy to determine the required access right.

5   Approach for Risk-Based Usage Control

Allowing access to a resource is always connected with a risk that the resource will be abused. It is not always possible to allow only trusted subjects to access a resource. This problem becomes even more important when we allow access for unknown users (using Trust Management, see Section 4). Such assignment could be too coarse. Therefore, we would like to allow access only to the subjects which, we believe, will not abuse its privileges. One way of doing this is to use reputation of the subject, as shown in Section 4. A more explicit way of taking this risk into account is to compute possible losses, using a well-known formula: $loss = probability \times impact$ and compare these losses with potential benefits.

The behaviour of the system we consider is the following. A resource provider and a resource consumer (subject) make an agreement about the usage of a resource (object). The resource consumer pays the agreed amount in advance the the resource provider shares the resources. In case the resource provider decides that the access should be revoked it pays money back (full amount). Naturally, the resource provider suffers from some losses if the resource consumer abuses its privileges as well as when the access is revoked while the resource consumer behaves well (loss of reputation). Revoking access of a resource consumer which misbehaves does not result in any loss (though, some benefit can be assigned to this case if needed).

Let C_B be the benefit a resource provider gets if it allows access to its resources; C_L be the losses the resource provider suffers if the resource consumer abuses its privileges in some way; C'_L be the losses the resource provider suffers if it revokes the access when the resource consumer behaved well; and p be the probability that the privileges will be abused by the consumer. In order to make a rational decision we should compare the resulting cost in case access is allowed with the cost when the access is revoked. Algebraically, we can show this relation for access decision making as follows:

$$C_B - C_L * p \lessgtr -C'_L(1-p) \tag{1}$$

The decision to allow access should be made if the left part of the Equation 1 is greater than the right one. Such situation means that it is more profitable to allow access rather than to deny access. Naturally, the access should be denied/revoked if we have the reverse condition.

A subject can abuse its privileges in different ways (make a server unavailable, install a back door, damage sensitive data, etc.) and every specific abuse cause different amount of losses. Thus, we need to consider every loss separately (C_L^i). In order to collect and process statistics required for determining the probabilities of some violation (p^i) we can use a limited set of such violations. Now, every entity in the GRID can collect such statistics about violations done by its users and share this statistics with other providers. E.g., in the simplest case we can use three well-known aspects of security for identifying these types of violation: i) loss of Confidentiality; ii) loss of Integrity iii) loss of Availability similar to [7]. For a more fine-grained analysis more elaborated list is required.

Equation 1 can be rewritten as follows:

$$C_B - \sum_{\forall i} C_L^i * p^i \lessgtr -C'_L \prod_{\forall i}(1 - p^i) \tag{2}$$

Access control models empowered with risk analysis [28,7,22,2] use a similar strategy to decide if access should be allowed or denied. Such model is based on the idea that the required values (benefits, probabilities, and costs) do not change during the whole session. But GRID projects may last for hours and days. Some parameters may change during a usage session and the validity of access decision made long time ago must be reconsidered. Moreover, existing access control models consider that access decision is based on attributes of the resource requestor only. In fact, in some situations environment and attributes of other resource requestors may affect the decision making process.

There are two parameters which can change during the access session: benefit and amount of losses. These values often depend on the attributes of other partners and environmental conditions. Naturally, probability of some misbehaviour for a concrete subject also may change, though this change happens not so sharply.

Example 2. Benefit, which ItUni gains, can be increased if there is a need for the ItUni to receive points to use the GRID for its purposes (points are given for allowing other partners to use the resources and consumed when resources of others are used). Benefits can be decreased if one of primary partners asks for resources while a third party uses most of them. On the other hand, losses can be increased when some sensitive data are processed by the servers.

In other words, losses and benefits are not constant during the access session, but a result of some function which depends on some attributes. Both these function require knowledge of the context and can be defined precisely only by experts. Sometimes it is a manager which simply should change the values. Note, that this change does not required rewriting of policies and evolvement of security staff. The probabilities of violation are simply attributes of subjects.

Example 3. The computation of losses in ItUni can be a simple summing function, which sums up losses of all sensitive data processed in by the servers. The need of points can be expressed as the losses caused by idle of the projects ItUni wants to execute with GRID. This value is added to the overall payment (benefit) for usage of the resources.

A risk manager can be easily added to our architecture shown in Figure 1. This manager is just another manager block. In order to make a decision about the access the risk manager needs to know: 1) what kind of threats must be taken into account; 2) functions or values for losses and benefits and required attributes; 3) probabilities of violation, which are just attributes of the subject. Possible threats and functions for benefits and losses are described in access policies. Current values required for computation of risk are taken from the PDP which, in its turn, gets attributes from the Attribute and Condition Managers. As a result, the risk manager returns a boolean result to the PDP: allow or deny access.

6   Conclusion and Related Work

In the paper we described our architecture for usage control on GRID. This architecture allows to check conditions, authorisations, and obligations during various time of a session. Moreover, the architecture also supports the trust management functionality. This functionality allows to grant access to unknown subjects on the basis of the trust relationships that he collected with other members of the VO. Reputation is added to the functionality of the architecture in order to deny access for those subjects which are considered not trustworthy enough. Finally, risk assessment helps to make a rational decision about access based on the analysis of losses and benefits. The architecture also considers that some parameters may change in time (e.g., reputation and risk) and, thus, provides more flexibility in access management.

There is some related work on the topics of this paper. As a matter of fact, some attempts have been done to enhance GRID security adopting standard authorization engines, such as VOMS, CAS, PERMIS and Akenti [1,3,12,26], but none of them provide continuous monitoring of service usage. Instead, in [29] the inventors of UCON also propose the adoption of their model in collaborative computing systems, such as the GRID. Their approach is based on a centralized repository for attribute management, and the authors adopt the push mode for immutable attributes, i.e. these attributes are submitted to GRID services by the user itself, and the pull mode for mutable attributes, i.e. the values of these attributes are collected when the policy evaluation is executed. Security policies are expressed using XACML.

Although risk assessment has been applied to access control by several authors, we are only aware of two papers on UCON and risk, namely [16,15]. In these papers we considered different aspects of applying risk in the UCON model: in [15] we assessed the risk caused by unfresh values of attributes, while in [16] the problem was to select the less risky service provider and control usage of client's data after granting the access. On the other hand, the notion of risk has been applied to several access control models. Indeed, risk for access control can be used as a static parameter to help a policy designer to assign privileges having possible losses in mind [19,14]. But a more promising scenario is when risk is considered to be dynamic [28,7,22]. N. N. Diep et. al., [7] explicitly show that risk should be competed and the decision is made comparing the risk value with a threshold. On the contrary, L. Zhang et. al., [28] R. W. McGraw [22] do not pay attention to how risk is computed, but state that the decision should be made comparing possible losses and benefits. Q. Ni et. al., [24] considered most of the parameters required for computation of risk as static, but used access quota which reduces with increasing of the amount of performed actions (aggregating risk of these actions). This change of quota can be seen as the change of the benefit value in terms of our model. There are also several papers which pay more attention to how to integrate risk in access control policies rather than how to use risk for making an access decision [2,8].

References

1. Alfieri, R., Cecchini, R., Ciaschini, V., dell Agnello, L., Frohner, A., Gianoli, A., Lorentey, K., Spataro, F.: VOMS: An authorisation system for virtual organizations. In: Proceedings of 1st European Across Grid Conference (2003)

2. Aziz, A.B., Foley, A.S., Herbert, A.J., Swart, A.G.: Reconfiguring role based access control policies using risk semantics. Journal of High Speed Networks 15(3), 261–273 (2006)

3. Chadwick, D., Otenko, A.: The PERMIS X.509 role-based privilege management infrastructure. In: Seventh ACM Symposium on Access Control Models and Technologies, pp. 135–140. ACM Press, New York (2002)

4. Colombo, M., Lazouski, A., Martinelli, F., Mori, P.: Controlling the usage of grid services. International Journal of Computational Science (2010)

5. Colombo, M., Martinelli, F., Mori, P., Petrocchi, M., Vaccarelli, A.: Fine grained access control with trust and reputation management for globus. In: Meersman, R., Tari, Z. (eds.) OTM 2007, Part II. LNCS, vol. 4804, pp. 1505–1515. Springer, Heidelberg (2007)

6. Colombo, M., Martinelli, F., Mori, P., Vaccarelli, A.: Extending the globus architecture with role-based trust management. In: Moreno Díaz, R., Pichler, F., Quesada Arencibia, A. (eds.) EUROCAST 2007. LNCS, vol. 4739, pp. 448–456. Springer, Heidelberg (2007)

7. Diep, N.N., Hung, L.X., Zhung, Y., Lee, S., Lee, Y.-K., Lee, H.: Enforcing access control using risk assessment. In: ECUMN '07: Proceedings of the Fourth European Conference on Universal Multiservice Networks, Washington, DC, USA, pp. 419–424. IEEE Computer Society, Los Alamitos (2007)

8. Dimmock, N., Belokosztolszki, A., Eyers, D., Bacon, J., Moody, K.: Using trust and risk in role-based access control policies. In: Proceedings of the 9th ACM Symposium on Access Control Models and Technologies, pp. 156–162. ACM, New York (2004)

9. Foster, I.: The anatomy of the grid: Enabling scalable virtual organizations. In: Sakellariou, R., Keane, J.A., Gurd, J.R., Freeman, L. (eds.) Euro-Par 2001. LNCS, vol. 2150, p. 1. Springer, Heidelberg (2001)

10. Foster, I.: Globus toolkit version 4: Software for service-oriented systems. In: Jin, H., Reed, D., Jiang, W. (eds.) NPC 2005. LNCS, vol. 3779, pp. 2–13. Springer, Heidelberg (2005)

11. Foster, I., Kesselman, C., Nick, J., Tuecke, S.: The physiology of the grid: An open grid service architecture for distributed system integration. Globus Project (2002), http://www.globus.org/research/papers/ogsa.pdf

12. Foster, I., Kesselman, C., Pearlman, L., Tuecke, S., Welch, V.: A community authorization service for group collaboration. In: Proceedings of the 3rd IEEE Int. Workshop on Policies for Distributed Systems and Networks (POLICY 2002), pp. 50–59 (2002)

13. Foster, I., Kishimoto, H., Savva, A., Berry, D., Djaoui, A., Grimshaw, A., Horn, B., Maciel, F., Siebenlist, F., Subramaniam, R., Treadwell, J., Reich, J.V.: The open grid service architecture (ogsa), version 1.5. Open Grid Forum Document Series: GFD-I.080 (2006), http://www.ogf.org/documents/GFD.80.pdf

14. Han, Y., Hori, Y., Sakurai, K.: Security policy pre-evaluation towards risk analysis. In: Proceedings of the 2008 International Conference on Information Security and Assurance (ISA 2008), Washington, DC, USA, pp. 415–420. IEEE Computer Society, Los Alamitos (2008)

15. Krautsevich, L., Lazouski, A., Martinelli, F., Yautsiukhin, A.: Risk-aware usage decision making in highly dynamic systems. In: Proceedings of the Fifth International Conference on Internet Monitoring and Protection, Barcelona, Spain (May 2010)

16. Krautsevich, L., Lazouski, A., Martinelli, F., Yautsiukhin, A.: Risk-based usage control for service oriented architecture. In: Proceedings of the 18th Euromicro Conference on Parallel, Distributed and Network-Based Processing. IEEE Computer Society Press, Los Alamitos (2010)
17. Lazouski, A., Martinelli, F., Mori, P.: A survey of usage control in computer security. Computer Science Review (4), 81–99 (2010)
18. Li, N., Mitchell, J., Winsborough, W.: Design of a role-based trust management framework. In: Symposium on Security and Privacy, pp. 114–130. IEEE Computer Society, Los Alamitos (2002)
19. Li, Y., Sun, H., Chen, Z., Ren, J., Luo, H.: Using trust and risk in access control for grid environment. In: Proceedings of the 2008 International Conference on Security Technology, Washington, DC, USA, pp. 13–16. IEEE Computer Society, Los Alamitos (2008)
20. Martinelli, F., Mori, P.: On usage control for grid systems. Future Generation Computer Systems 26(7), 1032–1042 (2010)
21. Martinelli, F., Mori, P., Vaccarelli, A.: Towards continuous usage control on grid computational services. In: ICAS-ICNS '05: Proceedings of the Joint International Conference on Autonomic and Autonomous Systems and International Conference on Networking and Services, p. 82. IEEE Computer Society, Los Alamitos (2005)
22. McGraw, R.W.: Risk-adaptable access control (radac), http://csrc.nist.gov/news_events/privilege-management-workshop/radac-Paper0001.pdf (September 16, 2009)
23. Nagaratnam, N., Janson, P., Dayka, J., Nadalin, A., Siebenlist, F., Welch, V., Foster, I., Tuecke, S.: Security architecture for open grid services. Global Grid Forum Recommendation (2003)
24. Ni, Q., Bertino, E., Lobo, J.: Risk-based access control systems built on fuzzy inferences. In: Proceedings of the 5th ACM Symposium on Information, Computer and Communications Security, pp. 250–260. ACM Press, New York (2010)
25. Park, J., Sandhu, R.: The UCON ABC usage control model. ACM Transactions on Information and System Security (TISSEC) 7(1), 128–174 (2004)
26. Thompson, M., Essiari, A., Mudumbai, S.: Certificate-based authorization policy in a pki environment. ACM Transactions on Information and System Security (TISSEC) 6(4), 566–588 (2003)
27. Winsborough, W., Mitchell, J.: Distributed credential chain discovery in trust management. Journal of Computer Security 11(1), 36–86 (2003)
28. Zhang, L., Brodsky, A., Jajodia, S.: Toward information sharing: Benefit and risk access control (barac). In: Proceedings of the 7th International Workshop on Policies for Distributed Systems and Networks, Washington, DC, USA, pp. 45–53. IEEE Computer Society, Los Alamitos (2006)
29. Zhang, X., Nakae, M., Covington, M.J., Sandhu, R.: Toward a usage-based security framework for collaborative computing systems. ACM Transactions on Information and System Security (TISSEC) (2008)
30. Zhang, X., Parisi-Presicce, F., Sandhu, R., Park, J.: Formal model and policy specification of usage control. ACM Transactions on Information and System Security (TISSEC) 8(4), 351–387 (2005)

Attacking Image Recognition CAPTCHAs
A Naive but Effective Approach

Christoph Fritsch, Michael Netter, Andreas Reisser, and Günther Pernul

Department of Information Systems,
University of Regensburg, 93053 Regensburg, Germany
{christoph.fritsch,michael.netter,andreas.reisser,guenther.pernul}
@wiwi.uni-regensburg.de
http://www-ifs.uni-regensburg.de

Abstract. The landscape of the World Wide Web today consists of a vast amount of services. While most of them are offered for free, the service providers prohibit their malicious usage by automated scripts. To enforce this policy, CAPTCHAs have emerged as a reliable method to setup a Turing test to distinguish between human and computers. Image recognition CAPTCHAs as one type of CAPTCHAs promise high human success rates. In this paper however, we develop an successful approach to attack this type of CAPTCHA. To evaluate our attack we implemented a publicly available tool, which delivers promising results for the HumanAuth CAPTCHA and others. Based upon our findings we propose several techniques for improving future versions of image recognition CAPTCHAs.

Keywords: CAPTCHA, Image Recognition CAPTCHA, HumanAuth, Experimentations, Security Analysis.

1 Introduction

Today's highly networked world is based on a vast amount of electronic services provided and requested via the world wide web. A large number of these services, i.e. e-mail and social networks, is available free of charge, solely requiring the user to register with the service provider. Yet the last decade has shown an increasing interest in abusing Internet services for malicious economical reasons. E-mail accounts, frequently available free of charge after initial registration, are misused for sending SPAM and phising mails to a plethora of plagued Internet users. There are still many more impermissible but still feasible and reasonably economic ways to abuse services trough the Internet.

To prevent corruptive usage of these services by automated scripts and thereby mitigate the threads illustrated above, in the majority of cases it is sufficient to remotely distinguish between humans and machines. Different approaches for such so-called Turing tests, generally known as CAPTCHAs[1], HIPs[2] or POSHs[3]

---

[1] Completely Automated Public Turing test to tell Computers and Humans Apart.
[2] Human Interactive Proof.
[3] Puzzle Only Solvable by Humans.

S. Katsikas, J. Lopez, and M. Soriano (Eds.): TrustBus 2010, LNCS 6264, pp. 13–25, 2010.
© Springer-Verlag Berlin Heidelberg 2010

have been proposed and are currently under active development and deployed to various systems. All of them are built upon problems that can easily be solved by humans but are very hard for machines to solve. Likewise, problems that emerged to be very hard challenges in the field of artificial intelligence (AI) are often implemented in one form or another into CAPTCHAS.

In this paper we present an approach, that does not try to solve the hard AI problem behind CAPTCHAS but forges a different solution, also known as side-channel attack. We focus on elementary image processing and color value distribution calculations to precompute characteristic attributes for all images of the chosen image recognition CAPTCHA implementation. Based on these characteristic attributes, our approach is able to recognize randomly distorted CAPTCHA images with impressive precision. We evaluated the applicability of our approach against several implementations (HumanAuth, Microsoft ASIRRA, UMIST FACES) to prove its reliability.

The main contributions of this paper are the following: We develop an attack on image recognition CAPTCHAS, called PixelMap. We evaluate our approach, attacking several image recognition CAPTCHAS with very promising results. Based upon our findings we propose several techniques to harden future image recognition CAPTCHAS from being vulnerable to this kind of attacks. Furthermore we implemented a prototype tool to show the practical applicability of the presented approach.

The remainder of this work is structured as follows: We start in Chapter 2 with an overview of related work and other approaches for automatically solving CAPTCHAS. Subsequently, in Chapter 3 we briefly explain the general CAPTCHA approach and different kinds of CAPTCHAS before we comprehensively introduce and evaluate our approach for attacking image recognition CAPTCHAS in general and the HumanAuth scheme in particular in Chapter 4. In Chapter 5 we infer ideas for both, improving our attack and tweaking image modification procedures to impede future attacks. Finally, Chapter 6 summarizes our findings.

2   Related Work

The first thoughts related to the field of 'Automated Turing Tests' were written down by Naor in 1997 [9]. Since the introduction of the term CAPTCHA by von Ahn et al. [12] a wide variety of CAPTCHAS showing different characteristics have been developed. Banday and Sha differ between three classes: Text-based (OCR), image-based and audio-based CAPTCHAS [1]. As CAPTCHAS are used for security purposes, different attack-schemes have emerged. Most attacks are based on OCR, meaning that they try to solve the underlying AI problem [8], [7], [14].

Furthermore, side-channel attacks exist trying to circumvent the AI problem. For example, Hernandez-Castro et al. propose a side-channel attack scheme on Microsoft's image-recognition based CAPTCHA ASIRRA [6] and the HumanAuth CAPTCHA (see Chapter 3.2), using different statistical test on the ASIRRA database and the HumanAuth image library. In [5] another attack on ASIRRA has been published, using support vector machines together with color and text processing for classification.

Yan and El Ahmad published an attack, using both, side-channel techniques as well as tackling the AI-problem, on an OCR-resistant text-based CAPTCHA [16]. The authors combine different techniques: First, they automatically separate foreground text from background to perform a text-segmentation. By counting the number of foreground pixels in each segment, they are able to identify characters according to an unique pixel count in most of the time, using a dictionary approach additionally in order to reveal unidentified characters.

3 CAPTCHA – A Modern Kind of Turing-Test?

In the following we shortly lay out background and implementation of different kinds of CAPTCHAs before we briefly pick up image recognition CAPTCHAs and HumanAuth as the implementation we attacked in particular.

3.1 Background and Alternatives

A CAPTCHA is defined as a challenge-response test, generated by a computer, that only a human can solve. Hence CAPTCHAs are suitable to prevent corruptive usage of web services by automated scripts. Since Ahn et al. [12] proposed the concept of CAPTCHAs, industry and researchers have developed a variety of different CAPTCHAs. Usually CAPTCHAs are based on the three principles developed by Chew and Tygar [3]: (1) Easy for humans to solve. (2) Hard for computers to solve. (3) Easy to generate and verify.

Hard artificial intelligence (AI) problems are often used to construct CAPTCHAs fulfilling the first and the second principle. Those problems are difficult to solve without special knowledge, i.e. the problem context, which is usually available to humans but not to computers. Several types of CAPTCHAs exist relying on various human sensory abilities, such as seeing and hearing.

The third principle is hard to fulfill. Similar to cryptographic functions and for security reasons, the algorithm to create a CAPTCHA is usually publicly available. Therefore a CAPTCHA generation algorithm must be able to quickly create a large number of unpredictable tests. Furthermore, the verification algorithm must know the solution a priori, since the verification is done by a computer that itself cannot solve the generated CAPTCHA.

To solve the verification problem two types of CAPTCHAs have emerged [4]: Algorithm- and database-based CAPTCHAs. The first uses an algorithm that is initialized with a secret random number to derive a challenge, allowing the verification to prove or disprove the test response. Thus the security and effectiveness for this type of CAPTCHAs depends on the secrecy of the random number. The second type employs a large database of preclassified challenges and an algorithm to randomly select single challenges. Using the classification, the verification algorithm can evaluate the test response.

The underlying principle of the most widespread type of CAPTCHAs is optical character recognition (OCR). The correct identification of characters in an image

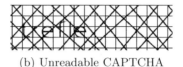

(a) Google CAPTCHA   (b) Unreadable CAPTCHA

Fig. 1. OCR-based CAPTCHAS

is a hard AI problem, especially if the characters are distorted (see Figure 1(a)). Using the definition introduced above, OCR CAPTCHAS are usually algorithm-based. The advantage of this type of CAPTCHA is the ability to easily generate a large number of text strings, that are distorted and displayed as a CAPTCHA. However this approach has a major shortcoming. Text with minimal distortion is easily readable by current OCR algorithms. Introducing more noise makes the CAPTCHA very hard to solve even for humans (see Figure 1(b)) [15]. Thus there is a small gap between human and non-human success rates [4] and human computer interaction (HCI) research is heavily involved.

To overcome the shortcomings of OCR-based CAPTCHAS, several approaches have been proposed using different types of AI problems, such as the recognition of spoken letters (so-called audio CAPTCHAS) and image classification.

3.2 Image Recognition CAPTCHAS

Chew and Tygar [3] were among the first to use images (usually photographs) to create a new type of CAPTCHAS, called image CAPTCHA. While several variations of image CAPTCHAS exist, the kind we focus on – image recognition CAPTCHAS – requires to understand what is depicted on an image which constitutes a hard AI problem [2]. Image recognition CAPTCHAS are usually database-based, thus requiring a database of preclassified images. Microsoft's ASIRRA is a well-known example [4]. ASIRRA presents a list of cat and dog images, asking the user to identify the cat images.

Studies indicate that the biggest advantage of image recognition CAPTCHAS is the improved human success rate compared to OCR-based CAPTCHAS [3], [4]. The main shortcoming is the dependency on a database of images that are preclassified by humans. Furthermore the database needs to be large and updated frequently with new images. Otherwise an adversary can create hashes of all images (similar to the rainbow table approach in cryptography [10]) and lookup a questioned image hash in his database.

3.3 The HumanAuth CAPTCHA

HumanAuth[4] is an image recognition CAPTCHA implementation, written in PHP and released under the GPL version 2 license. It presents to the user nine images chosen from an enclosed image database, three of them being *nature* and the

---

[4] http://sourceforge.net/projects/humanauth/

other six images being *nonnature* images. To solve the CAPTCHA, the user has to select the three *nature* images. HumanAuth constitutes a hard AI problem as the user has to understand what the images represent.

In order to protect from side-channel attacks, HumanAuth places a randomly positioned watermark on every image, rendering a precalculation of image hashes for each image in the database useless.

4   PixelMap – An Approach to Attack Image CAPTCHAS

Within this section we present PixelMap as our approach to attack image recognition CAPTCHAS, especially the previously mentioned HumanAuth implementation. The basic idea behind PixelMap is that even distorted images are at least very similar for the better part of the image area.

4.1   General Approach

Based on a CAPTCHA's freely available database of categorized source images (the learn images), we first pre-calculate a characteristic and distinguishing attribute, our so-called PixelMap (see Section 4.2) for each image (step 1 in Figure 2). To automatically solve a CAPTCHA, we calculate the PixelMap for each of the 'test images' (step 2 in Figure 2) and compare it to the pre-calculated PixelMaps of the original image database (step 3 in Figure 2). This comparison detects the 'learn image' which is most similar to the current test image. We know the learn image's category from the learning phase and assume the same classification for the test image. For the HumanAuth example this means that we finally pick a test image as *nature* image if the most similar learn image is classified as *nature* and vice versa.

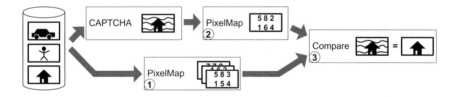

Fig. 2. PixelMap – Approach Outline

Please note that the image comparison has to be conducted in a fuzzy manner as the test image is distorted in some way or another, for example by an overlaid watermark. These image distortions however, do regularly not affect the whole image but only a minor part of the image area. Our analysis has shown that throughout the remaining image area, corresponding learn and test are at least very similar if not completely identical.

4.2   Fuzzy Image Recognition Algorithm

Algorithms 1, 2 and 3 show the foundations of our fuzzy image comparison approach. As mentioned above, we calculate a PixelMap based on which we compare two images fuzzily.

Algorithm 1. Image Classification Algorithm

```
function COMPUTEPIXELMAP(img)
    pixelMap ← ARRAY[img.WIDTH * img.HEIGHT]
    k ← 0
    for all pxl ∈ img do
        pixelMap[k] ← pxl.ALPHA + pxl.RED + pxl.GREEN + pxl.BLUE
        k ← k + 1
    end for
    return pixelMap
end function
```

Each single pixel of an image consists of red, green, blue (RGB) and alpha values. The mixture of the RGB-values establishes the color of the pixel while the alpha value represents its transparency. All four values vary within the range from 0 to 255. Our PixelMap is simply calculated by summing up the RGB and alpha values for each single pixel of an image, resulting in a sum between 0 and 1020. For example a purely red pixel thus gets the value 510 as its red value is 255, its alpha value is as well 255 because pixel opacity is 100%, and the remaining green and blue values are 0. Please note that consequently the resulting PixelMaps for i.e. purely red and purely green images do not differ but are exactly identical. Algorithm 1 shows the calculation of the PixelMap in pseudo code. This PixelMap is pre-calculated and cached together with the classification for each undistorted image of the underlying image database.

Algorithm 2. Image Identification Algorithm

```
 1: function UNCOVERIMAGE(testimg, img_class_db)
 2:     max_sim_img
 3:     max_sim ← 0
 4:     for all img ∈ img_class_db do
 5:         sim ←CompareImages(testimg, img)
 6:         if sim > max_sim then
 7:             max_sim_img ← img
 8:             max_sim ← sim
 9:         end if
10:     end for
11:     return max_sim_img
12: end function
```

To uncover the classification of a test image, we check it against the image database. Algorithm 2 shows the basic procedure. Based on its previously calculated PixelMap we compare the possibly distorted test image fuzzily against each single undistorted learn image in the image database. As a result we receive the most similar learn image from which we know its classification.

Algorithm 3. Fuzzy Image Comparison Algorithm

1: **function** COMPAREIMAGES($img1$, $img2$)
2:     $no\_identical\_pxls \leftarrow 0$
3:     **for all** $pxl\_id1 \in img1$ and $pxl\_id2 \in img2$ **do**
4:         $sim \leftarrow$ Compare(pxl_id1, pxl_id2)
5:         **if** $sim < THRESHOLD$ **then**
6:             $no\_identical\_pxls \leftarrow no\_identical\_pxls + 1$
7:         **end if**
8:     **end for**
9:     **return** ($no\_identical\_pxls/all\_pxl$)
10: **end function**

Finally, the pseudo code of our unpretentious image comparison algorithm is shown in Algorithm 3. It simply accepts two images as inputs which are fuzzily compared pixel by pixel based on the values of their PixelMaps. The fuzziness is implemented by a threshold which defines by which amount the pixel values of a single pixel in both images may differ before this pixel is rated as not matching. For our current approach a threshold of 20, which is about 2 percent of the maximum pixel sum, shaped up as suitable from several tests. The fuzzy image comparison algorithm simply returns the percentage of pixels that are similar between both images within the defined threshold.

As a result of these three fundamental building blocks of our image comparison approach, we receive for each distorted test image the unmodified image that is most similar to it together with its classification and a numeric similarity value ranging between 0-100 percent. Figure 3(a) shows the result in a graphical form. The abscissa marks all images, i.e. nature and non-nature images, from the image database while the ordinate marks the similarity of the test image to each of the learn images. Figure 3(a) is calculated using the original HumanAuth image database and a test image generated by the original HumanAuth implementation therefore containing a watermark. As can be seen from the graph, the similarity between the test image and the learn image most similar to it is about 85 percent. In other words, almost 85 percent of all pixels of the learn and the test image do not vary more then the previously defined threshold. Of particular interest is the significant gap between the similarity to the single most similar image (the peak in Figure 3(a)) and the much smaller similarity to all all other images. This result suggests that test images have to be distorted significantly before our algorithm does no longer accurately match correct test and base images (see Figure 6).

4.3 Evaluation

As we have shown in Figure 3(a), our image identification approach quite clearly identifies single distorted images based on the HumanAuth CAPTCHA implementation. To evaluate our approach in more detail, we checked it more accurately against HumanAuth and applied it to several other CAPTCHA image databases.

To effectively evaluate our approach, we implemented a HumanAuth simulator within our prototype (see Section 4.4). The simulator randomly choses 3 nature and 6 non-nature images from the image database and embeds the HumanAuth default watermark using the default opacity. In a second step we fed these distorted images into our image identification algorithm from which we receive the 9 most similar undistorted images. Finally, we checked whether the correct undistorted images have been uncovered. If and only if (a) the 3 nature images have been uncovered correctly as nature images and (b) no further actually non-nature image has wrongly been classified as nature image, the CAPTCHA is solved correctly. Figure 3(b) shows the results for one hundred simulator rounds (marked on the abscissa). The lower dotted black line shows the minimum similarity of correctly identified nature images to the image it has been derived from. The upper dashed blue line shows the success rate for solving the HumanAuth CAPTCHA, i.e. the percentage of correctly classified distorted nature images. As can easily be seen, our approach exhibits a 100 percent accuracy for the default HumanAuth settings. These results remained stable for several test runs with randomly selected images and watermark positions.

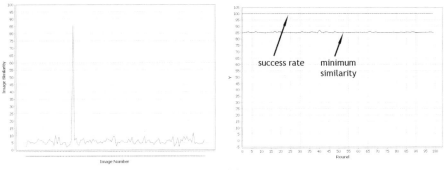

(a) Similarity between Distorted Test Image and Original Base Images   (b) Image Identification Results from our Simulator

Fig. 3. Evaluation of the Image Identification Algorithm

Please note that for solving the HumanAuth CAPTCHA it is not essential to correctly identify the base image of each distorted image. It rather suffices to correctly classify each image correctly as (non-)nature even if the correct base image is not uncovered. In case our algorithm uncovered an image as a nature one but not as the correct base image, Figure 3(b) would have shown an spacious dashed red line below the blue one.

Additionally, we performed a broader evaluation against two more image databases, Microsoft's ASIRRA[5] and the UMIST FACES database[6]. We applied our attack on a publicly available excerpt of the ASIRRA database, which contains 30000 images. The large amount of images leads to a higher similarity among the images. However since the images are not modified, this does not affect our fuzzy image comparison algorithm. The UMIST FACES database consists of black and white images, showing peoples' faces photographed in front of a white background. This setting implies that large parts are similar for all images. However, identical pixels, i.e. the pixels showing a white background are implicitly ignored by our algorithm, leaving the rest of the image for comparison. Hence the results of our attack on this database are identical to attack on the HumanAuth database.

4.4 Prototypical Implementation

We have implemented a prototype to attack image recognition CAPTCHAS. The prototype is available for download and testing on our Web site[7]. We integrated the HumanAuth images as a sample image database to allow a broad audience to easily evaluate the tool. The prototype comes with a variety of functions that are shortly explained hereafter.

Figure 4 depicts the HumanAuth solver which allows solving CAPTCHAS created by an arbitrary HumanAuth instance. Our prototype fetches the images from a HumanAuth instance we set up at our Web site[8] (see Figure 4(a)) and can easily solve it using our PixelMap approach (see Figure 4(b)).

Furthermore, to evaluate the effectiveness of our approach we implemented a generic CAPTCHA simulator. This allows for rapdily testing our attack against all database-based CAPTCHA with an arbitrary number of iterations. The simulator also implements a variety of image modification functions to test the success rate of our approach against hardened CAPTCHA instances.

For analytical reasons the prototype also contains image comparison functionalities to examine our PixelMap approach in a controlled environment. Analogous to the simulator it also implements the image modification functions. To enable an in-depth analysis of the results, most functions allow for a graph visualization (see for instance Figure 3(a) and 3(b)).

5 Ideas for Improvement and Future Work

Based on the results of our current PixelMap approach depicted in Chapter 4 we identified several ideas for both improving our attack and improving image choice and distortion to generate improved CAPTCHAS. These ideas are described shortly in the following.

---

[5] http://research.microsoft.com/en-us/projects/Asirra/corpus.aspx

[6] http://www.shef.ac.uk/eee/research/vie/research/face.html

[7] http://www-ifsresearch.wiwi.uni-regensburg.de/paper/captcha/solver/

[8] http://www-ifsresearch.wiwi.uni-regensburg.de/paper/captcha/humanauth/

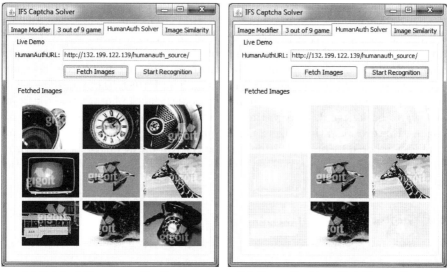

(a) Fetched CAPTCHA Challenges   (b) Correctly Identified Nature Images

Fig. 4. IFS Captcha Solver

5.1   Improving the Attack

Although delivering promising results compared to other approaches [6], we identified several starting points for improving our approach. As stated in Section 3.2,
a major shortcoming of many image CAPTCHAs is the dependency on a preclassified image database. In the majority of cases the image database is packaged
with the CAPTCHA and thus available to an attacker. Other types of CAPTCHAs,
such as ASIRRA [4] are based on a secret image database which is constantly being extended by new images. To prove the general applicability of our approach,
we sketch two strategies to attack this second kind of CAPTCHAs.

Using the secrecy of the image database as the main pillar for the security
of a CAPTCHA protects only poorly from exploitation by an attacker. Unlike
classical cryptosystems where the key remains always secret, a CAPTCHA reveals
a small portion of its database each time a new test is created and new images
are displayed. An attacker is able to store these images and classify them e.g.
using a crowd-sourcing approach such as the ESP Game [13]. This process can
be repeated until the whole database is downloaded and classified, making the
CAPTCHA fully exploitable with our approach. Thus the security solely depends
on the increased effort to reconstruct the secret database, rendering the security
of this type of CAPTCHA an economical question.

Another strategy to attack secret database CAPTCHAs without the need to
download the whole image database might be used to correctly classify previously unclassified images. Based on our PixelMap approach, we examined the
color distribution of the HumanAuth images and found an interesting property.

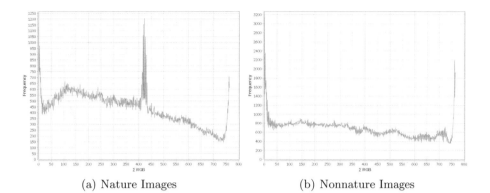

(a) Nature Images   (b) Nonnature Images

Fig. 5. RGB Value Frequency for HumanAuth Nature and Nonnature Images

Figure 5 depicts the cumulated and aggregated RGB value frequency for nature and non-nature images. The abscissa contains the cumulated, i.e. Alpha + Red + Green + Blue values and the ordinate holds frequency of those values among all images in the database. While both graphs in Figure 5 show a similar aggregated RGB value frequency the peak between 410 and 430 on the abscissa is evident. Nature images contain an above-average frequency of a certain small range of RGB values, which is reducible to their high portion of green and/or blue pixels. Using this characteristic property a fuzzy image comparison algorithm might be employed to classify previously unknown images. This approach is slightly similar to a method for classifying images in two semantic classes, namely photographs and graphics developed by Oliviera et al. [11].

5.2   Improving Image Choices

Section 3.2 identified a public image database as one of the major shortcomings of many image recognition Captchas like HumanAuth making them vulnerable to our attack. Furthermore in Section 5.1 we demonstrated the general applicability of our approach even for secret image database Captchas. In this section, we outline several improvements for image Captchas preventing fuzzy classification attacks like our PixelMap approach.

It must be acknowledged that an attacker can always obtain the image database and preclassify all images. Therefore the security of image Captchas must not depend on the image database at all. To effectively improve the security of image recognition Captchas, preclassification of all images and all potential variations and modifications thereof has to be uneconomically.

We propose to randomly modify each image using several image modification algorithms simultaneously. A randomly placed watermark prevents hashtable attacks, since the hash of an image is different for each position of the watermark. However we have showen in Section 4.2 that a watermark alone does not protect from fuzzy image classification. To improve that, we propose a combination of

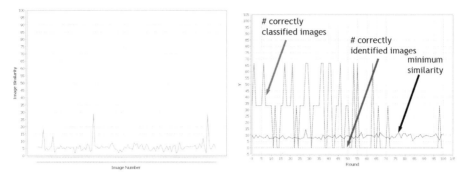

(a) Image Recognition Rate After Slight Zoom

(b) Combined Variation of Several Parameters

Fig. 6. Image Modification Improvements Applied

several image modification algorithms: Watermark size, watermark alpha, image zoom, image alpha, image color and image flip. Figure 6(a) depicts the similarity of a slightly zoomed test image to all other images. Please note the decrease in similarity from 85 percent for original HumanAuth images (see Figure 3(a)) to 30 percent after applying our image modification techniques. As a result the previously evident gap between similarities of the test image and the single most similar image is nonexistent.

The combined application of several image modification algorithms creates a slight variation of the original image which is still easily recognizable by humans. To evaluate the effectiveness of our approach, we implemented a modified version of the HumanAuth CAPTCHA that applies the proposed image modification algorithms. Figure 6(b) depicts the associated success rate for our modified HumanAuth implementation. Compared to the original HumanAuth, where the success rate of our attack is 100 percent, the modified version of HumanAuth lowers the success rate depending on the applied image modifications to 0-3 percent. Further iterations show that these results remain stable.

6   Conclusions

In this paper we present PixelMap, a side-channel attack on image recognition CAPTCHAs. Based on a fuzzy image comparison, our approach clearly identifies the shortcomings of several currently existing image recognition CAPTCHAs. To evaluate our approach we applied our attack on several image recognition CAPTCHAs, especially on HumanAuth with very promising results. We implemented a prototype tool that is available for download to demonstrate the practical applicability of our attack. Building upon our findings we develop several image modification techniques to protect future versions of image recognition CAPTCHAs, preventing image preclassification while not having an impact on human recognition success rates.

References

1. Banday, M.T., Shah, N.A.: Image flip captcha. ISC International Journal of Information Security (ISeCure) 1(2), 105–123 (2009)
2. Barnard, K., Duygulu, P., Forsyth, D.A., de Freitas, N., Blei, D.M., Jordan, M.I.: Matching words and pictures. Journal of Machine Learning Research 3, 1107–1135 (2003)
3. Chew, M., Tygar, J.D.: Image recognition captchas. In: Zhang, K., Zheng, Y. (eds.) ISC 2004. LNCS, vol. 3225, pp. 268–279. Springer, Heidelberg (2004)
4. Elson, J., Douceur, J.R., Howell, J., Saul, J.: Asirra: a captcha that exploits interest-aligned manual image categorization. In: Proc. of the 14th ACM Conference on Computer and Communications, CCS '07 (2007)
5. Golle, P.: Machine learning attacks against the asirra captcha. In: Proc. of the 15th ACM Conference on Computer and Communications Security, CCS '08 (2008)
6. Hernandez-Castro, C.J., Ribagorda, A., Saez, Y.: Side-channel attack on labeling captchas. Computing Research Repository (08/2009)
7. Mori, G., Malik, J.: Recognizing objects in adversarial clutter: Breaking a visual captcha. In: Proc. of the 16th IEEE Computer Society Conference on Computer Vision and Pattern Recognition, CVPR '03 (2003)
8. Moy, G., Jones, N., Harkless, C., Potter, R.: Distortion estimation techniques in solving visual captchas. In: Proc. of the 17th IEEE Computer Society Conference on Computer Vision and Pattern Recognition, CVPR '04 (2004)
9. Naor, M.: Verification of a human in the loop or identification via the turing test, available electronically,
http://www.wisdom.weizmann.ac.il/~naor/PAPERS/human.ps
10. Oechslin, P.: Making a faster cryptanalytic time-memory trade-off. In: Boneh, D. (ed.) CRYPTO 2003. LNCS, vol. 2729, pp. 617–630. Springer, Heidelberg (2003)
11. Oliveira, C.J.S., de Albuquerque Araújo, A.: Classifying images collected on the world wide web. In: Proc. of the 15th Brazilian Symposium on Computer Graphics and Image Processing, SIBGRAPI 2002 (2002)
12. von Ahn, L., Blum, M., Hopper, N.J., Langford, J.: Captcha: Using hard AI problems for security. In: Proc. of the International Conference on the Theory and Applications of Cryptographic Techniques (EUROCRYPT 2003) (2003)
13. von Ahn, L., Dabbish, L.: Labeling images with a computer game. In: Proc. of the 22th Conference on Human Factors in Computing Systems, CHI '04 (2004)
14. Yan, J., El Ahmad, A.S.: A low-cost attack on a microsoft captcha. In: Proc. of the 15th ACM Conference on Computer and Communications Security, CCS '08 (2008)
15. Jeff, Y., Ahmad Salah, E.A.: Usability of captchas or usability issues in captcha design. In: Proc. of the 4th Symposium on Usable Privacy and Security, SOUPS '08 (2008)
16. Jeff, Y., Ahmad Salah, E.A.: Captcha security: A case study. IEEE Security & Privacy 7(4), 22–28 (2009)

An Insider Threat Prediction Model

Miltiadis Kandias, Alexios Mylonas, Nikos Virvilis,
Marianthi Theoharidou, and Dimitris Gritzalis

Information Security & Critical Infrastructure Protection Research Group
Dept. of Informatics, Athens University of Economics and Business,
76 Patission Ave., GR-10434, Athens, Greece
{kandiasm,amylonas,nvir,mtheohar,dgrit}@aueb.gr
http://www.cis.aueb.gr

Abstract. Information systems face several security threats, some of
which originate by insiders. This paper presents a novel, interdisciplinary
insider threat prediction model. It combines approaches, techniques, and
tools from computer science and psychology. It utilizes real time monitoring, capturing the user's technological trait in an information system
and analyzing it for misbehavior. In parallel, the model is using data
from psychometric tests, so as to assess for each user the predisposition
to malicious acts and the stress level, which is an enabler for the user to
overcome his moral inhibitions, under the condition that the collection
of such data complies with the legal framework. The model combines the
above mentioned information, categorizes users, and identifies those that
require additional monitoring, as they can potentially be dangerous for
the information system and the organization.

Keywords: Insider   Threat,   Information   Security,   Taxonomy,
Prediction.

1   Introduction

Information systems face several security threats, a number of which may initiate
from the "trusted" inside of an organization. This is a problem with a technical
and a behavioral nature. The paper proposes a prediction model, which combines
a number of different approaches and techniques. The ultimate goal of the paper
is to identify some of the factors influencing a user's decision to act, as well as
a number of indicators and precursors of malicious acts, especially those that
leave a technological, detectable trail on a system.

Currently, the information security literature does not adopt a common definition of the "insider". The identified attributes of an insider usually are: logical
or physical location, authorization, expected behavior, motivation, and trust.
For the purposes of this paper, an insider is "a human entity that has/had access to the information system of an organization and does not comply with the
security policy of the organization". This definition does not define the type of
access (logical or physical, existing or revoked). Also, it does not define the level
of skill required by the insider to meet his objectives.

S. Katsikas, J. Lopez, and M. Soriano (Eds.): TrustBus 2010, LNCS 6264, pp. 26–37, 2010.
© Springer-Verlag Berlin Heidelberg 2010

In this paper we will focus on threats that are malicious, i.e., in cases where the insider intends to cause harm to an organisation; as a result of this, we would consider accidental threats to be out of scope of this work.

The paper draws upon the fields of computer science, as well as upon industrial and organizational psychology. It first examines current approaches as per the insider threat (Section 2). Then, a detailed description of the model follows (Section 3). Its requirements and limitations are discussed in Section 4. The paper concludes with plans and ideas for future work.

2   Current Approaches

Several insider models have been proposed in the literature. One of them uses multiple, but difficult to quantify, indicators, such as the personality traits and verbal behavior, so as to be able to predict insider attacks [1]. On the contrary, another model uses the attributes of user's knowledge, privileges and skills as metrics [2]. Hidden Markov Models have also been used to infer divergence between the activity patterns of a user and a set of activity models that are in place [3]. Psychological attributes of an insider have also been identified and dealt with [4], such as introversion and depression. The connection between intent and user action has also been investigated through experiments [5]. Finally, user sophistication (computer skills) has been used as a metric for the detection of insiders or as a component of a more general insider detection model [6]. The previously mentioned models focus on both the prevention and the detection of the insider threat, and draw upon other sciences, such as Psychology. The potential role of criminology theories has also been examined [7]. Moreover, best practices for the prevention and detection of the insider threat have been also proposed [8].

The technical approaches rely mainly on the detection of insider activity. In [5], the system detects violations of an already existing set of policies. Another system detects anomalous user search behavior by applying machine learning algorithms so as to analyze collected search events [9]. Finally, system dynamics have been applied, in order to model user life cycle that analyzes user interaction with insider security protection strategies [10].

These approaches detect violations of the security policy by monitoring the user behavior within an information system, and they are often called Intrusion Detection Systems (IDS). An IDS constantly monitors the interaction of each user with the information system, i.e. system call activity [11], access to files or applications [12], and watches for indications of unusual (or abnormal) behavior. Another technique is the use of baits to lure potential insiders, namely honeypots. It inserts resources with no production value into the system [13], varying from systems (i.e. servers, routers etc.) to spreadsheets or password files (commonly referred as honeytokens). Any user interaction with these resources is considered an anomaly, thus indicating a potential insider. It is worth mentioning that the deviations from an expected behavior imply the existence of a dynamic set of rules of acceptable behavior, which is usually described in a Security Policy. An extended set of rules is typically created after a period where all user interactions with the Information system are being captured. Techniques such as data mining [14] can then be utilized for the rule creation.

There are several insider taxonomies, the first of which was proposed by [15]. A user centric taxonomy classifies users according to their system role, reason of misuse and system consequences [16]. On the contrary, the taxonomy proposed in [17] models network attacks. In this case, insider attacks can be classified as network-level misuses, system-level misuses and application and data-level misuses [18]. Computer misuse incidents can also be classified based on incidents, response, and consequences; each of the three dimensions is further analyzed in the taxonomy of [19]. Alternatively, every attack can be classified using four dimensions: attack class, target, vulnerabilities and exploits, and payload [20].

In the following section, we present a prediction model which combines a user taxonomy with approaches from psychology and monitoring techniques (i.e. system call analysis, IDS and honeypots).

3   Insider Prediction Model

The proposed model (see Fig. 1) collects two types of information about a user. The first type is user characteristics, collected by the Psychological Profiling component. The model also analyses data from the IT components of the information system in order to collect usage information about the user. This is the role of the Real Time Usage Profiling component. All the information collected serve as input in the Decision Manager, which assesses whether a user is potentially dangerous or not. We assume that a security team is assigned for implementing, monitoring, and managing the model. The model is used as a decision making tool for the team and indicates whether a user is potentially dangerous and, thus, requires further monitoring.

When an organization uses monitoring techniques and psychological tests as in our model, two conflicting requirements emerge: the security of the organization (assuring business continuity and profit) vs. the employees' privacy [21]. This issue is highly dependent on the organisation's context. Thus, the above conflicting requirements should be weighed and the model should be developed in a way that fully complies with the organization security policy, its culture, and its legal framework.

3.1   Component: User Taxonomy

The user taxonomy is the first building block of the threat prediction model. More specially, each user is categorized on four dimensions.

System Role {Novice, Advanced, Administrator}. This dimension determines the access level of a user. This is a value that is not expected to change often and is defined in advance by the management team. Although an administrator is expected to receive a high user sophistication score, this is a different category than this one. For example, a department manager can be an advanced user, in terms of access rights, but his computer skills may not be advanced.

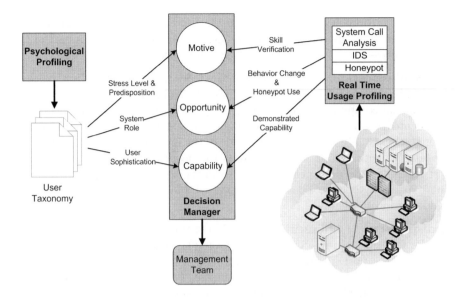

Fig. 1. Insider threat prediction model

Sophistication {Low, Medium, High}. The user's capabilities are examined under the prism of three further dimensions: "range of knowledge", "depth of knowledge" and "skill" [6]. User sophistication is assessed using the formula: $F_{sophistication} = F_{breadth} + F_{appscore} + F_{resutil}$, where $F_{breadth}$ indicates how many different applications has the user utilized, $F_{appscore}$ indicates user's sophistication regarding the type of applications he invokes and $F_{resutil}$ that represents the arithmetic sum of three computational resource consumption indicators (CPU, RAM and simultaneous applications running). Magklaras and Furnell proposed this technique as a method to measure the actual computer skills of a user. We also use this technique in order to verify the accuracy of the stated "computer skills" of a user in parallel with the psychological profiling. Later, when usage information is available (by the system call analysis module), these values can be updated.

The following two dimensions are assessed during the psychological profiling of the user:

Predisposition {Low, Medium, High}. This refers to the tendency of a user to demonstrate malevolent behavior.

Stress Level {Low, Medium, High}. It measures the current degree of personal and professional stress that a user experiences.

3.2 Component: Psychological Profiling

This component draws upon Industrial and Organizational Psychology. In specific, it applies techniques of the Social Learning Theory [7]. The profiling contains three stages: the first determines a user's sophistication, the second assesses predisposition to malicious behavior, and the third assesses stress level. The results of the test are used to populate the user taxonomy and also as part of the decision process ("motive" and "capability" dimension).

User Sophistication. The questionnaire includes questions regarding the computer skills of a user. These questions require from the user to evaluate his knowledge on computer usage, in terms of operating systems in use, techniques implemented, familiarization with specific technologies, etc. These questions, although technical, are used in the beginning of the interview, in order to make the user familiar with the process, as well as to encourage his cooperation. These questions allow the management team to initialize the user sophistication attribute in the taxonomy. This is later updated and verified by the technique of Magklaras and Furnell [6].

Predisposition. It utilizes the CCISLQ questionnaire [22] in order to measure the following parameters for each user: (1) Demonstration of delinquent behavior in the past, (2) Imitation and ability to reproduce ideas, (3) Level of influence from family and friendly environment, (4) Differential association, (5) Perception of punishment and balance of punishment and rewards, (6) Moral disengagement, (7) Sense of collective responsibility, and (8) Blaming or devaluation of a victim. Depending on the answers given, each user can be categorized as: "Low", "Medium" or "High".

Stress level. Regardless of predisposition, a user has to experience something stressful to trigger the above tendency [23]. This parameter is assessed by a psychometric test, which evaluates both personal and professional stress [24]. The factors examined include personal stressful triggers (e.g. death of spouse, financial difficulties, etc.), or triggers from the work environment. Such tests already exist and they can be customized, so as to embody characteristics of various organizations (e.g. military employees are expected to experience higher stress levels than others). The test we selected is based on the multidimensional Rasch model [25]. The output represents a snapshot of the user's current state of stress as "Low", "Medium", or "High".

3.3   Component: Real Time Usage Profiling

This component monitors the user interaction with the technical components of an information system. User behavior is monitored in real time. Usage information is collected from networks, operating systems, databases, and applications. The modules of the model are described in the sequel.

System calls analysis. The idea of using system call analysis to detect potentially malicious actions is not new [11]. There have been attempts to detect attacks using n-grams [26], [27], frequency analysis [28], etc. For example, it has been demonstrated that the average user presents predictable behavior regarding daily file usage [12]. Also, it appears that users have a concrete behavior when accessing specific files for a standard number of times daily [12]. System call analysis can be used to create behavioral patterns that trigger an alarm when violated, with a low false positive rate. This behavior pattern can be reinforced by application execution analysis, which is a variation of system call analysis, and searches for usage patterns of applications [12].

The previous module is used as part of the decision model, measuring several parameters (see Section 3.4). It examines whether a user's behavior has changed or not, which is the "change of behavior" parameter (dimension "opportunity"). It also examines whether the user is demonstrating behavior, which exceeds his defined skills. This is determined by two parameters, i.e., the boolean parameter "skills verification" (dimension "motive") and the scale parameter "demonstrated capability" (dimension "capability"). It can also provide data for the assessment of the "user sophistication" attribute in the taxonomy.

Intrusion Detection System. An IDS can detect both known and unknown attacks; there are lots of variations: anomaly-based, signature-based, or hybrid, which can be self trained, programmable, or both. These systems can detect an ongoing attack as well as behavior patterns violation[14].

We propose the use of a hybrid intrusion detection, as it tends to be more effective in detecting new attacks. The output of an IDS can be used in order to decide whether a user has modified his behavior, which affects the following parameters of the decision module (see Section 3.4): "behavior change", "skills verification", and "demonstrated capability" attributes. Like above, it can also provide data for the assessment of the "user sophistication" taxonomy attribute.

Honeypot. The honeypot technique is used to attract malicious users. Its advantages include the collection of a small amount of data, the low percentage of false positives/negatives, flexibility and adaptability [13]. A honeynet is a network of (usually) virtual computers, which wait to be targeted. Any interaction with these systems is an indication of an attack, as users are not expected to connect to them. A honeytoken can be anything from a file or database entry to a search engine registration. For example, a file honeytoken can be named as "password.txt" to lure attackers to access it. The model uses them, so as to evaluate whether a user is trying to exploit an opportunity to attack the information infrastructure (dimension opportunity), or not.

3.4   Component: Decision Manager

The previous components include a number of heterogeneous techniques. When these components are properly combined with the user taxonomy, they can assess potential insider behavior. We adopt Wood's assumption that each threat requires: (a) motive, (b) opportunity, and (c) capability [2], and we describe how each of these three factors are assessed. Each factor receives an assessment of the following form: (1-2) low, (3-4) medium, and (5-6) high.

Factor: Motive. The last dimension of the first stage of the model is the motive of the user to launch an attack (see Table 1). The motive of a user M_i is assessed using three parameters: (a) predisposition to malicious behavior P_i, (b) current stress level S_i, and (c) skill verification V_i.

$$M_i = f(P_i, S_i, V_i) \tag{1}$$

At first, the user's predisposition to malicious behavior is accessed through the test mentioned in section 3.2. This parameter is important, as it indicates the user's tendency to attacks. Users of "High" predisposition are not considered as an a priori insider threat. The second parameter is the stress level that the user experiences before he decides to commence an attack. A high level of stress can be an enabler for a user to start an attack, as it helps him overcome his moral inhibitions [23]. The last parameter is the verification of skills. The user has declared his skills during the psychometric tests that measure predisposition to malicious behavior. They are verified via the relevant modules described in Section 3.3. Our model considers unexpected the fact that a user was proven to have considerably higher skills than he initially declared.

Table 1. Motive Score

Skill Verification	Stress Level	Predisposition		
		Low	Medium	High
	Low	1	2	3
False	Medium	2	3	4
	High	3	4	5
	Low	2	3	4
True	Medium	3	4	5
	High	4	5	6

Factor: Opportunity. A malevolent user usually requires an opportunity in order to launch an attack. The opportunity level O_i of a user i depends on three parameters: change of work behavior B_i, system role R_i, and honeypot use H_i.

$$O_i = f(B_i, R_i, H_i) \tag{2}$$

Any change in the user behavior during the interaction with the information system may theoretically indicate that the user is in the process of finding a possible target in the system, or that he is trying to exploit one. The second parameter is the user role in the system, which can be "novice", "advanced" or "administrator". The last parameter is the potential user interaction with the honeypots; a user is not expected to access a honeypot for a legitimate purpose. However, any user may accidentally access a honeypot (even an administrator), as we have assumed that all users are not aware of the specific honeypot[1]. The opportunity factor can be assessed through on a scoring table (see Table 2).

Factor: Capability. The skills of a user are already defined by the user sophistication attribute in the user taxonomy S_i as a numerical value. However, the IDS and the Call analysis module may indicate that the user has the ability to

---

[1] Assumption: The honeypots are implemented by the management team of the model, which may not include all administrators.

Table 2. Opportunity Score

Behavior Change	Honeypot Use	System Role		
		Novice	Advanced	Administrator
False	False	1	2	3
	True	2	3	4
True	False	3	4	5
	True	4	5	6

use considerably more advanced skills than the ones assessed. This is indicated by the parameter "Demonstrated Capability" D_i, which is measured by these two modules as "Low", "Medium", "High", "Very High". These parameters may seem similar but, if a user uses advanced skills e.g. use of an automated exploitation tool, this does not mean per se that his user sophistication is advanced. The capability factor can be assessed by using a scoring table like Table 3.

$$C_i = f(D_i, S_i) \tag{3}$$

Table 3. Capability Score

Demonstrated Capability	User Sophistication		
	Low	Medium	High
Low	1	2	3
Medium	2	3	4
High	3	4	5
Very High	4	5	6

Decision algorithm. After the above mentioned factors have been assessed, the model has a component that can decide whether the user arouses suspicions and should be closely monitored. Every organization that uses this model must set a scoring system for the dimensions mentioned above. This system cannot be universal, because every organization has different security needs, demands, staff, and philosophy. As a result, every organization adopting this model should study several parameters before deciding which scoring system to use. Some of these parameters are the average and the fluctuation of the results, the required strictness, possibly a risk analysis, etc.

Herein we propose a simple scoring system, so as to demonstrate the role of the Decision Manager. As already mentioned, every dimension classifies the users into three categories: low (1), medium (2), high (3). Hence, if user i is assessed as user with "high" motivation ($M_i = 3$) , "medium" opportunity, ($O_i = 2$), and "high" capability ($C_i = 3$), then his threat score T_i equals to 8 points.

$$T_i = M_i + O_i + C_i \tag{4}$$

After assessing each user's final score, a scoring system is used to map the user into a category indicating how potentially dangerous he can be. Each organization has to choose the score intervals that classifies each user to a category. For example, we can use four intervals (3, 4), (5, 6), (7, 8), and (9), which map the user into the categories: "harmless", "medium risk", "dangerous", and "very dangerous", respectively (Table 4).

Table 4. Overall Threat Score

Motive	Opportunity	Capability		
		Low	Medium	High
	Low	3	4	5
Low	Medium	4	5	6
	High	5	6	7
	Low	4	5	6
Medium	Medium	5	6	7
	High	6	7	8
	Low	5	6	7
High	Medium	6	7	8
	High	7	8	9

Note: Low =1, Medium = 2, High = 3.

These results are then examined and evaluated by the management team. It is important to mention that the model determines an estimated value of the potential danger a user may pose to the organization. However, it does not receive any automated decision regarding the particular user access rights.

4   Requirements and Limitations

In the previous section we have described the model and its components. Here we will discuss its requirements, as well as the limitations of each component and of the overall model. First, we will examine the requirements of the real time usage profiling, in terms of network, application, database, and operating system, which are the data sources of the component.

In order to analyze alerts from the IDS, sensors have to be placed in the appropriate network areas (depending on the network topology). Ideally this will be the monitor port (SPAN - Switched Port Analyzer) of the switch(es). However, the network traffic has to be unencrypted; otherwise the IDS will not be able to analyze the data. This vulnerability might be exploited by a skillful insider, who can launch an attack over an encrypted channel (VPN, SSL/TLS tunnel, SSH tunnel), thus evading detection from the IDS.

Sensitive applications that may be targeted by insiders should have logging capabilities, so that all user actions can be logged and analyzed for potentially malicious behavior. Ideally, the logging of user actions has to be in real time.

The storage space for the log file should be taken into consideration, as - depending on the application - the size can increase rapidly, making storage and analysis practically infeasible. This is particularly important in databases, where in production environments, database logging mechanisms may be disabled due to the performance burden. Analysis of these log files has to be done locally, i.e., on the system that generates them, to avoid network overhead from the continuous transfer of the log data. Hence, a software agent - that will be able to perform the analysis locally and securely report back to the Decision Manager component - has to be installed in every security critical system.

All widely used operating systems can audit and control access to specific resources. These two parameters are mandatory for the model, in order to detect unauthorized access to resources. Again, logging and analyzing of all access requests to a specific resource can be a very demanding task.

Additionally, all sensors should be able to communicate directly and in a secure way with the Decision Manager, which will analyze all reported data and decide if a particular user action/behavior has to be further analyzed. A considerable level of expertise is also required from the network and system administrators, as monitoring the aforementioned resources requires manual reconfiguration of the operating systems and network devices. Performance issues have, also, to be addressed, as logging can severely affect performance. As IDS are not able to analyze encrypted communication, certain attacks may pass under the radar of network monitoring tools. A clever insider can change his behavior slowly, trying to fool the Decision System and prevent it from identifying his attack as not normal behavior and raising an alarm. Furthermore, in case the insider has authorized access to specific resources, he can access a small part of them each day, simulating a normal work behavior, knowing that accessing all information at the same time could raise an alarm. His attack will succeed and probably pass undetected, but he will need much more time to conduct it. Another important fact is that malicious administrators can disable/tamper the sensors/logging mechanisms. As some of them may be required to participate in the management team, additional measures should be put in place (i.e. organizational controls). Use of honeytokens can be a partial solution to this problem, as honeytokens do not require administrative privileges, so the administrators will not be aware of their existence and thus they will be detected by our model if they access them. Finally, our model does not address incidents caused by human error, incidents that happened outside the monitored environment, or attacks based on social engineering.

Regarding psychological profiling, when it is applied in different organizations, it is likely that its statistical parts may vary significantly. For example, the user computer skills in a software house can vary significantly from another organization. This could be addressed, if every organization adopts different statistical constants according to its own needs and characteristics. This also applies to the algorithm for the classification of users in categories. Every organization can develop its customized system of classification. Furthermore, the model should study each user's stress level throughout time, in comparison with the results of the user's predisposition to malicious behavior and his behavior in the information infrastructure.

Finally, as we have already mentioned, when an organization applies monitoring techniques and psychological tests as in our model, compliance with the legal requirements is imperative.

5   Discussion

This paper presented a model that aims in predicting insider behavior. It uses a user taxonomy, psychological profiling, real time usage data, and a decision algorithm in order to identify potentially dangerous users. The novelty of the model is that it is an interdisciplinary approach, in the sense that it combines technical solutions with approaches that draw upon psychology. We have presented a number of ranking and decision algorithms, in order to demonstrate how the model can be utilized. We have, also, identified the requirements and the possible restrictions that need to be taken into account.

Future work will focus on the implementation of the model in test and real environment, in order to evaluate its effectiveness and address performance issues. We plan to add an attack taxonomy, so as to produce IDS patterns of insider attacks. Also, we will explore the use and optimisation of more sophisticated scoring systems (formulae and weights), in order to implement the decision component. Finally, we will explore ways to identify non human threats.

Acknowledgements. Alexios Mylonas receives founding from the Propondis Foundation.

References

1. Schultz, E.E.: A framework for understanding and predicting insider attacks. Comput. Secur. 21(6), 526–531 (2002)
2. Wood, B.: An Insider Threat Model for Adversary Simulation. In: Anderson, R.H. (ed.) Research on Mitigating the Insider Threat to Information Systems-#2, RAND (2000)
3. Thompson, P.: Weak Models for Insider Threat Detection. In: Carapezza, E.M. (ed.) Sensors, & Command, Control, Communications, & Intelligence (C3I) Technologies for Homeland Security & Homeland Defense III, vol. 5403, pp. 40–48 (2004)
4. Shaw, E., Ruby, K.G., Post, J.M.: The Insider Threat to Information Systems, The Psychology of the Dangerous Insider. Sec. Awareness Bulletin 2, 98 (1998)
5. Caputo, D., Marcus, A., Maloof, M., Stephens, G.: Detecting Insider Theft of Trade Secrets. IEEE Secur. Privacy 7(6), 14–21 (2009)
6. Magklaras, G.B., Furnell, S.M.: A preliminary model of end user sophistication for insider threat prediction in IT systems. Comput. Secur. 24(5), 371–380 (2004)
7. Theoharidou, M., Kokolakis, S., Karyda, M., Kiountouzis, E.: The insider threat to information systems and the effectiveness of ISO17799. Comput. Secur. 24(6), 472–484 (2005)

8. Cappelli, D.M., Moore, A.P., Trzeciak, R.F., Shimeall, T.J.: Common Sense Guide to Prevention and Detection of Insider Threat, 3rd edn. Carnegie Mellon University, Pittsburgh (2009)

9. Bowen, B., Salem, M., Hershkop, S., Keromytis, A., Stolfo, S.: Designing Host and Network Sensors to Mitigate the Insider Threat. IEEE Secur. Privacy 7(6), 22–29 (2009)

10. Duran, F., Conrad, S., Conrad, G., Duggan, D., Held, E.: Building A System For Insider Security. IEEE Secur. Privacy 7(6), 30–38 (2009)

11. Liu, A., Martin, C., Hetherington, T., Matzner, S.: A comparison of system call feature for insider threat detection. In: Proc. of the 6th Annual IEEE Systems, Man & Cybernetics, Information Assurance Workshop, pp. 341–347 (2005)

12. Nguyen, N., Reiher, P., Kuenning, G.: Detecting Insider Threats by Monitoring System Call Activity. In: IEEE Workshop on Information Assurance. United States Military Academy, West Point (2003)

13. Spitzner, L.: Honeypots: Catching the Insider Threat. In: 19th Annual Computer Security Applications Conference, Las Vegas, Nevada (2003)

14. Velpula, V.B., Gudipudi, D.: Behavior-Anomaly-Based System for Detecting Insider Attacks and Data Mining. Int. J. of Rec. Tr. in Eng. 1(2), 261–266 (2009)

15. Anderson, J.P.: Computer Security Threat Monitoring and Surveillance. Technical Report. James P Anderson Co., Fort Washington (1980)

16. Magklaras, G.B., Furnell, S.M.: Insider Threat Prediction Tool: Evaluating the probability of IT misuse. Comput. Secur. 21(1), 62–73 (2002)

17. Cheswick, W.R., Bellovin, S.M.: Firewalls and Internet Security: Repelling the Wily Hacker. Addison-Wesley Publishing Company, Reading (1994)

18. Phyo, A.H., Furnell, S.M.: Detection-Oriented Classification of Insider IT Misuse. In: Proc. of the 3rd Security Conference, Las Vegas (2004)

19. Tuglular, T.: A Preliminary Structural Approach to Insider Computer Misuse Incidents. In: EICAR 2000 Best Paper Proceedings, pp. 105–125 (2000)

20. Hansman, S., Hunt, R.: A taxonomy of network and computer attacks. Comput. Secur. 24(1), 31–43 (2005)

21. Mitrou, L., Karyda, M.: Employees' privacy vs. employers' security: Can they be balanced? Telematics Inf. 23(3), 164–178 (2006)

22. Rogers, M.K.: A social learning theory and moral disengagement analysis of criminal computer behavior: an exploratory study. PHD Thesis. Dept. of Psychology, University of Manitoba (2001)

23. Heuer, R.J.: The insider espionage threat. In: Anderson, R.H. (ed.) Research on Mitigating the Insider Threat to Information Systems-#2, RAND (2000)

24. Puleo, A.J.: Mitigating insider threat using human behavior influence models. Master Thesis. Dept. of the Air Force, Air University Wright-Patterson Air Force Base, Ohio (2004)

25. Rasch, G.: Probabilistic models for some intelligence and attainment tests. Copenhagen, Danish Institute for Educational Research (1960)

26. Forrest, S., Hofmeyr, S.A., Somayaji, A.: A sense of self for unix processes. In: Proc. of the 1996 IEEE Symposium on Research in Security & Privacy, p. 0120 (1996)

27. Forrest, S., Hofmeyr, S.A., Somayaji, A.: Intrusion Detection Using Sequences of System Calls. J. of Comp. Sec. 6(3), 151–180 (1998)

28. Liao, Y., Vemuri, V.R.: Using Text Categorization Techniques for Intrusion Detection. In: Proc. of 11th USENIX Security Symposium, pp. 51–59 (2002)

A Call Conference Room Interception Attack and Its Detection

Nikos Vrakas[1], Dimitris Geneiatakis[2], and Costas Lambrinoudakis[1]

[1] Department of Digital Systems, University of Piraeus
150 Androutsou St., Piraeus 18532 Greece
{nvra,clam}@unipi.gr
[2] Dept. of Telecommunications Science and Technology, University of Peloponnese
End of Karaiskaki St., GR-22100, Tripolis, Greece
dgen@uop.gr

Abstract. The IP Multimedia Subsystem (IMS) infrastructure is currently considered to be the main core of Next Generation Networks (NGNs), integrating IP and other network types under one common infrastructure. Consequently, IMS inherits security flaws and vulnerabilities residing in all those technologies. Besides, the protection against unauthorized access in NGN services is of great importance. In this paper we present a call conference room interception attack and we propose a new cross layer architecture to shield IMS against it.

Keywords: SIP, IMS, Interception, Spoofing Detection, VoIP.

1 Introduction

The Session Initiation Protocol (SIP) [1] is an application layer protocol responsible for handling multimedia sessions and conferences in Next Generation Networks (NGNs). Although various protocols have been proposed for the administration of call sessions like H323 [2], SIP is considered the predominant one since 3GPP proposes its utilization in IP Multimedia Subsystem (IMS) [3].

Various researchers [4, 5] have focused their research on the identification of security vulnerabilities of SIP-based voice services offered over the Internet (VoIP). Similar security flaws are exhibited by any infrastructure that deploys the SIP protocol. Consequently, IMS services are subjected to attacks like SIP flooding, SIP malformed messages and SIP signaling attacks. In the latter case, a malicious user exploits the lack of the appropriate authentication and integrity protection mechanisms in SIP [4] and IMS correspondingly, in order to (illegally) "modify" a session in progress. Under this context, in this paper we demonstrate a call conference interception attack that could be launched against IMS services. Specifically, an internal user may act maliciously (Internal Attack – IA), as a man in the middle during a multimedia conference, in order to join the conference by exploiting the SIP REFER method. At this point one might argue that such security flaws could be prevented through the deployment of the appropriate integrity mechanisms [6, 7], however, such mechanisms require the modification of the IMS client side. Furthermore, those solutions have not

S. Katsikas, J. Lopez, and M. Soriano (Eds.): TrustBus 2010, LNCS 6264, pp. 38–44, 2010.

taken into consideration IMS client side's limited resource capabilities. Besides, it should be noted that in IMS deployments where User's Equipment (UE) lacks IP Multimedia Service Identity Module / Universal Subscriber Identity Module (ISIM/USIM), the IP Security (IPSec) Authentication and Key Agreement (AKA) [8] cannot be utilized. Consequently, the UE should use alternative solutions proposed in IMS specifications [9] like SIP Digest [8], NIBA [10] or GIBA [11]. Note that such mechanisms do not provide integrity protection to signaling messages, allowing a malicious user to participate in an unauthorized way in a multimedia conference. To this end, we propose a transparent server side cross-layer mechanism towards the detection of spoofing and man in the middle attacks in order to deter such behaviors.

The rest of this paper is structured as follows. In section 2 an interception attack, utilizing the SIP REFER method, which can be implemented in an IMS infrastructure is described. Section 3 presents a cross-layer framework capable to detect such behaviors and other more general spoofing attacks, like ARP poisoning, which could compromise a VoIP channel. Finally we conclude the paper with some pointers for future work.

2 Call Interception Attack Utilizing REFER Requests

The SIP REFER method is a non default request described in RFC 3515 [12]. Particularly, SIP REFER is used by an authorized entity (referrer) in order to request some other entity to access a resource on behalf of the "referrer". Fig. 1 depicts a multimedia

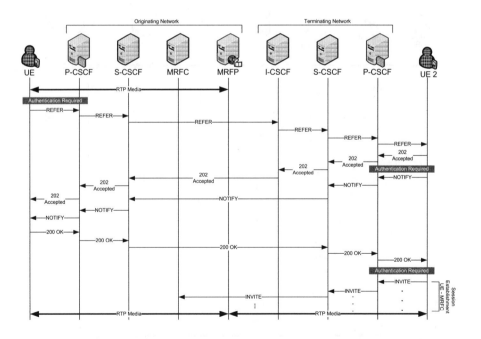

Fig. 1. Successful Invitation to a Call Conference

conference invitation in an IMS architecture. Note that the resource, to be accessed, is identified by the corresponding Uniform Resource Indicator (URI) included in the SIP Refer-To header and can be any type of existing URIs such as SIP and HTTP [13]. This method extends existing multimedia service capabilities providing extra functionality like call transfer, conference rooms etc. However, a malicious user can avail of this request by inviting itself or another UE of his choice in order to participate (illegally) in the session. In this case the attacker spoofs a legitimate REFER request of a valid user by adding his UE URI/public ID in the "Refer-To" or "To" header depending the type of conference invitation.

2.1 Attack Description

In this attack scenario a malicious user acts as an intermediate (Man in the Middle - MitM) between the Proxy Call Session Control Function (P-CSCF) and the UE, utilizing well-known attack techniques such as Domain Name System (DNS) [14, 15] and Address Resolution Protocol (ARP) poisoning [16]. We assume that a legitimate UE has already established a multimedia conference room and would like to invite one more user (UE3) to join. At the very first stages, a malicious user changes DNS binding in order to force the traffic passing through his domain. Consequently, whenever a legitimate UE sends a SIP REFER message, the DNS resolution procedure will force the CSCF components to forward traffic towards the attacker's domain. Afterwards the malicious user poisons the ARP correlating legitimate user's IP with his own MAC address in order to receive the responses directed to a legitimate UE.

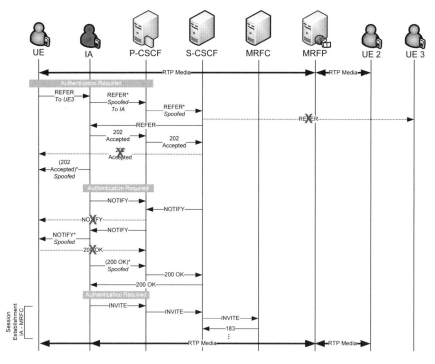

Fig. 2. REFER – Interception Attack

As soon as the malicious user catches a SIP REFER, spoofs the "To" header value with his URI/public ID, while the remaining message is retained as is, and forwards it to P-CSCF. Afterwards, the SIP REFER request is processed by the Server-CSCF (S-CSCF), which by its turn sends it to the destination that the "To header" points to, namely the IA. The IA responds with a "202 Accepted" to the S-CSCF as well as the former sends a spoofed "202 Accepted" towards the UE. Subsequently, the IA sends a "legitimate" SIP NOTIFY message to the P-CSCF, while the IA is the "legitimate" referee. The IA is able to authenticate successfully the NOTIFY request as he holds a valid subscription (considering that the IA is an internal user).

After the successful authentication, the P-CSCF sends a NOTIFY to UE through the IA who acts as MiTM, while the IA spoofs the included headers that points him ("From" and "Contact") with the corresponding of UE3. The UE accepts it by sending a 200 OK response message. In the same way the IA spoofs and forwards it to the P-CSCF. Finally, the IA executes an invitation handshake in order to establish a media session with the MRFP that will enable him to participate as a legitimate user in the conference room. For further information for the rest of the handshake refer to [17]. The whole attack procedure is depicted in Fig. 2. The green color denotes that the IA is able to fulfill the specific request or generally to bypass a security mechanism. Note that an external attacker will not be able to launch such an attack because of lack of valid credentials to authenticate SIP NOTIFY message.

3 Proposed Mechanism

The proposed mechanism relies on the information gathered from messages of different network layers, in order to correlate a specific UE with its MAC, IP, SIP addresses and private/public ID. This mechanism is able to detect IMS spoofed message attacks not only in cases where signaling messages lack authentication or integrity protection, but also in cases where the user establishes a security tunnel using IPSec [18] or Transport Layer Security (TLS) [19] with the corresponding server. For example an internal malicious user utilizes his legitimate tunnel in order to forward spoofed messages with stolen public IDs to Core Network (CN) [8].

3.1 Mechanism Description

The proposed mechanism monitors the incoming traffic and gathers information related to a specific UE. Particularly, it collects information from all Internet layers (SIP messages), Network (IP packets) and the frames of Data Link layer (MAC Address) relevant to the current UE request. Actually, this information is stored in a *cross layer correlating* table where a tuple denotes UE's specific connection characteristics which are the MAC address, IP addresses retrieved from IP and SIP protocol layers correspondingly, as well as the UE's identities and finally the method of the SIP request.

A stack of collected information is denoted by E_i, where i = {0,...,n} and n is the number of the incoming messages as illustrated in Table 1. For instance, MAC_0 denotes the MAC address of the UE that a user utilized in order to be initially registered to the service while the IP_0 denotes the IP address that the specific UE has been allocated during the same procedure. The SIP_0 and ID_0 come from the application layer denoting the IP address and the ID that have been included in the SIP header fields of the same message (E_0). All the subsequent messages come with a subscript increased by 1.

Table 1. Proposed Mechanism's Cross-Layer Correlation

	UE	IP Address		IMPI/IMPU	Method
E_0	MAC_0	IP_0	SIP_0	ID_0	Register
E_1	MAC_1	IP_1	SIP_1	ID_1	Refer
	Layer 2	**Layer 3**		**Layer 5**	

Every new collected message (E_i) for a specific UE is compared with the existing tuples in order to identify a spoof case. This is also true if the attacker is internal (and thus able to establish a security tunnel through IPSec) and tries to launch an identity theft attack as already described in section 2. For instance, for an incoming SIP message received by an IMS service we extract the following:

$$E_1=\{MAC_1, IP_1, SIP\text{-}IP_1, ID, Method_1\}$$

Furthermore, we define $K = MAC \cup IP \cup SIP\text{-}IP$ denoting a unique correlation with a specific UE. Consequently, for E_1 we compute the corresponding K_1 value. If K_1 matches some K_i (for every tuple in the table the corresponding K value is calculated) the incoming message E_1 has been generated by a legitimate user. Otherwise, the proposed mechanism compares the IP_1 and $SIP\text{-}IP_1$ field values in E_1. If these are different it is deducted that a malicious user has created a spoofed SIP message. Alternatively, it could be that IP_1 and $SIP\text{-}IP_1$ of message E_1 do have the same value, but there is no match with a record in the cross layer table. In such a case if the collected info (IP_1, $SIP\text{-}IP_1$ and MAC_1) has been extracted from an authenticated SIP REGISTER message, E_0 must be updated (as the legitimate user has been registered through a different UE), otherwise, a malicious user tries to impersonate a legitimate one.

3.2 Protecting against the Call Interception Attack

Considering the REFER interception attack that has been presented, we are able to detect it, through the conditional tests that detects IP spoofing and ARP poisoning. Specifically, when the IPs of both network (IP) and application layer (SIP) of an incoming message matched with a tuple in the cross layer table, while the corresponding MACs differ, we can deduce that: (a) IPs (network and application layer) or (b) MAC addresses has been spoofed.

Taking as an example the attack illustrated in Fig. 2, we assume that UE has the MAC AAA, UE2 the BBB and the attacker CCC (or a MAC of his choice but note that in order to achieve an ARP poison he must broadcast his real MAC). UE1 and UE2 have been registered and the corresponding E_i tuples have been generated in the cross layer table (E_0 and E_1). Afterwards, the IA gathers the UE's REFER and forwards it to the server (E_2). As depicted in Table 2, the E_2 K value does not match with any E_i K_i value in the table. Although, IP addresses (network and application level) have the same values, the E_2 record has been generated from a non-authenticated SIP REGISTER, consequently the incoming message is a spoofed one.

Table 2. An Instance During the Detection of Refer Attack

	UE	IP Address		IMPI/IMPU	Method
E_0	AAA	111	111	User1	Register
E_1	BBB	333	333	User3	Register
E_2	CCC	111	111	User1	Refer
	Layer 2	**Layer 3**		**Layer 5**	

4 Conclusions

NGNs infrastructures merge different network technologies under the umbrella of Internet architecture, constituting them vulnerable to similar threats and attacks residing in it. As IMS is the core of NGN it will attract the attention of malicious users who will try to identify new vulnerabilities or exploit existing ones. Under this context, in this paper we present a case of a signaling attack in IMS namely "A Call Conference Interception Attack", exploiting the lack of appropriate integrity protection mechanisms in SIP.

Furthermore, we propose a cross layer server based mechanism to detect illegal modifications in IMS signaling messages and consequently in established sessions. Such a method does not require any modification in client side as would be the case for an Integrity mechanism.

Currently, we focus on the evaluation of the proposed mechanism and we also investigate the case of broaden it in order to shield IMS infrastructure not only against signaling but also resource consumption attacks using a centralizing architecture.

References

1. Rosenberg, J., Schulzrinne, H., Camarillo, G., et al.: RFC 3261: SIP: Session Initiation Protocol (2002)
2. I.T.Union: H323 Packet Based Multimedia Communications Systems, Telecommunication Standardization Sector of ITU (1998)
3. 3GPP, TS 23.228: IP Multimedia Subsystems (IMS), Third Generation Partnership Project, Technical Specification Group Services and System Aspects (2008)
4. Geneiatakis, D., Dagiouklas, A., Kambourakis, G., et al.: Survey of security vulnerabilities in Session Initiation Protocol. IEEE Communications Surveys and Tutorials 8, 68–81 (2006)
5. Sisalem, D., Kuthan, J., Ehlert, S., et al.: Denial of Service Attacks Targeting a SIP VoIP Infrastructure: Attack Scenarios and Prevention Mechanisms. IEEE Network 20(5), 26 (2006)
6. Geneiatakis, D., Lambrinoudakis, C.: A lightweight protection mechanism against signaling attacks in a SIP-based VoIP environment. Telecommunication Systems 36(4), 153–159 (2007)
7. Ramsdell, B.: RFC 2633: S/MIME version 3 message specification (1999)
8. 3GPP, TS 33.203: 3G security; Access security for IP-based services (Release 9), Third Generation Partnership Project, Technical Specification Group Services and System Aspects (2009)

9. 3GPP, TS 24.229: IP Multimedia Call Control Based on SIP and SDP, Techincal Specification Group Core Network and Terminals (2009)
10. 3GPP, TR 33.978 Security aspects of early IP Multimedia Subsystem (IMS), Third Generation Partnership Project, Technical Specification Group Services and System Aspects (2008)
11. ETSI, TS 187 003: Telecommunications and Internet converged Services and Protocols for Advanced Networking (TISPAN): Security Architecture (2008)
12. Sparks, R.: RFC 3515: The Session Initiation Protocol (SIP) Refer Method (2003)
13. Johnston, A.B.: SIP: Understanding the Session Initiation Protocol. Artech House (2004)
14. Klein, A.: BIND 9 DNS cache poisoning,
    http://www.trusteer.com/docs/bind9dns.html
15. Zhang, R., Wang, X., Farley, R., et al.: On the feasibility of launching the man-in-the-middle attacks on VoIP from remote attackers, pp. 61–69
16. Wagner, R.: Address resolution protocol spoofing and man-in-the-middle attacks. The SANS Institute (2001)
17. 3GPP, TS 24.147: Conferencing using the IP Multimedia (IM) Core Network (CN) subsystem, Technical Specification Group Core Network and Terminals (2009)
18. Kent, S., Atkinson, R.: RFC 2401: Security Architecture for the Internet Protocol. Network Working Group (1998)
19. Dierks, T., Allen, C.: RFC 2246: The TLS Protocol Version 1.0, RFC Editor (1999)

Safe and Efficient Strategies for Updating Firewall Policies*

Zeeshan Ahmed[1], Abdessamad Imine[2], and Michaël Rusinowitch[1]

[1] INRIA Nancy Grand Est
{ahmedzee,rusi}@loria.fr
[2] INRIA Nancy Grand Est & Nancy-Université, France
imine@loria.fr

Abstract. Due to the large size and complex structure of modern networks, firewall policies can contain several thousand rules. The size and complexity of these policies require automated tools providing a user-friendly environment to specify, configure and safely deploy a target policy. When activated in online mode, a firewall policy deployment is a very difficult and error-prone task. Indeed, it may result in self-Denial of Service (self-DoS) and/or temporary security breaches. In this paper, we provide correct, efficient and safe algorithms for two important classes of policy editing. Our experimental results show that these algorithms are fast and can be used safely even for deploying large policies.

Keywords: Firewall Policy Management, Firewalls, Network Security.

1 Introduction

Motivation. A firewall is an essential component of any network security infrastructure. Network firewalls are devices or systems that control the flow of traffic between networks employing different security postures [17]. The network traffic flow is controlled according to a firewall policy. The large size and complexity of modern networks result in large and complex firewall policies. Firewall policies containing 10K rules are not uncommon and firewalls configured with as many as 50K rules exist [22].

A policy *deployment* is the process by which the running policy is replaced by a new policy. In most mission-critical network-based applications (such as Voice-OverIP and online e-commerce), the *deployment should be performed in online mode in order to keeping these applications available and accessible*. Different firewalls support different policy editing commands: inserting a new rule, appending a new rule at the end, deleting a rule and moving a rule from one position to another one. Due to intervening nature of firewall rules, correct deployment of such large policies is a very difficult and error-prone task.

For example, consider the initial policy I (the running policy) and the target policy T (the policy to be deployed) given in Figure 1. To obtain T, if we delete rules a and c and next we insert these rules at right positions the deployment will be slow. A deployment

* This work has been supported by the INRIA ARC 2010 ACCESS and FP7-ICT-2007-1 Project No.216471 AVANTSSAR.

S. Katsikas, J. Lopez, and M. Soriano (Eds.): TrustBus 2010, LNCS 6264, pp. 45–57, 2010.

should be *efficient* i.e. it should issue the minimum number of commands to accomplish the deployment. A slow deployment is unpleasant for users and may partly defeat the purpose of deployment [22]. In our example, instead of four commands, we have only to issue two move commands (either moving a and c or moving b and d).

Now consider a packet p with source address of 10.1.1.1. Clearly, rule a denies p, while rule c accepts it. It is evident that both I and T deny p. If we first move a, then we get the intermediate running policy $R = [b, c, d, a]$. Now rule c appears before rule a, while it appears after a in both I and T. The running policy accepts p, which is denied by both I and T. A deployment is *safe* if no legal packet is rejected and no illegal packet is accepted during the deployment. A naive deployment strategy may result in self-Denial of Service (self-DoS) and/or temporary security breaches. Deployment safety is a new and challenging area of research.

I	T
a. deny tcp 10.1.1.0/24 any	b. permit ip 192.168.1.0/24 any
b. permit ip 192.168.1.0/24 any	d. permit tcp 192.168.2.0/24
c. permit tcp 10.1.0.0/16 any	a. deny tcp 10.1.1.0/24 any
d. permit tcp 192.168.2.0/24 any	c. permit tcp 10.1.0.0/16 any

Fig. 1. Example of Policy Deployment

Related Work. Much research has addressed policy specification [10, 7, 15], conflict detection [18, 14, 9], and optimization [20, 16]. However, very little research has been done on firewall policy deployment. To the best of our knowledge, the work presented in [22] is the first that addresses deployment safety and efficiency. In [22], the authors classify policy editing languages into two representative classes, Type I and Type II, and provide deployment algorithms for both types of languages. In [6], it is shown that these algorithms have serious flaws related to efficiency and safety properties.

Contributions. In this paper, we present a safety formalization that can be used as a basis for formulating safe deployment strategies (Section 3). We provide a linear algorithm for Type I deployment (Section 4). This algorithm is most-efficient and it ensures that either no legal traffic is rejected or no illegal traffic is permitted. We also give an approximately linear, most-efficient and safe algorithm for Type II languages (Section 5). Finally, we present experimental results of our Type II algorithm, and give conclusions.

2   Overview of Firewalls

A firewall is a perimeter security device that filters packets that traversing across the boundaries of a secured network. The filtering decision is based on a *policy* defined by the network administrator. A firewall policy is an ordered list of rules. A firewall rule r defines an action, typically *accept* or *reject*, for the set of packets matching its criteria. Most of firewalls filter traffic according to first-match semantics. When a packet p arrives, it is compared against the rules in a top-down fashion until a matching rule is found and the process is repeated for the following packet. All policies admit a hidden match-all default rule at the end. Therefore, when a packet does not match a rule in the policy, then the default action is followed. In most firewalls, the default rule is *deny-all*, however a *permit-all* default rule is also possible. A rule is given with a set of fields, where each field can have an atomic value or a range of values. It is possible to use any field of IP, UDP, or TCP headers [22]. However, the following five fields are most commonly used: protocol type, source IP address, source port, destination IP address and destination port [11].

Any field in packet's header can be used for the matching process. However, the same five fields are most commonly used. In a packet, each of these fields has an atomic value. If all the fields of a packet p match with the corresponding fields of a rule r, then p is accepted or rejected according to the decision field of r. If p does not match to any rule in policy, then the default match-all rule is applied. Most of firewalls do not allow identical rules in the same policy. *Therefore, we assume this restriction and do not allow duplication of rules within a policy.*

3   Policy Deployment

Policy deployment is the process by which policy editing commands are issued on firewall, so that the target policy becomes the running policy.

3.1   Policy Editing Languages

A network administrator or a management tool issues commands on firewall to transform the running policy R into the target policy T. The set of commands that a firewall supports is called its policy editing language. Policy editing languages can be classified into two representative classes [22]: Type I and Type II.

Type I Editing. This type supports only two commands, append and delete. Command *(app r)* appends a rule r at the end of the running policy R, unless r is already in R, in which case the command fails. Command *(del r)* deletes r from R, if it is present. As Type I editing can transform any running policy into any target policy, therefore it is complete. Most older firewalls and some recent firewalls, such as FWSM 2.x [1] and JUNOSe 7.x [5], only support Type I editing.

Type II Editing. This type allows random editing of firewall policy. It supports three operations: *(ins i r)* inserts rule r as the ith rule in running policy R, unless r is already present; *(del i)* deletes ith rule from R; *(mov i j)* moves the ith rule to the jth in R position. Type II editing can transform any running policy into any target policy without accepting illegal packets or rejecting legal packets. It is obvious that for a given set of initial and target policies, a Type II deployment normally uses fewer editing commands than an equivalent Type I deployment. Examples of Type II editing firewalls include SunScreen 3.1 Lite [13] and Enterasys Matrix X [2].

3.2   Deployment Efficiency

A deployment is *most-efficient* if it utilizes the minimum number of editing commands in a given language, to correctly deploy a target policy on a firewall. Therefore for a given deployment scenario, a most-efficient Type I (resp. Type II) deployment uses the minimum number of *append* and *delete* commands (resp. *insert*, *delete* and *move* commands). Usually a policy editing command takes constant time, and the variation in deployment time is negligible for different types of commands. Accordingly, the most-efficient deployment minimizes the overall deployment time. Deployment efficiency for Type I and Type II languages are discussed in more detail in Sections 4 and 5 respectively.

3.3   Deployment Safety

A deployment is *safe* if no security hole is introduced and no legal traffic is denied at any stage during the deployment. A temporary security hole permits malicious traffic to pass through the firewall and this may cause serious damage to the network infrastructure. Similarly, rejection of legal traffic during deployment may interrupt critical operations and result in serious losses. This is like inflicting a self-DoS attack and hence it is intolerable in mission-critical networks, even for a short duration of time.

Deployment safety is particularly important in cases where many changes are to be made to a large firewall policy. In such cases, a deployment can last up to several minutes, which may provide sufficient opportunity to a malicious party to exploit a vulnerability. Fast spreading worms, such as Conficker [4] and Slammer [3], can infect million of systems across the globe within minutes. Furthermore, a skilled hacker can use automated tools to continuously probe for vulnerabilities and instantly exploit these as they appear during an unsafe deployment.

The first fundamental work on deployment safety is presented in [22] where a safe deployment formalization is presented. The formalization defines a safe deployment as follows: Policy A is *denial-safe* w.r.t. policies B and C iff every packet that A denies is also denied by B or C. A deployment is denial-safe iff at every moment during the deployment the running policy is denial-safe w.r.t. the initial and the target policies. Similarly, policy A is *permission-safe* w.r.t. policies B and C iff every packet that A permits is also permitted by B or C. A deployment is permission-safe iff at every moment during the deployment the running policy is permission-safe w.r.t. to initial and the target policies.

Definition 1. *Deployment Safety.* *A policy is* safe *iff it is both denial-safe and permission-safe. A deployment is* partial-safe *if it is either permission-safe or denial-safe but not both w.r.t. initial and final policies.*

In the rest of this paper, we denote the initial policy by I and the target policy by T. A firewall has a new running policy every time an editing command is applied. Thus deployment can be viewed as a sequence of running policies $I = R_0, R_1, ..., R_{n-1}, R_n = T$, where R_{i+1} is derived by applying an editing command to R_i. Let $P(R)$ denotes the set of packets permitted by Policy R and $D(R)$ denotes the set of packets denied by Policy R. Formally, we can define that R is safe w.r.t. policies I and T as follows:

$$Safe(R, I, T) \equiv (P(I) \cap P(T)) \subseteq P(R) \subseteq (P(I) \cup P(T))$$
$$Safe(R, I, T) \equiv (D(I) \cap D(T)) \subseteq D(R) \subseteq (D(I) \cup D(T))$$

This is semantic characterization for the safety deployment as it is based on the set of packets. It should be noted that it is very hard to verify $Safe(R, I, T)$ because it depends on the data contained in all fields of every policy rule. Unlike [22], we define a *sufficient* condition to verify whether or not a deployment is safely performed. Indeed, Theorem 1 gives syntactic characterization for the deployment safety because all rules within policies are considered as a black box. Let r_e represent the hidden default rule at the end of policy (i.e $r_e = deny - all$ or $r_e = permit - all$). For a rule r, α_r represents the set of rules that precede r in I, and β_r represents the set of rules that precede r in T.

Theorem 1. *An intermediate policy R is safe w.r.t. I and T, if the following conditions hold for all rules r_i in $I \cup T \cup \{r_e\}$: (i) If $r_i \in I \cap T$, then r_i is preceded by an improper superset of α_{r_i} or β_{r_i}. (ii) If $r_i \in I$ (or $r_i \in T$) but $r_i \notin I \cap T$ and r_i appears in R, then r_i is preceded by an improper superset of α_{r_i} (or β_{r_i}).*

Due to the space limit, the proof of Theorem 1 is given in [6].

Example 1. Consider the following initial and target policies described as a list of rules:

$$I = [a, b, c] \text{ and } T = [d, e, f]$$

Let R_1 and R_2 be intermediate policies where $R_1 = []$ and $R_2 = [b, e]$. Note that $\alpha_{r_e} = \{a, b, c\}$ and $\beta_{r_e} = \{d, e, f\}$. The intermediate policy R_1 may not be safe because an empty set of rules precedes r_e, which is neither an improper superset of α_{r_e} nor β_{r_e}. Also, b appears only in I, and $\alpha_b = \{a\}$. But the set of rules that precede b in R_2 is not an improper superset of α_b. Hence, R_2 may not be safe w.r.t. I and T.

Example 2. Consider the following initial and target policies:

$$I = [b, c] \text{ and } T = [d, c]$$

such that b and d permit a packet p, while c denies p. Obviously, both I and T permit p. There are two cases where p is rejected by an intermediate policy R: (i) when both b and d are not in R i.e. $R_1 = [c]$, and; (ii) when c appears at the first position in R i.e. $R_2 = [c, b]$. However, $\alpha_{r_e} = \{b, c\}$ and $\beta_{r_e} = \{d, c\}$. Therefore, b or d (or both) must precede r_e in R and case (i) cannot occur in safe deployment. Furthermore, $\alpha_c = \{b\}$ and $\beta_c = \{d\}$. Therefore, b or d (or both) must also precede c in R and case (ii) is also not possible in a safe deployment. The four possible safe running policies w.r.t. I and T are:

$$R_3 = [b, c]$$
$$R_4 = [d, c]$$
$$R_5 = [b, d, c]$$
$$R_6 = [d, b, c]$$

Theorem 2 gives syntactic characterization to verify the partial-safety. Due to the space limit, the proof of this theorem is given in [6].

Theorem 2. *An intermediate running policy R is partial-safe w.r.t. I and T, if the conditions of Theorem 1 hold for all rules r_j in $I \cup T$.*

Example 3. Let r_e be the hidden default rule at the end of policy. Consider the following policies where b and d deny a packet p, while c and e accept p:

$$I = [b, c, r_e = deny - all]$$

$$T = [d, e, r_e = deny - all]$$

Clearly, both I and T deny p. The only case where p is accepted by a running policy is when c or e appear as first rule in R. However, $\alpha_c = \{b\}$ and $\beta_e = \{d\}$. Therefore, c appears in R only when it is preceded by b. Similarly, if e appears in R, then it must be preceded by d. Therefore, this case in not possible. This also implies that if both b and d are not in R, then c and e cannot be in R. In this case, p matches r_e and it is denied. Hence, R is permission-safe. Alternatively, consider the same I and T, and the case where both b and d permit p, while c and e deny p. In this case, if both b and d are not in R, then p matches r_e and it is falsely denied. Hence, R is not denial-safe.

4   Type I Deployment

Recall that two types of security problems may arise during an unsafe deployment: (i) Rejection of legal traffic; (ii) Creation of temporary security holes. To be safe, a firewall policy deployment must avoid both types of problems. However, safe deployment is not always possible by using only the rules of I and T and Type I editing commands [22]. In Algorithm 1, called PARTIALSAFEDEPLOYMENT, we give a most-efficient algorithm that provides a *partial-safe* deployment; that is it can avoid either situation (i) or (ii) but not both. For firewall policies with permit-all semantics, the algorithm ensures that situation (i) will never occur. Similarly, for firewall policies with deny-all semantics situation (ii) is avoided.

It is worth mentioning that some types of security threats cannot be dealt by firewalls alone and additional security mechanism such as Intrusion Detection and Prevention System (IDPS) [8] may be required. If the situation (ii) temporarily arises during a deployment, an IDPS can be configured to block the illegal packets that may pass through the firewall. Therefore, in the presence of an IDPS, a firewall policy with permit-all semantics can avoid both types of problem.

It is assumed that both the initial policy I and the final one T are stored in separate arrays and the running policy R is initiallay equal to I. The algorithm is efficient, as it deploys the target policy using the minimum number of Type I editing commands. The algorithm selectively deletes all rules that are in I but not in T, in reverse order and appropriately append rules to running policy R. The algorithm begins by finding the longest prefix T' of T that is a subsequence of I. Starting from first rule in I, all rules of I – but not in T' – are then pushed to the stack and added to the hash table (lines $3 - 11$). Next, starting from the first rule in T that is not in T', each rule r is taken and placed at a correct position in R. If r is present in the hash table, this implies that r is present in R and needs to be deleted first. In this case, all rules in I that are not in T' and occur after r in I are deleted from R (lines $13 - 20$). Then r is deleted from R and appended back at the end. This ensures that r appears in R, only if it is preceded by an improper superset of α_r or β_r (see Sub-section 3.3). Thus, the condition of Theorem 2

```
 1: PARTIALSAFEDEPLOYMENT(I,T)
 2: // Find longest prefix T' of T such that T' ⊆ I
 3: j ← 1
 4: for i ← 1 to sizeOf(I) do
 5:    if I[i] = T[j] then
 6:       j ← j + 1
 7:    else
 8:       stack.push(I[i])
 9:       hash.add (I[i])
10:    end if
11: end for
12: // Place each rule of T that is not in T' at correct position
13: for t ← j to sizeOf(T) do
14:    if hash.contains(T[t]) then
15:       repeat
16:          y ← stack.pop()
17:          IssueCommand (del y)
18:          hash.delete(y)
19:       until y = T[t]
20:    end if
21:    IssueCommand (app T[t])
22: end for
23: // Delete all rules in I that are not in T
24: while NOT stack.empty do
25:    IssueCommand (del stack.pop())
26: end while
```

Algorithm 1. Partial Safe Deployment

is satisfied and the algorithm PARTIALSAFEDEPLOYMENT is *partial-safe*. Finally, the stack contains rules that are in I but not T and therefore must be deleted from R. After the deletion of these rules (lines 24-26), R becomes T. Hence, the deployment is also correct. Let $|X|$ represents the total number of rules in policy X , then $|I| + |T| - 2|T'|$ editing commands are generated by the algorithm. The algorithm takes $O(n)$ time and space,where $n = max(|I|, |T|)$.

Due to the limited set of operations and the restriction that repetition of rules is not allowed, not all deployments can be done safely using Type I languages. For instance, if $I = [a, b]$ and $T = [b, a]$ the deployement can never be safe. The restriction, that all rules must be distinct, can be overcome by using semantically equivalent rules or by breaking a rule r into sub-rules r_1 and r_2, such that $r_1 \cup r_2 = r$. Two rules r_1 and r_2 are considered semantically equivalent, if both rules match exactly the same set of packets. The union $r_1 \cup r_2$ provides a semantic equivalence to r. Regardless of firewall policy architecture, it is always possible to split a rule with a multi-value field into several rules [21]. In [6], we presented an algorithm providing a safe strategy for Type I deployment by splitting r into equivalent r_1 and r_2. Due to the space limit, this algorithm is not presented here.

5 Type II Deployment

Type II deployment allows for random modification of a running policy. Therefore, for a given set of I and T, a safe Type II deployment usually utilizes less editing commands than an equivalent Type I deployment. If I and T have identical set of rules, then T can be considered as a permutation of I. In this case, the optimal edit sequence preserves a Longest Common Subsequence LCS(I,T) of the two sequences, and the optimal edit sequence have length equal to $|I| - |LCS(I,T)|$ [12]. That is, a move command has to be generated for each rule that is not in LCS(I,T). In the general case, where I has some rules that are not in T and T has some rules that are not in I, a command has to be generated to insert/delete each such rule. Therefore, the optimal edit sequence will have a length of $|I| + |T| - c - |LCS(I,T)|$, where c is the number of rules common to both I and T.

5.1 Deployment Algorithm

In this section we present a correct, safe and most-efficient near linear running time type II deployment algorithm called EFFICIENTDEPLOYMENT (see algorithms 2 and 3). For a most-efficient deployment, we need to issue exactly one command for each rule that is in $I \cup T$ but not in one of the longest common subsequences of I and T [19]. EFFICIENTDEPLOYMENT issues exactly $|I \cup T| - |LCS(I,T)|$ commands to transform I to T. Firstly, the algorithm issues commands to selectively move rules upwards and to insert rules that are in T but not in I. An array T_2 is maintained that facilitates in the calculation of positional parameters for ins, del and mov operations. After commands are issued for all the rules to be moved upwards and inserted, T_2 becomes the running policy.

EFFICIENTDEPLOYMENT maintains two variables i and t that point to the rules in I and T respectively that are currently under consideration to be appended to T_2. The rules still to be moved upwards and inserted are also appended to an array χ and later on commands are generated for these rules, as described below.

The algorithm starts by traversing T from $T[t = 1]$. If $T[t]$ is neither in T_2 nor in $LCS(I,T)$, then it is appended to T_2 and χ (lines 9-10). While if $T[t]$ is in $LCS(I,T)$ but not in T_2, then I is traversed by incrementing i until $I[i] = T[t]$ and any rule $I[i]$ that is not in T_2 is appended to T_2 and pushed to the stack (lines 12-23). Then, $T[t]$ is appended to T_2 and the variable t is incremented. Next, a command is issued for each rule r in χ and then r is deleted from χ (lines 26-37). If r is not in I, then an $insert$ command is issued and the variable M is incremented, otherwise a $move$ command is issued that places r closer to the beginning of R. Each rule to be moved upwards that appear after r in I but before r in R causes the r to be shifted down one position in R. The number of such rules, N, is calculated by using binary search technique in the function $Count$ and stored in the array C_1. Similarly the number of rules, M, inserted above r causes r to be shifted down M position. Therefore, the current position of r in R is the sum of its initial position in I, M, and N. The value of N is calculated in $O(log|I|)$ steps.

```
 1: EFFICIENTDEPLOYMENT(I,T)
 2:   i ← 1, L ← LCS(I,T)
 3:   C₁ ← empty array of size sizeOf(I)
 4:   C₂ ← empty array of size sizeOf(T)
 5:   T₂ ← empty_array, χ ← empty_array
 6:   for t ← 1 to sizeOf(T) + 1 do
 7:     if T[t] ∉ T₂ then
 8:       if T[t] ∉ L then
 9:         χ.append(T[t])
10:         T₂.append(T[t])
11:       else
12:         while I[i] ≠ T[t] do
13:           if I[i] ∉ T₂ then
14:             T₂.append(I[i])
15:             if I[i] ∈ T then
16:               stack.push(I[i], count(indexOf(I[i], T), C₂))
17:             else
18:               stack.push(I[i], 0)
19:               V ← V + 1
20:             end if
21:           end if
22:           i ← i + 1
23:         end while
24:         T₂.append(I[i])
25:         i ← i + 1
26:         if sizeOf(χ) > 0 then
27:           j ← 1
28:           while sizeOf(χ) > 0 do
29:             if χ[j] ∉ I then
30:               issueCommand(insert indexOf(χ[j], T₂), χ[j])
31:               M ← M + 1
32:             else
33:               issueCommand(move            indexOf(χ[j], I)              +
                   count(indexOf(χ[j], I), C₁) + M, indexOf(χ[j], T₂))
34:             end if
35:             χ.delete(χ[j])
36:             j ← j + 1
37:           end while
38:         end if
39:       end if
40:     end if
41:   end for
42:   //MoveDowns and Delete
43:   while NOT stack.empty do
44:     [r, U] ← stack.pop()
45:     if r ∉ T then
46:       issueCommand(delete indexOf(r, T₂))
47:       V ← V - 1
48:     else
49:       issueCommand(move indexOf(r, T₂), indexOf(r, T) + U + V + 1)
50:     end if
51:   end while
```

Algorithm 2. EFFICIENTDEPLOYMENT algorithm

```
 1: Count(nodePos, arr) {
 2:   start ← 1, last ← sizeOf(arr)
 3:   adjust ← 0
 4:   mid ← Trunc((start + last)/2)
 5:   while mid ≠ nodePos AND start ≤ last do
 6:     if mid > nodePos then
 7:       adjust ← adjust + arr[mid]
 8:       last ← mid − 1
 9:     else
10:       start ← mid + 1
11:       arr[mid] ← arr[mid] + 1
12:     end if
13:     mid ← Trunc((start + last)/2)
14:   end while
15:   arr[mid] ← arr[mid] + 1
16:   return(adjust + arr[mid] − 1) }
```

Algorithm 3. Count function

After all the rules in χ are processed, the traversal is resumed at T[t] and the steps described in the previous paragraph are repeated until $T[|T|+1]$ is reached. We assume that $I[|I|+1] = T[|T|+1] = r_e$, where r_e is the default rule at the end of each policy. After traversal is finished T_2 becomes the running policy.

Finally, a command is issued for each rule s in stack (lines 43-51). If s is not in T, then a *delete* command is issued, otherwise a *move* command is issued. The current position of s is its index in T_2. The final position for *move* command is the sum of index of s in T, the rules still need to be deleted (V), and the number of rules (U) that appear before s in I but after s in T. The value of U is determined in $O(log|T|)$ steps in the function $Count$ and stored in array C_2. The total running time for issuing all commands is $O(n + x\ log\ n)$, where x is the number of rules to be moved and $n = max(|I|, |T|)$. The running time can be further improved if a balance tree such as AVL tree is used to compute positional parameters leading to a running time complexity of $O(n + x\ log\ x)$.

5.2   Safety and Correctness of EFFICIENTDEPLOYMENT

Recall that α_x represents the set of rules that precede a rule x in I, and β_x represents the set of rules that precede x in T. EFFICIENTDEPLOYMENT starts by traversing T from the beginning and if a rule $r = T[t]$ is encountered, which is not in T_2, it is immediately appended to T_2.

If a rule $\Sigma = T[t]$ is encountered that is in $LCS(I, T)$, then i is incremented until $I[i] = \Sigma$ and any rule $s = I[i]$ that is not in T_2 is appended to T_2. If s is not in T_2, this means that either s does not appear in T or it appears after Σ in T and therefore must be moved downwards. Similarly r is not in $LCS(I, T)$ and it appears before Σ in T, this implies that either r is not present in I or it appears after Σ in I and therefore must be moved upwards.

As all rules that appear before r in T are appended to T_2 before r, therefore r is preceded by an improper superset of β_r in T_2. Also, all rules that appear before Σ in I and/or T precede Σ in T_2. In other words, Σ is preceded by $\alpha_\Sigma \cup \beta_\Sigma$ in T_2. Similarly, some rules in T and all rules in I that precede s are appended to T_2 before s, therefore s is preceded by an improper superset of α_s in T_2.

Initially I is the running policy. The algorithm starts by issuing commands for rules to be inserted and move upwards. The final position of a move (or insert) operation for r is $indexOf(r, T_2)$. Therefore, after the move operation r is preceded by an improper superset of β_r. Since r is moved upwards, so it still precedes the rules that appear below it in I. Therefore according to Theorem 1 (see Sub-section 3.3), R remains safe w.r.t. I and T.

After commands are issued for all the rules to be moved upwards and inserted, T_2 becomes the running policy and s is preceded by an improper superset of α_s. However, some rules in β_s may still appear below s in R. The correct position of s is calculated as described in previous section, which causes s to be preceded by an improper superset of $\alpha_s \cup \beta_s$. Therefore according to theorem 1, R remains safe w.r.t. I and T. When all the rules, to be moved down and deleted, above s are processed then s is preceded by exactly β_s. Thus, after commands are issued for all rules to be moved downwards and deleted, each rule x is preceded by exactly β_x. In other words, each rule in R is preceded by exactly the same set of rules that precedes it in T; this implies that I is converted to T and hence the deployment is safe and correct.

6 Performance Evaluation

To evaluate the performance of EFFICIENTDEPLOYMENT, we try to follow the same set of test cases as in [22]. We use four firewall policies with 2000, 5000, 10000, and 25000 rules. For each policy, we perform five different tests. In a most-efficient deployment test 1, test 2, test 3,test 4 and test 5 requires 10, 500, 1000, 60%, and 90% of commands respectively to convert initial policy to the target policy. Note that these percentages are taken from the initial policy. The algorithm is implemented in C++, and all tests are performed on *Dell Precision 370* with Intel Pentium IV 2.0 Ghz processor and 1 GB of RAM[1]. The results of each test on policies 1-4 are given in Table 1. The time taken by EFFICIENTDEPLOYMENT is specified in the column ED, while the column SI specifies the total time taken by *diff* and SANITIZEIT algorithm given in [22] for computing a safe deployment. All times are shown in seconds.

It is clear that EFFICIENTDEPLOYMENT takes a fraction of second to calculate safe and most-efficient deployment for policies as large as Policy 4. Also, EFFICIENTDEPLOYMENT generates a most-efficient and safe deployment much faster than the SanitizeIt algorithm. However, as no details are given about nature of changes in [22], it might not be appropriate to directly draw conclusion for tests 2-5. For example, consider Test 5 on Policy 4, 90% edit distance means 22500 commands need to be issued to turn I to T. If 22,500 insert commands are required that means T has 47,500 rules, while if 22,500 delete commands are required then T has only 2500 rules. Therefore, reliable comparison can only be done if size of I and T used in [1] is known, so that policies of same size could be used for testing EFFICIENTDEPLOYMENT. However, Test 1 involves only 10 changes and it can be used to compare the two algorithms, as shown in figure 2.

---

[1] An executable program is available at
`http://webloria.loria.fr/~imine/program.zip`

Table 1. Performance tests

Tests	Policy 1 (2,000)		Policy 2 (5,000)		Policy 3 (10,000)		Policy 4 (25,000)	
	ED	SI	ED	SI	ED	SI	ED	SI
Test 1	.00635	.01200	.01542	.02300	.03023	.04400	.07567	.24200
Test 2	.00662	.01200	.01622	.02800	.03111	.04900	.07580	.28300
Test 3	.00697	.03800	.01641	.04900	.03154	.07000	.07592	.32500
Test 4	.00703	.04000	.01757	.20500	.03518	1.3820	.08943	12.582
Test 5	.00732	.07000	.01859	.38700	.03722	4.3920	.09421	26.983

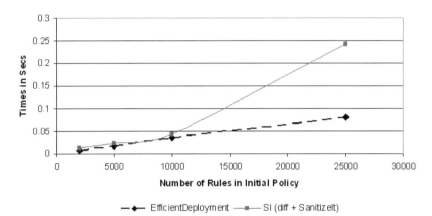

Fig. 2. Comparison of EFFICIENTDEPLOYMENT and SANITIZEIT for Test 1

From the curve illustrated in Figure 2, it can be concluded that EFFICIENTDEPLOY-MENT is more efficient than SANITIZEIT and the running time is close to linear. Furthermore, SANITIZEIT appears to have a polynomial running time. This effect is more notable in case of test 5 and Policy 4, where SI takes almost 27 secs to compute a deployment sequence.

7   Conclusion

Firewall policy deployment safety is a new and area of research. In this paper, we have presented a formalization for deployment safety and used this formalization as a basis to provide safe and efficient algorithms for both Type I and Type II languages. We have proposed for type I policy editing languages a correct algorithm that is efficient and partial-safe. For Type II policy editing languages, we have presented an approximately linear, most-efficient and safe algorithm. Our experimental results showed that this algorithm does not add any overhead and it is practical even for very large policies. In future work, we plan to investigate the deployment problem in two kinds of firewalls: stateful firewalls and distributed firewalls.

References

1. Cisco Security Manager,
   http://www.cisco.com/en/US/products/ps6498/index.html

2. Entrasys Matrix X Core Router,
   `http://www.entrasys.com/products/routing/x/`
3. F-Secure. Malware information pages: Slammer,
   `http://www.f-secure.com/v-descs/mssqlm.shtml`
4. F-Secure. Malware information pages: Worm:w32/downadup.al,
   `http://www.f-secure.com/v-descs/worm_w32_downadup_al.shtml`
5. Juniper Network and Security Manager,
   `http://www.juniper.net/us/en/local/pdf/datasheets/`
   `1100018-en.pdf`
6. Ahmed, Z., Imine, A., Rusinowitch, M.: Safe and Efficient Strategies for Updating Firewall Policies. Research Report RR-6940, INRIA (2009),
   `http://webloria.loria.fr/~imine/rep2009.pdf`
7. Al-Shaer, E., Hamed, H.: Modeling and Management of Firewall Policies. IEEE Transactions on Network and Service Management 1(1), 2–10 (2004)
8. Anwar, M., Zafar, M., Ahmed, Z.: A Proposed Preventive Information Security System. In: International Conference on Electrical Engineering, ICEE '07, pp. 1–6 (2007)
9. Baboescu, F., Varghese, G.: Fast and Scalable Conflict Detection for Packet Classifiers. In: ICNP, pp. 270–279 (2002)
10. Bartal, Y., Mayer, A.J., Nissim, K., Wool, A.: Firmato: A Novel Firewall Management Toolkit. In: IEEE Symposium on Security and Privacy, pp. 17–31 (1999)
11. Cobb, S.: ICSA Firewall Policy Guide v2.0. Technical report. NCSA Security White Paper Series (1997)
12. Cormode, G., Muthukrishnan, S., Sahinalp, S.C.: Permutation Editing and Matching via Embeddings. In: Orejas, F., Spirakis, P.G., van Leeuwen, J. (eds.) ICALP 2001. LNCS, vol. 2076, pp. 481–492. Springer, Heidelberg (2001)
13. Englund, M.: Securing systems with host-based firewalls. In: Sun BluePrints Online (September 2001)
14. Fu, Z., Wu, S.F., Huang, H., Loh, K., Gong, F., Baldine, I., Xu, C.: IPSec/VPN Security Policy: Correctness, Conflict Detection, and Resolution. In: Sloman, M., Lobo, J., Lupu, E.C. (eds.) POLICY 2001. LNCS, vol. 1995, pp. 39–56. Springer, Heidelberg (2001)
15. Gouda, M.G., Liu, A.X.: Firewall Design: Consistency, Completeness, and Compactness. In: ICDCS, pp. 320–327 (2004)
16. Hamed, H., Al-Shaer, E.: Dynamic rule-ordering optimization for high-speed firewall filtering. In: ASIACCS, pp. 332–342 (2006)
17. Karen, S., Paul, H.: Guidelines on Firewalls and Firewall Policy. NIST Recommendations, SP 800-41 (July 2008)
18. Liu, A.X.: Change-impact analysis of firewall policies. In: Biskup, J., López, J. (eds.) ESORICS 2007. LNCS, vol. 4734, pp. 155–170. Springer, Heidelberg (2007)
19. Myers, E.W.: An o(nd) difference algorithm and its variations. Algorithmica 1(2), 251–266 (1986)
20. Qian, J.: ACLA: A framework for Access Control List (ACL) Analysis and Optimization. In: Proceedings of the IFIP TC6/TC11 International Conference on Communications and Multimedia Security Issues of the New Century, Deventer, The Netherlands, p. 4. Kluwer, B.V. (2001)
21. Qiu, L., Varghese, G., Suri, S.: Fast firewall implementations for software and hardware-based routers. In: International Conference on Network Protocols, pp. 155–170 (2001)
22. Zhang, C.C., Winslett, M., Gunter, C.A.: On the Safety and Efficiency of Firewall Policy Deployment. In: SP '07: Proceedings of the 2007 IEEE Symposium on Security and Privacy, Washington, DC, USA, pp. 33–50. IEEE Computer Society, Los Alamitos (2007)

A Privacy-Preserving Architecture for the Semantic Web Based on Tag Suppression

Javier Parra-Arnau, David Rebollo-Monedero, and Jordi Forné

Department of Telematics Engineering, Technical University of Catalonia (UPC),
E-08034 Barcelona, Spain
{javier.parra,david.rebollo,jforne}@entel.upc.edu*

Abstract. We propose an architecture that preserves user privacy in the semantic Web via tag suppression. In tag suppression, users may wish to tag some resources and refrain from tagging some others in order to hinder privacy attackers in their efforts to profile users' interests. Following this strategy, our architecture helps users decide which tags should be suppressed. We describe the implementation details of the proposed architecture and provide further insight into the modeling of profiles. In addition, we present a mathematical formulation of the optimal trade-off between privacy and tag suppression rate.

1 Introduction

The World Wide Web constitutes the largest repository of information in the world. Since its invention in the nineties, the form in which information is organized has evolved substantially. At the beginning, web content was classified in directories belonging to different areas of interest, manually maintained by experts. These directories provided users with accurate information, but as the Web grew they rapidly became unmanageable. Although they are still available, they have been progressively dominated by the current search engines based on web crawlers, which explore new or updated content in a methodic, automatic manner. However, even though search engines are able to index a large amount of web content, they may provide irrelevant results or fail when terms are not explicitly included in web pages. A query containing the keyword *accommodation*, for instance, would not retrieve web pages with terms such as *hotel* or *apartment* not including that keyword.

Recently, a new form of conceiving the Web, called the *semantic Web* [1], has emerged to address this problem. The semantic Web, envisioned by Tim Berners-Lee in 2001, is expected to provide the web content with a conceptual structure so that information can be interpreted by machines. The semantic Web requires to explicitly associate meaning with resources on the Web. This process is normally referred to as *semantic tagging*, or simply tagging, and is supposed to play a key

---

* This work was supported in part by the Spanish Government under Projects CONSOLIDER INGENIO 2010 CSD2007-00004 "ARES" and TSI2007-65393-C02-02 "ITACA", and by the Catalan Government under Grant 2009 SGR 1362.

S. Katsikas, J. Lopez, and M. Soriano (Eds.): TrustBus 2010, LNCS 6264, pp. 58–68, 2010.

role for the semantic Web to become a reality. One of the benefits of associating concepts with web pages is the semantic interoperability in web applications. Furthermore, tagging allows applications to decrease the interaction with users, to obtain some form of semantic distance between web pages and to ultimately process web pages whose content is nowadays only understandable by humans.

Despite the many advantages the semantic Web is bringing to the Web community, the continuous tagging activity prompts serious privacy concerns. More specifically, tags submitted to a web server could be used to derive user's preferences [2] or expertise [3], and thus obtain precise user profiles containing sensitive information such as health, political affiliation, salary or religion. This could be the case of recommendation web sites such as *Last.fm*, *Movielens* or *Jinni*, where user profiles are normally shown by some kind of histogram or tag cloud, as depicted in Fig. 1.

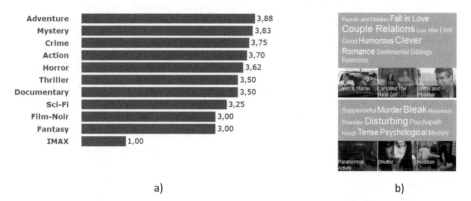

a)   b)

Fig. 1. A histogram (a) and a tag cloud (b) displaying user profiles in *Movielens* and *Jinni*, respectively

1.1   Contribution and Plan of This Paper

In this paper, we present an architecture that preserves user privacy in the semantic Web via *tag suppression*. More specifically, users may wish to tag some resources and refrain from tagging some others when their privacy is being compromised. The proposed architecture helps users decide which tags should be suppressed in order to hinder privacy attackers in their efforts to profile users' interests. Consequently, this approach guarantees user privacy to a certain extent, at the cost of processing overhead and the semantic loss incurred by suppressing tags, but without having to trust the web server or the network operator.

Additionally, we present an information-theoretic formulation of the trade-off between privacy and tag suppression rate, which arises from our definition of privacy risk. In particular, we measure privacy risk as a divergence between a user's apparent tag distribution and the population's.

Sec. 2 explores the basics of the semantic Web and reviews some relevant approaches related to privacy. Sec. 3 describes our privacy-preserving architecture and focuses on its internal components. Sec. 4 presents our privacy measure and a formulation of the trade-off between privacy and tag suppression rate. Conclusions are drawn in Sec. 5.

2   State of the Art

This section describes the fundamentals of the semantic Web and includes some relevant contributions to privacy within this context.

As mentioned in Sec. 1, the semantic Web requires to explicitly associate meaning with resources on the Web. In order to achieve this meaningful structure, the conceptual description of resources must be described formally. For this purpose, the World Wide Web Consortium (W3C) proposes to use the resource description format (RDF), which is a general-purpose language for representing information on the Web. In RDF, the meaning is encoded by a triple consisting of a *subject*, a *predicate* and an *object*. According to this format, a resource on a web page (subject) is associated with a property (predicate), to which a value (object) is assigned. For instance, in the statement "1984 was written by George Orwell", "1984" would be the subject, "was written by" the predicate, and "George Orwell" the object.

Although RDF provides the technology to describe meaning, the semantic Web requires also that concepts and terms share a common definition. Ontologies, which are defined in [4] as "a formal, explicit specification of a shared conceptualization", arise with this aim. In the semantic web context, an ontology is a set of statements where terminology is defined using a specific language. Several languages such as RDF schemas (RDF-S) [5] or ontology web language (OWL) [6] are used to express ontologies.

A number of approaches have been suggested to preserve user privacy in the semantic Web, most of them focused on privacy policies. In the traditional Web, the majority of web sites interact with users to provide them with privacy policies, and allowing them to find out how their private information will be managed. Unfortunately, users do not frequently understand [7] or even read [8] privacy policies. The platform for privacy preferences (P3P) is created to deal with this situation and provides a framework with informed online interactions. More specifically, when a web site supports the P3P, it establishes a set of policies to define how user's private information will be used. Users, in turn, set their own privacy policies to determine what kind of personal information they are willing to disclose to the web sites they browse. Accordingly, when a user browses a web site, P3P compares both the web site's and the user's privacy policies. If they do not match, P3P informs the user about this situation and consequently they decide how to proceed. In the semantic Web, this process is intended to be carried out by autonomous agents. In this context, several policy languages to define privacy and security requirements have been proposed. In [9], the authors suggest a new semantic policy language based on RDF-S to express access control requirements over concepts defined in ontologies. In [10], privacy and authentication policies are incorporated into the descriptions of an ontology called OWL *for services* (OWL-S). Furthermore, the authors implement algorithms for the requester to verify the provider's adherence to policies.

In the context of private information retrieval (PIR), users send general-purpose queries to an information service provider. An example would be a user sending the query: "What was George Orwell's real name?". In this scenario, query forgery, which consists in accompanying genuine with false queries, appears as an approach to guarantee user privacy to a certain extent at the cost of traffic and processing overhead. Building on this principle, several PIR protocols, mainly heuristic, have been proposed and implemented. In [11, 12], a solution is presented, aimed to preserve the privacy of a group of users sharing an access point to the Web while surfing the Internet. The authors propose the generation of fake transactions, i.e., accesses to a web page to hinder eavesdroppers in their efforts to profile the group. Privacy is measured as the similarity between the actual profile of a group of users and that observed by privacy attackers [11]. Specifically, the authors use the cosine measure, as frequently used in information retrieval [13], to capture the similarity between the group genuine profile and the group apparent profile. Based on this model, some experiments are conducted to study the impact of the construction of user profiles on the performance [14]. In line with this, some simple, heuristic implementations in the form of add-ons for popular browsers have recently started to appear [15, 16].

Despite the simplicity of the mechanism described above, an analogous *tag forgery* would clearly not be convenient for the semantic Web, which is the motivating application of our work. Submitting a tag implies the construction of conceptual relations, a much more complex process than just sending a simple query to a service provider. Therefore, users might not be willing to manually tag web content they are not interested in.

3   An Architecture for Privacy Preservation in the Semantic Web

This section presents the main contribution of this work: a privacy-preserving architecture in the semantic Web via tag suppression. More specifically, Sec. 3.1 provides further insight into the construction of user profiles. Sec. 3.2 examines our architecture from a global point of view. Sec. 3.3 focuses on the user-side architecture and goes into the details of its internal functional blocks. The specification of one of these blocks will be given in Sec. 4.

3.1   User Profile Construction

Our architecture contemplates that the profile of a user is directly obtained from specific modules integrated into the user's system. Before giving any details on the construction of user profiles, we will first explore how this information could be represented.

Sec. 1 already mentioned that some recommendation web sites commonly use some kind of histogram to show a user profile, as in the case of *Movielens*, or tag clouds, as in *Jinni*. Bearing in mind these examples, we propose a first-approximation, mathematically-tractable model of user profile as a probability mass function (PMF). Accordingly, we suggest two alternatives to model a user profile. Our first proposal entails certain information loss, as it uses categories into which tags are mapped. On the one hand, this could be difficult to carry out, as the meaning of tags would have to be interpreted in order to classify them into categories, but on the other hand, the description of user profiles could be simplified. Our second alternative represents a user profile by means of tags, which do not necessarily coincide with the semantic tags in the RDF format discussed in Sec. 2. Consequently, this approach could provide a much more accurate description of user profiles, although at the expense of a higher complexity.

Once we have described our proposals to represent a user profile, we will now focus on how to extract this information from a user tag activity. We shall assume that user profiles are modeled by tags, although all considerations also apply to category-based profiles. The naive solution is to locally keep a histogram of all the submitted tags, and to calculate the relative frequency of each tag. Accordingly, this PMF would be updated every time a new tag is generated. However, an improved version would explore contextual information to derive a more accurate profile. A possible approach would be using the vector space model [17], as normally done in information retrieval, to represent web pages as tuples containing their most representative terms. More specifically, the term frequency-inverse document frequency (TF-IDF) would be applied to calculate the weights of each term appearing in a web page. Afterwards, the most weighted terms could be combined with the semantic tag submitted by the user in order to obtain an enriched tag. In the remainder of this section, we shall refer to this enriched tag as *profile tag*, as it will be used by the system to construct the user profile, whereas we shall call *semantic tag*, or simply *tag*, the one created by the user in a format such as RDF. For instance, consider a user browsing a web page and submitting the tag "A conference was held in Copenhagen". Instead of using this tag to update the user profile, the system would first extract contextual information from the web page as described above, and later, the profile tag "Copenhagen climate conference" would be used to update the user profile, resulting in a more precise description.

Although this section just describes how to construct user profiles, analogous arguments would apply to the modeling of the population profile. Sec. 3.3 gives more details on this.

3.2   Architecture Overview

Our architecture is built on the simple principle of tag suppression. More specifically, a user may wish to tag some resources and refrain from tagging some others when their privacy is being compromised. Our proposal is motivated by the intuitive observation that a privacy attacker will have actually gained some information about a user whenever the user profile differs from the population profile. Accordingly, we now describe an architecture that helps users decide which tags should be suppressed in order to hinder privacy attackers in their efforts to construct a user profile too different from the population profile.

The main component of this architecture is the web and tag server (WTS), a single entity in which web pages and their semantic tags are stored. Users browsing the Web would retrieve those data from the WTSs. The web browser would represent this information so that it could be understood by users. Afterwards, users would generate their own semantic tags and would submit them to the WTSs.

Users would calculate the population profile as the relative frequency of the tags stored in a particular WTS. This could be done by a crawler application collecting the tags submitted to that WTS. Later, this profile would be used to prevent that WTS from deriving accurate user profiles. As the population would be restricted to users tagging in the same WTS, they would have to store a different population profile for each WTS. More details are given in the next section.

3.3   User-Side Architecture

This section examines the internal components of the proposed architecture and goes into the details of a practical implementation.

The user-side architecture is depicted in Fig. 2. As it can be seen there, our proposal is composed by a number of modules, each of them performing a specific task. Next, we provide a functional description of all of their components.

Web Browser. This module is essentially responsible for the communication with the WTS. Specifically, it downloads both the web content and the semantic tags that the user specifies by means of a URL. Afterwards, the web content is delivered to the *context analyzer*, which extracts contextual information from the web page. The web browser is also in charge of submitting the tags proposed by the user to the WTS. Last but not least, this module also retrieves the tags requested by the *tag crawler* component.

Context Analyzer. This module is aimed to process the web content that is either requested by the user or explored by the tag crawler. Particularly, it performs this task by using the vector space model and the TF-IDF weights commented on in Sec. 3.1. As a result, a tuple of weighted terms is internally generated for each web page. Later, the context analyzer takes a number of the most weighted terms of each tuple, and sends them to the *profile tag generator* module. The selection of these terms could be done according to these two possible alternatives: a user could choose either a fixed number of terms n, or those terms with weights above a threshold t. This selection poses an inherent compromise between accuracy and complexity, regardless the alternative chosen. The higher the resulting number of terms, the higher the accuracy in the description of the profile tag, but the higher the difficulty to handle that user profile.

Tag Crawler. This module retrieves the tags stored in a WTS. Namely, the web browser gives the tag crawler the URL specified by the user. The tag crawler browses then the web pages stored in the corresponding WTS and retrieves the other users' tags. These retrieved tags are submitted to the profile tag generator module linked to the *population profile constructor* block.

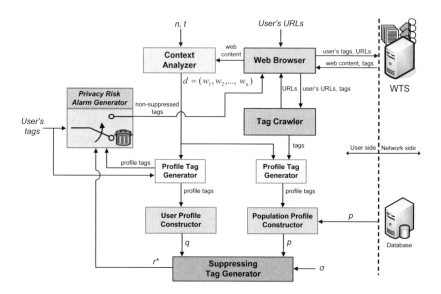

Fig. 2. Internal components of the user-side architecture

Profile Tag Generator. This component generates profile tags from both the semantic tags and the contextual information given by the context analyzer. The architecture is composed of two profile tag generator modules. One of these modules derives profile tags from the tags proposed by the user, and the other generates them from the population's tags retrieved by the tag crawler. The resulting profile tags are delivered respectively to the modules *user profile constructor* and population profile constructor. In addition, the user's profile tags are sent to the *privacy risk alarm generator* block.

Population Profile Constructor. It is responsible for the estimation of the population's tag profile. As the concept of population is limited to users tagging in a common WTS, this module requires to store a population profile for each WTS. Specifically, this module obtains profile tags from one of the profile tag generators. Based on these profile tags, the population profile constructor proceeds as follows: if the profile tag is not included in the population profile, a new entry for it will be automatically created. However, if the profile tag already exists the population profile will be just updated. Alternatively, this block could query databases containing this kind of information. This would be the case, for example, of a future application similar to *Google Insight*.

User Profile Constructor. Analogously to the population profile constructor, this component generates the user's tag profile. Specifically, this module receives profile tags from the profile tag generator dealing with the tags proposed by the user. These profile tags update the user profile like the population profile constructor module does.

Suppressing Tag Generator. This module is the core of the proposed architecture as it is directly responsible for the user privacy. First, this component is provided with both the user and the population profile. In addition, the user specifies a *tag suppression* rate σ, which is a parameter reflecting the proportion of tags that the user is willing to suppress. Next, this module computes the optimum tuple of suppressing tags r^*, which contains information about the profile tags that should be suppressed. Finally, this tuple is given to the *privacy risk alarm generator* module. The suppressing tag generator block is specified in Sec. 4 by means of a mathematical formulation of the trade-off between privacy and tag suppression rate.

Privacy Risk Alarm Generator. The functionality of this module is to warn the user when their privacy is being compromised. When the user submits a tag to the system, this module waits for the profile tag generator to send the profile tag corresponding to the semantic tag. Additionally, this module receives the tuple r^* and proceeds as follows: if the probability of that profile tag in r^* is positive, a privacy risk alarm is generated to warn the user, and it is then for the user to decide whether to eliminate the tag or not. However, if that probability is zero, the system is not aware of any privacy risk and then sends the tag to the web browser.

Having examined each individual component, we will next describe how this system would work. Initially, the user would browse a web page and would submit tags to a WTS. The contextual information derived by the context analyzer would be used to transform these tags into profile tags, and then construct the user profile. At the same time, the tag crawler would retrieve semantic tags from that WTS, and analogously the population profile would be constructed. Both the user profile and the population profile would be used to calculate the tuple r^* every time these profiles were updated. At a certain point, the user could receive a privacy risk alarm when trying to submit a new tag. If this was the case, the user would have to decide whether to eliminate the tag or not.

4   Formulation of the Trade-Off between Privacy and Tag Suppression Rate

This section presents our privacy criterion and a formulation of the trade-off between privacy and tag suppression rate in the semantic Web, which is used to specify one of the functional blocks in Sec. 3.3.

Sec. 3.1 explained how certain recommendation web sites show user profiles. In particular, we mentioned that this information is normally displayed using histograms or tag clouds. Now, we provide a more formal approach to describe user profiles. Specifically, we model user *tags* as random variables (r.v.'s) on a common finite alphabet of n categories or topics, or more specific tags. This model allows us to describe user profiles by means of a PMF, leading to a similar representation than that shown in Fig. 1a. Accordingly, we define q as the probability distribution of the tags of a particular *user* and p as the distribution of the *population*'s tags. In line with Sec. 3.3, we introduce a *tag suppression rate* $\sigma \in [0,1)$, which is the ratio of suppressed tags to total tags. Thus, we define the user's *apparent* tag distribution s as $\frac{q-r}{1-\sigma}$ for some suppression policy $r = (r_1, \ldots, r_n)$ satisfying $0 \leqslant r_i \leqslant q_i$ and $\sum r_i = \sigma$ for $i = 1, \ldots, n$.

Inspired by the privacy criteria proposed in [18], we use an information-theoretic quantity to reflect the intuition that an attacker will be able to compromise user privacy as long as the user's apparent tag distribution diverges from the population's. Specifically, we consider the Kullback-Leibler (KL) divergence [19], which may be interpreted as a measure of discrepancy between probability distributions. Accordingly, we define *privacy risk* as the KL divergence between the apparent distribution and the population's, that is,

$$D(s \parallel p) = D\left(\frac{q-r}{1-\sigma} \middle\| p\right).$$

Supposing that the population is large enough to neglect the impact of the choice of r on p, we define now the *privacy-tag suppression rate* function

$$\mathcal{R}(\sigma) = \min_{\substack{0 \leqslant r_i \leqslant q_i \\ \sum r_i = \sigma}} D\left(\frac{q-r}{1-\sigma} \middle\| p\right), \tag{1}$$

which characterizes the optimal trade-off between privacy (risk) and tag suppression rate, and formally expresses the intuitive reasoning behind tag suppression: the higher the tag suppression rate σ, the lower the discrepancy in terms of the KL divergence between the apparent distribution and the population's, and the lower the privacy risk. In addition, this formulation allows us to describe the functional block *suppressing tag generator* in Sec. 3.3. Namely, this module will be responsible for solving the optimization problem in (1).

Our privacy criterion in the formulation of the privacy-tag suppression rate function is justified, on the one hand, by the arguments in the literature advocating entropy maximization [20], as our privacy measure may be regarded as an extension of Shannon's entropy [19], and on the other hand, by the rationale behind divergence minimization and information gain minimization [18].

5   Concluding Remarks

There exists a large number of proposals for privacy preservation in the semantic Web. Within these approaches, tag suppression arises as a simple technique in terms of infrastructure requirements, as users need not trust an external entity. However, this strategy comes at the cost of processing overhead and the semantic loss incurred by suppressing tags. Recall that we assumed that only a small number of users adhere to this privacy strategy, in contrast to the large population of Internet users. In that case, the global detriment in semantic functionality is small.

Our main contribution is an architecture that implements tag suppression in the semantic Web. The proposed architecture helps users refrain from proposing certain tags in order to hinder attackers in their efforts to profile users' interests.

We describe the implementation details of our architecture. Specifically, the core of the system is a module responsible for calculating a tag suppression policy. The system uses this information to warn the user when their privacy is being compromised and it is then for the user to decide whether to eliminate the tag or not.

We present a mathematical formulation of the optimal trade-off between privacy and tag suppression rate in the semantic Web, which arises from the definition of our privacy criterion.

References

1. Berners-Lee, T., Hendler, J., Lassila, O.: The semantic web. Scient. Amer. (May 2001)
2. Michlmayr, E., Cazer, S.: Learning user profiles from tagging data and leveraging them for personal(ized) information access. In: Proc. Workshop Tagging and Metadata for Social Inform. Org. Workshop in Int. WWW Conf. (2007)
3. John, A., Seligmann, D.: Collaborative tagging and expertise in the enterprise. In: Proc. Col. Web Tagging Workshop WWW (2006)
4. Gruber, T.R.: A translation approach to portable ontology specifications. Knowl. Acquisition 5(2), 199–220 (1993)
5. Brickley, D., Guha, R.V.: RDF vocabulary description language 1.0: RDF schema. W3c recommendation, W3C (February 2004),
   http://www.w3.org/TR/2004/REC-rdf-schema-20040210/
6. OWL Working Group, W.: OWL 2 Web Ontology Language: Document Overview. W3C Recommendation (October 27, 2009),
   http://www.w3.org/TR/owl2-overview/
7. Mcdonald, A.M., Reeder, R.W., Kelley, P.G., Cranor, L.F.: A comparative study of online privacy policies and formats. In: Proc. Workshop Privacy Enhanc. Technol. (PET), pp. 37–55. Springer, Heidelberg (2009)
8. Jensen, C., Potts, C., Jensen, C.: Privacy practices of internet users: Self-reports versus observed behavior. Int. J. Human-Comput. Stud. 63(1-2), 203–227 (2005)
9. Kagal, L., Finin, T., Joshi, A.: A policy based approach to security for the semantic web. In: Proc. Int. Semantic Web Conf., pp. 402–418 (2003)
10. Kagal, L., Paolucci, M., Srinivasan, N., Denker, G., Finin, T., Sycara, K.: Authorization and privacy for semantic web services. IEEE J. Intelligent Syst. 19(4), 50–56 (2004)
11. Elovici, Y., Shapira, B., Maschiach, A.: A new privacy model for hiding group interests while accessing the web. In: Proc. ACM Workshop on Privacy in the Electron. Society, pp. 63–70. ACM, New York (2002)
12. Shapira, B., Elovici, Y., Meshiach, A., Kuflik, T.: PRAW – The model for PRivAte Web. J. Amer. Soc. Inform. Sci., Technol. 56(2), 159–172 (2005)

13. Frakes, W.B., Baeza-Yates, R.A. (eds.): Information Retrieval: Data Structures & Algorithms. Prentice-Hall, Englewood Cliffs (1992)
14. Kuflik, T., Shapira, B., Elovici, Y., Maschiach, A.: Privacy preservation improvement by learning optimal profile generation rate. In: Brusilovsky, P., Corbett, A.T., de Rosis, F. (eds.) UM 2003. LNCS, vol. 2702, pp. 168–177. Springer, Heidelberg (2003)
15. Howe, D.C., Nissenbaum, H.: TrackMeNot (2006)
16. Toubiana, V.: SquiggleSR (2007)
17. Salton, G., Wong, A., Yang, C.S.: A vector space model for automatic indexing. ACM Commun. 18(11), 613–620 (1975)
18. Rebollo-Monedero, D., Forné, J., Domingo-Ferrer, J.: From t-closeness-like privacy to postrandomization via information theory. IEEE Trans. Knowl. Data Eng. (October 2009)
19. Cover, T.M., Thomas, J.A.: Elements of Information Theory, 2nd edn. Wiley, New York (2006)
20. Jaynes, E.T.: On the rationale of maximum-entropy methods. Proc. IEEE 70(9), 939–952 (1982)

Context-Aware Privacy Design Pattern Selection

Siani Pearson and Yun Shen

HP Labs Bristol
Long Down Avenue
Stoke Gifford
Bristol BS34 8QZ UK
{Siani.Pearson,Yun.Shen}@hp.com

Abstract. User-related contextual factors affect the degree of privacy
protection that is necessary for a given context. Such factors include: sensitivity of data, location of data, sector, contractual restrictions, cultural
expectations, user trust (in organisations, etc.), trustworthiness of partners, security deployed in the infrastructure, etc. The relationship between
these factors and privacy control measures that should be deployed can be
complex. In this paper we propose a decision based support system that
assesses context and deduces a list of recommendations and controls. One
or more design patterns will be suggested, that can be used in conjunction to satisfy contextual requirements. This is a broad solution that can
be used for privacy, security and other types of requirement.

1 Introduction

There is increasing awareness that privacy should be integrated into design rather
than being bolted on afterwards, and for the need to take privacy into account
[1]. New regulations, consumer concerns and high profile cases of personal or
sensitive data exposure are forcing companies to design more privacy-aware systems. Contextual and environmental factors should be taken account of in product and service design, but this can be very complex. Sometimes the time and
expertise to do this is not readily available even with the presence of system administrators: this is especially the case for dynamic environments. User-related
contextual factors affect the degree of privacy protection that is necessary for a
given context. Such factors include: sensitivity of data, location of data, sector,
contractual restrictions, cultural expectations, user trust (in organisations, etc.),
trustworthiness of partners, security deployed in the infrastructure, etc. The relationship between these factors and privacy control measures that should be
deployed is too complex to be modelled in a tabular form. By breaking the complex modelling issue down to relatively simple rules and combining these using
the proposed reasoning engine, we are able to model the complex relationships
mentioned above.

The core problems we address in this paper are:

- How to aid product and service design, whilst taking into account the context
  and environment in which the product or service is to be deployed.

S. Katsikas, J. Lopez, and M. Soriano (Eds.): TrustBus 2010, LNCS 6264, pp. 69–80, 2010.
© Springer-Verlag Berlin Heidelberg 2010

– How to help non-expert developers/architects locate design patterns [2] that are particularly relevant to their problem space.

In essence, our solution to these problems is a system that gathers context relating to the design required and inputs this to a rule-based system, to trigger decisions about which control measures it could be appropriate to use within that context. The tool helps to determine appropriate design patterns that could be used to address privacy, security and other requirements. The solution is targeted at non-expert developers and architects. It may be useful in management products for servers, storage, networking, etc., in cloud environments and in other domains.

The rest of the paper is organised as follows. We describe our solution in Section 2. A detailed example is further discussed in Section 3 showing how the system can generate a list of candidate privacy design patterns with regard to specific contextual factors. We consider related work in Section 4 and finally conclusions are given in Section 5.

2   Framework Overview

Our approach is to use a specialised tool in order to aid a designer to make decisions. It is a type of decision-based support system that interacts with designers in order to gather appropriate context, and that assesses this context and outputs a list of recommendations and controls that it would be appropriate for the designer to use within this context. One or more design patterns [2] will be suggested, that can be used in conjunction to satisfy contextual requirements. (Further information about design patterns and how they are extended within our solution will be given in Sections 3 and 4). The solution is rule-based and functions as an expert system. A domain expert (or experts) will create the rules and patterns, based upon industry standard techniques and patterns for specific domains. There can be a feedback process by which an architect can choose a lower ranked pattern and this goes to improve the selection process. In the rest of this section, we consider in more detail the component parts of this system and their interactions, both internal and external.

An overview of the system is shown in Figure 1. An expert administrator can tailor the rules if required, and the user of the system is the designer that wishes to obtain advice about which controls (in the form of design patterns) they should consider using for their situation. The user interacts with the system via a questionnaire, which asks the user questions about their current goals, context and preferences. This questionnaire could be static, but ideally would be generated via an expert system such that the questions will vary according to the previous answers of the user. When the questionnaire is completed, the system outputs a ranked list of design pattern candidates. For example, it might suggest usage of Design Pattern 1 for the current context, with confidence being 1.0, and also Design Pattern 2, with confidence that this is appropriate for the current context being 0.8.

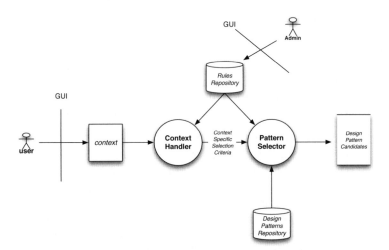

Fig. 1. Context Aware Design Pattern Selection

A central aspect to this approach is the mechanism that selects design patterns in a context-aware manner, such that design pattern candidates are selected with regard to the context (e.g. customer requests, regulations, policies) and pre-defined rules/knowledge base. This mechanism includes:

1. a rules repository that has two major kinds of rules: rules that apply to a context handler and rules that apply to a design pattern selection processor
2. a context handler that quantifies the context factors by applying contextual rules
3. a design patterns repository that contains fine-grained design patterns with additional parameters relating to selection criteria
4. a pattern selector which (either through a graphical user interface (GUI) to manually or a programmed process to automatically) selects a list of design pattern candidates by finding a reasonable matching between the parameters expressed in the design patterns and the selection criteria generated by the context handler and the pattern filter rules.

The main features of the system are as follows:

- **Design Stage Context** is collected from the user (in this case, the designer) through the GUI. The user can specify contexts using pre-defined keywords such as sensitive information, limited contractual restrictions, etc.
- **Context Processing Rules (CPR)** are defined by system administrator to handle contextual information specified by user. CPR will process applicable contextual information and output a set of selection criteria based on the context processing rules combination configuration
- **Context Processing Rules Combination (CPRC)** are defined to combine the results generated by the CPR process

- **Selection Criteria** are generated by the CPRC and used by the design pattern selection rules
- **Design Pattern Selection Rules (DPSR)** process selection criteria generated by the CPRC to determine a list of design pattern candidates that are close to the contextual information input by the user
- **Design Pattern Selection Rules Combination (DPSRC)** defines the algorithm to output a ranked list with regard to the DPSR

The generic process works as follows. A set of fine-grained design patterns are carefully formulated. Each design pattern has a criteria field in which a list of parameters relating to different context setup and selection criteria are defined. Two sets of rules are also constructed: one is context-related and another is pattern selection-related. The context handler responds to specific context setup at the design stage. Context-related rules are applied to quantify contextual information, e.g. 'sensitivity is high' is converted to 'sensitivity = 1.0'. After this process, contextual information collected through the GUI from the user is transformed into a list of quantified selection criteria. The pattern selector, either as a GUI or automatic process, applies a set of selection rules to match the previously generated selection criteria against the design patterns stored in the repository. The pattern selector outputs a list of design pattern candidates with a double value identifying how suitable the design pattern is to a specific context. We take an approach similar to Thesaurus [3]; this enables a better interaction between the system and the users.

3   Example of Our Approach

In this section we give a worked example where we base the representation used upon the design pattern format used within [2], and show what the corresponding rules look like in our system.

3.1   Design Stage Context

The supported privacy context is defined by the system administrator, i.e. designer of our solution (and referred to within the GUIs and rules, as explained above). It can include aspects such as:

- Sensitivity of data: {No Personally Identifiable Information (PII), PII, sensitive}
- Location of (stored) data
- Potential locations of transferred data
- Sector
- Number of users of system
- Whether an anonymous data set could be usable
- Contractual restrictions
- Cultural expectations
- User's role in the organisation

– Security deployed in the infrastructure
– Intent of system designer

Note that these are not the same as the context within the design pattern, nor the intent of the pattern (see Section 3.8, where we refer to this privacy context as a new category called 'applicable context' within the design patterns).

This Design Stage Context is collected from the user through the GUI. The user can specify contexts using pre-defined keywords such as sensitive information, limited contractual restrictions, etc. A natural language processing module can also be applied in this stage. Examples include the following context, where some phrases may be varied across pre-set options (e.g. {a large number, a small number, one, no}; {personal information, sensitive information, not personal information}):

1. Protected storage of data should be enabled over a large number of distributed servers in different countries.
2. Data is not sensitive personal information.
3. Assurances are required that the data cannot be re-assembled within a jurisdiction that is either not permitted to process the data set, or by a single malicious entity within the storage chain.
4. There are limited contractual restrictions between data storage locations.

3.2   Context Handler (CH)

The Context Handler (CH) processes and quantifies context information input by the user with regard to mutual agreement between the CH and Context Processing Rules. For example, the CH will process the context stated above as:

1. data.Location is cross-border
2. data.Sensitivity is non-sensitive
3. purposeOfProcessingData is restricted
4. contractualRestrictions is limited

3.3   Context Processing Rules (CPR)

Context Processing Rules (CPR) are stored in the Rules Repository and retrieved by the CH. They are defined by the system administrator to handle contextual information specified by the user. CPR will process applicable contextual information and output a set of selection criteria based on the context processing rules combination configuration. For example:

1. CPR.r1: If (data.Location is undetermined or data.Location is cross-border) then transborderDataFlow = true else transborderDataFlow = false;
2. CPR.r2: If (data.Sensitivity = sensitive) then sensitivity of information = 1.0 else sensitivity of information = 0.0;
3. CPR.r3: If(securityLevel < idealLevel & transborderDataFlowRestrictions = true) then sensitivity of information = 1.0
4. CPR.r4: If(purposeOfProcessingData is restricted) then limited usage = 0.4 else limitedUsage =0.0;
5. CPR.r5 If(contractualRestrictions is limited) then limitedLiability = 0.7;

3.4   Context Processing Rules Combination (CPRC)

Context Processing Rules Combination (CPRC) is defined to combine the results generated by CPR process. An example is listed below. It will generate four selection criteria: one criterion from CPR.r1, one criterion from maximum value between CPR.r2 and CPR.r3, one criterion from CPR.r4 and one criterion from CPR.r5.

1. CPR.r1 append max(CPR.r2, CPR,r3) append CPR.r4 append CPR.r5

3.5   Selection Criteria (Generated by CPRC)

Selection Criteria are generated by CPRC within the CH and are passed to the Pattern Selector. They are used by the Pattern Selector in conjunction with design pattern selection rules. For example:

1. Sensitivity of information = 1.0 (result from max(CPR.r2, CPR.r3))
2. transborderDataFlow = true; (result from CPR.r1)
3. limited usage = 0.4 (result from CPR.r4)
4. limited liability = 0.8 (result from CPR.r5)

3.6   Design Pattern Selection Rules (DPSR)

Design Pattern Selection Rules (DPSR) are used by the Pattern Selector to process selection criteria generated by the CPRC to determine a list of design pattern candidates that are close to the contextual information input by the user. For example:

1. DPSR.r1. If (Sensitivity of information = 1.0) then DP1 = 1.0, DP2 = 0.6;
2. DPSR.r2 If (transborderDataFlow = true & limited usage > 0.3) then DP2 = 0.8, DP1 = 0.3;
3. DPSR.r3 If (limitedLiability > 0.5) then DP2 = 0.8, DP1 = 0.6

3.7   Design Pattern Selection Rules Combination (DPSRC)

Design Pattern Selection Rules Combination (DPSRC) defines the algorithm to output a ranked list with regard to the DPSR. For example:

1. Max(DPSR.result.all.DP1) append Max(DPSR.result.all.DP2)

Result
The system outputs a ranked list of design pattern candidates.

1. DP1, confidence is 1.0
2. DP2, confidence is 0.8

3.8   Example Design Patterns

Our solution is independent of any particular format of design pattern: an additional *applicable context* field just needs to be added into the pattern format used that is reasoned about within the pattern selection process. We show below some privacy-related design patterns that we have defined to illustrate the type of patterns that might be deployed in the knowledge base. Note that these two design patterns have the same set of Selection Rules which generate different results with regard to specific contextual factors.

1. Design Pattern 1 (DP1)   Obligation Management

Applicable Context:

- Sensitivity of data
- Location of (stored) data
- Potential locations of transferred data
- Cultural expectations
- Number of users of system
- Would an anonymous data set be usable?
- Contractual restrictions
- Security deployed in the infrastructure
- Conformance to existing agreements between parties or compatibility with legacy systems

Selection Rule Repository: DPSR

Selection Rules: DPSR1.r1, DPSR1.r2, DPSR1.r3

Name: Obligation **Classification:** Data and policy management

Intent: to allow obligations relating to data processing to be transferred and managed when the data is shared.

Motivation: A scenario where this would be useful is when a service provider (SP) subcontracts services, but wishes to ensure that the data is deleted after a certain time and that the SP will be notified if there is further subcontracting

Context: You are designing a service solution. You want to make sure that multiple parties are aware of and act in accordance with your policies as personal and sensitive data is passed along the chain of parties storing, using and sharing that data.

Problem: Data could be treated by receivers in ways that the data subject or initiator would not like, and/or the data subject may be contacted in ways that they would not like e.g. being contacted by a call centre when they had expressed that they did not wish to be contacted. Furthermore, the original service provider may be legally liable if this happens (e.g. according to APEC accountability-related legislation). In addition, data could be received by receivers in ways that they would not agree with or is not conforming to the initial agreement between parties, e.g. data subject or initiator changes the data transfer protocols or pre-defined communication channels.

Solution: all the service providers use an obligation management system. Obligation management can handle information lifecycle management, driven by individual preferences and organisational policies. A scalable obligation management system could be deployed, driven by obligation policies and individuals preferences that would manipulate data over time, including data minimisation, deletion and management of notifications to individuals.

Consequences:

Benefits - privacy preferences and policies can be conveyed along the chain and acted on in an operational manner.

Liabilities - extra workload in that users or organisations need to set obligations.

Known uses: Pretschner et al [4] provide a framework for evaluating whether a supplier is meeting customer data protection obligations in distributed systems. IBM proposed Enterprise Privacy Authorization Language (EPAL) [5] to to govern data handling practices in IT systems according to fine-grained positive and negative authorisation rights. Casassa Mont [6] discussed various important aspects and technical approaches to deal with privacy obligations.

Related patterns: sticky policies (obligations can be stuck to data), identity management (e.g. user-centric obligations managed by identity management system)

2. Design Pattern 2 (DP2) Sticky Policies

Applicable Context:

- Sensitivity of data
- Location of (stored) data
- Potential locations of transferred data
- Number of users of system
- Would an anonymous data set be usable?
- Contractual restrictions
- Security deployed in the infrastructure

Selection Rule Repository: DPSR

Selection Rules: DPSR1.r1, DPSR1.r2, DPSR1.r3

Name: Sticky policies **Classification:** Policy enforcement

Intent: to bind policies to the data it refers to

Motivation: A scenario where this would be useful is to ensure that policies relating to data are propagated and enforced along all chains through which the data is stored, processed and shared

Context: You want to make sure that multiple parties are aware of and act in accordance with your policies as personal and sensitive data is passed along the chain of parties storing, using and sharing that data.

Problem: Data could be treated by receivers in ways that the data subject or initiator would not like. The policy could be ignored, or separated from the data it should refer to. **Solution:** Enforceable sticky electronic privacy policies: personal information is associated with machine-readable policies, which are preferences or conditions about how that information should be treated (for example, that it is only to be used for particular purposes, by certain people or that the user must be contacted before it is used) in such a way that this cannot be compromised. When information is processed, this is done in such a way as to adhere to these constraints. These policies can be associated with data with various degrees of binding and enforcement. Trusted computing and cryptography can be used to stick policies to data and ensure that that receivers act according to associated policies and constraints, by interacting with trusted third parties or Trust Authorities.

Consequences:

Benefits - Policies can be propagated throughout the cloud, strong enforcement of these policies, strong binding of data to policies, traceability. Multiple copies of data are OK, as each has the policy attached.

Liabilities - Scalability and practicality: if data is bonded with the policy, this makes data heavier and potentially not compatible to current information systems. It may be difficult to update the policy once the data is sent to the cloud, as there can be multiple copies of data and it might not be known where these are. Once the data is decrypted and in clear, the enforcement mechanism becomes weak, i.e. it is hard to enforce that the data cannot be shared further in clear, but must instead be passed on in the sticky policy form; therefore, audit must be used to check that this does not happen.

Known uses: Policy specification, modelling and verification tools include EPAL, OASIS XACML , W3C P3P and Ponder. Notably, a technical solution for sticky policies and tracing services can leverage Identifier-Based Encryption (IBE) and trusted technologies; this solution requires enforcement for third party tracing and auditing parties. An alternative solution that relies on a Merkle hash tree has been proposed by Pöhls [7]. A Platform for Enterprise Privacy Practices (E-P3P) [8] separates the enterprise-specific deployment policy from the privacy policy and facilitates the privacy-enabled management and exchange of customer data.

Related patterns: obligations (obligations can be stuck to data), identity management (e.g. polices bound to data managed in identity management system), audit, Digital Rights Management (DRM).

4   Related Work

Privacy design techniques are not a new concept: various companies, notably Microsoft [9], have produced detailed privacy design guidelines. Cannon has described processes and methodologies about how to integrate privacy considerations and engineering into the development process [10]. Privacy design guidelines in specific areas are given in [11,12]. In November 2007 the UK Information Commissioners Office (ICO) [13] (an organisation responsible for regulating and enforcing access to and use of personal information), launched a Privacy Impact Assessment (PIA) [13] process (incorporating privacy by design) to help organisations assess the impact of their operations on personal privacy. This process assesses the privacy requirements of new and existing systems; it is primarily intended for use in public sector risk management, but is increasingly seen to be of value to private sector businesses that process personal data. Similar methodologies exist and can have legal status in Australia, Canada and the USA [14]. This methodology aims to combat the slow take-up to design in privacy protections from first principles at the enterprise level, see [15] for further discussion, [16] for further background, and [17] for a useful classification system for online privacy.

In addition to this body of privacy design guidelines, practical techniques can be specified using design patterns [2]. These can be defined in various different forms, ranging from fairly informal to formal, but all having substructure. Work is currently in place to define these: for example, use-cases that drive cloud computing are familiar ones and so design patterns to fit these have started to be produced [18]. Some previous work has been carried out in the privacy design pattern area, but not for cloud computing: [19] describes four design patterns that can aide the decision making process for the designers of privacy protecting systems. These design patterns are applicable to the design of anonymity systems for various types of online communication, online data sharing, location monitoring, voting and electronic cash management and do not address use within an enterprise. In our system, we extend the usage of design patterns to cover privacy architectural options and controls that can be deployed - particularly within an organisation, with the option of providing detail right down to example code level. Furthermore, we build upon this approach to allow automated determination of a set of recommendations for designers. With the existing guidelines, these are distributed and used in an off-line way, and it can be difficult for developers to find appropriate advice.

In expert systems, problem expertise is encoded in the data structures rather than the programs and the inference rules are authored by a domain expert. Techniques for building expert systems are well known [20]. A key advantage of this approach is that it is easier for the expert to understand or modify statements relating to their expertise. Our system can also be viewed as a decision support system. Again, there is a large body of preceding research [21]. Many different DSS generator products are available, including [22,23,24,25].

Halkidis et al. [26] perform risk analysis of software systems based on the security patterns that they contain. The first step is to determine to what extent specific security patterns shield from known attacks. This information is fed to a mathematical model based on the fuzzy-set theory and fuzzy fault trees in order to compute the risk for each category of attacks. However, this approach does not handle context information and there is no rule engine provided. There has been related work carried out in the Serenity project (see especially [27,28]): a general framework was proposed to develop secure applications based on security patterns. They used an extension of TROPOS called SI* modelling framework for modelling and analysis of security requirements. The context of security patterns was discussed, and executable components can be selected upon client request by matching the context of pre-defined patterns. Delessy et al. [29] also discussed how to build upon two different approaches to secure SOA applications: model-driven development and the use of security patterns. Laboto et al. [30] proposed to use patterns to support the development of privacy policies. However, unlike our approach, a rule engine was not proposed to automatically select appropriate patterns at the design stage, and the focus was on security.

5 Conclusions

We have presented a novel approach for automatically selecting design patterns based on context. Our approach enables contextual and environmental factors to be taken account of in product and service design, by providing suitable options for the given context to designers. This procedure is independent of the chosen format of the design patterns. One or more design patterns will be suggested, that can be used in conjunction to satisfy contextual requirements. This is a broad solution that can be used for privacy, security and other types of requirement. We are currently extending this approach within the EnCoRe project [31] in order to generate privacy controls (with a focus on consent and revocation mechanisms) that are appropriate for different contexts, such as: to what level of granularity of data should the policy be attached? any economically feasible mechanism to enforce the policy? whether compatible to legacy systems? whether the obligations will be an extension of access control policies, or separate policies that are dealt with in a separate manner? etc.

References

1. Information Commissioneres Office: The Privacy Dividend; the business case for investing in proactive privacy protection (2010)
2. Alexander, C., Ishikawa, S., Silverstein, M., Jacobson, M., Fiksdahl-King, I., Angel, S.: A Pattern Language: Towns, Buildings, Construction. Oxford University Press, Oxford (1977)
3. Miller, G.A.: WordNet: A Lexical Database for English. Communications of the ACM 38(11), 39–41
4. Pretschner, A., Schtz, F., Schaefer, C., Walter, T.: Policy Evolution in Distributed Usage Control. Electron. Notes Theor. Comput. Sci. 244 (2009)
5. IBM: The Enterprise Privacy Authorization Language (EPAL), EPAL specification, v1.2 (2004),
   http://www.zurich.ibm.com/security/enterprise-privacy/epal/
6. Casassa Mont, M.: Dealing with Privacy Obligations, Important Aspects and Technical Approaches. In: Katsikas, S.K., López, J., Pernul, G. (eds.) TrustBus 2004. LNCS, vol. 3184, pp. 120–131. Springer, Heidelberg (2004)
7. Phls, H.G.: Verifiable and Revocable Expression of Consent to Processing of Aggregated Personal Data. In: Chen, L., Ryan, M.D., Wang, G. (eds.) ICICS 2008. LNCS, vol. 5308, pp. 279–293. Springer, Heidelberg (2008)
8. Ashley, P., Hada, S., Karjoth, G., Schunter, M.: E-P3P privacy policies and privacy authorization. In: WPES '02, pp. 103–109 (2002)

9. Microsoft Corporation: Privacy Guidelines for Developing Software Products and Services, Version 2.1a (2007),
   http://www.microsoft.com/Downloads/details.aspx?
   FamilyID=c48cf80f-6e87-48f5-83ec-a18d1ad2fc1f&displaylang=en
10. Cannon, J.C.: Privacy: What Developers and IT Professionals Should Know. Addison Wesley, Reading (2004)
11. Patrick, A., Kenny, S.: From Privacy Legislation to Interface Design: Implementing Information Privacy in Human-Computer Interactions. In: Dingledine, R. (ed.) PET 2003. LNCS, vol. 2760, pp. 107–124. Springer, Heidelberg (2003)
12. Belloti, V., Sellen, A.: Design for Privacy in Ubiquitous Computing Environments. In: Proc. 3rd European Conference on Computer-Supported Cooperative Work, pp. 77–92 (1993)
13. Information Commissioneres Office: PIA handbook (2007),
    http://www.ico.gov.uk/
14. Office of the Privacy Commissioner of Canada: Fact sheet: Privacy impact assessments (2007), http://www.privcom.gc.ca/
15. Information Commissioners Office: Privacy by Design. Report (2008),
    http://www.ico.gov.uk
16. Jutla, D.N., Bodorik, P.: Sociotechnical architecture for online privacy. IEEE Security and Privacy 3(2), 29–39 (2005)
17. Spiekermann, S., Cranor, L.F.: Engineering privacy. IEEE Transactions on Software Engineering, 1–42 (2008)
18. Arista: Cloud Networking: Design Patterns for Cloud Centric Application Environments (2009),
    http://www.aristanetworks.com/en/CloudCentricDesignPatterns.pdf
19. Hafiz, M.: A collection of privacy design patterns. In: Proc. 2006 Conference on Pattern Languages of Programs, pp. 1–13. ACM, NY (2006)
20. Russel, S., Norvig, P.: Artificial Intelligence A Modern Approach, 2nd edn. Prentice Hall, Englewood Cliffs (2003)
21. Wikipedia, http://en.wikipedia.org/wiki/Decision_support
22. Dicodess: Open Source Model-Driven DSS Generator,
    http://dicodess.sourceforge.net
23. XpertRule: Knowledge Builder, http://www.xpertrule.com/pages/info_kb.htm
24. Lumenaut: Decision Tree Package, http://www.lumenaut.com/decisiontree.htm
25. OC1 Oblique Classifier 1,
    http://www.cbcb.umd.edu/~salzberg/announce-oc1.html
26. Halkidis, S.T., Tsantalis, N., Chatzigeorgiou, A., Stephanides, G.: Architectural Risk Analysis of Software Systems Based on Security Patterns. IEEE TDSC 5(3) (2008)
27. Kokolakis, S., Rizomiliotis, P., Benameur, A., Kumar Sinha, S.: Security and Dependability Solutions for Web Services and Workflows: A Patterns Approach, Security and dependability for Ambient Intelligence, May 2009. Springer, Heidelberg (2009)
28. Benameur, A., Fenet, S., Saidane, A., Khumar Sinha, S.: A Pattern-Based General Security Framework: An eBusiness Case Study. In: HPCC, Seoul, Korea (2009)
29. Delessy, N.A., d Fernandez, E. B.: A Pattern-Driven Security Process for SOA Applications. In: ARES, pp. 416–421 (2008)
30. Lobato, L.L., d Fernandez, E.B., Zorzo, S.D.: Patterns to Support the Development of Privacy Policies. In: ARES, pp. 744–774 (2009)
31. EnCoRe - Ensuring Consent and Revocation, http://www.encore-project.info/

Real-Time Remote Attestation with Privacy Protection

Aimin Yu[1,2,*] and Dengguo Feng[1,2]

[1] State Key Laboratory Of Information Security, Institute of Software,
China Academy of Sciences, Beijing, China, 100190
[2] National Engineering Research Center of Information Security, Beijing, China, 100190
yuaimin@is.iscas.ac.cn, fdg@is.iscas.ac.cn

Abstract. How to ensure the freshness of measurement and protect the concrete system configuration from leaking are two major challenges faced by existing remote attestation solutions. This paper proposes a new attestation architecture, called RTRA, to resolve these problems. In RTRA the real-time state of the attester is collected and reported. And the privacy about the attester's binary configuration is protected through extending traditional property-based remote attestation architecture. Compared with existing property attestation architecture, RTRA is more scalable and secure since a unique proxy who is trusted totally to protect the whole configuration from leaking is not needed anymore.

Keywords: TPM, property attestation, measurement freshness.

1 Introduction

With the rapid spread of malicious code and the tremendous loss caused by them, it is in urgent demand to build a distributed and flexible trusted computing environment which ensures the participants behave as expected. For example, before providing online-bank service to a user the server has to evaluate the security of current client application to protect the confidentiality of the user account information.

For this purpose, the computer industry has founded Trusted Computing Group (TCG) and developed Trusted Platform Module (TPM)[1] to support remote attestation[2] of system state. A typical remote attestation framework includes an attester and a verifier. The attester is responsible to produce the measurement of its own hardware and software state and report it to the verifier. The verifier checks the integrity reports and evaluates the security of the attester. Since the hardware configuration of a platform is not subject to change and easier to be measured, attesting the software state running in the attester has become the main issue.

By far there have been many integrity measurement architectures designed to realize remote attestation. These approaches put forth different mechanism to identifying the software running on the system. Nevertheless there are still some shortcomings. The

---

* The work was supported by The National High-Tech Research and Development Plan of China under Grant No.2007AA01Z412, the National Science & Technology Pillar Program of China under Grant No.2008BAH22B06, CAS Innovation Program under Grant No ISCAS2009-DR14, ISCAS2009-GR.

S. Katsikas, J. Lopez, and M. Soriano (Eds.): TrustBus 2010, LNCS 6264, pp. 81–92, 2010.
© Springer-Verlag Berlin Heidelberg 2010

main two problems are how to ensure freshness of the measurement result and how to protect privacy about the attester's concrete configuration. In this paper we design and implement a new remote attestation architecture, RTRA, to overcome these problems.

The contributions of RTRA can be concluded into two aspects. On one hand RTRA supports measurement of the real-time state of a target running application. The experiments showed that RTRA can detect those malicious behaviors such as code injection attacks.

On the other hand, RTRA extended traditional property-based remote attestation architecture and the scalability and privacy are enhanced. In traditional property attestation architecture a unique verification proxy is needed who maps the attester's trust chain into privacy-friendly property and prevents the configuration from leaking. However, since the trust chain includes the whole configuration of the attester from hardware to application, in scenarios such as Internet it is difficult to find such a verification proxy who is fair-and-square enough to treat the whole configuration without any discrimination. For example a proxy owned by a company or organization would give higher evaluation to their own software than those developed by others. The second problem is that the verification proxy itself tends to be the security bottleneck in the whole architecture. For example, if the online-bank server need evaluate the integrity of end-user's system each time it is accessed, then the verification proxy must be online all along, as necessarily increases the possibility that the proxy is attacked. In RTRA the property relation model adopted by traditional property attestation is extended and a new *prove* relation is introduced. Based on the extended model, new property-based remote attestation architecture is proposed. With these improvements the attester need not trust one unique proxy totally and report the whole configuration to it, so the risk is decreased that the privacy is leaked when one proxy is attacked.

The remaining part of this paper is organized as follows. Section 2 describes related works. Then the architecture of RTRA is given in section 3. Section 4 describes the detailed design and implementation of a real system. Section 5 discussed the advantage and shortcoming of RTRA. Finally we summarize the paper and outline the future work.

2   Related Work

IMA[3] is the first remote attestation architecture based on TPM. It was realized into a LSM module. All executable files and kernel module files are measured when they are loaded into memory. The attestation protocol is defined according to the integrity report protocol specified in TCG specification[4]. PRIMA[5] is an improvement of IMA. It made progress in privacy protection through reducing the number of measured objects. Only the target application itself and others which have information flow with it need to be measured. However PRIMA still report binary measurement of file to the verifier directly, so it remains that some privacy such as what application is running in the attester may be leaked.

Terra[6] is an integrity measurement architecture used in virtual machine (VM) environment. The trusted virtual machine monitor(TVMM) signs a hash of all persistent objects that identify the loaded VM, including the BIOS, executable code, and constant data of the VM and not including temporary data on persistent storage or

NVRAM that constantly change over time. It put forward the concept of "closed box" and "open box". The "closed box" is used to process critical task and software running in it can be modified specially to counteract security attack. Terra facilitates the use of TPM in virtual machine.

An attestation approach based on language analysis is proposed in [7]. The authors of [7] proposed semantic remote attestation using language-based trusted virtual machines (VM) to remotely attest high-level program properties. The general idea behind this approach is to use of a trusted virtual machine that checks the security policy of the code. Since the trusted VM still has to be binary attested, semantic remote attestation is a hybrid solution with code analysis.

In [8] a mechanism to measure the target program and all the objects it depends on is proposed. The attestation of the target program begins with a program analysis on the source code or the binary code in order to find out the relevant executables and data objects. Whenever such a data object is accessed or a relevant executable is invoked due to the execution of the target program, its state is measured for attestation. This approach enhances the granularity of attestation while the privacy protection problem is not resolved.

To protect privacy, in[9] and [10], the authors propose an approach called property attestation to prevent the deficiencies of the existing binary attestation. The basic idea in[10] is to engage a protocol between verifier and attester to prove that the attested platform satisfies the verifier's security requirements. Their solution is based on property certificates that are used by a verification proxy to translate binary attestations into property attestations. Moreover, this work briefly discusses two deployment scenarios: The verification proxy as a dedicated machine and the verification proxy on the verified platform. Whereas [10] proposes a high-level protocol for property-based attestation, [9] proposes and discusses several protocols and mechanisms that differ in their trust models, efficiency and the functionalities offered by the trusted components. [11] and [12] are two major work based on these ideas. The former implemented property-based attestation through extension of bootloader. The enhanced bootloader translates between binary measurements and properties and attest properties of unmodified operating systems loaded. Based on the work of [9], [12] proposes a concrete efficient property-based attestation protocol within an abstract model for the main functionalities provided by TCG-compliant platforms. The security of this protocol is proved under the strong RSA assumption and the discrete logarithm assumption in the random oracle model. The protocol allows blind verification and revocation of mappings between properties and configurations.

3 RTRA Overview

The section describes the property relation used in RTRA firstly. Then the logical architecture of RTRA is presented.

3.1 Property Relation Definitions

In this paper *property* is used to denote a quantity that describes an aspect of the platform with respect to certain requirements[9, 10]. Examples of properties are the absence of certain vulnerabilities or the ability to enforce certain policies. The binary measurement of a system component is equal to a specific value can be considered as a property also. In the context of remote attestation we define *map* and *prove* relations for property. A property *p1 map p2* means that if a platform satisfies property *p1* then it can be conclude that it satisfies property *p2*. For example if the binary measurement of the running operating system is equal to the measurement of the common criteria evaluated Linux enterprise edition, then it can be concluded that the platform has the property that its operating system satisfies EAL2+ for the Controlled Access Protection Profile.

The *map* relation is ubiquitous and composes the base model of traditional property based remote attestation approaches. However, *map* relation is not enough to express the relations between properties in the context of TCG-based remote attestation. For example if the attester system behaves as what the TCG PC specification specified and it reports its binary configuration of MBR(Master Boot Record) using AIK-signed PCR4 (platform configuration register), then it can be trusted that the value of PCR4 represents the configuration of MBR actually. To express these cases we define *prove* relation. A property *p1 prove p2* denotes that if a platform has property *p1* and it says itself has property *p2* then it can be assured that the platform satisfies *p2*.

Given the terms defined above we construct *attest chain* for property *p*. An *attest chain* of *p* is a list of properties {*p1, p2, ..., pn*} where *pn* is property *p* itself and each pair *(pi , pi+1)* satisfies either *map* or *prove* relation. For clarity, we give out some concrete properties and the *map, prove* relations defined between them. Then we construct an attest chain for a property. It is commented that these examples are also used in the real system which will be described in section 4.

p1: the platform is compatible with the TCG PC-Client Specification [13]

p2: the binary measurement of MBR is equal to the measurement of Trusted Grub[14].

p3: the boot loader of the platform measures the operating system correctly

p4: the binary measurement of the operating system is equal to the measurement of the Linux edition which has been modified to measure the real-time state of applications

p5: the operating system of the platform measures the application correctly

p6: the measurement of the *sshd* in the platform is equal to the measurement of the up-to-date release of *sshd*.

p7: the secure shell service of the platform is secure

The *map* and *prove* relations between these properties are defined as follows:

$$map = \{(p2 , p3),(p4, p5),(p6, p7)\}$$
$$prove = \{(p1 , p2),(p3, p4),(p5, p6)\}$$

With the definitions above an attest chain of property *p7* is illustrated in figure1.

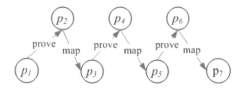

Fig. 1. Attest Chain Example

3.2 Architecture

Figure2 shows the logical entities composing RTRA architecture. The property authority is responsible to define concrete *map* and *prove* relations between properties. The relations definitions issued by it are trusted and admitted by all other entities. Multiple verification proxies exist in the architecture. The attester and the verifier trust each verification proxy partly, as means that the proxy here is only trusted to prevent partial system configurations from leaking and handle them according to the property relation honestly. We use verification proxy-*p* to represent the proxy who is trusted to treat the configuration representing property *p* from leaking and indiscriminatingly. In real deployment the attester and the verifier could have a privacy policy specifying which one proxy is trusted about what properties and multiple logical verification proxy-*p* may be realized into a physical verification proxy according the privacy policy.

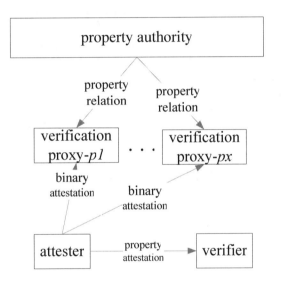

Fig. 2. RTRA Architecture

With the interaction among these entities the property of the attester is proved to the verifier. Typically when the verifier requests the attester to prove property p, the attester computes the attest chain $\{p_1, p_2, ..., p_n\}$ for p. It is pointed out that under the context of TPM-based remote attestation p_1 is always the property that the platform is compatible with the TCG PC-Client Specification. Then according to the attest chain the attester sends the binary configuration representing property p_x to verification proxy-p_x, and gets the assertion which is issued by the verification proxy according to the *map* and *prove* relation. The assertion is used to represent the properties that the attester satisfies. Finally the assertion representing property p is sent to the verifier. The detailed attestation flow will be described in section 4.3.

4 Design of Real System

This section gives the detailed design and implementation of the real system. We use the sample properties and the relation instances which were given in section 3.1. As an example we selects property *p7*, the secure shell service of the platform is secure, as the objective property which is to be attested. Figure 3 shows the real components contained in the real system. The property authority is realized through extending X.509 attribute certificate. Three verification proxies are deployed. The vp-HW is the verification proxy which is trusted to protect the binary configuration of hardware and firmware including MBR. The vp-os and vp-app are trusted about the binary configuration of operating system and application respectively. In the follows detailed implementation of the system are described.

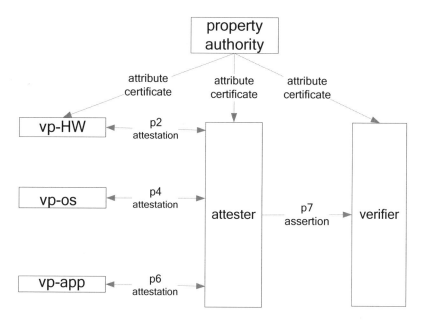

Fig. 3. Real System Architecture

4.1 Property Authority

In the real system a property is represented as a list of attributes. Each attribute contains a name-value pair. We added special flags in the X.509 attribute certificate to denote the *map* and *prove* relation between properties. In terms of the measurement mechanism described in section 4.2, the property relation certificates generated in our system are illustrated in Figure 4.

The attester's hardware platform is a PC (personal computer) which is compatible with TCG PC-Client Specification. When system starts up, the boot loader in MBR would be measured and the measurement result is extended into PCR4. The Trusted Grub[14] is used as our boot loader, so the operating system kernel will be measured and the result is extended into PCR8.

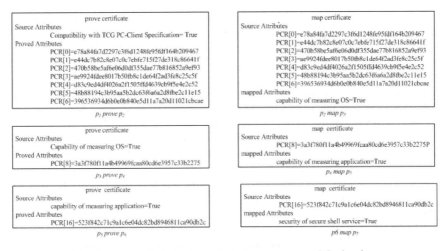

Fig. 4. Property Relation CertificatesMeasurement Mechanism

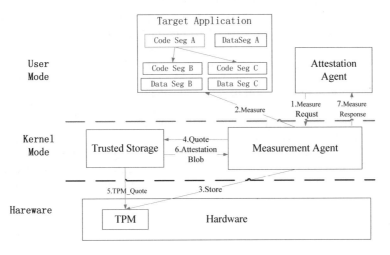

Fig. 5. Measurement Architecture

Figure 5 shows the architecture to realize measurement of application's real-time state. Measurement Agent (MA) is responsible to produce measurement of target application's real-time state. Trusted Storage (TS) is designed to be the only entity which can execute TPM_quote operation with AIK(Attestation Identity Key). Attestation Agent(AA) is the entity communicating with the verification proxy and verifier to exchange attestation information. When a verifier requests an attestation, the AA would request the MA to measure the target application firstly. Then MA measures the process image corresponding to the application and stores the measurement result in the TPM. Then it send Quote request. TS checks the request is received form the trusted MA, and do TPM_quote operation and return the measurement signed by AIK to the MA. After receiving this blob MA composes the measurement response and sends it to the AA. Then AA composes the attestation response and sends it back to the Verifier.

Typically the process image of an application is composed of code/data segments which are corresponding to the executable files. These segments decide how the process behaves. So MA need measure all these segments. Furthermore considering an scenario where library *A* is loaded dynamically and function Foo() included in it will be called by the application. So before Foo() is called the correctness of *A* would not impact the behavior of the process. To represent such situation, the measurement should also include the dynamic dependency on those libraries. According these analyses we implemented MA as follows. For data segments, MA would create the measurement when they are created for the first time when an executable file is loaded. For the code segments MA would scan the address space of the running application to measure them. For the dynamic dependency on shared library MA would decides them through checking the *got (global offset table)* table. After measurement MA will reset PCR16 and extend the result into PCR 16.

In order to make TS the only entity which can execute TPM_quote operation, we realized TS through making it be the only entity to store *TPM_Owner AuthData..* In the implementation the TS is implemented as a Linux kernel module and compiled in the kernel. The *TPM_Owner AuthData* is sealed with the system configuration including the trusted hardware platform, boot loader and the Linux kernel. Moreover the Linux kernel has been modified to load the sealed *AuthData* blob into an internal variable. For fear that a malicious user release the blob with the specific configuration, the kernel would delete it from the external storage after system starts up. When system shuts down, the kernel will seal the Auth_Data with the configuration and store it on external storage again. In order to limit only trusted MA can request quote operation, we implemented MA as a Linux kernel module and compiled it in the kernel also. Then TS would check the caller's address to restrict only the trusted MA can request to quote.

Figure 6 shows our measurement result for application *cat*. The ID is an identifier which is defined by us. The Name is used to describe the file which the current measured segment corresponds to. The Measurement is the hash of current in-memory content of the code/data segment. The Time shows the time when measurement is done and the Status show whether the process has executed the function included in the segment.

Fig. 6. Measurement of *cat*

Then we input something to the process *cat* and do measurement again. Figure 7 shows the results.

Fig. 7. Measurement of cat after input

As is shown in Figure 7, the dependency relationship has changed. The Status column depicts that library */usr/lib/locale/locale-archive* has been referenced after our input.

Next we show that our measurement mechanism can detect code injection attacks. Figure 8 is used to show the correct measurement of an s*shd* daemon.

File View Option Test Key Help

ID	Name	Measurement	Time	Status ▽
0xB058C6F8	/lib/libc-2.3.6.so	EDFB1FEB545183A1A2C086A228EDC114...	Thu May 29 20:45:33 G...	Referenced
0xB058C6F8	/usr/lib/i686/cmo...	D50E5C7B3BDBA0853D891AAF72FCCCD...	Thu May 29 20:45:33 G...	Referenced
0xB058C6F8	/usr/sbin/sshd	AB017813375E9C408F526879821DAF57...	Thu May 29 20:45:33 G...	Referenced
0xB058C6F8	/lib/libcrypt-2.3.6...	CE5F6CE0C870C520173712762B0D1E4C...	Thu May 29 20:45:33 G...	UnReferenced
0xB058C6F8	/lib/libdl-2.3.6.so	1BFA3F518D99C8A13E2D5D8D1D7E3A6...	Thu May 29 20:45:33 G...	UnReferenced
0xB058C6F8	/lib/libnsl-2.3.6.so	858F95C5160FE36348E4378DB64DBE3E...	Thu May 29 20:45:33 G...	UnReferenced
0xB058C6F8	/lib/libnss_compat...	4D9F24547AF940610C86AE8FBAFF4D01...	Thu May 29 20:45:33 G...	UnReferenced
0xB058C6F8	/lib/libnss_files-2...	C912E914CB494AABE8CAA037755CD55...	Thu May 29 20:45:33 G...	UnReferenced
0xB058C6F8	/lib/libnss_nis-2.3...	AE81EC4B3F8A517403AFBA31A6057208...	Thu May 29 20:45:33 G...	UnReferenced
0xB058C6F8	/lib/libpam.so.0.79	DCDCE876FC0BF2E08988D7F1D44B897...	Thu May 29 20:45:33 G...	UnReferenced
0xB058C6F8	/lib/libresolv-2.3.6...	27F969259387AFF2BEDA0BBC994FFB09F...	Thu May 29 20:45:33 G...	UnReferenced
0xB058C6F8	/lib/libselinux.so.1	46895DF94F540197E4DDF9F4AF3CBB63...	Thu May 29 20:45:33 G...	UnReferenced
0xB058C6F8	/lib/libsepol.so.1	AFA19A6AC50DC5913644CE7A02D5283...	Thu May 29 20:45:33 G...	UnReferenced
0xB058C6F8	/lib/libutil-2.3.6.so	CA3D912BB71B0118FAE8CFD8397DA04...	Thu May 29 20:45:33 G...	UnReferenced
0xB058C6F8	/lib/libwrap.so.0.7.6	6A1D110ABB61594D0F64B6AAA54C8E6...	Thu May 29 20:45:33 G...	UnReferenced
0xB058C6F8	/lib/ld-2.3.6.so	C440A8749C421433B65D3CCDEA887B7...	Thu May 29 20:45:33 G...	UnReferenced
0xB058C6F8	/usr/lib/libqssapi...	814EA7EC88A2BC12510FCBB045461CB5...	Thu May 29 20:45:33 G...	UnReferenced
0xB058C6F8	/usr/lib/libk5crypt...	4D1CC7967DC076B5B05697619B719507...	Thu May 29 20:45:33 G...	UnReferenced
0xB058C6F8	/usr/lib/libkrb5.so...	1970B180D8707B826427BECA0D21D3A...	Thu May 29 20:45:33 G...	UnReferenced
0xB058C6F8	/usr/lib/libkrb5su...	2E4ADDD24F0DA5F80BE07902B66F6C77...	Thu May 29 20:45:33 G...	UnReferenced
0xB058C6F8	/usr/lib/libz.so.1.2.3	F6E223D25F916577AC79D301CFFC850E...	Thu May 29 20:45:33 G...	UnReferenced
0xB058C6F8	/lib/libcom_err.so...	A1F35FC4BBA2C54E0DF4F80EB75ED475...	Thu May 29 20:45:33 G...	UnReferenced

Fig. 8. Measurement of *sshd*

Then we enforced an attack on the running *sshd* through shared library injection. This attack is done in following steps:

1. use *ptrace()* to attach to the *sshd* process.

2. find out the location of *dl_open()* and load a specific library in the process. Here we loaded the *libREAD.so*.

3. modify the entry in *got* table of the destined function to the function defined in the new loaded library. Here we modify original *read()* to the *newRead()* defined in *libREAD.so*

4. the *newRead()* is implemented to append an entry in the */etc/passwd* file as a user type '#', then if a user logins using *ssh* , he will get root privilege.

Figure 9 manifests the measurement of sshd after such attack. The result shows that libREAD.so has been referenced.

ID	Name	Measurement	Time	Status ▽
0xB058C6F8	/lib/libREAD.so	54AE5E006BE0541D1F2F2CB44F12312D...	Thu May 29 20:51:58 ...	Referenced
0xB058C6F8	/lib/libc-2.3.6.so	EDFB1FEB545183A1A2C086A228EDC114...	Thu May 29 20:51:58 ...	Referenced
0xB058C6F8	/usr/lib/i686/cmo...	D50E5C7B3BDBA0853D891AAF72FCCCD...	Thu May 29 20:51:58 ...	Referenced
0xB058C6F8	/usr/sbin/sshd	AB017813375E9C408F526879821DAF57...	Thu May 29 20:51:58 ...	Referenced
0xB058C6F8	/lib/libcrypt-2.3.6...	CE5F6CE0C870C520173712762B0D1E4C...	Thu May 29 20:51:58 ...	UnReferenced
0xB058C6F8	/lib/libdl-2.3.6.so	1BFA3F518D99C8A13E2D5D8D1D7E3A6...	Thu May 29 20:51:58 ...	UnReferenced
0xB058C6F8	/lib/libnsl-2.3.6.so	858F95C5160FE36348E4378DB64DBE3E...	Thu May 29 20:51:58 ...	UnReferenced
0xB058C6F8	/lib/libnss_compat...	4D9F24547AF940610C86AE8FBAFF4D01...	Thu May 29 20:51:58 ...	UnReferenced
0xB058C6F8	/lib/libnss_files-2...	C912E914CB494AABE8CAA037755CD55...	Thu May 29 20:51:58 ...	UnReferenced
0xB058C6F8	/lib/libnss_nis-2.3...	AE81EC4B3F8A517403AFBA31A6057208...	Thu May 29 20:51:58 ...	UnReferenced
0xB058C6F8	/lib/libpam.so.0.79	DCDCE876FC0BF2E08988D7F1D44B897...	Thu May 29 20:51:58 ...	UnReferenced

Fig. 9. Measurement of *sshd* after attack

4.2 Attestation Flow

According to the attest chain of property $p7$, the detailed attestation flow is depicted in Figure 10.

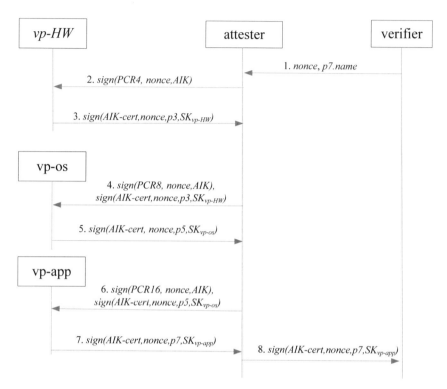

Fig. 10. Detailed Attestation Protocol

Step 1: the verifier sends attestation request to the attester. *nonce* is used to ensure the freshness of the attestation and p_7.*name* denotes the names of the property that the verifier wants to know. Here it is "security of secure shell service".

Step 2: the attester reports the attestation representing property $p2$ to *vp-HW*. Here the value of PCR4, *nonce* and the AIK signature of them are sent.

Step 3: *vp-HW* decides the mapped property and responses the assertion to the attester. Here the assertion contains the AIK certificate, *nonce* and property $p3$. All of them are signed by SK_{vp-HW} which is the private key of *vp-HW*.

Step 4: The attester reports the attestation representing property $p4$ and the assertion received in Step3 to *vp-os*. Here the attestation includes the value of PCR8, *nonce* and the AIK signature of them.

Step 5: *vp-os* sends the assertion for property $p5$ to the attester.

Step 6: The attester sends the attestation of property $p6$ and the assertion for property $p5$ to vp-app. Here PCR16 is included in the attestation.

Step 7: *vp-app* sends the assertion for property $p7$ to the attester.

Step 8: The attester forwards the assertion of $p7$ to the verifier.

5   Discussion

In this section RTRA is analyzed in the following aspects:

Privacy: Privacy protection is a main motivation of RTRA. Since *map* relation remains in our architecture, the privacy protection which can be achieved in traditional property-based attestation can be realized in RTRA also. Additionally the whole configuration of the attester is not required to be reported to one unique verification proxy in RTRA. The attester can define its own privacy policy and complete the attestation. So it can be concluded that the new framework made improvements in privacy protection.

Scalability: In the new framework the user can select multiple verification proxies according to his own privacy policy and construct corresponding property-based attestation architecture, as is more flexible than those frameworks where one unique proxy is needed. Considering the potential shortcoming that multiple verification proxies will reduce the availability of the whole architecture, some means can be taken. On one hand the user can relax his privacy policy, and then the number of the verification proxies will be reduced. On the other hand some special methods, such as utilizing TPM tick count or duplicating each verification proxy, can be enforced. In a word the new framework provides more freedom to the user and can be used in different scenarios.

As far as how to manage property relation is concerned, the traditional PKI/PMI infrastructure can be extended to create, publish and revoke the property relation. For example, in our implementation special flags are added in the X.509 attribute certificate to represent prove and map relation between properties.

Freshness: In our architecture the real-time state of target application is measured. The measurement result represents the behavior of the application more exactly.

6   Conclusion and Future Work

RTRA improve the freshness of measurement result. Moreover it is an extension of traditional property attestation and binary attestation. It brings forward the *prove* relation between properties. Based on the idea the unique verification proxy is not needed anymore.

In future, how to monitor the state change of target application continuously would be an important work. We would pay attention to enhance current virtual machine monitor such as Xen to achieve the goal. At the same time the algorithms of computing the attest chain for a property and finding out the conflict occurred in the property relation are important part of our future work too.

References

[1] Trusted Computing Group: TPM Main Part 1 Design Principles Specification Version 1.2 (2007)
[2] Trusted Computing Group: TCG Specification Architecture Overview v1.2 (2004)
[3] Sailer, R., Zhang, X., Jaeger, T., Doorn, L.v.: Design and implementation of a tcg-based integrity measurement architecture. In: Proceedings of the 13th Conference on USENIX Security Symposium, San Diego, CA, USA (August)

[4] Trusted Computing Group: TCG Infrastructure Working Group Architecture Part II - Integrity Management (2006)

[5] Jaeger, T., Sailer, R., Shankar, U.: PRIMA: policy-reduced integrity measurement architecture. In: Proceedings of the Eleventh ACM Symposium on Access Control Models and Technologies, New York, USA, pp. 19–28

[6] Garfinnkel, T., Phaff, B., Chow, J., Rosenblum, M., Boneh, D.: Terra: a virtual machine-based platform for trusted computing. In: SOSP 2003: New York, USA (October 2003)

[7] Haldar, V., Chandra Franz, D.: Semantic remote attestation: a virtual machine directed approach to trusted computing. In: Proceedings of the 3rd conference on Virtual Machine Research And Technology Symposium USENIX, San Jose, California (2004)

[8] Liang, G., Xuhua, D., Robert, H.D., Bind, X., Hong, M.: Remote attestation on program execution. In: Proceedings of the 3rd ACM workshop on Scalable trusted computing. ACM, Alexandria (2008)

[9] Poritz, J., Schunter, M., Herreweghen, V.E., Waidner, M.: Property Attestation–Scalable and Privacy-friendly Security Assessment of Peer Computers. Technical Report RZ 3548, IBM Research (May 2004)

[10] Sadeghi, A.R., Stüble, C.: Property-based attestation for computing platforms: caring about properties, not mechanisms. In: Proceedings of the 2004 Workshop on New Security Paradigms, September. ACM Nova Scotia, Canada (2004)

[11] Kühn, U., Selhorst, M., Stüble, C.: Realizing property-based attestation and sealing with commonly available hard- and software. In: Proceedings of the 2007 ACM Workshop on Scalable Trusted Computing. ACM Alexandria, Virginia (2007)

[12] Chen, L., Landfermann, R., Löhr, H., Rohe, Sadeghi, A.R., Stüble, C.: A protocol for property-based attestation. In: Proceedings of the, ACM Workshop on Scalable Trusted Computing. ACM Alexandria, Virginia (2006)

[13] Trusted Computing Group: TCG PC Client Specific Implementation Specification For Conventional BIOS (2005)

[14] Trusted Grub, http://www.prosec.rub.de/trusted_grub.html

Private Searching on MapReduce

Huafei Zhu and Feng Bao

I²R, A*STAR, Singapore
{huafei,baofeng}@i2r.a-star.edu.sg

Abstract. In this paper, a private searching protocol on MapReduce is introduced and formalized within the Mapping-Filtering-Reducing framework. The idea behind of our construction is that a map function Map is activated to generate (key, value) pairs; an intermedial filtering protocol is invoked to filter (key, value) pairs according to a query criteria; a reduce function Reduce is then applied to aggregate the resulting (key, value) pairs generated by the filter. The map function Map and the reduce function Reduction are inherently derived from the MapReduce program while the intermedial filtering algorithm is constructed from the state-of-the-art filtering protocol which in turn can be constructed from a Bloom-Filter with Storage and an additively homomorphic public-key encryption scheme. We show that if the underlying additively homomorphic public-key encryption is semantically secure, then the proposed private searching protocol on MapReduce is semantically secure.

Keywords: Bloom-Filter with Storage, Homomorphic encryption, MapReduce.

1 Introduction

MapReduce introduced by Dean and Ghemawat [3–5] is automatically parallelized and executed on a large cluster of the commodity machines. An atomic MapReduce program supporting distributed computing on large data sets, consists of two functions: a map function Map and a reduce function Reduce. A map function Map transforms a piece of data into (key, value) pairs whereas a reduce function Reduce merges the emitted values (value$_1$ ... value$_i$) of the same key into a single result (key: value$_1$ ... value$_n$). Considering a scenario where a document is split in words $(w_1, \ldots, w_n)$ and each word w_i is counted initially with a "1" value by the Map function. The Reduce function is invoked by using a word w_i as a resulting key and aggregating all the pairs with the same key w_i to output the resulting pairs $(w_i, \text{value}_1, \ldots, \text{value}_m)$. As a result, when the MapReduce is applied to the invert index problem, this function just needs to sum all of its input values to find the total appearances of that word. Many real world tasks are expressible in the Map-then-Reduce model including distributed grep, count of URL access frequency, reverse Web-link graph, term-vector per host, invert index and distributed sort(see [3–5] for details). Further applications of Mapreduce in the cloud computing scenarios are discussed in [1, 6, 7].

1.1 The Motivation Problem

This paper studies private searching protocols in the context of MapReduce. The motivation of our work is supported by the following illustrative applications:

S. Katsikas, J. Lopez, and M. Soriano (Eds.): TrustBus 2010, LNCS 6264, pp. 93–101, 2010.

– Obliviously retrieving documents: Assuming that a client wants to know whether a Cloud $\mathcal{C}$ stores documents containing a keyword key, and in case that a document contains key, the client would like to obliviously retrieve this document from $\mathcal{C}$ so that the server knows nothing about what is the specified keyword and which document is retrieved. A quick solution is to apply the MapReduce program directly to this scenario by extracting a set of words from the data (this phase is run by the Map and Reduce function) and obliviously retrieving all reduced documents (intuitively, this can viewed as a privacy-preserving MapReduce program applied here). To the best of our knowledge, no privacy-preserving MapReduce program projected on the extracted keyword set is known so that it can be applied immediately to ensure that the Cloud learns nothing about the specified keyword and the retrieved document.

– Obliviously managing documents: suppose, a client stores his/her encrypted documents in a remote server $\mathcal{C}$ and wishes to update all encrypted documents if they contain some specified keywords. An obvious solution is that the client requires the server to send back all encrypted documents stored at the server $\mathcal{C}$ to the client and then searches the document containing the specified keywords in a safety environment. The communication overhead of this solution is expensive since $\mathcal{C}$ must send all the data to the client. A promising approach would be that the client searches all encrypted documents in the remote environment of the server but ensures that the server learns nothing about the retrieved documents. If we are able to provide a secure searching protocol in the context of MapReduce, then we can solve the problems mentioned above by activating the Map function generate key/value pairs and then invoking an intermedial filtering to filter key/value pairs according to a query criteria associated with the filter.

We stress the technique on private searching protocol defined over MapReduce is general and it can be immediately applied to the other scenarios such as private searching on streams and public-key encryption allowing PIR quires as well (see [2, 9] for more details).

1.2   This Work

In this paper, a private searching protocol on MapReduce is introduced and analyzed. The protocol is formalized within the Mapping-Filtering-Reducing framework in the context of the MapReduce.

THE IDEA: The idea of private searching protocol on MapReduce is simple: a mapping function Map is first activated to generate key/value pairs (key, $value_1$, $\ldots$, $value_m$). That is, the key in the Map function is a document d stored and the values are lists of words $(w_1, \ldots, w_m)$ contained in the document d. An intermedial filtering protocol is designed and invoked to filter key/value pairs according to a query criteria associated with the filter defined over the extracted word lists $(w_1, \ldots, w_m)$. A reducing function Reduce is finally applied to aggregate the resulting key/value pairs generated by the filter, where the notion key different from that described in the Map function, is a word that one is interested in while the values are documents $d_1, \ldots, d_n$ each contains the key (a word, say w_i). We stress that the map function and the reduce function are inherently derived from the MapReduce program while the intermedial filtering algorithm is constructed from a Bloom-Filter with Storage (to ensure the correctness of the proposed searching protocol on MapReduce) and a homomorphic public-key encryption scheme (to ensure the privacy of the proposed searching protocol). Our design style is thus consistent with the programming model of MapReduce while the privacy of MapReduce is provided.

THE TECHNIQUE: Our protocol in essence, is constructed from the Ostrovsky and Skeith III private searching on streaming data protocol [8, 9] which in turn can be constructed from a Bloom-Filter with Storage and an additively homomorphic public-key encryption scheme. The private filtering algorithm is defined over a query type at the remote resource. A query type $\mathcal{Q}$ is a class of Boolean logical expressions. Given a set of keywords K, we define Q_K takes a document as input and returns 1 if and only if the checked document matches the criteria. Keeping this query type classified is clearly essential since otherwise adversaries could easily present their messages from being collected by simply avoiding the criteria that is used to collect such documents. The challenging task is how can this be accomplished while keeping the filtering criteria classified, even if the adversary is given ability to access the filtering algorithm. To solve the problem, we will encode key/value pairs as ciphertexts of a homomorphic public-key encryption scheme to ensure the privacy of the proposed searching protocol. The ciphertext of key/value pairs are then randomly thrown into bins of a Bloom-Filter with Storage so that sieved documents are efficiently retrievable and thus ensures the correctness of the searching protocol on MapReduce.

THE RESULT: We claim that if the underlying public-key encryption is semantically secure, then the searching protocol on MapReduce is semantically secure.

ROADMAP: The rest of this paper is organized as follows: Syntax, correctness and security of searching protocol on MapReduce is defined in Section 2. Building blocks are sketched in Section 3. A construction of searching protocol on MapReduce is presented and analyzed in Section 4. We conclude this work in Section 4.

2   Private Searching on MapReduce: Syntax, Correctness and Security

2.1   Syntax

We consider a universe of words $W = \{0, 1\}^*$, and a dictionary $D \subseteq W$. A set of keywords K is any subset of D. Let $d(i)$ (=: $\{d(i,j), 1 \leq j < \infty\}$) be finite documents stored in the cloud $\mathcal{C}_i$. Let $\mathcal{M}$ be the map function of a MapReduce program: $d(i,j) \rightarrow \{w(i,j,1), \ldots, w(i,j,l_{i,j})\}$, where $w(i,j,\iota) \in D$, $1 \leq \iota \leq l_{i,j}$; Let $\mathcal{Q}$ be a class of query type. A query type $\mathcal{Q}$ could be a class of logical expressions in $\wedge$, $\vee$ and $\neg$. Given a set of keywords $K \subset D$ and a query $Q \in \mathcal{Q}$, where $K = \{k_1, \ldots, k_{|K|}\}$, we define $Q_K: d \rightarrow \{0, 1\}$ that takes a document d and returns 1, if and only if a document matches the criteria. $Q_K(d)$ is computed simply by evaluating on input of the form $k_i \in d$. Following the previous works [2, 8], we call Q_K a query over keywords K.

Definition 1. *For a query Q_K over a set of keywords K, and for a document d, we say d matches query Q_K if and only if $Q_K(d) = 1$.*

For a fixed query type $\mathcal{Q}$, a private searching protocol for MapReduce can be defined. Our searching protoocl consists of two probabilistic polynomial time (PPT) algorithms: an initial algorithm and a filtering algorithm. The details of protocol is depicted below

- An initial algorithm $\mathcal{I}$ comprises two PPT algorithms $(\mathcal{I}_1, \mathcal{I}_2)$ which is defined below.
    1. On input a security parameter 1^k, $\mathcal{I}_1$ is invoked to generate a pair of public/secret keys (pk, sk) for an homomorphic encryption scheme $E_{pk}()$ and $D_{sk}()$ of the Paillier's public-key encryption scheme [10];
    2. On input a dictionary D and a set of keywords K, $\mathcal{I}_2$ invokes $E_{pk}()$ to generate ciphertexts of $\{\widehat{w}_i\}_{i=1}^{|D|}$) of the dictionary D projected on the keywords set K. Let $\widehat{w} = E_{pk}(1, r_w)$ if $w \in K$ and $\widehat{w} = E_{pk}(0, r_w)$ if $w \in D \setminus K$ and let $\widehat{D} = \{\widehat{w}_i\}_{i=1}^{|D|}$).
- A filtering algorithm $\mathcal{F}$ comprises three PPT algorithms $(\mathcal{F}_0, \mathcal{F}_1, \mathcal{F}_2)$ which is defined below.
    1. On input a document $d(i)$, $\mathcal{F}_0$ invokes a map function $\mathcal{M}$ of the MapReduce to generate a set of words W. Let $\widehat{W}$ be an encoding of W, i.e., $\widehat{w} = E_{pk}(1, r_w)$ if $w \in K$ and $\widehat{w} = E_{pk}(0, r_w)$ if $w \in D \setminus K$;
    2. On input $\widehat{W}$, $\mathcal{F}_1$ invokes a (m, n)-Bloom Filter with Storage to store the ciphertetxts $\widehat{W}$; By B^*, we denote the current statement of the (m, n)-Bloom Filter.
    3. Given B^*, $\mathcal{F}_2$ is invoked to retrieve the document $d(i)$ from the (m, n)-Bloom Filter.

2.2   The Correctness

The correctness of a searching protocol means that we must save matched documents with overwhelming probability and saves non-matched documents with negligible probability. That is, the buffer decryption algorithm can distinguish collisions in the buffer from the valid documents.

Definition 2. *(correctness) Let $neg(k)$ be a negligible function and k be a security parameter. Let D be a dictionary and Q_K be a query for keywords K. Let $d(i)$ be documents stored at Cloud C_i and B^* be the state of the (m, n)-Bloom Filter with Storage, i.e., $B^* = \mathcal{F}_1(d(i))$. We say that a searching protocol is correct if*

$$\Pr[\mathcal{F}_2(B^*) = \{d(i, j) \in d(i) | Q_K(d(i, j) = 1\}] > 1 - neg(k)$$

2.3   The Security

To define the security of private searching on MapReduce, we consider the following game between an adversary $\mathcal{A}$ and a challenger $\mathcal{C}$.

- C first invokes a key generation algorithm $\mathcal{I}_1$ to obtain (pk, sk), and then sends pk to $\mathcal{A}$;
- $\mathcal{A}$ chooses two queries for two sets of keywords Q_{K_0}, Q_{K_1} with $K_0, K_1 \subset D$, and sends (Q_{K_0}, Q_{K_1}) to C;
- C chooses a bit b and invokes $\mathcal{I}_2$ to generate $\widehat{W_b}$;
- C invokes $\mathcal{F}$ to create an instance of filtering algorithm $\widehat{\mathcal{F}}$ with $\widehat{W_b}$, and sends $\widehat{\mathcal{F}}$ to $\mathcal{A}$;
- $\mathcal{A}$ can experiment with the code of $\widehat{\mathcal{F}}$ and finally outputs $b' \in \{0, 1\}$

The adversary $\mathcal{A}$ wins the game if $b' = b$ and loses otherwise. We define the adversary's advantage in this game to be $\text{Adv}_\mathcal{A}(k) = |\Pr(b' = b) - 1/2|$.

Definition 3. *A searching protocol is semantically secure if for any adversary $\mathcal{A}$ we have that $\text{Adv}_\mathcal{A}(k)$ is a negligible function, where the probability is taken over coin-tosses of the challenger and the adversary.*

3 Building Blocks

This section sketches building blocks that will be used to construct private searching protocols on MapReduce: Bloom Filter and Paillier's public-key scheme.

3.1 Bloom Filters

Let $[m] = [1, \ldots, m]$. A (m, n)-Bloom Filter consists of an array of n-bits $B[1], \ldots, B[n]$, initially set to 0 using m independent random hash functions $h_1, \ldots, h_m$ with range $[1, \ldots, n]$. This work will use a variation of a Bloom Filter, called (m, n)-Bloom Filter with Storage first introduced and formalized in [2].

Definition 4. *A (m, n)-Bloom Filter with Storage is a collection $\{h_i\}_{i=1}^m$ of functions together with a collection of sets $\{B_j\}_{j=1}^n$, where $h_i: \{0, 1\}^* \to [1, \ldots, n]$. To insert a pair (u, v) into this structure, v is added to $B_{h_i(u)}$ for all $i \in [m]$. To determine whether or not v is stored in a set U, one examines all of the sets $v \in B_{h_i(u)}$ and returns true if all checks are valid.*

As usual, we model h_i as uniform, independent randomness. For each $u \in U$, we define $H_u = \{h_i(u) | i \in [m]\}$. The correctness of our construction relies on the following lemma due to Boneh et al [2].

Lemma 1. *Let $(\{h_i\}_{i=1}^m, \{B_j\}_{j=1}^n)$ be a (m, n)-Bloom Filter with Storage. Suppose the filter has been initialized to store some set U of size $|U|$ and associated values. Suppose also that $n = \lceil cm|U| \rceil$, where $c > 1$ is a constant. Denote the relationship of element-value associates by $R(\cdot, \cdot)$. Then for any $u \in U$, the following statements hold true with probability $1 - neg(k)$, where the probability is over the uniform randomness used to model the h_i and $neg(k)$ is a negligible function*

1. *$u \in U$ if and only if ($B_{h_i(u)} \neq \emptyset, \forall i \in [m]$);*
2. *$\bigcap_{i \in [m]} B_{h_i(u)} = \{v | R(u, v) = 1\}$*

3.2 Paillier's Public-Key Scheme

Paillier investigated a novel computational problem called the composite residuosity class problem (CRS), and its applications to public key cryptography in [10].

Decisional composite residuosity class problems: Let $N = pq$, where p and q are two large safe prime numbers. A number z is said to be a N-th residue modulo N^2, if there exists a number $y \in Z_{N^2}^*$ such that $z = y^N \bmod N^2$. The decisional composite residuosity class problem states the following thing: given $z \in_r Z_{N^2}^*$ deciding whether z is N-th residue or non N-th residue. The decisional composite residuosity class assumption means that there exists no polynomial time distinguisher for N-th residues modulo N^2.

Paillier's encryption scheme: The public key is a $2k$-bit RSA modulus $N=pq$, where p, q are two large safe primes with length k and the secret key is (p, q). The plain-text space is Z_N and the cipher-text space is $Z_{N^2}^*$. To encrypt a message $m \in Z_N$, one chooses $r \in Z_N^*$ uniformly at random and computes the cipher-text as $E_{PK}(m, r) = g^m r^N \bmod N^2$, where $g = (1 + N)$ has order N in $Z_{N^2}^*$. The private key is (p, q). To decrypt a ciphertetxt $c = (1 + N)^m r^N \bmod N^2$ with the help of the trapdoor information (p, q), one first computes $c_1 = c \bmod N$, and then computes r from the equation $r = c_1^{N^{-1} \bmod \phi(N)} \bmod N$; Finally, one can compute m from the equation $cr^{-N} \bmod N^2 = 1 + mN$.

The Paillier's public-key cryptosystem is homomorphic, i.e., $E_{PK}(m_1, r_1) \times E_{PK}(m_2, r_2) \bmod N^2 = E_{PK}(m_1 + m_2 \bmod N, r_1 \times r_2 \bmod N)$ and it is semantically secure if the decisional composite residuosity class problem is hard. We refer to the reader [10] for more details.

4　MapReduce Filter: Construction and Security Analysis

In this section, we will describe our implementation of MapReduce filter which is based on the Ostrovsky and Skeith III's private searching on streaming data protocol [8, 9] and then show that it is semantically secure assuming that the underlying public-key encryption scheme is semantically secure.

4.1　A Description of MapReduce Filter

A MapReduce filter $(\mathcal{I}, \mathcal{F})$ consists of an initialization algorithm $(\mathcal{I})$ and a filtering algorithm $\mathcal{F}$. The details of protocol is described below

The initial algorithm $\mathcal{I}$ comprises two algorithms: a key generation algorithm $\mathcal{I}_1$ and an array generation algorithm $\mathcal{I}_2$:

- Key generation algorithm $\mathcal{I}_1$: on input a security parameter 1^k, $\mathcal{I}_1$ generates two large safe prime numbers p and q such that $|p| = |q| = k$. Let $N = pq$, $pk = N$ and $sk = (p, q)$. Let $E_{pk}()$ be Paillier's encryption scheme defined over pk and $D_{sk}()$ be the corresponding decryption algorithm.
- Array generation algorithm $\mathcal{I}_2$: on input a dictionary D and a set of keywords K, $\mathcal{I}_2$ invokes $E_{pk}()$ to generate an encryption $\widehat{D}$ ($= \{\widehat{w}_i\}_{i=1}^{|D|}$) of the dictionary D projected on the keywords set K, where $\widehat{w} = E_{pk}(1, r_w)$ if $w \in K$ and $\widehat{w} = E_{pk}(0, r_w)$ if $w \in D \setminus K$.

The filtering algorithm $\mathcal{F}$ comprises three algorithms: a collection algorithm $\mathcal{F}_0$ and a buffer encoding algorithm $\mathcal{F}_1$ and a buffer decoding algorithm $\mathcal{F}_2$. On a receiving document $d(i,j)$ stored in the cloud $\mathcal{C}_i$ for $1 \leq j \leq l_i$ (here the notation l_i stands for the number of documents stored in $\mathcal{C}_i$)

- $\mathcal{F}_0$ performs the following computations
  1) $\mathcal{F}_0$ invokes the map function $\mathcal{M}$ (of a MapReduce function) to obtain a sequence words $\{w(i,j,1), \ldots, w(i,j,l_{i,j})\}$, where $w(i,j,\iota) \in D$ $(1 \leq \iota \leq l_{i,j})$;
  2) For $\iota = 1, \ldots, \leq l_{i,j}$, the collection algorithm $\mathcal{F}_0$ constructs a temporary collection $\widehat{W}(i,j) = \{\widehat{w}(i,j,\iota) \in \widehat{D} | w(i,j,\iota) \in d(i,j)\}$; Let $c(i,j) = \prod_{\widehat{w}(i,j,\iota) \in \widehat{W}(i,j)} \widehat{w}(i,j,\iota)$;
- Let $u(i,j) \leftarrow c(i,j)$ and $v(i,j) \leftarrow (c(i,j), c(i,j)^{d(i,j)})$; Given $(u(i,j), v(i,j))$, the encoding algorithm $\mathcal{F}_1$ invokes a (m,n)-Bloom Filter to throw m copies of $v(i,j)$ to n bins of the (m,n)-Bloom Filter uniformly at random. Let B be the current state of the (m,n)-Bloom Filter.
- Given B, the decoding algorithm $\mathcal{F}_2$ performs the following computations
  1) $\mathcal{F}_2$ computes the locations $h_i(u(i,j))$ $(1 \leq i \leq m, 1 \leq j \leq l_{i,j})$ and then checks each specified location is stored by some data; if some of the specified location is empty, $\mathcal{F}_2$ outputs 0 indicating the failure of the buffer storage;
  2) In case that the output is 1, $\mathcal{F}_2$ parses $v(i,j)$ as $(c(i,j), c'(i,j))$ and checks that $u(i,j) \overset{?}{=} c(i,j)$; If the check is valid, $\mathcal{F}_2$ decrypts $c(i,j)$ and $c'(i,j)$ to obtain $(z(i,j), z'(i,j))$.
     Notice that $z(i,j)$ is number of keywords in the set K and $z'(i,j)$ is the multiplication of the document $d(i,j)$ containing certain number of keywords in K and $z(i,j)$, i.e., $z'(i,j) = z'(i,j)d(i,j)$.

This ends the description of the protocol.

4.2   The Correctness

Before providing the security of the scheme, we illustrate the correctness of the protocol. Let l_i be the number of documents $d(i,j)$ filtered in the cloud $\mathcal{C}_i$. Each document has m copies that are thrown into the m-out-of-n bins randomly specified by the hash functions $\{h_i\}_{i=1}^{m}$. Thus we have total ml_i documents thrown n bins.

Borrowing the notation from [8, 9], we call each document $d(i,j)$ a color C_j ($j = 1, \ldots, l_i$) and call each copy of color C_j a ball $B(j,k)$, where $k = 1, \ldots, m$. Thus, we have total ml_i balls that are thrown into n bins. We say a color C_j survives if at least one ball of color C_j survives. We say that the color-survival game succeeds of all l_i colors survives, otherwise, we say that it fails.

Let E be an event that a single specified ball survives this process. Then $\Pr[E]$ $= (\frac{n-1}{n})^{ml_i - 1} > \frac{1}{\sqrt{e}}$ assuming that $n = 2ml_i$.

Let E_j be an event that the j-th ball of a certain color does not survive. Then the probability that all m balls of this color does not survive is $\Pr[\bigcap_{j=1}^{m} E_j] \leq (1 - \frac{1}{\sqrt{e}})^m$ $< (1/2)^m$.

Let E^* be an event that the at least one of the color does not survive and E_j^* be an event that the color C_j does not survive. Then $\Pr[E^*] \leq \Pr[\bigcup_{j=1}^{l_i} E_j^*] \leq \sum_{j=1}^{m} \Pr[E_j^*]$

$\leq \frac{l_i}{2^m}$, which is clearly negligible in m. This means that with overwhelming probability that all colors survive and hence with the overwhelming probability that the all l_i documents are retrievable in our Bloom-Filter with storage, and hence all can be decrypted with overwhelming probability.

4.3 The Proof of Security

The correctness of the protocol immediately follows from the Lemma 1 and thus omitted. The rest of our work is thus to show that the proposed searching protocol is secure in the sense of the definition 3.

Theorem 1. *Assuming that the Paillier public-key encryption is semantically secure, then the searching protocol on MapReduce from the preceding construction is semantically secure according to Definition 3*

Proof. Suppose there exists an adversary that can gain a non-negligible advantage ϵ in our semantic security game from the definition 3. We will show that $\mathcal{A}$ can be used to gain an advantage in breaking semantic security of the underlying public-key encryption scheme. A challenger $\mathcal{C}$ is given an encryption c of a message $m_b \in \{0,1\}$, i.e., $c = E_{pk}(m_b)$ (note that the challenger $\mathcal{C}$ is also given the public key pk but not the secret key sk of the underlying Paillier's encryption scheme). The challenger $\mathcal{C}$ is also given two set of keywords K_0 and K_1 and then chooses a bit b uniformly at random. The challenger $\mathcal{C}$ now generates a ciphertext $\widehat{D}$ of the given dictionary D by the following procedure: re-randomized encryption $E_{pk}(0)$ if $w \in D \setminus K_b$ and $E_{pk}(0)c$ if $w \in K_b$

- if $m_b = 1$, then the construction of MapReduce Filter is exactly same as that real protocol described above, hence in this case with probability $1/2 + \epsilon$ the adversary returns b' such that $b' = b$.
- if $m_b = 0$, then the simulated MapReduce Filter searches nothing, hence in this case with probability $1/2$ the adversary returns b' such that $b' = b$.

The $\mathcal{C}$ now outputs what the adversary outputs. As a result, the challenger $\mathcal{C}$ obtains the non-negligible advantage $1/2 + \epsilon/2$ to break the semantic security of the Pailler's encryption.

4.4 Further Discussion

To ensure the correctness of the protocol, we assume that the size of bins $n \geq ml_i$, where l_i is the size of the documents stored in the cloud $\mathcal{C}_i$. Note that in the cloud computing environment, the size of document l_i is very large while the size of a buffer could be limited. This means that the protocol described in this paper suitable for the case where the size searched documents is limited, i.e., the size of l_i should be not very large. Thus, to apply the technique to the cloud environment, we should make use of distributed Bloom filters for saving outputs of the map functions. Recall that an atomic MapReduce program supporting distributed computing, and thus it is not a problem when the proposed protocol applies the cloud environment.

5   Conclusion

We have implemented a searching protocol on MapReduce and have shown that the proposed protocol is semantically secure if the underlying homomorphic public-key encryption scheme is semantically secure. We also have demonstrated that the proposed private searching protocol can be immediately applied to obliviously retrieve documents and obliviously manage documents scenarios.

References

1. Armbrust, M., Fox, A., Griffith, R., Joseph, A.D., Katz, R.H., Konwinski, A., Lee, G., Patterson, D.A., Rabkin, A., Stoica, I., Zaharia, M.: Above the Clouds: A Berkeley View of Cloud Computing, Technical Report No. UCB/EECS-2009-28
2. Boneh, D., Kushilevitz, E., Ostrovsky, R., Skeith III, W.E.: Public Key Encryption That Allows PIR Queries. In: Menezes, A. (ed.) CRYPTO 2007. LNCS, vol. 4622, pp. 50–67. Springer, Heidelberg (2007)
3. Dean, J., Ghemawat, S.: MapReduce: Simplified Data Processing on Large Clusters. In: OSDI 2004, pp. 137–150 (2004)
4. Dean, J., Ghemawat, S.: MapReduce: simplified data processing on large clusters. ACM Commun. 51(1), 107–113 (2008)
5. Dean, J., Ghemawat, S.: MapReduce: a flexible data processing tool. CACM Commun. 53(1), 72–77 (2010)
6. Grossman, R.L.: The Case for Cloud Computing. IT Professional 11(2), 23–27 (2009)
7. Grossman, R.L., Gu, Y., Sabala, M., Zhang, W.: Compute and storage clouds using wide area high performance networks. Future Generation Comp. Syst. 25(2), 179–183 (2009)
8. Ostrovsky, R., Skeith III, W.E.: Private Searching on Streaming Data. In: Shoup, V. (ed.) CRYPTO 2005. LNCS, vol. 3621, pp. 223–240. Springer, Heidelberg (2005)
9. Ostrovsky, R., Skeith III, W.E.: Private Searching on Streaming Data. J. Cryptology 20(4), 397–430 (2007)
10. Paillier, P.: Public-Key Cryptosystems Based on Composite Degree Residuosity Classes. In: Stern, J. (ed.) EUROCRYPT 1999. LNCS, vol. 1592, pp. 223–238. Springer, Heidelberg (1999)

In Search of Search Privacy

Wesley Brandi and Martin S. Olivier

Information and Computer Security Architectures (ICSA) Research Group
Department of Computer Science, University of Pretoria, Pretoria

Abstract. We present findings from an analysis of a database released by an online search provider in 2006. We show that there exists a significantly large number of queries which are shared by users when searching on the Web today. We then propose a network which uses shared queries to preserve the privacy of its participants.

1 Introduction

Bellotti and Sellen [4] point out that any definition of privacy must be dynamic. They then define privacy as a subjective notion which may be influenced by culturally determined expectations and perceptions of one's environment. When one considers the diverse nature of the Web, this definition of privacy is apt.

There are a number of Privacy Enhancing Technologies (PET) on the Web today. They offer users of the Web a number of options when protecting their general privacy is of utmost importance. It is surprising to note that despite the growing number of privacy concerns on the Web, these PETs receive a minuscule amount of support: Anonymizer.com claims to have approximately one million users whilst its free (and arguably more secure) counterpart mentions users in the order of hundreds of thousands.

It may be argued that many users do not employ the usage of PETs simply because they do not consider their actions online of having the potential to violate their privacy. This may be the case when one considers users that access a number of different and independent Web sites in a manner where no private information is ever divulged.

But what of a handful of Web sites that are integral to the online experience of millions of users each and every day? Search engines have become an important part of our experience on the Web. In fact, so much so that this experience would be drastically different if it were not for search engines. They serve as a central point of enquiry, an index of what is on the Web and how relevant it may be in so far as what one is searching for.

This dependence on search engines as a source of information and a starting point on the Web today can be viewed upon as a privacy nightmare. Whilst it may not be a violation of privacy when a single day's worth of queries is stored for a single user, the implication of years of queries stored for millions of users worldwide can not be overlooked. Fortunately, there are a number of PETs that serve users in a bid to thwart some of these privacy problems. A common pitfall of these PETs is that they are not specifically designed to preserve the

S. Katsikas, J. Lopez, and M. Soriano (Eds.): TrustBus 2010, LNCS 6264, pp. 102–116, 2010.
© Springer-Verlag Berlin Heidelberg 2010

privacy of millions of users using search engines in addition to delivering the functionality that one expects from search engines. As a general solution to private communications on the Web today, modern PETs tend to be too slow to deliver the functionality that one expects from search. Anonymizer.com on the other hand, although quite able to deliver the functionality expected when using search, does not protect the user from itself, i.e., Anonymizer.com still submits the search query on behalf of the user to the search engine. Since the user is directly associated with Anonymizer.com, a record of queries submitted through this service over time may result in a violation of privacy.

The aim of this paper is firstly to identify the need for protecting the privacy of users conducting search queries on the Web. We do this by discussing a privacy violation that occurred in 2006 that was directly related to search. We then use the database involved in the privacy violation to show that the search queries of users are not necessarily always mutually exclusive. With this in mind, we outline the basic architecture of a search network that is solely intended to protect the privacy of its users when searching on the Web in addition to providing the functionality that they expect.

This paper is structured as follows: we begin with a look at various definitions of anonymity and briefly discuss an instance of an anonymity model. We then introduce Privacy Enhancing Technologies and provide an overview of several modern day implementations. We move on to present the search query database that was released by an online search engine in 2006. In this section, we discuss the database search profiles and identify the underlying privacy problem therein. In the next section, we use the database to make a case for sharing queries in a network aimed at preserving the privacy of its users. We then present such a network and discuss its most important characteristics. After formalising the notion of a search query log and discussing the difficulties faced by a search engine within the context of the network proposed, we conclude this paper and discuss possible future work.

2 Background

2.1 Anonymity

Pfitzmann and Koehntopp [14] define anonymity as "the state of being not identifiable within a set of subjects"

Various papers [12,9] briefly discuss the advantages and disadvantages that anonymity on a network the likes of the Internet brings. In favour of anonymity is the extended support for members of support groups (rape victims, recovering alcoholics and others), whistleblowing, refereeing for academic conferences, anonymous tips to investigative journalists, personal privacy protection etcetera. Disadvantages of anonymity include exploiting email services to spam the masses, launching massive denial of service attacks and illegally distributed copyrighted software.

Pfitzmann et al [15] discuss exactly what forms of anonymity are possible on a network:

> Receiver anonymity - referring to the receiver of a message. The sender may be known, the message itself may be observed but the receiver of the message is anonymous (the degree of anonymity associated with the entity is discussed later in this section).
>
> Sender anonymity - referring to the entity from which the message originated. This is the same as receiver anonymity except it applies to the sender only.
>
> Unlinkability of Receiver and Sender - this form of anonymity hides the relation between the sender and the receiver of a message.

There are a number of anonymity models that employ numerous techniques to provide anonymity in one form or another. Chaum [6] employs the use of *mix* machines to delay the delivery of encrypted messages so as to hide the source of the message (typically used for email). Wright et al [20] provide an overview on a host of different mix implementations and discuss the basic technologies employed in modern day anonymity models.

2.2   Privacy Enhancing Technologies

There are a number of techniques that can be used to obtain varying degrees of anonymity on the Internet. A relatively cost-effective and easily configurable solution lies in the usage of anonymous proxies the likes of Anonymizer.com. One is effectively anonymous to the end server being visited when traffic is passed through an anonymising proxy. Unfortunately, although some degree of anonymity is offered from the end server, this is not the case from the proxy itself.

To circumvent this problem there are a number of Privacy Enhancing Technologies that offer anonymity from an end server as well as from the entities used to obtain the anonymity (in most cases, this is a network of machines). Most of these technologies are based, in one way or another, on the mix proposed by Chaum [6].

Tor[1] is an example of an anonymising network that is based on second generation onion routing [7,16] (which in turn is based on the mix). Developed by the Naval Research Laboratory and the Free Haven Project, Tor has approximately 450 server nodes participating in its network [13] and effectively provides a high degree of unlinkability between the sender and receiver of a message even in the case of compromised mixes.

The JAP[2] network is similar to Tor in that it is also based on the mix. It differs slightly since it offers a very limited selection of static mix machines (mix cascades) through which requests can be routed. As a result, many users of the JAP network are likely to share a single static IP address.

---

[1] An anonymous Internet communication system - http://www.torproject.org

[2] Anonymity & Privacy - http://anon.inf.tu-dresden.de/index_en.html

3   A Privacy Problem

In 2006, an online search engine made one of its own databases available with the intention that it be used exclusively for research[3]. The database contained the search profiles of approximately 650,000 of its users over a period of three months. A search profile is a history of search queries. Each query in the profile consists of the username, the time of the query, the query itself and when applicable, the link the user followed after the query was submitted.

The owners of the database *anonymised* the data by replacing the username for each profile with a random number. What followed was a privacy catastrophe. Within a few days of its release the private lives of a number of users in the database were on the Web and open to scrutiny by anyone with basic SQL knowledge and a bit of curiosity. On the subject of releasing search profiles for research in a privacy preserving manner, Adar [2] and Korolova et al [11] refer to the AOL incident and propose their solutions.

Since the release of AOL's logs, there have been a number of communities and users on the Web[4] that have taken a keen interest on inferring what they can about users in this database. In some cases[5], users have been identified in so far as where they live, what they do and even what car they drive.

With this in mind, the definition of privacy presented in the beginning of this paper suits us well. At what point was the privacy of these individuals violated: (1) when the search engine kept a log of queries? (2) when the search engine kept a log of queries associated with usernames? (3) when the search engine kept a log of queries for more than a day, a week or a month? or (4) when the search engine released the queries online (after they were supposedly anonymised)? Since privacy is a subjective notion, the point at which privacy was lost (or threatened) is not clear. What is clear, is that each user's search queries were recorded.

It can be argued that had the users' search profiles been anonymised more effectively then the privacy problem that followed (regardless of its definition) could have been minimised, or perhaps even avoided entirely. Despite the simple anonymisation process, one can easily look over each user's profile and draw a number of conclusions from the time a query is conducted and what other queries followed/preceded it. The underlying problem is essentially that each query has context. A lone query is not nearly as important as a query which has context. For example, a single query for a wig has a lot more meaning when it is preceded by queries for information on cancer treatment or the location of cancer clinics a few weeks earlier.

One approach to anonymising the data (and still deem it somewhat usable) is that of having the queries lose their context. Instead of assigning each profile a

---

[3] "AOL Search Queries Open Window Onto Users' Worlds", The Washington Post, August 17, 2006.

[4] http://www.aolpsycho.com/, http://www.dontdelete.com/

[5] "A Face Is Exposed for AOL Searcher No. 4417749", New York Times, August 9, 2006.

random number, each query is assigned a random profile and only then is each profile's username replaced with a random number.

This simple process of scrambling the queries is surely far more effective when thwarting the inference of private information for an individual (a profile) based on search queries alone. Since the queries have lost their context, and since context is obviously an important factor, we say that in the search domain each profile has been anonymised.

The aim of this paper is to contribute towards the anonymity of users when searching on the Web. If we can propose a method of querying search engines in a manner that their records/logs are inherently anonymised in the fashion described in this section (the queries have lost their context) then we believe that we will be successful in realising our goal.

4   A Case for Sharing

If the online search engine mentioned in the previous section had scrambled the queries before releasing the database it may have certainly minimised the privacy questions that were raised upon its release. Of course, the online search engine itself is still storing millions of queries for millions of profiles each and every day. Whether or not they make a small part of their queries available (even in an anonymised form), the potential for the most dire form of privacy violation lies with the online search engine themselves.

The mechanism for search is simple: a user submits a text-based query to a search engine, this is processed and a results page is returned from which a user may decide to follow a number of the links within. It is common practice for search engines to have links on the results page redirect through them. This allows the search engines to log the interaction. There are a number of existing PETs that address this potential privacy problem.

The focus of this paper is on the first step of the search process. We show that it may not be necessary at all to query the search engine since it is probable that someone else has already conducted the query.

4.1   Analysis of Search Data

With the 650,000 search profiles discussed in the previous section, we chose to work with a random sample from this data. This was made up of 65,517 profiles with a combined total of 3,558,412 queries (t). A unique query (Q_u) is a query that was issued only once in the sample. A shared query (Q_s) is defined as a query that has been issued more than once by any user/profile in the sample. Query 1 (Q_1) is said to be unique if it has only been issued once by a single user in the system. Q_2 on the other hand, is said to be shared if user x has used it multiple times, or if user x and user y have each used it once or more times.

Analysis of the sample showed that $n(Q_s i) < n(Q_u j)$ where $Q_s i$ is the set consisting of all shared queries, $Q_u j$ the set of all unique queries and n the function returning the number of elements in a set. Specifically $n(Q_si) = 479,688$ and $n(Q_uj) = 736,967$.

Figure 1 depicts the relationship between users and the types of queries that they have submitted. Each user has two points of interest: (1) the number of shared queries he/she issued in black ($n(Q_si)$ for the user) and (2) the number of unique queries he/she issued in gray ($n(Q_uj)$ for the user).

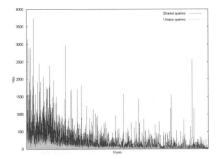

Fig. 1. Each user is plotted against the number of shared and unique queries that he/she submitted

Despite the apparent contradiction, the large amount of shared queries is consistent with our previous observation of $n(Q_si) < n(Q_uj)$. This may not seem initially evident but must certainly be the case since we know that there were a total of approximately 3.5 million queries (t) issued. If 736,967 of those queries were unique then the remaining Q_si queries must make up the difference. What is now clear is that although $n(Q_uj)$ is almost double the amount of $n(Q_si)$, if each Q_s were treated as a separate query then shared queries are far more popular than unique queries: $n(Q_si) = t - n(Q_uj) = 2,821,445$.

It may be the case however that each user is simply reissuing their own queries. If this is so then a network which depends on sharing query results amongst its users would be useless since there would not be many queries to share.

Figure 2 depicts the number of different users that used each query. The figure shows that at least 50% of the shared queries were used by two or more different users: $0.5 * n(Q_si) = 1,410,723$. Since this is almost half of the total number of queries issued, we believe this makes an excellent case for a network dependent on sharing search queries.

5   A Search Network

We have shown that there is a surprisingly large number of shared search queries. The network we propose leverages off of this fact in a bid to better protect the privacy of its users. In this section, we discuss a high level design of the network. This is achieved through an analysis of its requirements:

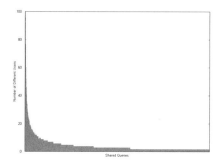

Fig. 2. In this figure the number of users that used each shared query is plotted

1. The network must be scalable. The number of search queries per day for single search providers alone may be in the hundreds of millions [5]. A network which aims to operate as a source of search query results for multiple search engines across the Web must scale to accommodate a staggering number of users and queries.
2. The network must be fast. A search query conducted through the network should be comparable to querying the search engine directly.
3. The network must protect the privacy of its users not only from the search engines, but from each other. We must assume that not all users of the network are trustworthy.

5.1   A Scalable Network

A centralised search network would not lend itself well to massive scalability unless tremendous costs were incurred. From a privacy perspective, this approach would also mean a single point of vulnerability. A decentralised approach on the other hand, may be far more cost effective in addition to not forcing users to trust a single entity.

A decentralised and scalable approach is that of P2P networking. There are a number of P2P networks which exhibit scalability [1,21,18,19,8]. Most of these networks are based on the notion of a Distributed Hash Table (DHT) [3].

A DHT is essentially a decentralised approach to storing and retrieving data. Load in a DHT is distributed in a manner that facilitates change in the set of participants with minimal impact to the network itself. Participants in a DHT employ a consistent hash function [10] so as to establish a keyspace partitioning scheme amongst themselves that balances the load fairly.

From a very high level perspective, a DHT offers two sets of functions:

1. $put(k, data)$: k represents a hash of the key used to index *data* into the DHT. When putting data into the DHT, the key and the data will *hop* through nodes of the DHT until the node responsible for that key is reached (this is determined by the globally known hashing function), it is this node where the data will be stored.

2. $get(k)$: returns the *data* indexed by k.

If we briefly examine the search process, a search network built upon a DHT seems to be a logical fit: a user issues a query ($get(k)$) to a search engine which responds with a search results page (*data*). The network we propose would act as a scalable storage depot operating in conjunction with the basic search process. Once a search results page has been retrieved from the search engine it would be stored in the DHT ($put(k, data)$) so as to save other users from having to query the search engine in the future.

5.2   A Fast Network

Besides the benefit of being scalable, DHTs offer the advantage of only needing a small number of hops through neighbouring nodes in order to satisfy requests. The order differs across varying implementations of DHTs but it is typically $O(log(n))$ or better (where n is the number of nodes participating in the DHT). Unfortunately, a disadvantage of the quick lookup scheme using the hashing function means that only exact matches for k can be returned.

5.3   A Privacy Preserving Network

As the reader has probably inferred from the discussion thus far, the proposed search network works as follows:

- Results of queries submitted to a search engine are stored in a DHT.
- Users wishing to make the same queries (this has been shown to be a likely occurrence) have the option of retrieving the results from the DHT instead of making a submission to a search engine.

At this point, the contribution of the network is that of anonymity from the search engine. We assume that search queries and their associated results are not personalised. This assumption means that there is a one to many relationship between a result for a query and the number of consumers of the result, i.e., a result for one user can be provided as a result for another user submitting the same query.

Unfortunately, anonymity from the search engine is not the only concern. Since there may be users of the network that can not be trusted, the proposed solution must provide all users with a degree of privacy from each other. In a bid to maintain the scalability and speed of the search network, we adopt a simple approach to privacy.

Since the users will be relying on each other to retrieve and store results, anonymity within the network is not our goal, i.e., the network does not employ any anonymisation techniques in so far as *who* is searching for data. Privacy is provided in the sense of *what* is being searched for. We know that the DHT stores a search result (*data*) for the hashed version of a query (k). At the very least, we will not store the query or the search result in plain text. Since k is a result of a one way hashing function this only leaves the problem of ensuring that *data* can not be observed. In the absence of a centralised authority or third party we propose an encryption scheme that uses the plain text version of the query (*q* before it is hashed) as the key when encrypting the result: $data = E_q(result)$. Since *q* will form part of the one way hash, the search results will only be accessible to those who already know what they are looking for, in other words, they know *q*.

At this stage, we have only dealt with storing the results of a query in the DHT. We have discussed a solution where participants of the network are offered anonymity from the search engines and a degree of privacy from each other. Unfortunately, the privacy introduced in this section brings with it another problem: if the query is hashed and unobservable in plain text, then who is going to submit the query on behalf of a user when a cached result does not exist in the DHT? After all, the search engine can not be queried with a hashed version of the query.

5.4 Submitting a Query

Submitting a lone query to a search engine is not as much of a problem as submitting a number of queries over time since a search engine may construct a sequential log (search profile) of the user's queries which may be used to infer something private about him or her.

A search profile consisting of other users' queries contributes to the privacy of the user in question since each query has lost its context. In order to submit queries to a search engine so that they are inherently stored this way, users make submissions on behalf of each other. Whilst this approach seems to be the simplest solution it has an obvious disadvantage: if user U_2 is to submit query Q_1 to a search engine on behalf of U_1, then U_2 must know what Q_1 is. This may be considered a violation of privacy. However, if our goal is to prevent the search engine from violating privacy, then it could be the case that this potential for violation of privacy may be acceptable in the event that not all queries from U_1 are submitted by U_2. This would have U_2 only submitting ad hoc queries for U_1 and, just like the search engine, these queries would have no context.

Since a DHT is essentially treated as a decentralised collection of nodes used to store data, we introduce a simple rule that each node must obey in order to have users successfully submitting queries on behalf of each other. The rule is simple: if a predefined data structure is present in the data to be stored, the necessary elements required to make a submission to a search engine must be extracted from this data. The search engine is then queried, the result of which is encrypted and stored in place of the original data.

The data structure serves only as a means for nodes to recognise when to store the data and when to use the contents thereof to formulate a query to a search engine. For example, *data* containing "**BING,Anonymity**" may signal a node to send the query "Anonymity" to the bing.com search engine. The result would then be encrypted (using "Anonymity" as the key) and stored. Note that the proposed search network is not bound to a specific search engine.

Of course, a large number of colluding nodes could possibly thwart the search network's attempt to preserve the privacy of users from each other. Increasing the number of attackers in the DHT increases the probability of receiving a number of queries on behalf of the user under attack and, in doing so, increase the likelihood of generating a log with context. There are a number of options for this scenario. The first option is to bypass the DHT nodes entirely and have a foreign node join the DHT to submit the request on the user's behalf. The foreign node could be part of another PET, for example, Tor [7]. Unfortunately, making use of another network will most likely introduce the very problems the search network proposed in this paper tries to remedy: scalability and performance.

Another option is a variation on the technique employed by "John Doe" nodes in the Crowds model [17]. In this model, a John Doe picks a random node from the crowd (which could be itself) and forwards the message to the node. This node, upon receiving the message, flips a biased coin to determine whether to send the message to another John Doe node or to deliver the message to its recipient. Nodes in the search network could employ a simpler process: upon determining that a search result is not available for a particular query, a node can flip a coin to determine whether to issue a request into the DHT to have the query addressed (using the predefined data structure) or address the query itself and place the result into the DHT. Since the node is part of the DHT it will have already conducted a number of queries on behalf of other nodes. As a result, detecting the user's queries from a search engine's perspective will be cumbersome. Ultimately, the queries still have no context.

We have opted to adopt the latter approach when submitting queries in the proposed search network.

6   Formalisation

In this section, we highlight the relationship between an accurate search profile and a log of queries submitted by a user. We then analyse a number of methods that can be used to submit queries to a search engine. The focus of our analysis deals with the logs that can be derived by an entity the likes of a proxy or search engine. We will show that constructing an accurate search profile of a user participating in a search network requires collusion with all parties in the network.

A log of search queries can be prepared from any one of the following perspectives: the user issuing the queries, a proxy user issuing the queries or the search engine for which the queries are destined. In this section we place emphasis on the number of queries in a log. Correct knowledge of a log (and its contents) implies that one knows how many queries have been issued. Similarly, if one does not know how many queries were issued then the contents of the log are not entirely known.

Within the context of this paper, if a user submits n queries to a search engine, the log of this user from his/her perspective is entirely known and will contain n

queries. If the log generated for this user from the perspective of a search engine contains the *same* n queries then the search engine has correct knowledge of the log.

L is a function with the set of users, U, as its domain and the number of queries associated with his/her log, V, as its range. With $U = \{u_1, u_2, \ldots, u_n\}$ and $V = I\!N$, L is the function that maps a user to the number of queries issued.

$$L : U \mapsto V \tag{1}$$

For any user u_i, the number of search queries issued is $L(u_i) = n_i$.

Let $L_s(u_i)$ denote the number of queries issued by u_i from the perspective of search engine s. Similarly, $L_{u_j}(u_i)$ denotes the number of queries issued by u_i from the perspective of u_j where $j \neq i$. If $L_s(u_i) \neq L(u_i)$ then the contents of u_i's log are not entirely known by the search engine (it does not have an accurate search profile for u_i).

6.1   Submitting Queries Directly

In the absence of a proxy, all search queries issued by u_i are submitted directly to the search engine. Since the number of queries in the log generated from the perspective of the search engine equals the number of queries in the user's log, the search engine has correct knowledge of the log (also referred to as an accurate search profile), i.e., $L_s(u_i) = L(u_i) = n_i$.

6.2   Submitting Queries through a Proxy

Consider the introduction of a proxy where u_j submits queries on behalf of u_i. From the perspective of a search engine, the logs generated yield the following: $L_s(u_j) = n_i$ (there are n_i queries for user u_j) and $L_s(u_i) = 0$ (there were no queries for user u_i). Whilst the search engine can't derive anything about user u_i (there is no log of his/her queries), the user through which u_i is proxying is in a much better position to build a search profile since $L_{u_j}(u_i) = L(u_i) = n_i$. Essentially, the problem for user u_i is that the accurate search profile has now been shifted from the search engine to the user that is acting as a proxy.

6.3   Using a Proxy and Direct Submission

We try to alleviate the problem of shifting the profile from one entity to another by introducing the flipped coin approach discussed in the previous section. Instead of forwarding all queries to a proxy we let p denote the probability of forwarding a query to a proxy. Since there are n_i queries submitted by u_i, an average of pn_i of these will be forwarded to the proxy and $(1-p)n_i$ to the search engine. The result is that a number of queries go to u_j and a number to s (note that we are now dealing with expected values):

$$L_{u_j}(u_i) = L_s(u_j) = pn_i \tag{2}$$

$$L_s(u_i) = (1-p)n_i \tag{3}$$

By splitting the queries between the two entities, we decrease the chance of a single entity forming an accurate search profile.

However, if it is known that u_j is only a proxy for u_i, the search engine can easily construct the complete search profile by combining its log of u_i with the log of u_j. We refer to this log as $L_s\prime(u_i)$:

$$L_s\prime(u_i) = L_s(u_i) + L_s(u_j) \tag{4}$$

Using equation 2 and 3:

$$L_s\prime(u_i) = (1-p)n_i + pn_i = n_i = L(u_i)$$

6.4   Using Multiple Proxies and Direct Submission

If we increase the number of users acting as proxies for u_i to m, constructing $L_s\prime(u_i)$ becomes tedious for s since it would have to know each of the m users that u_i is proxying through. We know that the probability of forwarding a query to a proxy is p. With m proxies, the chance of forwarding a query to any particular proxy is $\frac{p}{m}$. As a result

$$L_s(u_j) = \frac{pn_i}{m} \tag{5}$$

Compiling the search profile for u_i from the perspective of s would be achieved by adding the logs of all m proxies to $L_s(u_i)$:

$$L_s\prime(u_i) = L_s(u_i) + \sum_{j=1}^{m} L_s(u_j) \tag{6}$$

Using equation 5, 6 expands so that $L(u_i)$ is determined:

$$L_s\prime(u_i) = (1-p)n_i + \sum_{l=1}^{m} \frac{pn_i}{m} = (1-p)n_i + m(\frac{pn_i}{m}) = n_i = L(u_i)$$

As the number of proxies for u_i increases, a successful attack from a search engine perspective becomes difficult only in the sense that it has to know which users are acting as proxies for u_i.

6.5   Submission of Queries through a DHT

In this paper, we have proposed a network where all users act as proxies for one another. This very simple act adds significant complexity to an attack from a search engine since, as we are going to show, it would have to collude with each of the users proxying for the victim in addition to knowing who is proxying for the victim. For the sake of simplicity, in this section we assume that users in the search network act as non-caching proxies.

Since all users in the proposed network submit queries on behalf of other users in the network, the log of queries submitted by any user from the perspective of the search engine will include all queries submitted by the user directly (remember from 3 that this is $(1 - p)n_i$) in addition to queries for which the user acted as a proxy. To be precise, in a network of m users:

$$L_s(u_i) = (1 - p)n_i + \sum_{j=1}^{m} \frac{pn_j}{m}; i \neq j \qquad (7)$$

Applying this to 6, we have

$$L_{s'}(u_i) = (1 - p)n_i + \sum_{j=1}^{m} \frac{pn_j}{m} + \sum_{j=1}^{m} L_s(u_j) \qquad (8)$$

We have shown that the search engine must take into account that u_i is submitting queries on behalf of other users (depicted in 7). Note that each proxy u_i is using is also acting as a proxy to users other than u_i. Furthermore, the proxies are submitting queries themselves. Unless the search engine colludes with each of the proxies (ensuring that they are not submitting any queries themselves), then the log of queries submitted to the search engine from each proxy is similar to that of u_i in 7:

$$L_s(u_j) = (1 - p)n_j + \sum_{l=1}^{m} \frac{pn_l}{m}; l \neq j \qquad (9)$$

With this in mind, we expand 8:

$$L_{s'}(u_i) = (1 - p)n_i + \sum_{j=1}^{m} \frac{pn_j}{m} + \sum_{j=1}^{m} L_s(u_j)$$

$$= (1 - p)n_i + \sum_{j=1}^{m} \frac{pn_j}{m} + \sum_{j=1}^{m} ((1 - p)n_j + \sum_{l=1}^{m} \frac{pn_l}{m})$$

Note that in the search network approach, a search engine colluding with a number of proxies will only be successful (generate an accurate search profile) when the number of proxies colluding in the network equals $m - 1$.

7 Conclusion

In the beginning of this paper we discussed the privacy problems that were raised when a search engine placed its search database online in 2006. We suggested how this may have been avoided through a simple process of anonymisation. We then argued that queries without context are not as prone to privacy violation as queries with context. With this in mind, we proposed a network which would protect a user from a search engine violating his or her privacy.

Using the database of 2006, we took a random sample and showed that there is a significantly large number of queries which are shared by users when using search engines. If we assume that the results of these queries are not specific to the user conducting the initial query, then the results from a single query can be shared with other users of the network, sparing them from having to conduct the query themselves.

The notion of sharing queries is introduced and forms the basis upon which the search network is proposed. Essentially, the search network acts as a cache of search queries and search results. Built on top of a distributed hash table, the search network allows users or nodes to place and retrieve queries and their associated search results from the cache. A simple encryption scheme using the query to encrypt the search results allows for a small degree of privacy between the users of this network. The major contribution is that of privacy from the search engines. This privacy is in the form of sender anonymity as defined earlier in this paper.

The search network is built on top of a Distributed Hash Table. DHTs have shown themselves to be fast and massively scalable. These two characteristics are of paramount importance in a network of this nature. A greater number of users will result in a higher probability of a query already being conducted by someone else on the network. If the network can not scale well, there would not be more incentive to use it over conventional PETs.

Ultimately, the search network is a form of distributed proxy. It differs from conventional privacy preserving proxies the likes of Anonymizer.com because the queries, in addition to not always being in the clear, lack context. This is not the case with a centralised proxy since although one is protected from the search engine, the proxy itself has the potential for privacy violation.

References

1. Aberer, K.: P-Grid: A Self-Organizing Access Structure for P2P Information Systems. In: Batini, C., Giunchiglia, F., Giorgini, P., Mecella, M. (eds.) CoopIS 2001. LNCS, vol. 2172, pp. 179–194. Springer, Heidelberg (2001)
2. Adar, E.: User 4xxxxx9: Anonymizing query logs. In: Amitay, E., Murray, C.G., Teevan, J. (eds.) Query Log Analysis: Social And Technological Challenges. A workshop at the 16th International World Wide Web Conference (WWW 2007) (May 2007)
3. Araújo, F.: Position-Based Distributed Hash Tables. PhD thesis, Department of Informatics, University of Lisbon, DI/FCUL TR-06-7 (May 2006)
4. Bellotti, V., Sellen, A.: Design for Privacy in Ubiquitous Computing Environments. In: Proceedings of the Third European Conference on Computer Supported Cooperative Work (ECSCW'93), pp. 77–92. Kluwer, Dordrecht (1993)
5. Brin, S., Page, L.: The anatomy of a large-scale hypertextual Web search engine. Computer Networks and ISDN Systems 30(1-7), 107–117 (1998)
6. Chaum, D.: Untraceable electronic mail, return addresses, and digital pseudonyms. Communications of the ACM 4(2) (February 1981)
7. Dingledine, R., Mathewson, N., Syverson, P.: Tor: The second-generation onion router. In: Proceedings of the 13th USENIX Security Symposium (August 2004)
8. Garcés-Erice, L., Ross, K.W., Biersack, E.W., Felber, P., Urvoy-Keller, G.: Topology-centric look-up service. Networked Group Communication, 58–69 (2003)

9. Goldberg, I., Wagner, D., Brewer, E.: Privacy-enhancing technologies for the internet. In: Proc. of 42nd IEEE Spring COMPCON. IEEE Computer Society Press, Los Alamitos (February 1997)
10. Karger, D., Lehman, E., Leighton, T., Levine, M., Lewin, D., Panigrahy, R.: Consistent hashing and random trees: Distributed caching protocols for relieving hot spots on the world wide web. In: ACM Symposium on Theory of Computing, pp. 654–663 (May 1997)
11. Korolova, A., Kenthapadi, K., Mishra, N., Ntoulas, A.: Releasing search queries and clicks privately. In: 18th International World Wide Web Conference, WWW 2009 (April 2009)
12. Levine, B., Shields, C.: Hordes: A multicast based protocol for anonymity. Journal of Computer Security 10(3), 213–240 (2002)
13. Øverlier, L., Syverson, P.: Locating hidden servers. In: Proceedings of the 2006 IEEE Symposium on Security and Privacy, May 2006, pp. 100–114. IEEE Computer Society, Los Alamitos (2006)
14. Pfitzmann, A., Koehntopp, M.: Anonymity, unobservability, and pseudonymity - A proposal for terminology. In: Federrath, H. (ed.) Designing Privacy Enhancing Technologies. LNCS, vol. 2009, p. 1. Springer, Heidelberg (2001)
15. Pfitzmann, A., Waidner, M.: Networks without user observability. Computers and Security 2(6), 158–166 (1987)
16. Reed, M.G., Syverson, P.F., Goldschlag, D.M.: Anonymous connections and onion routing. IEEE Journal on Selected Areas in Communications 16(4), 482–494 (1998)
17. Reiter, M.K., Rubin, A.D.: Crowds: anonymity for Web transactions. ACM Transactions on Information and System Security 1(1), 66–92 (1998)
18. Rowstron, A., Druschel, P.: Pastry: Scalable, decentralized object location and routing for large-scale peer-to-peer systems. In: IFIP/ACM International Conference on Distributed Systems Platforms (Middleware), November 2001, pp. 329–350 (2001)
19. Stoica, I., Morris, R., Karger, D., Kaashoek, M.F., Balakrishnan, H.: Chord: A scalable peer-to-peer lookup service for internet applications. In: Proceedings of the ACM SIGCOMM '01 Conference, San Diego, California (August 2001)
20. Wright, J., Stepney, S., Clark, J.A., Jacob, J.L.: Designing Anonymity - A Formal Basis for Identity Hiding. Internal yellow report, York University, York, UK (December 2004)
21. Zhao, B., Kubiatowicz, J., Joseph, A.D.: Tapestry: An infrastructure for fault-tolerant wide-area location and routing. Technical Report UCB/CSD-01-1141, University of California Berkeley, Electrical Engineering and Computer Science Department (April 2001)

Untraceability and Profiling Are Not Mutually Exclusive[*]

Sébastien Canard[1] and Amandine Jambert[1,2]

[1] Orange Labs, 42 rue des Coutures, BP6243, 14066 Caen Cedex, France
[2] IMB, Université Bordeaux 1, 351 cours de la Libération, 33405 Talence, France

Abstract. In this paper, we study the concept of privacy-preserving multi-service subscription systems. With such system, service providers can propose to their customers, by the way of a subscription, several distinct services that users can access while being anonymous. We moreover study how users can be untraceable *w.r.t.* the service provider during the subscription process, in such a way that it is additionally possible to make profiling on the users' customs. This permits the service provider to propose some advertisements to users while protecting the privacy of the latter, even this may be seen as contradictory. We also propose concrete instantiations, based on signature schemes with extensions from Camenisch and Lysyanskaya.

1 Introduction

Nowadays, more and more services are available on the internet. Some of them are free but, some others imply a payment from the customers. Users may pay each time they use the provided service, or subscribe to this service to use it once [12,8], a fixed number of time, or each time they want during a fixed time period [2]. In this paper, we focus on the latter case: a user subscribes to a service (or a set of services) and can use it as she wants. More precisely, we focus on the case where service providers propose to their customers several distinct services for which it is necessary to subscribe before using them.

Such subscription should not be done to the detriment of privacy principles and users may not want to be traced in their actions. It should be possible for a user to be anonymous and untraceable when she access a subscribed service, as described by Blanton in [2], or in [18]. It is also possible to do better than the Blanton system by additionally making the user anonymous and untraceable *w.r.t.* the service provider during the subscription process. Note that in this case, it is necessary to add a privacy-preserving payment system such as Secure Electronic Transaction (SET) [16], e-cash [5] or multi-coupon [8] systems. In the following, we only focus on the subscription part and do not treat this payment phase.

---

[*] This work has been financially supported by the French Agence Nationale de la Recherche and the TES Cluster under the PACE project.

S. Katsikas, J. Lopez, and M. Soriano (Eds.): TrustBus 2010, LNCS 6264, pp. 117–128, 2010.

In this paper, we also study "profiling", that is the analysis of a group of customers to determine what characteristics they might have in common. This permits a service provider to know what set of services one user is interested in, such that this service provider is able to put some well-chosen advertisements for a particular user in a personalized web page, influencing this user to buy some new services, according to her preferences.

The untraceability of a user during a subscription or an access to some services may be considered as contradictory with the possibility for the service provider to make such profiling. In this paper, we show that this is not true. We thus study different levels of untraceability during use and/or subscription in order to allow the service provider to make such profiling. More precisely, we propose different multi-service subscription schemes which permit to balance both untraceability and profiling during purchase, while keeping the user untraceable during the use of one service.

The paper is organized as follows. In the next section, we introduce the concept of multi-service subscription scheme. Then, we propose a new system based on signature schemes with extensions proposed by Camenisch and Lysyanskaya. Finally we introduce different extensions balancing untraceability and profiling before to conclude.

2 Multi-service Subscription Systems

A multi-service subscription system is composed of two types of actors: users, denoted $\mathcal{U}$, who want to subscribe and use services provided by a service provider $\mathcal{SP}$. A service provider provides a set of f different services, each of them being identified by a unique identifier denoted s_i. Each user can use a specific service as soon as she subscribes to it. A user is known to be a subscriber by owning a subscription certificate. At any time, the user can subscribe to more services provided by the same (or not) service provider. Concerning privacy, the user is anonymous and untraceable when she uses a specific service. In the following, we more formally describe this concept.

2.1 Procedures

Formally speaking, a multi-service subscription system is composed of the following procedures, where λ is a security parameter.

- SETUP is an algorithm executed by some designated entities which on input 1^λ outputs the parameters param of the system. These parameters can be common for several service providers.
- SPSETUP is an algorithm executed by $\mathcal{SP}$ providing f different services to generates the set $\mathcal{S}$ of service identifiers $s_1, \cdots, s_f$, on input 1^λ and param. The service provider also outputs a pair of keys (spsk, sppk). The public key is certified by some designated authorities, for example using a PKI.
- USETUP is a procedure which permits the user to obtain a pair of keys (usk, upk), upk being published. As for sppk, this public key may be certified.

- SUBSCRIBE is a protocol between $\mathcal{U}$ and $\mathcal{SP}$, in which $\mathcal{U}$ subscribes to some services. $\mathcal{U}$ gives to $\mathcal{SP}$ a subset $\mathcal{S_U}$ of the set $\mathcal{S}$ of all provided services. $\mathcal{U}$ takes as input usk, upk, param, $\mathcal{S_U}$, $\mathcal{S}$ and sppk and $\mathcal{SP}$ takes as input spsk, sppk, param and $\mathcal{S}$. The user outputs a subscription certificate cert.
- ADDSUBSCRIBE permits a user $\mathcal{U}$ owning a certificate cert to subscribe to new services and thus to update cert so that it incorporates the new services. More formally, this is a protocol between $\mathcal{U}$, taking on input usk, param, $\mathcal{S_U}$, $\mathcal{S}$, sppk and the initial certificate cert, and $\mathcal{SP}$, taking on input spsk, param, $\mathcal{S}$ and sppk. The user outputs an updated subscription certificate $\widetilde{\text{cert}}$ which corresponds to her subscription to a subset $\tilde{\mathcal{S}}_\mathcal{U} \subset \mathcal{S}$ such that $\mathcal{S_U} \subset \tilde{\mathcal{S}}_\mathcal{U}$.
- USE permits to $\mathcal{U}$ to prove to $\mathcal{SP}$ that she has the right to use a service $s \in \mathcal{S}$. The user takes on input cert, usk, param, the service $s \in \mathcal{S_U} \subset \mathcal{S}$ and sppk, while the service provider uses spsk, param, $\mathcal{S}$ and sppk. The output of this protocol is either 1 if the user has the right to obtain the service s or 0.

2.2   Security and Efficiency Issues

There are several security and efficiency issues in our context, which ones are based on the work from [2].

- **Correctness:** any subscriber can use, thanks to the USE protocol with $\mathcal{SP}$, the services she subscribed thanks to the SUBSCRIBE or the ADDSUBSCRIBE procedure with that $\mathcal{SP}$.
- **Soundness:** even a coalition of legitimate users is unable to obtain access to non-subscribed services. The aim of an adversary, who may play several users, is to be accepted during a USE on a service s_i while having played no SUBSCRIBE or ADDSUBSCRIBE protocol on that service with this $\mathcal{SP}$.
- **Anonymity:** even the $\mathcal{SP}$ is unable to identify a user within legitimate users or to decide whether two executions of USE come from the same user. An adversary, playing the role of $\mathcal{SP}$, should be unable to decide between two chosen users which one is playing a USE with the fraudulent $\mathcal{SP}$.
- **Compactness:** the size of the certificate cert should not depend on the number of embedded services.

2.3   Profiling Definition

One of the aim of the $\mathcal{SP}$ is to profile costumers, *i.e.* to analyse his group of customers to determine what characteristics they have in common. This is used by $\mathcal{SP}$ to better direct their future sales and marketing programs. Unfortunately, this may interfere with privacy.

3   Our Basic Construction: Scheme 1

3.1   Notation and Building Blocks

In the following, a bilinear environment is denoted $(p, \mathbb{G}_1, \mathbb{G}_2, \mathbb{G}_T, g_1, g_2, e)$ where p is a prime number, $\mathbb{G}_1$, $\mathbb{G}_2$ and $\mathbb{G}_T$ are two groups of order p, g_1 (resp. g_2) is a generator of $\mathbb{G}_1$ (resp. $\mathbb{G}_2$) and $e : \mathbb{G}_1 \times \mathbb{G}_2 \longrightarrow \mathbb{G}_T$ is a bilinear map.

Zero-Knowledge Proof of Knowledge. Roughly speaking, a Zero Knowledge Proof of Knowledge (ZKPK) is an interactive protocol during which a prover $\mathcal{P}$ proves to a verifier $\mathcal{V}$ that she knows a set of secret values verifying a given relation without revealing anything else[1]. In the following, we denote by $\text{POK}(\alpha_1, \ldots, \alpha_q : \mathsf{R}(\alpha_1, \ldots, \alpha_q))$ a proof of knowledge of the secrets $\alpha_1, \ldots, \alpha_q$ verifying the relation R. In this paper, we only consider the case where secrets are discrete logarithms in relations constructed over a group of prime order: proof of knowledge of a discrete logarithm [19] $\text{POK}(\alpha : y = g^\alpha)$; proof of knowledge of a representation [17] $\text{POK}(\alpha_1, \ldots, \alpha_q : y = g_1^{\alpha_1} \ldots g_q^{\alpha_q})$; and proof of equality of discrete logarithms [11] $\text{POK}(\alpha : y = g^\alpha \wedge z = h^\alpha)$. Such proofs of knowledge can be turned to non-interactive proofs of knowledge (*a.k.a.* signatures of knowledge) by using the Fiat-Shamir heuristic [14].

Signature Schemes with Extensions. The concept of signature schemes with extensions was introduced by Camenisch and Lysyanskaya [6]. Such schemes are standard signature schemes with some additional features. The first additional feature is the possibility to sign a message (SIGN algorithm) which is decomposed into several blocks $m = m_0 \| \cdots \| m_\ell$. The second one is an algorithm, denoted CSIGN, which permits the signer to sign a commitment C on some unknown values $(m_0, \cdots, m_\ell)$, using the Pedersen commitment scheme. Finally, it is possible to prove the knowledge of a valid signature on a message divided into blocks without revealing the message nor the signature: $\text{POK}(m - m_0 \| \cdots \| m_\ell, \sigma : \text{VERIF}(m, \sigma, \mathsf{spk}) = 1)$.

It exists several constructions of such signature schemes with extensions [6,7]. We here focus on the one [7] based on the q-SDH assumption and related to the BBS group signature scheme [3].

3.2   High Level Description of Scheme 1

In our basic solution, each service provided by $\mathcal{SP}$ is known by a specific identifier s_i and is related to one generator h_i and one scalar n_i which is used to state that this service has not been subscribed. $\mathcal{SP}$ can generate signatures with extensions to sign the subscribed services $(s_{i_1}, \cdots, s_{i_k})$ and the unsubscribed ones $(n_{i_{k+1}}, \cdots, n_{i_f})$, together with the secret key usk of the subscriber, so that only her can use this subscription. This is done during the SUBSCRIBE procedure by using an interactive signing protocol (see below).

The ADDSUBSCRIBE procedure consists in executing a new signing protocol to add messages to a signature with extensions. For this purpose, we improve signature schemes with extensions by adding a new feature, making possible to update a previously obtained signature to add sub messages. Finally, the USE protocol consists for the user in proving her knowledge of a signature with extension on the wanted service, without revealing the signature nor the other

---

[1] These protocols are also used to prove that some public values are well-formed from known secret ones (*e.g.* a ciphertext *w.r.t.* a known secret plaintext).

subscribed services. We now detailed each procedure one by one, using the q-SDH based signature scheme with extensions from [7,3].

3.3 Setup Procedures

Let λ be a security parameter. The SETUP procedure consists in generating a bilinear environment $(p, \mathbb{G}_1, \mathbb{G}_2, \mathbb{G}_T, g_1, g_2, e)$. Let $g, h \in \mathbb{G}_1$. The SPSETUP algorithm consists in choosing, for each service provider, the number f of proposed services[2]. Each service is next associated to three different values: one scalar, denoted s_i, to state that the service is subscribed, one another scalar, denoted n_i, to state that the service is unsubscribed, and one group element $h_i \in \mathbb{G}_1$. $\mathcal{SP}$ also generates at random the signature secret key γ of the chosen signature scheme with extension and publishes the corresponding public key $w = g_2^\gamma$ in the service provider public key sppk. Finally, $\mathcal{U}$ is related to a secret key usk and known by the public key $\mathsf{upk} = g^{\mathsf{usk}}$, which one may be certified by using a PKI. We will see other possibilities in Section 4.

3.4 Subscription Procedure

We suppose that $\mathcal{U}$, with the key pair $(\mathsf{usk}, \mathsf{upk})$, wants to subscribe to $k \leq f$ services identified by $s_{i_1}, \cdots, s_{i_k}$ where the i_j's belong to $[1, f]$. We denote by $\mathcal{I} = \{i_1, \cdots, i_k\} \subset [1, f]$. This protocol is an interactive protocol of the signature scheme with extensions between the user $\mathcal{U}$ and the signer $\mathcal{SP}$, which permits the user to obtain a signature on the $f + 1$ following committed values: usk, all s_j for $j \in \mathcal{I}$ and all n_j for $j \in [1, f] \setminus \mathcal{I}$. During this protocol, the value usk is added by the user while the service identifiers s_j and n_j are committed by the service provider[3]. More precisely, we have the following steps.

1. The user first commits to a secret s' and her user secret key usk: $C' = h^{s'} h_0^{\mathsf{usk}}$.
2. She produces U as a proof of knowledge that C' is well-formed using known s' and usk. Note that during this step, the user should prove, within the U proof of knowledge, that the committed value usk is related to the given public key upk: $U = \mathrm{POK}(s', \mathsf{usk} : C' = h^{s'} h_0^{\mathsf{usk}} \wedge \mathsf{upk} = g^{\mathsf{usk}})$. The user sends to $\mathcal{SP}$ the commitment C', her public key upk (and, if needed, the X.509 certificate), the proof U and the wanted services $s_{i_1}, \cdots, s_{i_k}$.
3. $\mathcal{SP}$ adds to the commitment C' the values corresponding to the subscribed (the s_j's) and the unsubscribed (the n_j's) services, and modifies s' to $s = s' + s''$ in the new commitment $C = C' h^{s''} \prod_{j \in \mathcal{I}} h_j^{s_j} \prod_{j \in [1, f] \setminus \mathcal{I}} h_j^{n_j}$.
4. $\mathcal{SP}$ finally signs the commitment C so that $\mathcal{U}$ obtains a signature (A, x) on $(s, \mathsf{usk}, \{s_j\}_{j \in \mathcal{I}}, \{n_j\}_{j \in [1,f] \setminus \mathcal{I}})$. For this purpose, x is chosen at random in $\mathbb{Z}_p^*$ and A is computed as $A = (g_1 h^s h_0^{\mathsf{usk}} \prod_{j \in \mathcal{I}} h_j^{s_j} \prod_{j \in [1,f] \setminus \mathcal{I}} h_j^{n_j})^{\frac{1}{\gamma + x}}$. $\mathcal{SP}$ also saves the commitment C and the services $s_{i_1}, \cdots, s_{i_k}$ subscribed by $\mathcal{U}$. The subscription certificate cert is finally the signature with extension $\sigma = (A, x)$.

---

[2] This number can be updated by generating the corresponding triple (s_i, n_i, h_i).
[3] The values n_j are necessary to improve the untraceability, since one can learn some information on $\mathcal{U}$ by knowing that she has e.g. registered to only 3 services.

3.5   Addition of Services

We now suppose that $\mathcal{U}$ has previously subscribed to k services. Thus, she knows a certificate represented by the signature $\sigma = (A, x)$ on the message $(s, \mathsf{usk}, \{s_j\}_{j \in \mathcal{I}}, \{n_j\}_{j \in [1,f] \setminus \mathcal{I}})$ (also written $C = h^s h_0^{\mathsf{usk}} \prod_{j \in \mathcal{I}} h_j^{s_j} \prod_{j \in [1,f] \setminus \mathcal{I}} h_j^{n_j}$). $\mathcal{U}$ now wants to subscribe to l additional services (for simplicity, we denote $\ell = k + l$) identified by $s_{i_{k+1}}, \cdots, s_{i_\ell}$. In the following, we denote by $\tilde{\mathcal{I}} = \{i_{k+1}, \cdots, i_\ell\} \cup \mathcal{I}$. Our aim is to make one single certificate incorporating the previously obtained services and the new ones. More precisely, we have the following steps.

1. The user first sends to $\mathcal{SP}$ her public key upk and the previously signed message in the form C above. She finally produces the proof of knowledge

$$V = \text{POK}(s, \mathsf{usk} : C / \prod_{j \in \mathcal{I}} h_j^{-s_j} \prod_{j \in [1,f] \setminus \mathcal{I}} h_j^{-n_j} = h^s h_0^{\mathsf{usk}} \wedge \mathsf{upk} = g^{\mathsf{usk}})$$

2. We consider that the aggregation of subscribed services is done by $\mathcal{SP}$ since it knows the identity of $\mathcal{U}$. $\mathcal{SP}$ retrieves in its database the value C and the services $s_{i_1}, \cdots, s_{i_k}$ already subscribed by $\mathcal{U}$, verifies U, adds to C the values $s_{i_{k+1}}, \cdots, s_{i_\ell}$ and modifies s to $\tilde{s} = s + \tilde{s}'$ in the new commitment $\tilde{C} = C h^{\tilde{s}'} \prod_{j \in \tilde{\mathcal{I}} \setminus \mathcal{I}} h_j^{s_j - n_j} = h^{\tilde{s}} h_0^{\mathsf{usk}} \prod_{j \in \tilde{\mathcal{I}}} h_j^{s_j} \prod_{j \in [1,f] \setminus \tilde{\mathcal{I}}} h_j^{n_j}$.

3. $\mathcal{SP}$ finally signs $\tilde{C}$ so that $\mathcal{U}$ obtains a signature $(\tilde{A}, \tilde{x})$ on $(s, \mathsf{usk}, \{s_j\}_{j \in \tilde{\mathcal{I}}}, \{n_j\}_{j \in [1,f] \setminus \tilde{\mathcal{I}}})$, that is such that $\tilde{A} = (g_1 h^{\tilde{s}} h_0^{\mathsf{usk}} \prod_{j \in \tilde{\mathcal{I}}} h_j^{s_j} \prod_{j \in [1,f] \setminus \tilde{\mathcal{I}}} h_j^{n_j})^{\frac{1}{\gamma + \tilde{x}}}$, where $x \in_R \mathbb{Z}_p^*$. $\mathcal{SP}$ should not take the same x used during SUBSCRIBE since it permits $\mathcal{U}$ to forge signatures. $\mathcal{SP}$ saves the new services $s_{i_{k+1}}, \cdots, s_{i_\ell}$ subscribed by $\mathcal{U}$. The new subscription certificate $\widetilde{\mathsf{cert}}$ is finally $\tilde{\sigma} = (\tilde{A}, \tilde{x})$.

3.6   The Use Protocol

We next imagine that $\mathcal{U}$, who has subscribed to services $s_{i_1}, \cdots, s_{i_\ell}$, wants to use e.g. s_{i_1}. The USE protocol is based on the ZKPK of a signature with extension $\tilde{\sigma} = (\tilde{A}, \tilde{x})$ on the message $(s, \mathsf{usk}, \{s_j\}_{j \in \tilde{\mathcal{I}}}, \{n_j\}_{j \in [1,f] \setminus \tilde{\mathcal{I}}})$ without revealing the signature nor the values $s, \mathsf{usk}, \{s_j\}_{j \in \tilde{\mathcal{I}}}, \{n_j\}_{j \in [1,f] \setminus \tilde{\mathcal{I}}}$. The only sub-message known by $\mathcal{SP}$ is, obviously, the value s_{i_1}. In the q-SDH case, the user first computes $C_1 = A h^r$ and $C_2 = g^r h^u$, where r and u are randomly chosen in $\mathbb{Z}_p^*$, and next makes the proof

$$\text{POK} \ (\tilde{s}, \mathsf{usk}, s_{i_2}, \cdots, s_{i_\ell}, \{n_j\}_{j \in [1,f] \setminus \tilde{\mathcal{I}}}, x, rx, r, s, sx : C_2 = g^r h^s \wedge$$
$$1 = C_2^x g^{-rx} h^{-sx} \wedge e(g_1, g_2) e(h_j, g_2)^{s_1} / e(C_1, w) =$$
$$e(C_1, g_2)^x e(h, g_2)^{-rx} e(h, w)^{-r} \prod_{j \in \tilde{\mathcal{I}}} e(h_j, g_2)^{-s_j} \prod_{j \in [1,f] \setminus \tilde{\mathcal{I}}} e(h_j, g_2)^{-n_j}).$$

3.7   Security Issues

We here give some words on the security and efficiency issues that have been described before for multi-service subscription systems.

- **Correctness:** this is obvious that a user having subscribe to a service will be able to produce the proof of knowledge underlying the USE protocol.
- **Soundness:** the unforgeability property is verified due to the unforgeability property of the signature scheme with extension. Since the used one is secure (in our case under the q-SDH assumption), it means that an adversary is not able to output a signature on a new message, even with access to the verification public key and to a signing oracle.
- **Anonymity:** this property is verified due to the use of a zero-knowledge proof of knowledge which blinds the subscribed services to the service provider during the USE procedure. There is no way for $\mathcal{SP}$ to make a link between the SUBSCRIBE and the USE procedures other than by breaking the commitment scheme or the zero-knowledge proof of knowledge.
- **Compactness:** It is obvious that our system is compact since the size of the certificate is the one of the signature scheme with extension (in our case (A, x)) which does not depend on the number of subscribed services.

3.8   Profiling vs. Privacy of Scheme 1

With the above system, we have reached a first level of untraceability of the user. In fact, the service provider does not know the identity of the user during the USE protocol, and can not make the link with a SUBSCRIBE or an ADDSUBSCRIBE procedure since the other subscribed services are blinded. With such system, it is clear that the service provider can make some profiling since it knows which set of services a specific user has subscribed. Thus the service provider can make some statistics on the sets of services that are appreciated by users so as to propose new existing services to its customers by using well-chosen advertisements.

In some cases, a user may want to better protect her privacy *w.r.t.* the service provider by not giving her identity when subscribing services. One may think that this goes against profiling but, in the following, we show that the user can be anonymous and sometimes untraceable by the service provider, while permitting some profiling by the $\mathcal{SP}$.

4   Untraceability during Subscription

In this section, we show how $\mathcal{U}$ can be anonymous *w.r.t.* $\mathcal{SP}$ during both the SUBSCRIBE and ADDSUBSCRIBE procedures. For this purpose, we use a variant of the concept of group signatures called Direct Anonymous Attestations.

4.1   Group Signatures and Direct Anonymous Attestations

Concept of Group Signature. A group signature scheme permits group members to sign messages such that they are anonymous and unlinkable but for a designated authority which is able to revoke the anonymity of a signature. It is possible to design a group signature scheme [13,1,3] using a signature schemes with extensions (see Section 3.1) and an encryption scheme [15,3]. Most of current constructions are based on the same basis. For example, the XSGS scheme [13] uses the above q-SDH based signature scheme with extensions. In this case, the encryption scheme can be the (double) El Gamal encryption [15,13] or the linear encryption [3].

Concept of DAA. The concept of list signature schemes has been introduced in [10,9]. It is a variant of group signature schemes which permits, in some cases, to link the signatures from the same user. The same technique has later been used in [4] for Direct Anonymous Attestations (DAA) where the signatures from a group member can be linked if they are related to the same receiver.

The main difference between a group signature and a DAA is the addition, during the signature process, of a value $T = h_{\mathcal{SP}}^{\mathsf{usk}}$ where $h_{\mathcal{SP}}$ is specific to the receiver. Thus, for one group member and one receiver, this value is always the same, and this group member can be traced with T, but two different service providers cannot make any link between two attestations with two different $h_{\mathcal{SP}}$. For this purpose, it should not exist any link between two values $h_{\mathcal{SP}_1}$ and $h_{\mathcal{SP}_2}$ of two different services providers $\mathcal{SP}_1$ and $\mathcal{SP}_2$. This is done by computing e.g. $h_{\mathcal{SP}}$ using a hash function on public values such as name and address of $\mathcal{SP}$.

4.2   Anonymity but Traceability of the User: Scheme 2

In Section 3.4, we have seen that, during the subscription process of Scheme 1, the user has to prove that she has the right to subscribe to some chosen services. For this purpose, U should include the proof of knowledge of usk such that the revealed value upk equals g^{usk}. As shown previously, this also permits us to obtain non repudiation of the user. But as $\mathcal{SP}$ may do the link between upk and the true identity of $\mathcal{U}$, the latter is not anonymous. $\mathcal{U}$ may belong to the group of people who are authorized to access the services provided by $\mathcal{SP}$ but she needs to be anonymous. As we need non-repudiation, the anonymity should be revoked, in case of dispute, in a proven way: we thus need a group signature scheme. But, as one user needs to be recognized by $\mathcal{SP}$ (to ensure the compactness property) during the ADDSUBSCRIBE, we need a DAA.

Setup. The SETUP protocol is different from the one in Section 3.3 since $\mathcal{U}$ needs to be able to produce a DAA. This is done using a GJOIN protocol with a "group" manager during the USETUP, so that $\mathcal{U}$ now owns a user secret key usk and a group member certificate $\tau = (Z, u)$ such that $Z = (g_1 h_0^{\mathsf{usk}})^{\frac{1}{\gamma+u}}$ (see [13]). The role of the group manager can here be played by $\mathcal{SP}$ in case there is only one service provider (and since the anonymity is also verified w.r.t. the group manager) or by any other designated entity with no commercial link with $\mathcal{SP}$. Finally, let $(\theta_1, k_1 = h^{\theta_1})$ and $(\theta_2, k_2 = g^{\theta_2})$ be two pairs of the El Gamal cryptosystem [15,13].

Subscribe Procedure. During the SUBSCRIBE process, instead of the proof of knowledge that the committed usk in $C' = h^{s'} h_0^{\mathsf{usk}}$ is related to a revealed and known $\mathsf{upk} = g^{\mathsf{usk}}$, $\mathcal{U}$ needs to prove that the key usk is related to the DAA. This is possible using the subscription process described in Section 3.4 while replacing U by the following one, including a proof that usk is related to a group member certificate $\tau = (Z, u)$ by $Z = (g_1 h_0^{\mathsf{usk}})^{\frac{1}{\gamma + u}}$.

$$U = \text{POK}(s', \alpha, \beta, u, u\alpha, \mathsf{usk} : C' = h^{s'} h_0^{\mathsf{usk}} \wedge T = h_{\mathcal{SP}}^{\mathsf{usk}} \wedge$$
$$T_1 = h^\alpha \wedge T_3 = h^\beta \wedge T_2/T_4 = k_1^\alpha/k_2^\beta \wedge$$
$$e(T_2, g_2)^u e(k_1, w)^{-\alpha} e(k_1, g_2)^{-u\alpha} e(h_0, g_2)^{-\mathsf{usk}} = e(g_1, g_2)/e(T_2, w)),$$

where $T_1 = h^\alpha$, $T_2 = Zk_1^\alpha$, $T_3 = h^\beta$, $T_4 = Zk_2^\beta$, with $\alpha, \beta \in \mathbb{Z}_p^*$. The other steps of the subscription protocol are unchanged and the user finally obtains the signature with extension $\sigma = (A, x)$ on the message $(s, \mathsf{usk}, \{s_j\}_{j\in\mathcal{I}}, \{n_j\}_{j\in[1,f]\setminus\mathcal{I}})$ as before. As the user proves that she belongs to the group of authorized persons, we keep authorization. Moreover, as the DAA can be opened in our case, we also keep non repudiation. Note moreover that $\mathcal{SP}$ can here store on its database the link between the value T and the subscribed services $s_{i_1}, \cdots, s_{i_k}$, with the value $C = h^s h_0^{\mathsf{usk}} \prod_{j\in\mathcal{I}} h_j^{s_j} \prod_{j\in[1,f]\setminus\mathcal{I}} h_j^{n_j}$.

Addition of Services. The ADDSUBSCRIBE protocol is modified as the same way as above, that is replacing the proof that $\mathsf{upk} = g^{\mathsf{usk}}$ by the proof underlying a DAA. As $\mathcal{SP}$ can retrieve the previously subscribed services by using $T = h_{\mathcal{SP}}^{\mathsf{usk}}$ in its database (see above), it can easily make the aggregation of all the services and provide stronger profiling capabilities. The proof V now becomes

$$V = \text{POK}(s, \alpha, \beta, u, u\alpha, \mathsf{usk} : C/ \prod_{j\in\mathcal{I}} h_j^{-s_j} \prod_{j\in[1,f]\setminus\mathcal{I}} h_j^{-n_j} = h^s h_0^{\mathsf{usk}} \wedge$$
$$T = h_{\mathcal{SP}}^{\mathsf{usk}} \wedge T_1 = h^\alpha \wedge T_3 = h^\beta \wedge T_2/T_4 = k_1^\alpha/k_2^\beta \wedge$$
$$e(T_2, g_2)^u e(k_1, w)^{-\alpha} e(k_1, g_2)^{-u\alpha} e(h_0, g_2)^{-\mathsf{usk}} = e(g_1, g_2)/e(T_2, w)),$$

where $T_1 = h^\alpha$, $T_2 = Zk_1^\alpha$, $T_3 = h^\beta$, $T_4 = Zk_2^\beta$, with $\alpha, \beta \in \mathbb{Z}_p^*$.

Use Procedure. The USE procedure is the same as the one in Section 3.6 and is not repeated again here. Note that $\mathcal{U}$ does not have to prove the link between usk and her group membership, as for the SUBSCRIBE procedure.

Profiling vs. Privacy of Scheme 2. With such system, the privacy of the user is more protected than for the Scheme 1 since she is anonymous *w.r.t.* the service provider. Moreover, as we use DAA, the service provider $\mathcal{SP}$ can make the link between the SUBSCRIBE and the ADDSUBSCRIBE procedure regarding services, and consequently the profiling is the same as for Scheme 1.

4.3   The Case of Group Signatures

It is possible to replace a DAA by a group signature. In fact, such solution may seem strange since the group signature provides unlinkability between SUBSCRIBE and ADDSUBSCRIBE while, as $\mathcal{U}$ needs to give her previously obtained services to obtain the aggregation property, we permit $\mathcal{SP}$ to make some link between SUBSCRIBE and ADDSUBSCRIBE. But the use of group signature is interesting since it is possible to study the untraceability of services, that is to prevent the link between SUBSCRIBE and ADDSUBSCRIBE as we will see in the next section.

5   Service Untraceability

In this section, we complete the group signature based solution where $\mathcal{U}$ is anonymous and untraceable and provide a better privacy protection of users. In the scheme 3, we prevent $\mathcal{SP}$ to make any link between a SUBSCRIBE and an ADDSUBSCRIBE procedure. In the scheme 4, $\mathcal{SP}$ is no more able to make any profiling on user preferences since it can not make any link between two sub-scribed services. All the techniques below are only applicable when using a group signature. In fact, with the above Schemes 1 and 2, $\mathcal{SP}$ can make the link be-tween SUBSCRIBE and ADDSUBSCRIBE by construction and $\mathcal{SP}$ thus necessarily knows which services are subscribed by a unique user.

5.1   Aggregation by the User: Scheme 3

As said in Section 4.3, the Scheme 2 described above when using a group signa-ture provides anonymity and unlinkability of the user $w.r.t.$ the service provider. But, as we ask for compactness, the service provider should know the previously obtained services. One solution is to let the user do the aggregation during the ADDSUBSCRIBE protocol, without revealing the link with the related SUBSCRIBE protocol. This way, the user does not have to give to $\mathcal{SP}$ her subscribed services, and thus becomes truly untraceable by $\mathcal{SP}$.

Subscription and Use Procedures. Using such solution, the SUBSCRIBE and the USE procedures of Scheme 2 remain unchanged, except that during the SUBSCRIBE, which now includes a group signature, the value $T = h_{\mathcal{SP}}^{\mathsf{usk}}$ is no more used. Thus, the proof of knowledge becomes:

$$U = \mathrm{POK}(s', \alpha, \beta, u, u\alpha, \mathsf{usk} : C' = h^{s'} h_0^{\mathsf{usk}} \wedge T_1 = h^{\alpha} \wedge T_2/T_4 = k_1^{\alpha}/k_2^{\beta} \wedge$$
$$T_3 = h^{\beta} \wedge e(T_2, g_2)^u e(k_1, w)^{-\alpha} e(k_1, g_2)^{-u\alpha} e(h_0, g_2)^{-\mathsf{usk}} = e(g_1, g_2)/e(T_2, w)),$$

where $T_1 = h^{\alpha}$, $T_2 = Zk_1^{\alpha}$, $T_3 = h^{\beta}$, $T_4 = Zk_2^{\beta}$, with $\alpha, \beta \in \mathbb{Z}_p^*$.

Addition of Services. As the user now aggregates the subscribed services by not revealing the previously obtained one, we need to modify the U proof of knowledge. In fact, the user still sends to $\mathcal{SP}$ the commitment on all previously obtained services, that is $C = h^s h_0^{\mathsf{usk}} \prod_{j \in \mathcal{I}} h_j^{s_j} \prod_{j \in [1,f] \setminus \mathcal{I}} h_j^{n_j}$ (see Section 3.5). But, this time, she has to prove that this commitment is well-formed while keep-ing secret the already subscribed services $s_{i_1}, \cdots, s_{i_k}$. Before that, we remark that the user should not send as it is the above commitment C since this one is known by $\mathcal{SP}$ during the SUBSCRIBE protocol (see Section 3.4). Thus, she has beforehand to modify it. This is done by the user who first chooses at random one $\hat{s} \in \mathbb{Z}_p^*$ and computes $\hat{C} = h^{\hat{s}}C$. Moreover, the user has to prove that she has truly already subscribed the services included into $\hat{C}$ by proving her knowledge of a signature with extension (A, x) on these services.

The user first computes $C_1 = Ah^r$ and $C_2 = g^r h^u$, where r and u are random, and the proof of knowledge V becomes in this case

$$V = \text{POK}(s, \hat{s}, x, r, rx, sx, \alpha, \beta, u, u\alpha, \mathsf{usk}, s_{i_1}, \cdots, s_{i_k}, \{n_j\}_{j \in [1,f]\backslash \mathcal{I}} :$$

$$\hat{C} = h^s h^{\hat{s}} h_0^{\mathsf{usk}} \prod_{j \in \mathcal{I}} h_j^{s_j} \prod_{j \in [1,f]\backslash \mathcal{I}} h_j^{n_j} \wedge C_2 = g^r h^s \wedge 1 = C_2^x g^{-rx} h^{-sx} \wedge T_1 = h^\alpha \wedge$$

$$T_3 = h^\beta \wedge T_2/T_4 = k_1^\alpha/k_2^\beta \wedge e(T_2, g_2)^u e(k_1, w)^{-\alpha} e(k_1, g_2)^{-u\alpha} e(h_0, g_2)^{-\mathsf{usk}} =$$

$$e(g_1, g_2)/e(T_2, w) \wedge e(g_1, g_2)e(h_j, g_2)^{s_{i_1}}/e(C_1, w) =$$

$$e(C_1, g_2)^x e(h, g_2)^{-rx} e(h, w)^{-r} \prod_{j \in \mathcal{I}} e(h_j, g_2)^{-s_j} \prod_{j \in [1,f]\backslash \mathcal{I}} e(h_j, g_2)^{-n_j}),$$

where $T_1 = h^\alpha$, $T_2 = Zk_1^\alpha$, $T_3 = h^\beta$, $T_4 = Zk_2^\beta$, with $\alpha, \beta \in \mathbb{Z}_p^*$. Next the service provider uses $\hat{C}$, chooses at random $\tilde{s}'$, and computes $\tilde{C} = \hat{C}h^{\tilde{s}'} \prod_{j \in \tilde{\mathcal{I}}\backslash \mathcal{I}} h_j^{s_j - n_j}$. $\mathcal{SP}$ finally computes the final signature with extension $\tilde{\sigma} = (\tilde{A}, \tilde{x})$ on the message $(s, \mathsf{usk}, \{s_j\}_{j \in \tilde{\mathcal{I}}}, \{n_j\}_{j \in [1,f]\backslash \tilde{\mathcal{I}}})$.

Profiling vs. Privacy of Scheme 3. On one side, the user privacy is protected since she is anonymous and unlinkable *w.r.t.* $\mathcal{SP}$ all the time. On the other side, $\mathcal{SP}$ is able to make profiling by storing the *subsets* of services users are interested in. In fact, $\mathcal{SP}$ can make such profiling for one SUBSCRIBE or one ADDSUBSCRIBE procedure, but not between both such procedures.

5.2   The No-Profiling Case: Scheme 4

The privacy protection can be higher than the previous section, at the cost of a less interesting profiling for $\mathcal{SP}$. The procedures are similar to the previous one, except that SUBSCRIBE and ADDSUBSCRIBE are only used with one single service at a time. This way, the user privacy is completely protected. On the other hand, $\mathcal{SP}$ is no more able to profile users with this solution.

6   Conclusion

We have presented in this paper several schemes which allows users to protect their privacy while permitting them to subscribe to services. In some of our proposals, service providers are moreover able to make some kind of profiling. Note that using current benchmarks on elliptic curve point multiplications and pairing evaluations, our systems can be implemented such that most of the procedures need less than 200 ms to be performed.

References

1. Ateniese, G., Camenisch, J., Joye, M., Tsudik, G.: A practical and provably secure coalition-resistant group signature scheme. In: Bellare, M. (ed.) CRYPTO 2000. LNCS, vol. 1880, pp. 255–270. Springer, Heidelberg (2000)
2. Blanton, M.: Online subscriptions with anonymous access. In: ASIACCS, pp. 217–227. ACM, New York (2008)
3. Boneh, D., Boyen, X., Shacham, H.: Short group signatures. In: Franklin, M. (ed.) CRYPTO 2004. LNCS, vol. 3152, pp. 41–55. Springer, Heidelberg (2004)
4. Brickell, E.F., Camenisch, J., Chen, L.: Direct anonymous attestation. In: ACM Conference on Computer and Communications Security - ACM CCS 2004, pp. 132–145. ACM Press, New York (2004)
5. Camenisch, J., Hohenberger, S., Lysyanskaya, A.: Compact E-cash. In: Cramer, R. (ed.) EUROCRYPT 2005. LNCS, vol. 3494, pp. 302–321. Springer, Heidelberg (2005)
6. Camenisch, J., Lysyanskaya, A.: A signature scheme with efficient protocols. In: Cimato, S., Galdi, C., Persiano, G. (eds.) SCN 2002. LNCS, vol. 2576, pp. 268–289. Springer, Heidelberg (2003)
7. Camenisch, J., Lysyanskaya, A.: Signature schemes and anonymous credentials from bilinear maps. In: Franklin, M. (ed.) CRYPTO 2004. LNCS, vol. 3152, pp. 56–72. Springer, Heidelberg (2004)
8. Canard, S., Gouget, A., Hufschmitt, E.: A handy multi-coupon system. In: Zhou, J., Yung, M., Bao, F. (eds.) ACNS 2006. LNCS, vol. 3989, pp. 66–81. Springer, Heidelberg (2006)
9. Canard, S., Schoenmakers, B., Stam, M., Traoré, J.: List signature schemes. Discrete Applied Mathematics 154(2), 189–201 (2006)
10. Canard, S., Traoré, J.: List Signature Schemes and Application to Electronic Voting. In: WCC 2003, pp. 81–90 (2003)
11. Chaum, D., Pedersen, T.P.: Transferred cash grows in size. In: Rueppel, R.A. (ed.) EUROCRYPT 1992. LNCS, vol. 658, pp. 390–407. Springer, Heidelberg (1993)
12. Chen, L., Enzmann, M., Sadeghi, A.-R., Schneider, M., Steiner, M.: A privacy-protecting coupon system. In: S. Patrick, A., Yung, M. (eds.) FC 2005. LNCS, vol. 3570, pp. 93–108. Springer, Heidelberg (2005)
13. Delerablée, C., Pointcheval, D.: Dynamic fully anonymous short group signatures. In: Nguyên, P.Q. (ed.) VIETCRYPT 2006. LNCS, vol. 4341, pp. 193–210. Springer, Heidelberg (2006)
14. Fiat, A., Shamir, A.: How to prove yourself: Practical solutions to identification and signature problems. In: Odlyzko, A.M. (ed.) CRYPTO 1986. LNCS, vol. 263, pp. 186–194. Springer, Heidelberg (1987)
15. Gamal, T.E.: A public key cryptosystem and a signature scheme based on discrete logarithms. In: Blakely, G.R., Chaum, D. (eds.) CRYPTO 1984. LNCS, vol. 196, pp. 10–18. Springer, Heidelberg (1985)
16. Mastercard and VIsa: Secure Electronic Transaction (SET) (1996)
17. Okamoto, T.: Provably secure and practical identification schemes and corresponding signature schemes. In: Brickell, E.F. (ed.) CRYPTO 1992. LNCS, vol. 740, pp. 31–53. Springer, Heidelberg (1993)
18. Persiano, P., Visconti, I.: A secure and private system for subscription-based remote services. ACM Trans. Inf. Syst. Secur. 66(4), 472–500 (2003)
19. Schnorr, C.P.: Efficient identification and signatures for smart cards. In: Brassard, G. (ed.) CRYPTO 1989. LNCS, vol. 435, pp. 239–252. Springer, Heidelberg (1990)

Privacy Policy Referencing

Audun Jøsang[1], Lothar Fritsch[2], and Tobias Mahler[3,2]

[1] UNIK University Graduate Center - University of Oslo
josang@unik.no
[2] Norwegian Computing Center
Lothar.Fritsch@NR.no
[3] Norwegian Research Center for Computers and Law - University of Oslo
tobias.mahler@jus.uio.no

Abstract. Data protection legislation was originally defined for a context where personal information is mostly stored on centralized servers with limited connectivity and openness to 3rd party access. Currently, servers are connected to the Internet, where a large amount of personal information is continuously being exchanged as part of application transactions. This is very different from the original context of data protection regulation. Even though there are rather strict data protection laws in an increasing number of countries, it is in practice rather challenging to ensure an adequate protection for personal data that is communicated on-line. The enforcement of privacy legislation and policies therefore might require a technological basis, which is integrated with adequate amendments to the legal framework. This article describes a new approach called Privacy Policy Referencing, and outlines the technical and the complementary legal framework that needs to be established to support it.

1 Introduction

Data protection law regulates the processing of information related to individual persons, including their collection, storage, dissemination etc.

Privacy concerns exist wherever personally identifiable information is collected and stored – in digital form or otherwise. Some forms of processing personal information can be against the interests of the person the data is associated with (called the data subject). Data privacy issues can arise with respect to information from a wide range of sources, such as: Healthcare records, criminal justice investigations and proceedings, financial institutions and their transactions, private sector customer data bases, social communities, mobile phone services with context awareness, residence and geographic records, and ethnicity information. Amongst the challenges in data privacy is to share selected personal data and permit the processing thereof, while inhibiting unwanted or unlawful use, including further dissemination. The IT and information security disciplines have made various attempts at designing and applying software, hardware, procedures, policies and human resources in order to address this issue. National and regional privacy protection laws are to a large extent based on the OECD data privacy principles defined in 1980 [21], e.g. the EU Data Protection Directive [13]. The legal framework for data protection has been adapted to take into account some of the changes in technology, but the constant technological change has been challenging to follow up. In

S. Katsikas, J. Lopez, and M. Soriano (Eds.): TrustBus 2010, LNCS 6264, pp. 129–140, 2010.
© Springer-Verlag Berlin Heidelberg 2010

the 70s and 80s personal information was stored on mainframe computers, on punch cards or on tape rolls with limited connectivity. The Internet only existed in the form of the experimental ARPANET, and no commercial applications had been conceived. It is natural that the principles defined by the OECD in 1980 reflected the computing infrastructure at that time, and the principles can be judged as relatively adequate from that perspective. Since then, the legal framework has struggled in keeping up with changes in the technology.

On the technological side, a long track of information security research exists. Their focus is the development of privacy-enhancing technology (PET) in support of the - mostly legally derived - requirements for personal information handling. A brief historical overview over privacy regulation and PET is given in [15]:

> Starting in the 1970ies, regulatory regimes were put on computers and networks. Starting with government data processing, along the lines of computerization of communication and workflows, explicit rules like the European Data Protection Directive [7] have been put in place. With the adoption of Internet and mobile telephony in society in the past decade, the privacy challenges of information technology came to everyday life.The PET research perspective focused to a certain degree on the legal foundations of privacy protection, determined by constitutional and fundamental human rights that should be protected using technology. This view is shown in an analysis of the PET vocabulary in [18]. As rights are granted to individuals, much of the research has focused on the user-side, e.g. visible in Pfitzmann/Hansen's well-quoted terminology paper [23]. The legal view is propagated into contemporary frameworks like the Canadian [22] and Dutch [28] privacy legislation, which both define privacy audit schemes with detailed procedural definitions and responsibilities, but neglect to provide a decision support method for managers that would enable them to make feasible decisions about privacy needs based on quantifiable risks. Most of these criteria, including schemes like Datenschutz-Gütesiegel [16], provide checklists with questions for the auditors. They inherently call for competent – and well-paid – external experts when they are used by a company, but are rarely based on empirical data or metrics. The PET award winning taxonomy of privacy [26] is very visibly structured along the legal view on privacy.

Many assumptions underlying traditional PETs (Privacy Enhancing Technologies) are no longer valid. Users have little control over information they provide to service providers, which e.g. exposes them to various profiling risks [14]. M. Peter Hustinx, the European Data Protection Supervisor, said in his keynote talk at NordSec 2009[1] that the EU and OECD have recognized the erosion of the adequacy of the classic privacy principles after the emergence of the Internet. In 2009, these organizations therefore have initiated a process for defining new and more adequate privacy principles for networked environments. Similarly, in a keynote speech at the Data Protection Day on 28 January 2010 at the European Parliament, Brussels, Viviane Reding[2] expressed the intention to present a

---

[1] "Privacy in the Internet Age" URL: `NordSec2009.unik.no`

[2] Member of the European Commission responsible for Information Society and Media Privacy.

legislative proposal for reforming the European Privacy Directive before the end of the year (2010), and launched the concept of "privacy by design" [24] which specifies that privacy requirements must always be included in the design of new Internet technologies. In her speech she said that the new legal framework should address new challenges of the information age, such as globalisation, development of information technologies, the Internet, online social networking, e-commerce, cloud computing, video surveillance, behavioural advertising, data security breaches, etc.

Privacy policies are sometimes used by organizations that collect and process personal information. However, users often pay little or no attention to these privacy policies, and once the personal information has been collected, it is practically impossible to verify that the specified privacy policies are being adhered to. There is also scientific evidence that user-side reading of privacy policies is in conflict with basic market economic principles [30].

It can also be mentioned that the protection of personal data is sometimes in conflict with other interests of individuals, organizations or society at large. Several occasions, for example the 'war on terrorism', showed that the European Union delivers passenger flight databases, SWIFT financial transactions, and telecommunications data to authorities outside the EU legislation. In such cases, no consent is necessary, if such disclosure is lawful under the applicable law.

From this brief survey it seems timely to rethink how information privacy should be defined and enforced in the online environment. This paper looks at the inadequacy of the current approach to information privacy protection, and proposes a new approach based on attaching policy metadata to personal information. By requiring that the metadata follows personal information, it becomes easy to verify whether the policies are being adhered to. In addition, one should consider standardizing privacy policies in the form of a limited set of easily recognizable rules to improve the usability of privacy protection.

2   The Inadequacy of the Current Approach

2.1   Business Decision-Making and Privacy Technology

For any deployment of PET into information systems, the effectiveness of the PET measure against threats is important [15]. While PET cost of installation and operation could be assessed with experiments, the efficiency of their deployment remains unknown. In the computer science field, several contributions provide information theoretic models for anonymity, identifiability or the linkability of data, e.g. in [27]or in [10]. Both papers build mathematical models that are rather impractical for usage in the evaluation of large-scale information systems. Another suggestion comes from an article on intrusion detection by user context modeling [19], where the author tries to identify attacks by classification of untypical user behavior. Such behavioral analysis can be developed into a tool to measure effectiveness of PET. From some experiments on profiling people with publicly available data from the Internet [9], one might try to use profiling output as a measure of the quality of PET systems. But the definition of the information that counts as a part of a profile, as well as the question of how to distinguish leaked information from intentionally published personal information make profiling a rather impractical metric. With these difficulties in measuring effectiveness of PET, how will we judge efficiency? Also, for the deployment of PET on the business side, or the acceptance of some extra effort by users adapting to PETs, there are more questions to ask:

– Which PET will remove or reduce a particular risk? At what cost will a particular PET remove a particular risk?
– How much effort (instruction, change of system usage habits, change of behavior, self-control) had to be spent on the user-side for the PET to be effective?
– Is there a cheaper or more convenient alternative on how to deal with a particular risk instead of PET deployment?

2.2   Inadequacy of Technical Privacy Strategies

Public surveys indicate that privacy is a major concern for people using the Internet [6]. Privacy related complaints that are made to the US Federal Trade Commission include complaints about unsolicited email, identity theft, harassing phone calls, and selling of data to third parties [20]. One attempt to address privacy concerns and thereby increase user trust in the Web is the W3C's Platform for Privacy Preferences (P3P) Project [8]. P3P enables Web sites to express their privacy practices in a standardized, XML-based, format that can be automatically interpreted by user agents such as a Web browser. The aim is that discrepancies between a site's practices and the user's preferences can be automatically flagged. Nine aspects of online privacy are covered by P3P, including five that cover data being tracked by the site: who is collecting the data; what information is being collected; for what purposes is it being collected; which information is being shared with others; and who are the data recipients. Four topics explain the site's internal privacy policies: can users make changes in how their data is used; how are disputes resolved; what is the policy for retaining data; and where can the detailed policies be found in a 'human readable' form. It would be fair to say that P3P has been a failure because users and industry have not adopted it. One of the reasons might be that P3P is unable to guarantee or enforce the privacy claims made by Websites. Despite its potential, detractors say that P3P does not go far enough to protect privacy. They believe that the aim of privacy technology should be to enable people to transact anonymously [11]. Private privacy service providers or *anonymisers* have been proposed [29]. One example is iPrivacy, a New York based company that around 2002 professed on its Web site, "not even iPrivacy will know the true identity of the people who use its service". To utilize the technology, users first had to download software from the Web site of a company they trusted, for example a bank or credit card company. When they wished to purchase a product online, they used the software to generate a one-off fictitious identity (name, address and email address). Users were given the choice of collecting the goods from their local post office (their post or zip code is the only part of the address which is correct) or having the goods delivered by a delivery company or postal service that has been sent a decoded address label. Originally the iPrivacy software generated a one-off credit card number for each transaction. The credit card issuer matched the credit card number it received from the merchant with the user's real credit card number and then authorized payment. However, this proved to be a major job for banks to integrate and is no longer offered by iPrivacy. There are still other companies such as Orbiscom.com and Cyota.com (acquired by RSA) that do offer one-off credit card numbers,but these have captured limited use to date. Another type of privacy provider or *infomediary* is emerging which sells aggregated buyer data to marketers, but keeps individual identifying information private [29]. One example of this is Lumeria, a Berkley based company that provides royalties to people who participate. In the Lumeria system, users download free software that encrypts their profile and stores it on Lumeria's servers. The user accesses the Web via a Lumeria proxy server, which shields their identity from merchants and marketing companies whilst enabling marketing material that matches their profile to be sent to them. However, none of these initiatives have been a success, and many privacy providers have gone out of business. This is quite understandable, as the anonymity solutions result in significant additional complexity and cost.

2.3   Inadequacy of Specifying Privacy Policies

Many data controllers specify privacy policies that can be accessed from the interface where personal information is being collected or where consent to do so is given. Such policies are sometimes of 10 pages or longer, and can be written in a jargon that makes them inaccessible for most people. Users are normally required to accept the policies by ticking a box, which all but very few do in a semi-automatic fashion. Users quickly learn that reading such policies is very frustrating. In addition, users who might be opposed to some clauses in the policy faces the organization alone, although many others might be of the same opinion. It is difficult for users to organize themselves and exercise pressure on organizations to change their privacy policies, but both data protection authorities and consumer ombudsmen have succeeded in pressuring some organizations to change their policies. Once personal information has been collected, users have no practical way of verifying whether the policies are being adhered to. In practice, it would also be difficult to trace personal information back to the point where it was collected. Once inside the network or system of an organization, it often becomes very difficult to trace personal information back to the point of origin and the applicable privacy policy. This is precisely where our proposal offers a solution, whereby the applicable privacy policy always is referenced by the metadata associated with any personal information. This will be explained in further detail below.

The privacy policy interpretation and specification troubles are illustrated in a survey article that provides a taxonomy of 'privacy-supporting' and 'privacy-consuming' privacy clauses from real policies [1]. The survey clearly shows that most privacy policies on web pages are carefully drafted to lure the consumers into accepting privacy-consuming clauses.

A privacy policy may fulfill several different functions [4] (p.239). First, it can be used to provide information about how personal data is processed by the data controller, and such information may be mandatory according to the law. Second and somewhat related, a policy may provide the background for a statement of consent to certain forms of processing. Thus, the policy may explain what the data subject is consenting to. The existence of a privacy policy may also lead to some users increasing their trust in an organization. However, particularly regarding very lengthy, ambiguous and open privacy policies may one may sometimes suspect that the intention is not to provide clear information and rules for data processing, but rather to secure the flexibility of the data controller in processing the data in any desired manner.

However, if a privacy policy is in conflict with the applicable data protection law, then it may have a limited or no legal effect. The most important rules in data protection law can be expressed in relation to a number of basic principles [3] to be found in most international and national data protection instruments and laws.

- **Fair and lawful processing:** Personal data must be processed fairly and lawfully.
- **Purpose specification:** Personal data must be collected for specified, explicit and legitimate purposes and not further processed for other purposes.
- **Minimality:** The collection and storage of personal data should be limited to the amount necessary to achieve the purpose(s).
- **Information quality:** Personal data should be valid with respect to what they are intended to describe and relevant and complete with respect to the specified purpose(s).
- **Data subject participation and control:** Persons should be able to participate in the processing of data on them and they should have some measure of influence over the processing.
- **Limitation of fully automated decisions:** Fully automated assessments of a persons character should not form the sole basis of a decision that impinges upon the persons interest.
- **Disclosure limitation:** The data controllers disclosure of personal data to third parties shall be restricted, it may only occur upon certain conditions.
- **Information security:** The data controller must ensure that personal data is not subject to unauthorized access, alteration, destruction or disclosure.
- **Sensitivity:** Processing certain categories of especially sensitive data is subject to a stricter control than other personal data.

Thus, a privacy policy may be legally assessed under legislation that implements these principles. For example, if a particular policy does not provide for a fair processing, then the rules included in the policy may be void. Nevertheless, for most people it is challenging to assess whether they should consent to the processing of their personal data under a given privacy policy, particularly if it is ambiguous and permits a wide range of forms of processing personal data, possibly exceeding what would be permitted under the applicable data protection law. For the data subject it often remains unclear to what, exactly, she is consenting and for what purposes and by whom the data will be processed. This reflects the vast economic imbalance between the data subjects and the data controllers.

All of these factors make the practical protection of personal information rather challenging. The approach outlined in the remainder of this paper might, if successful, solve some of these shortcomings.

3   An Infrastructure for Privacy Policy Referencing

The fundamental principle of Privacy Policy Referencing is that all personal information must be tagged or associated with metadata that relates it to the applicable privacy policy, and possibly to the point and time of collection. This would enable users or authorities to audit systems and applications where personal information is being processed, and to determine whether they adhere to applicable privacy policies. By making it mandatory to always have policy metadata associated with personal information, it becomes a universal principle for referencing privacy policies. In other words, a pointer to the relevant privacy policy will always follow the data. The PRIME FP7 research project[3] developed concepts based on HP Labs 'Sticky Policies' approach, where personal data is stored and communicated in encrypted data containers with attached policies [5].Their approach, however, assumes that the underlying hardware platform, and the software running on it, are so-called trustworthy systems based on the Trusted Computing specification. To improve personal data processing in reality, all information systems that can get a hold of data must be based on such platforms. However, a complete market penetration is not realistic in the near future. Recently, concepts such as 'Obligations Management' and 'Audit Trails' have come into focus of the FP7 PRIMELife project[4], which shall provide organizational and technical awareness and auditability of personal data handling in corporate and large IT systems [2]. This will not put any extra burden on the users, but will require the establishment of totally new frameworks for organizations, which can be grouped into technical, policy, management and legal frameworks. These will be discussed below.

3.1   The Technical Framework

Privacy policy metadata will require the definition of a common metadata language in XML style. A conceptual visualization of personal information with associated privacy policy metadata is illustrated in Fig.1 below.

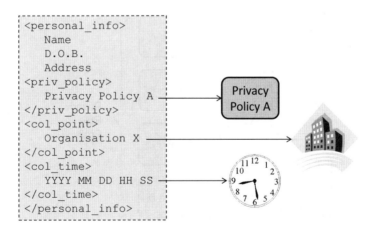

Fig. 1. Personal information with associated privacy policy metadata

---

[3] See http://www.prime-project.eu
[4] See http://www.primelife.eu/

Typical tags that need to be defined are the privacy policy identifier, date of collection, and type of consent given by the user. This means that each privacy policy must be uniquely identifiable, so that organizations must keep records of such identifiable privacy policies that have been used. The integrity of the policies can be ensured, e.g. with cryptographic means. The metadata does not need to contain any additional personal information, because that would be irrelevant for potential audits of policy adherence.

There are situations where it is impractical to have the metadata stored directly together with the personal information, e.g. when personal information is being processed with very high speed and high volume. The organizations must then find a solution for associating the personal information with metadata stored elsewhere.

It can be noted that our scheme has similarities with the scheme for electronic signature policies described in [25] where a specific signature policy has a globally unique reference which is bound to the signature by the signer as part of the signature calculation. This thereby provides non-repudiation for the applicable signature.

3.2   The Policy Framework

It is very difficult for users to understand privacy policies when each organization specifies a different policy and when typical policies are 10 pages or more. In order to increase the usability and accessibility of privacy policies, a set of standard privacy rules and policy profiles can be defined. Let a specific privacy rule be denoted as P-Rule n where n is a number. Then a set of compatible and coherent rules will constitute a specific profile denoted as PR-Profile X where X is a letter. The combination of rules into specific profiles can be denoted as the PRP (Privacy Rules Profile) framework. The purpose of defining PR-Profiles is that a specific privacy policy can simply be defined and expressed as a PR-Profile within this framework. The PRP framework is illustrated in Fig.2.

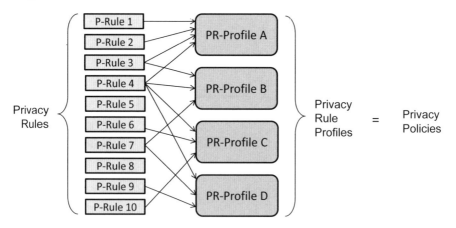

Fig. 2. The Privacy Rules Profile Framework

It is also possible to have more of less strict versions of each profile, so that a profile e.g. can be called "PRP-B level II", where "level II" indicates options within the specified profile. To some degree, elements of privacy policies could be standardized at least at a national or regional level, for example under the auspices of the Article 29 Working Party of the EU. Ideally, a standardization on an international level would also be desirable, so that it is possible to define meaningful policies that could be interpreted in a global context. However, this would be challenging, as such policies would have to be assessed under the different national legal frameworks of data protection laws.

In this respect, one might benefit from the experiences of standardizing other contract clauses. For example, in international trade law, the Incoterms [17] offer a widely used catalogue of specific contract terms that can be quoted when buying or selling goods. One of the advantages of the Incoterms are that they address very specific issues, enabling contract parties to simply reference a brief abbreviation (e.g. FCA) to agree on a number of basic terms. Characteristic for the Incoterms is, however, that they do not include a comprehensive set of rules for a contract, which is described in a lengthy contract text. This distinguishes this type of contract standardization from another example, which is arguably more well-known in the IT community. A number of IPR licensing issues regarding open source software can be easily regulated by referring to specific predefined licenses. For example, the Open Source Initiative publishes a list of approved licenses (http://opensource.org/licenses/alphabetical). In data protection law, contractual frameworks have been standardized, for example, in order to regulate the transfer of personal data to countries outside the EU legal framework [12].

Instead of specifying a lengthy policy, organizations could simply refer to a standardized policy profile that is specified elsewhere. By having limited set of standardized policies, it would be possible for users to become educated and familiar with what the respective policies actually mean, and the level of protection they provide. Assuming that users are familiar with privacy policies A, B, C and D in terms of their PRP (privacy rules profiles), a reference to e.g. Policy-B will be meaningful for users, without having to read several pages of text. Moreover, the recommendation of some trusted entity of certain policies could be informative for those users not wanting to read the whole policy themselves.

3.3 The Management Framework

Organizations would need to manage their privacy policies according to strict criteria, and define a way guaranteeing their integrity and authenticity. This can e.g. be achieved by letting independent third parties sign hashes of each particular policy or policy profile which would allow changes in policies or profiles to be noticed, or to deposit the privacy policies with independent third parties such as national information commissioners and data protection inspectorates. Privacy policy repositories that are suitable for long-term archival of verified policies might me necessary with respect to long-term legal validity. Organizations will also need to define processes for creating metadata and to adapt applications where personal information is being processed so that the metadata can be appropriately handled during storage, transfer and processing.

3.4 The Legal Framework

This approach could also be complemented with respective changes to the legal framework as e.g. through [24], in order to provide incentives for its adoption. Otherwise, data controllers might not be interested in this approach, as it may ultimately limit their possibilities of processing personal data.

For example, it could be considered to oblige certain data controllers – particularly those collecting vast amounts of personal data – to associate valid privacy policy metadata to all personal data. This could be seen as an extension of the purpose specification principle mentioned above, according to which personal data can only be collected for specified, explicit and legitimate purposes and not further processed for other purposes. An additional element might be that that certain classes of privacy policies could be mandatorily deposited with a respective national or regional data protection authority, and that the metadata points to the deposited copies of the privacy policies, who might also assess a policy's compliance with the applicable law. This might enhance the possibilities for auditors to review data controllers with regard to the personal information that that they process. Assume that the privacy policy referred to by the metadata specifies that the personal information shall not be transferred to third parties, and that the metadata also indicates a specific organization's web interface as the point of collection as well as the time of user consent. In case the audited organization is different from the organization specified in the metadata, the auditor will have an indication that the privacy policy has been infringed.

4   Conclusion

The current approach to ensuring personal information privacy on the Internet is ineffective in providing privacy protection in the age of distributed, networked services. In this paper, we have argued that the traditional method of accepting privacy policies by ticking boxes provides very poor user understanding, and hence poor consent as required by the law.

The approach described in this paper changes the way privacy policies can be specified by service providers, and compliance be verified by auditors or users. By providing certified template policies, users gain oversight of policies that have been verified. At the same time, auditors can verify system states against policy claims. Finally, based on using metadata as a pointer to applicable privacy policies, and by use of specifying policies as standardized profiles, a connection between data, user, consent and policy is maintained. Introducing this framework might also require the introduction of incentives, for example by making it mandatory to include privacy policy metadata with personal information. Remaining challenges, such as the international synchronization of policy templates, the reliable, auditable and secure implementation of personal data handling with policies, and the creation of the default policies and their supervision and archival, need to be further researched.

References

1. Antón, A.I., Earp, J.B., Reese, A.: Analyzing Website Privacy Requirements Using a Privacy Goal Taxonomy. In: IEEE Computer Society (ed.) Proceedings of the IEEE Joint International Requirements Engineering Conference 2002, September 9-13, pp. 605–612. IEEE Computer Society, Essen (2002)

2. Ardagna, C.A., Bussard, L., De Capitani di Vimercati, S., Neven, G., Pedrini, E., Paraboschi, S., Preiss, F., Samarati, P., Trabelsi, S., Verdicchio, M.: Primelife policy language (November 2009)

3. Bygrave, L.A.: Data Protection Law, Approaching its Rationale, Logic and Limits. Information Law Series, vol. 10, pp. 57–68. Kluwer Law International, Dordrecht (2002)

4. Carey, P.: Data protection: a practical guide to UK and EU law. Oxford University Press, Oxford (2004)

5. Mont, M.C., Pearson, S., Bramhall, P.: Towards Accountable Management of Identity and Privacy: Sticky Policies and Enforceable Tracing Services. In: Proceedings of the 14th International Workshop on Database and Expert Systems Applications (DEXA'03), p. 377. IEEE Computer Society, Los Alamitos (2003)

6. Cavoukian, A., Crompton, M.: Web Seals: A Review of Online Privacy Programs. In: A Joint Project of The Office of the Information and Privacy Commissioner/Ontario and The Office of the Federal Privacy Commissioner of Australia, Venice (September 2000), http://www.ipc.on.ca/english/pubpres/papers/seals.pdf

7. European Comission. Directive 2002/58/EC of the European Parliament and of the council concerning the processing of personal data and the protection of privacy in the electronic communications sector (Directive on privacy and electronic communications). Technical report (July 12, 2002)

8. Cranor, L., et al.: The Platform for Privacy Preferences 1.0 (P3P1.0) Specification. W3C Recommendation (April 16, 2002), http://www.w3.org/TR/P3P/

9. Diaz, C.: Profiling Game (2005)

10. Diaz, C., Preneel, B.: Anonymous communication. In: Swedish Institute of Computer Science (ed.) WHOLES - A Multiple View of Individual Privacy in a Networked World, Stockholm, January 30 (2004)

11. Dutton, P.: Trust Issues in E-Commerce. In: Proceedings of the 6th Australasian Women in Computing Workshop, pp. 15–26. Griffith University, Brisbane (July 2000)

12. EC: Standard Contractual Clauses for the Transfer of Personal Data to Third Countries, Commission Decision 2004/915/EC of 27 December 2004. In: Official Journal L 385 of 29.12.2004. European Commission (2004)

13. European Council. Directive 95/46/EC of the European Parliament and of the Council of October 24, 1995 on the protection of individuals with regard to the processing of personal data and on the free movement of such data (November 23, 1995)

14. Fritsch, L.: Profiling and location-based services. In: Hildebrandt, M., Gutwirth, S. (eds.) Profiling the European Citizen - Cross-Disciplinary Perspectives, Dordrecht, April 2008, pp. 147–160 (2008)

15. Fritsch, L., Abie, H.: A Road Map to the Management of Privacy Risks in Information Systems. In: Gesellschaft f. Informatik (GI) (ed.) Konferenzband Sicherheit 2008. LNI, vol. 128, pp. 1–15. Gesellschaft für Informatik, Bonn (2008)

16. Unabhängiges Landeszentrum für Datenschutz Schleswig-Holstein. Datenschutz-Gütesiegel (2003)

17. ICC. Incoterms 2000: ICC Official Rules for the Interpretation of Trade Terms. ICC Publication No.560, 2000 Edition (2000)

18. Koch, C.: Taxonomie von Location Based Services - Ein interdisziplinärer Ansatz mit Boundary Objects. PhD thesis, Johann Wolfgang Goethe - Universitt, Frankfurt am Main (2006)

19. Mazhelis, O., Puuronen, S.: Combining One-Class Classifiers for Mobile-User Substitution Detection. In: Proceedings of 6th International Conference on Enterprise Information Systems (ICEIS'04), Porto, pp. 130–137 (2004)

20. Mithal, M.: Illustrating B2C Complaints in the Online Environment. Presentation by the US Federal Trade Commission and Industry Canada, at the Joint Conference of the OECD, HCOPIL, ICC: Building Trust in the Online Environment: Business to Consumer Dispute Resolution (The Hague) (December 2000)
21. OECD - Organisation for Economice Co-Operation and Development. Recommendation of the Council Concerning Guidelines Governing the Protection of Privacy and Transborder Flows of Personal Data (September 23, 1980)
22. The Treasury Board of Canada. Privacy Impact Assessment Guidelines Version 2.0 - A Framework to Manage Privacy Risks (August 31, 2002)
23. Pfitzmann, A., Köhntopp, M.: Anonymity, Unobservability, and Pseudonymity - A Proposal for Terminology. In: Federrath, H. (ed.) Designing Privacy Enhancing Technologies. LNCS, vol. 2009, pp. 1–9. Springer, Heidelberg (2001)
24. Reding, V.: Privacy: the challenges ahead for the European Union (Keynote speech at the Data Proteciton Day), SPEECH/10/16. European Parliament, Brussels (January 28, 2010), http://europa.eu/rapid/pressReleasesAction.do?reference=SPEECH/10/16
25. Ross, J., Pinkas, D.: Pope. N. RFC 3125 - Electronic Signature Policies. IETF (September 2001), http://www.rfc-editor.org/
26. Solove, D.: A taxonomy of privacy - GWU Law School Public Law Research Paper No.129. University of Pennsylvania Law Review 154(3), 477 (2006)
27. Steinbrecher, S., Köpsell, S.: Modelling Unlinkability. In: Dingledine, R. (ed.) PET 2003. LNCS, vol. 2760, pp. 32–47. Springer, Heidelberg (2003)
28. Cooperation Group Audit Strategy. Privacy Audit Framework under the new Dutch Data Protection Act (WBP). Technical report, Den Haag (December 19, 2000)
29. The Economist. The Coming Backlash in Privacy. The Economist Technology Quarterly (December 9, 2000)
30. Vila, T., Greenstadt, R., Molnar, D.: Why we cant be bothered to read privacy policies: models of privacy economics as a lemons market. In: Proceedings of the 5th International Conference on Electronic Commerce (ICEC'03), pp. 403–407. ACM Press, Pittsburgh (2003)

Formal Proof of Cooperativeness in a Multi–Party P2P Content Authentication Protocol

Almudena Alcaide, Esther Palomar, Ana I. González–Tablas, and Arturo Ribagorda

Department of Computer Science,
University Carlos III of Madrid
{aalcaide,epalomar,aigonzal,arturo}@inf.uc3m.es

Abstract. The goal of this paper is to present a formal framework specially defined for the analysis of cooperative behavior in self–organizing multi–party security protocols. To illustrate the formalism, we formally analyze a multi–party peer to peer (MP–P2P) content authentication protocol which ensures content integrity in a decentralized P2P file sharing system. Our approach, based on Game Theory, will serve to formally analyze and verify cooperation among a variable number of selfish and untrustworthy participant peers.

1 Introduction

Currently, the majority of P2P networks sustains peer cooperativeness on two main concepts: trust and incentives (see [1] for a comparative study.)

Trust–based solutions generally rely on the exchange of reputation feedback (submit referrals on performance of their mutual transaction) among community nodes in order to globally/locally evaluate a certain node trustworthy value (see [2] for an excellent survey.) However, in general, building a trust system already requires some kind of cooperation between peers.

By contrast, **incentive–based** solutions apply incentive programs to encourage cooperation amongst peers. In many P2P systems the notion of reputation is actually considered as an incentive in view of future interactions ([3,4]). In such models, it is reasonable to assume that peers would cooperate aimed at maximizing the final payoff that they derive from the system in each interaction.

On the other hand, the idea of self–organized cooperation is being currently addressed by different research directions; for example, mobile robots connect in a MANET (mobile ad hoc network) to coordinate their movements. Furthermore, several approaches have taken inspiration from a number of natural phenomena allowing self–organizing behaviors to naturally emerge [5]. Others apply mechanisms inspired by biological evolution such as mutation and recombination, natural selection and survival of the fittest, to analyze the evolution of selfish and cooperative behaviors [6].

S. Katsikas, J. Lopez, and M. Soriano (Eds.): TrustBus 2010, LNCS 6264, pp. 141–152, 2010.
© Springer-Verlag Berlin Heidelberg 2010

1.1 P2P Security Protocols

P2P security protocols are at the heart of any P2P system. These protocols differ from any other type of security protocol as they are usually constrained by a total lack of predefined infrastructure, the absence of many of the services provided by trusted third parties (as a public key infrastructure), and a high transient topology network. All these aspects, coupled with the need of self–organization, make it very difficult to apply classic cryptographic protocols (e.g. for authentication and authorization services.) Numerous solutions proposed so far are in one way or another based on the idea of replacing a whole PKI (public key infrastructure) by a collaboration scheme. Put simply, a subgroup of peers must cooperate to perform tasks such as generating (or verifying) a digital signature, or negotiating a group key for a secure communication. This collaboration–based nature of the communication layers guarantees fault–tolerance though, however, imposes a number of drawbacks as well.

In previous works [7,8], we proposed a *secure content distribution* protocol, specially oriented to pure P2P file sharing systems (see Figure 1.) The global solution is divided into two sub–protocols:

- On the one hand, our model defines an *access control* protocol by means of a challenge–response mechanism. Contrary to classic trust systems where trust decisions are directly or indirectly given by nodes' past behavior, our scheme uses cryptographic proofs of work to discourage selfish behavior and to reward cooperation. A formal validation proof of this protocol was presented in [9].
- On the other hand, our solution also defines a *content authentication* protocol based on Byzantine agreement, which is able to detect if non–authorized alterations have been made on the published contents. The content authentication proposal is based on the collaboration among a fraction of peers in the system. No formal analysis of this part of the global solution had yet been carried out in any other previous work.

1.2 Formal Validation of P2P Security Protocols

Although the formal analysis of any P2P protocol is carried out infrequently (the emphasis is rather on the formal analysis of system performance), a formal approach to protocol validation serves to guarantee the necessary security properties and helps to detect vulnerabilities and errors at the initial states of system design.

Note that, in the same way as P2P security solutions must be carefully chosen when being deployed in one or another environment and when providing one or another service (different execution environments and other factors can influence the final output of a P2P solution), selecting the right analytical model must also be cautiously done to guarantee the validity of the formal proof.

Different attempts have been made to define a formal framework in which to analyze P2P systems. Some of those models are based on *Process Calculi* (Spi

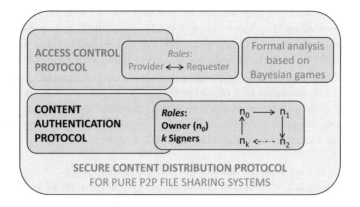

Fig. 1. Sub–protocols of a secure content distribution solution: Content Authentication and Access Control

calculus [10]), Secure Protocol Language (SPL) [11,12] (the use of SPL allows us to formalize protocol communication and to prove security properties by means of event–based semantics), while others apply general purpose tools to perform a whole system security analysis [13]. Additionally, game theoretical models have also been considered by several authors. In this regard, we have identified two different approaches:

- Approach 1. When the whole system is considered and analyzed as an N– player game in which nodes/players have got the option of being collabora- tive or non–collaborative ([14], [15]); and,
- Approach 2. When individual P2P protocols that nodes use to interact are analyzed as individual games ([9], [16]). In the latter, conclusions over the overall system analysis are derived from the analysis of single (*one–shot*) P2P interactions. In the following section we describe our approach.

1.3   Our Approach and Main Contributions

Security protocols for pure P2P systems can be designed such that, cooperation and well behavior exist based on the sole assumption of nodes *rational* nature, i.e.: nodes cooperate because it is in their own interest to do so. This way, it is considered that a potential adversary will only misbehave when it obtains greater benefit in doing so. In this context, Game Theory stands as a very suitable tool for the formal analysis of such P2P schemes. However, of the two game theoretical approaches aforementioned we favor Approach 2 attending the following criteria:

- By considering the whole system as an N–player game being played indef- initely, the resulting formalism fails to capture the high transient nature of

any P2P system. In general, nodes abandoning the system do not behave the same as when they intent to stay in the community and these individual behavioral differences will have an effect on the overall system performance.
– Moreover, the analysis of individual interactions will allow us to evaluate different types of malicious nodes not only those free–riding. For example, nodes which, intentionally or unintentionally, waste other node's resources by not completing the execution of a P2P protocol and quitting once other nodes have invested their resources. The extreme action of these nodes will be seen as a denial of service attack on the system.

Our approach is based on the analysis of individual P2P security protocols used for nodes to interact within the community. The main goal of our analysis is to obtain formal proof of protocol security properties based on the *protocol rationality*[1]. Informally, a protocol is said to be *rational* if, when all nodes follow the steps dictated by the protocol, the payoff values obtained at the end of the execution are the greatest possible. In other words, a rational protocol ensures nodes that unilaterally deviating from the protocol description will not render them a better outcome. Rationality of a protocol is an essential property for cooperativeness to naturally emerge in the absence of trusted third parties.

Formally, by definition, a protocol is said to be *rational* when the steps described in the protocol correspond to the *Nash equilibrium* of the corresponding *representative protocol game*. The *representative protocol game* of a protocol is a game in which protocol participants become players, and the turns and actions of the game are dictated by the protocol steps. A more formal definition of all these concepts will be given in Sections 2 and 3.

The formal framework presented in this paper is based on the analysis of representative protocol games. This methodology will allow us to formally reason and validate a multi–party peer to peer (MP–P2P) security protocol for any number of entities. This will be the first time that such a reasoning is formally carried out as previous attempts have failed to formalize the calculation of the Nash equilibria in an MP–P2P *representative protocol game* ([16]) or have had to reduce the problem to a two entity game ([14]). In summary, the main contributions of this paper are:

1. The description of a formal analytical framework which allows us to reason about MP–P2P protocols.
2. The formal rationality proof of a particular MP–P2P protocol allows us to:
   (a) Formally predict the outcome of the protocol.
   (b) Formally verify cooperation among participant peers.
3. The formalism can be extended for the analysis of selfish behavior in any self–organizing multi–party computation.

The rest of the paper is organized as follows. In Section 2, we introduce the terminology and game theoretical concepts that will be used throughout the paper. In Section 3, we describe the MP–P2P protocol subject of our study.

---

[1] In [16] authors use the term *protocol robustness* which results equivalent.

Section 4 is devoted to the presentation of the formal model and the validation of the described scheme. Finally, Section 5 concludes the paper and outlines some open issues.

2 Game Theory: Basic Concepts

For completeness of this work and to unify notation, we will briefly present some of the essential concepts which constitute the basis of Game Theory.

Definition 1 (Strategy)
In a game G, a strategy for player i, denoted by $s_i \in S_i$ where S_i is the set of all possible strategies, is a complete contingency plan for player i. It describes the series of actions that this player would take at each possible decision point in the game G.

Definition 2 (Strategy Profile). *A strategy profile is a vector of strategies $(s_1, \ldots, s_n)$, one for each player i of a game. The set of strategy profiles, denoted by S, is the Cartesian product of the strategy spaces over all players: $S = S_1 \times \cdots \times S_n$.*

A convention is to describe as s_{-i}, the strategies chosen by all other players except for a given player i. Any given strategy profile in a game may then be represented by the tuple (s_i, s_{-i}).

Definition 3 (Payoff function). *In a game G, a payoff function v_i (also called utility function) is defined for each player i. The domain of v_i is the set of strategy profiles S, and the range of the function is the set of real numbers, so that, for each strategy profile $(s_i, s_{-i}) \in S$, $v_i(s_i, s_{-i})$ represents the player i's payoff when i plays strategy s_i and the other players follow strategies s_{-i}.*

Definition 4 (Dynamic Game). *A dynamic game is defined by the tuple:*
$G = \langle P, S, \overrightarrow{v} \rangle$ *where:*

- $P = \{i\}$, $i \in \{1, \ldots, n\}$ *is a set of n players,*
- $S = S_1 \times \cdots \times S_n$ *is a set of strategy profiles and*
- $\overrightarrow{v} = [v_1(), \ldots, v_n()]$ *is a vector of payoff functions.*

In a dynamic game, players take it in turns to move, so their actions may depend on what actions other players have taken in previous turns.

Definition 5 (Nash equilibrium). *Given a game $G = \langle P, S, \overrightarrow{v} \rangle$, a strategy profile $s^* \in S$, represents a Nash equilibrium if and only if, for every player i, $i \in \{1, \ldots, n\}$:*

$$v_i(s_i^*, s_{-i}^*) \geq v_i(s_i, s_{-i}^*) \qquad \forall s_i \in S_i \tag{1}$$

In other words, a Nash equilibrium is a strategy profile s^* where no player has anything to gain by changing only her own strategy unilaterally. That is, given the other players' strategies s^*_{-i}, player i cannot increase her payoff by choosing a strategy different from s^*_i.

Finally, we will define sub–game of a dynamic game and we will also give a definition of what it is a refinement of the Nash equilibrium used in dynamic games.

Definition 6 (Sub–Game). *A sub–game of a dynamic game G, is a smaller game which takes any given point in the larger game as the start, and carries on until the end.*

Definition 7 (Sub–game perfect equilibrium). *A strategy profile is a sub–game perfect equilibrium if it represents a Nash equilibrium of every sub–game of the original game.*

Informally this means that if players, following a sub–game perfect equilibrium strategy, played any smaller game that consisted of only one part of the larger game, then their behavior would still represent a Nash equilibrium in that sub–game.

2.1   Rationality by Backward Induction

In Game Theory, backward induction is one of the dynamic programming algorithms used to compute *sub–game perfect equilibria*. The process proceeds by first considering the last actions of the final player of the game. It determines which actions the final mover should take in each possible circumstance to maximize his/her utility. Using this information and taking the induction one step backward, one can then determine what the second to last player will do, to also maximize his/her own utility function. This process continues until one reaches the first move of the game. The strategy profiles selected are all possible sub–game perfect equilibria in the game.

3   MP–P2P Content Authentication Protocol

In this section we will introduce an enhanced version of the MP–P2P content authetication protocol defined by Palomar et al. in [7] (see Figure 1). In later sections we will represent the described protocol as a dynamic game and finally, we will use backward induction to formally prove that the description of the protocol corresponds to the *Nash Equilibrium perfect in sub–games* of the *representative protocol game*. Hence, concluding the protocol is rational and the outcome of the protocol corresponds with the cooperative behavior of participant peers.

3.1   Protocol Description

The possibility of replicating the same content among different nodes, and download a specific content at any moment, is an attractive distinctive feature in P2P file sharing scenarios. In the vast majority of current systems, these tasks are not performed in a proactive way, but they are the result of a search and location mechanism. Once a user gets a file, it is usual that a local copy will remain in the node, in such a way that future queries will identify the node as one of the various locations from which the content can be obtained. However, it is unrealistic to assume that every integrating node will exhibit a honest behavior, even if they have always behaved correctly in the past. Once that a content is replicated through different locations, the originator loses control over it. A malicious party can modify the replica according to several purposes, e.g. insert malicious software into a highly demanded content or dishonestly claim ownership over other's content.

In this section, we briefly summarize the main steps of our content authentication protocol (for further details please refer to [17]). The scheme maintains content integrity based on the collaboration among a fraction of peers in the system, who play the role of a distributed PKI. Under certain restrictions, our proposal assures content integrity in a P2P file sharing system, i.e. a guarantee that the file has not been altered even if it is a replica of the original, and therefore the owner has lost control over it.

The basic idea is that contents will be associated to a digital certificate ensuring properties such as integrity and authenticity, much in the way an X.509 public key certificate can be used to ensure these properties for a public key. Let n_0 be the legitimate owner node of a given content m. After n_0 joins the system and shows interest in distributing m, she must first produce a content certificate for m as follows:

1. Select a subgroup $\{n_1, n_2, \ldots, n_k\}$ of k nodes. These k nodes are called *signers*.
2. Generate the content certificate structure, C (Figure 2(a)), with the following fields: n_0's identity (establishing who has generated the content and who is the legitimate owner), the identity of the content, a digest of the content, $h(m)$ (using a one–way cryptographically strong hash function, assuring its integrity), the ordered list of signers (OLS), the validity period (ts_1, ts_2) (establishing that the certificate is valid from ts_1 until ts_2) and the description of the hash and signature functions which have been used.
3. Finally, the previous items are recursively signed by the nodes listed in the OLS (Figure 2(b)). First, n_0 provides the first signature on C and passes it to the next node in the OLS, along with m. At each stage, the next node in the OLS adds its signature to the previous ones. The chained signature procedure is defined as follows:

$$E_0 = E_{K_{n_0}^{-1}}\big(h(C)\big)$$
$$E_{i+1} = E_{K_{n_{i+1}}^{-1}}\big(E_i\big) \tag{2}$$

where $E_{K_{n_i}}(x)$ is the asymmetric encryption of message x using K_{n_i} as key. The keys K_{n_i} and $K_{n_i}^{-1}$ represent the public and private keys respectively.

In summary, n_0 waits until C_m arrives from n_k, and then publishes the content m, along with the content certificate, (m, C_m).

Content certificate C_m

```
Certificate Body C:
    Holder: n_0
    ID: I_m
    Content: h(m)
    OLS: n_0, n_1, ..., n_k
    Validity Period: (ts_1, ts_2)
    Signing Algorithm: AlgorithmDesc.
Signatures:
```
$$E_k = E_{K_{n_k}^{-1}}(\cdots(E_{K_{n_1}^{-1}}(E_{K_{n_0}^{-1}}(h(C)))))$$

(a) Content Certificate C_m.

$$1.\ n_0 \rightarrow n_1\colon m_0 = E_{K_{n_1}}\left(m, E_0\right), \sigma_0$$
$$2.\ n_1 \rightarrow n_2\colon m_1 = E_{K_{n_2}}\left(m, E_1\right), \sigma_1$$
$$\vdots \ \vdots$$
$$k.\ n_k \rightarrow n_0\colon m_k = E_{K_{n_0}}\left(m, E_k\right), \sigma_k$$

$$\text{where } \sigma_i = E_{K_{n_i}^{-1}}(m_i)$$

(b) Certificate generation.

Fig. 2. Content certificate structure and generation

Cooperation is then crucial during the content certificate generation as a dishonest signer can delay the authentication process by not signing the certificate, wasting other peers' time and resources. We first informally evaluate whether it is reasonable to assume that signers would not misbehave (i.e. do not deviate from the protocol specification) if aimed at maximizing the expected payoff that they derive from the execution of the protocol. To this regard, the most realistic assumption is to consider that punishment to non–collaborative signers is not practical to implement. By contrast, nodes' signature over the content certificate will stand as formal evidence of her honest behavior. Therefore, the benefit for non–collaboration will be zero, whereas all cooperative participants will be rewarded at the end of a successful content authentication protocol run. We have chosen an arbitrary value $f_i > 0$ to represent the expected payoff of a cooperative action. Based on this assumption and on the rational nature of the peers we carry out the following analysis.

4   Protocol Formal Analysis

The description of any given MP–P2P protocol can be used to construct a *representative protocol game*. When a protocol game is constructed, each of the protocol participants becomes a *player* of the protocol game, and every player is given a series of possible *strategies* such as 'quit', or 'send a message' at each of their turns in the game. When the protocol game is over, every participant can assess the profit or loss they have incurred, by using a *payoff function*.

Definition 8. *Let $G_{MP-CA} = \{P, S, \overrightarrow{v}\}$ be the protocol game derived from the MP–P2P Content Authentication protocol previously described in Section 3.1, where:*

$$P = \{n_0, \ldots, n_k\} \text{ is the set of participant peers,}$$
each one with a pair of keys $(K_{n_i}, K_{n_i}^{-1})$.

$$S = S_0 \times \cdots \times S_k \text{ is the set of strategy profiles,}$$
where: $S_i = \{(send\_m_i, quit)\}$ is the set of
possible strategies for each entity n_i,
and $m_i = E_{K_{n_{i+1}}}(m, E_i)$.

$$\overrightarrow{v} = (v_0, \ldots, v_k) \text{ is a vector of } k+1 \text{ utility}$$
functions with domain over the
set S of strategy profiles and range over $\mathbb{R}$.

Each one of those utility functions can take the following values ($i \in \{0, \ldots, k\}$):

$$v_i(s) = \begin{cases} 0 & \text{if } \left[\exists j < i : s_j = quit\right] \vee \\ & \left[s_i = quit\right] \\ -f_i & \text{if } \left[s_i = send\_m_i\right] \wedge \\ & \left[\exists j, i < j \le k : s_j = quit\right] \\ f_i & \text{if } \left[s_j = send\_m_i \forall j \in \{0, \ldots, k\}\right] \end{cases} \tag{3}$$

Figures 3 represents, in an extensive form (a tree), the G_{MP-CA} game. The tree represents the different moves each participant can make and all the possible outcomes. The vectors assigned to each terminal node represent the values of the payoff function. The first value corresponds to participant n_0 and the rest are the payoff values for entities n_1 to n_k.

Our formal analysis of the MP–P2P Content Authentication protocol will be based on applying backward induction to the G_{MP-CA} game.

Theorem 1. *The strategy profile $s^* \in S$ defined as $s^* = (s_0^*, \ldots, s_k^*)$ where $s_i^* = (send\_m_i) \ \forall i \in \{0, \ldots, k\}$ represents a sub–game perfect Nash equilibrium in the G_{MP-CA} game.*

Proof. Entity n_k is the last player to move in the last phase of the protocol game. Entity n_k has to chose between quitting the protocol or sending message m_k to n_0. In other words, at the last round of the game, player n_k is presented with two options for which she would obtain different payoff values:

$$v_k(s_k, s_{-k}) = \begin{cases} 0 & \text{if } \left[s_k = quit)\right] \\ f_k & \text{if } \left[s_k = (send\_m_k)\right] \end{cases} \tag{4}$$

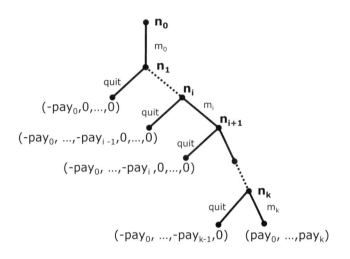

Fig. 3. Formal representation of the G_{MP-CA} game

All participant entities are considered to be rational, so all entities play to maximize their payoffs. Therefore strategy $(send\_m_k)$ is a dominant [2] strategy for n_k.

When it is entity n_{k-1}'s turn to play, n_{k-1} is aware of entity n_k's dominant strategy and behaves accordingly to maximize her payoff. In general, the backward induction process forces every entity n_i, to choose between the following two strategies with the following different payoffs:

$$v_i(s_i, s_{-i}) - \begin{cases} 0 \text{ if } \left[s_i = quit\right] \\ \\ f_i \text{ if } \left[s_i = (send\_m_i)\right] \end{cases} \tag{5}$$

Therefore, every entity n_i $i \in \{1, \ldots, k\}$ is *rationally* forced to play $send\_m_i$ instead of *quit*.

Summarizing, by applying backward induction to the G_{MP-CA} game, we have stated the following results:

- Strategies $s_i^* = send\_m_i$ $\forall i \in \{0, \ldots, k\}$ are dominant strategies for each participant entity.
- In all sub–games considered during the induction process, the described strategies represent local Nash equilibria, as no player has anything to gain by changing only his or her own strategy unilaterally.

Following Definition 7, we can then conclude that the strategy profile $s^* \in S$ defined as $s^* = (s_0^*, \ldots, s_n^*)$ where $s_i^* = (send\_m_i)$ $\forall i \in \{0, \ldots, k\}$ represents a sub–game perfect Nash equilibrium in the G_{MP-CA} game.

---

[2] A strategy is dominant if, regardless of what other players do, the strategy earns the player a greater payoff than any other possible strategy.

Corollary 1. *The MP–P2P Content Authentication protocol defined in Section 3.1 is a multiparty rational protocol.*

Proof. Theorem 1 defines a strategy profile representing an unique solution for the G_{MP-CA} game. Such a strategy profile corresponds exactly to the MP–P2P Content Authentication protocol description, and to what entities are dictated by the protocol specification given in Section 3.1. Such a solution is also a sub–game perfect equilibrium, so no other strategies result in higher benefits when any of the entities unilaterally changes their behavior. Therefore, deviating from the protocol description does not represent a profitable option. This, being the actual definition of a rational protocol is a conclusive result.

5   Conclusion and Future Work

In this paper we have formally proven that the MP–P2P Content Authentication protocol is rational. Despite the variable number of participant entities in the protocol, we were able to apply backward induction to compute the Nash Equilibrium of the dynamic game representing such a protocol.

Protocol rationality is an essential property for cooperativeness to naturally emerge in the absence of trusted third parties. Furthermore, rationality allows us to determine the outcome of each protocol interaction.

The content authentication protocol described in this paper is part of a global P2P secure file sharing system, introduced in [8] by Palomar et al. In their work, the authors define two sub–protocols as part of the global solution: (1) An MP–P2P Content Authentication protocol, described in [8] and of which an enhanced version has been presented and analyzed in this paper and, (2)An Access Control protocol [7,8]. This protocol has already been formally proven to be rational using Bayesian games [9]. Although extensive experimental work and simulation had been carried out to proof the viability and performance of such a global system, validation of the content authentication protocol was pending a formal approach. To this regard, this paper represents the final result of a series of works aimed at the formal definition and verification of a global solution for authenticated and secure file sharing in self–organizing P2P networks.

References

1. Zhang, Y., Lin, L., Huai, J.: Balancing trust and incentive in peer-to-peer collaborative system. Int. Journal of Network Security 5(1), 73–81 (2007)
2. Marti, S., Garcia-Molina, H.: Taxonomy of trust: Categorizing p2p reputation systems. Computer Networks 50, 472–484 (2006)
3. Andrade, N., Mowbray, M., Lima, A., Wagner, G., Ripeanu, M.: Influences on cooperation in bittorrent communities. In: Proceedings of the 2005 ACM SIGCOMM workshop on Economics of Peer-to-Peer systems, pp. 111–115. ACM, New York (2005)

4. Cheng, J., Li, Y., Jiao, W., Ma, J.: A utility-based auction cooperation incentive mechanism in peer-to-peer network. In: Zhou, X., Sokolsky, O., Yan, L., Jung, E.-S., Shao, Z., Mu, Y., Lee, D.C., Kim, D.Y., Jeong, Y.-S., Xu, C.-Z. (eds.) EUC Workshops 2006. LNCS, vol. 4097, pp. 11–21. Springer, Heidelberg (2006)
5. Zambonelli, F., Gleizesb, M., Mameia, M., Tolksdorf, R.: Spray computers: Explorations in self-organization. Pervasive and Mobile Computing 1, 1–20 (2005)
6. Ellis, T., Yao, X.: Evolving cooperation in the non-iterated prisoner's dilemma: A social network inspired approach. In: Proceedings of the IEEE Congress on Evolutionary Computation, Singapore, September 2007, pp. 25–28 (2007)
7. Palomar, E., Tapiador, J., Hernandez-Castro, J., Ribagorda, A.: Certificate-based access control in pure p2p networks. In: Proceedings of the 6th Int. Conference on Peer-to-Peer Computing, Cambridge, UK, September 2006, pp. 177–184. IEEE, Los Alamitos (2006)
8. Palomar, E., Estevez-Tapiador, J., Hernandez-Castro, J., Ribagorda, A.: Secure content access and replication in pure p2p networks. Computer Communications 31(2), 266–279 (2008)
9. Palomar, E., Alcaide, A., Estevez-Tapiador, J., Hernandez-Castro, J.: Bayesian analysis of secure p2p sharing protocols. In: Meersman, R., Tari, Z. (eds.) OTM 2007, Part II. LNCS, vol. 4804, pp. 1701–1717. Springer, Heidelberg (2007)
10. Abadi, M., Gordon, A.: A calculus for cryptographic protocols: the spi calculus. In: Proceedings of the 4th ACM Conference on Computer and Communications Security, pp. 36–47. ACM, New York (1997)
11. Aristizabal, A., Lopez, H., Rueda, C., Valencia, F.: Formally reasoning about security issues in p2p protocols: A case study. In: Proceedings of the 3rd Taiwanese-French Conference on Information Technology, Nancy, France, INRIA Technical report (March 2006)
12. Schneider, S., Borgstrom, J., Nestmann, U.: Towards the application of process calculi in the domain of peer-to-peer algorithms. In: Proceedings of the 8th Int. Workshop on Autonomous Systems–Self-Organization, Management and Control, Shanghai, China, October 2008. Springer, Heidelberg (2008)
13. Velipasalar, S., Chang-Hong, L., Schlessman, J., Wolf, W.: Design and verification of communication protocols for peer-to-peer multimedia systems. In: Proceedings of the IEEE International Conference on Multimedia and Expo., Toronto, Canada, July 2006, pp. 1421–1424. IEEE, Los Alamitos (2006)
14. Buragohain, C., Agrawal, D., Suri, S.: A game theoretic framework for incentives in p2p systems. In: Proceedings of the 3rd Int. Conf. on Peer-to-Peer Computing, Linkping, Sweden, September 2003, pp. 48–56. IEEE Computer Society, Los Alamitos (2003)
15. Gupta, R., Somani, A.K.: Game theory as a tool to strategize as well as predict nodes behavior in peer-to-peer networks. In: ICPADS, pp. 244–249 (2005)
16. Morselli, R., Katz, J., Bhattacharjee, B.: A game-theoretic framework for analyzing trust-inference protocols. In: Second Workshop on the Economics of Peer-to-Peer Systems (2004)
17. Palomar, E.: Content authentication and access control in pure peer-to-peer networks. Technical report, University Carlos III of Madrid. Computer Science Department. Spain, Ph.D. Thesis (2008)

Extending XACML Access Control Architecture for Allowing Preference-Based Authorisation

Gina Kounga, Marco Casassa Mont, and Pete Bramhall

Hewlett-Packard Laboratories
Long Down Avenue
Stoke Gifford
Bristol
BS34 8QZ
United Kingdom
{Gina.Kounga,Marco.Casassa-Mont,Pete.Bramhall}@hp.com

Abstract. European data protection regulation states that organisations must have data subjects' consent to use their personally identifiable information (PII) for a variety of purposes. Solutions have been proposed which generally handle consent in a coarse-grained way, by means of opt in/out choices. However, we believe that consent's representation should be extended to allow data subjects to express a rich set of conditions under which their PII can be used. In this paper we introduce and discuss an approach enabling the representation of consent as fine-grained preferences. To enforce such consent, we leverage and extend the current standard XACML architecture and framework. As data collectors maintain links between PII and associated preferences, preferences should also be considered as part of this PII. Therefore our solution prevents access control components from directly accessing any PII.

Keywords: Privacy, Access controls.

1 Introduction

Data protection regulations [1, 2] require organisations to process collected personal data only with data subjects' (e.g., end-users) consent for that processing. In the literature, this requirement is usually translated into opt in/out mechanisms that permit to capture data subjects' consent [3, 4]. However, opt in/out mechanisms do not provide any freedom to data subjects to fully specify how they would like to limit their personal data to be used. These mechanisms are indeed mainly associated with consent forms specified by data collectors (the entities that collect personal data items from data subjects) for the data subjects, which leaves data subjects only limited control of their personal data. We believe that the notion of consent has to be extended to encompass these needs. In the context of this paper, we define consent as *a set of fine-grained privacy preferences that define the actions that can be performed on a personal data item or a group of personal data items*. The data collectors still define the preference framework, but they explicitly share the management of preferences with

S. Katsikas, J. Lopez, and M. Soriano (Eds.): TrustBus 2010, LNCS 6264, pp. 153–164, 2010.

data subjects. Therefore, the value of the privacy preferences to be associated with each personal data item can be set by the data subject, along with the personal data items they apply to, before sending this information to the data collector. As proposed by Karjoth et al in [4], the data collector stores each personal data item as well as the corresponding preferences and maintains a link between both to guarantee that each preference can always be associated to the data item it applies to. Consequently, preferences can be linked to a living individual and therefore have to be considered as being personal data [1].

In this context, enforcing consent requires guaranteeing that each personal data item is accessed only if the conditions expressed by the associated preferences are met. As the data collector may collect thousands of data items from thousands of different data subjects, enforcing consent, as previously described, introduces a scalability problem. Further, as preferences are personal data, they also need to be securely maintained and only accessed by authorised principals – i.e., unique entities.

In this paper, we propose a solution that ensures that only the legitimate entities/data receivers can access personal data. For that, we propose an extension to the OASIS eXtensible Access Control Markup Language (XACML) [5] architecture and framework to enforce consent based on fine-grained preferences representing data subjects' consent. The XACML choice is influenced by the fact that this framework is currently a reference standard. Our solution builds on the observation that in most organisations, personal data are collected and managed by specific entities – e.g., the human resources service, the customer management service, etc. The manner in which these entities manage personal data is dictated by a set of regulations such as employment laws. Consequently, these organisations are constrained to use personal data as specified by these entities. In our solution, an *attribute authority* (AA) represents such an entity. The AA is the entity within the data collector which collects and stores personal data items and the associated preferences. It is composed of subcomponents that extend the XACML access control architecture to allow access control decisions to be made based on preferences' values. The goal is to ensure that no XACML component – i.e., neither the policy decision point (PDP) nor the policy enforcement point (PEP) – accesses the preferences and the personal data items. Only the AA and the authorised principals – that have been granted the access – do access them. As the AA is designed to adapt to any type of data repository or data store, our solution does not require heavy modifications to be performed on organisations' legacy systems to make it work. To the best of our knowledge, no other solution has been proposed which enforces consent based on fine-grained preferences, protects the access to these preferences and the associated personal data items and which, at the same time, can adapt to any legacy system.

This paper is organised as follows. In Section 2, we present the scenario that we consider. This will be used as a reference in the remainder of this paper. Then, in Section 3 we discuss the related work. In Section 4, we present the assumptions on which our solution relies. We present our proposed extended XACML architecture in Section 5, and detail in Section 6 the interactions allowing the enforcement of consent based on fine-grained preferences and the protection of personal data. Finally, we present the current status of our work in Section 7 and conclude our paper in Section 8.

2   Scenario

In this paper, we consider a scenario in which an organisation needs to collect some personal data from individuals in order to provide some services to these individuals. During collection, individuals specify fine-grained privacy preferences defining the conditions under which their personal data should be accessed. After being collected, these personal data need to be accessed and processed by various business processes within the organisation, in order for the relevant services be provided to individuals. To enforce consent, access to personal data by a business process is only to be granted if the conditions defined by individuals with their privacy preferences are fulfilled. An example of this scenario consists of employees who can be provided with services such as travel offers, ticket booking services, etc. by their company. To benefit from these services, employees need to fill registration forms where they disclose personal data, e.g., name, surname, age, address, etc. These forms also allow employees to specify the conditions under which their personal data can be accessed. As services offered by the company may be provided by entities internal to the company (e.g., a career development advice service) as well as entities external to the company (e.g., a travel agency) these conditions can, for instance, restrict the access to certain personal data items to entities within the company.

3   Related Work

A set of key requirements must be fulfilled in order to provide the data subject the means to control how a data collector uses their personal data items – see Section 1. First, (1) the data subject must be given the means to fully specify the actions that can be performed on their personal data items as well as the conditions under which they can be performed. Then, (2) as specified by Karjoth et al. in [4], after personal data items have been sent to the data collector, the data collector must maintain a link between each of the received personal data items and the associated preferences. This, to guarantee that the conditions under which each personal data item may be accessed can always be identified. This aspect has been dealt with by the PRIME project [6]. However, here we further refine that work by considering both consent and revocation aspects, i.e., we implement the lifecycle management of consent. Finally, (3) the previous conditions must be enforced each time that an access to the associated personal data item is requested. Mechanisms must be put into place that, for each data item and each data subject, check whether the values of the preferences allow the access to be granted. As previously discussed, the first of the previous requirements (cf. (1)) cannot be fulfilled by traditional opt in/out mechanism. A more suitable approach is the one introduced in the EnCoRe project [7] where the data subject consents to the use of their personal data by specifying, for each personal data item or group of personal data items, fine-grained privacy preferences defining how these data items must be used. This approach has the advantage of coping with situations, generally not dealt with in the literature, where the data subject decides to revoke the right they gave to a data collector to use their personal data. By properly updating the preferences stored by the data collector, the data subject can indeed make some of their personal data items be no longer validly accessible. Such preferences can for instance be: a date *authorised_date* until when a data item can be used by an authorised principal, a list *authorised_third_parties* of third parties to which the data item can be sent, a list *authorised_purposes* of purposes for which the access to the data item can be granted, etc.

Different solutions already proposed in the literature might be considered to fulfil the third requirement (cf. (3)). Hippocratic databases [8], for instance, are a specific type of database which rely on a relational data model to allow access to data to be granted based on ten privacy principles. Using Hippocratic databases to solve the considered problem would require to modify their data model and to make it adaptable to each data collector's requirements. Another strong limitation is that Hippocratic databases do not apply to other types of data repositories than relational databases. The solution proposed by Byun and Li in [9] only deals with purpose-based access control. The Enterprise Privacy Authorization Language (EPAL) [10] could also be considered. It is a language that allows the definition of fine-grained access control policies. As it is considered to be a subset of the XACML standard [11], XACML would suit better the resolution of our problem. However, XACML does not allow specifying, in the access control policies' rules, some conditions which depend on the values of some data stored in some repositories. It indeed only allows policies' rules to contain conditions specified on the "*subject*", "*resource*", "*action*" or "*environment*" attributes concerned by an access request. But none of these attributes corresponds to our privacy preferences. Fine-grained preferences, as proposed in our solution, are not dealt with by the XACML standard or by the XACML privacy profile [12] which only allows to make authorisation decisions based on the purpose for which an access is requested. Consequently, no mechanism is provided that permits XACML to make authorisation decisions based on fine-grained preferences. Casassa Mont et al. proposed in [13] a solution that does provide preference-based access control. However, it relies on a proprietary language. Hence, there is the need to ensure that the same can be achieved with open languages, such as XACML and/or their extensions. Kolter et al. proposed in [14] a solution relying on XACML in which clients specify privacy preferences by defining constrains that a PDP, trusted by the service provider, must fulfil in order this PDP to be chosen by the client to evaluate an access request. Therefore, it does not allow access control decisions to be based on privacy preferences specified by data subjects but only allows some policy to be evaluated by some PDP fulfilling access requester's privacy preferences. In [14] only access requesters' privacy is dealt with while in this paper, the goal is to protect both access requesters' and data subjects' privacy. Besides this, the solution proposed in [14] requires PDPs to be not only trusted to properly evaluate some policies but also to properly manage some received privacy-sensitive attributes, which goes beyond the traditional role of the PDP.

A solution to allow XACML to provide preference-based access control could be to import the preferences within access requests transmitted to the PDP. However, as a request can consist in accessing personal data from very large numbers of data subjects, providing preference-based access control in this case would require incorporating very large numbers of preferences within the request. This does not scale. The foregoing highlights that the XACML language needs to be extended to allow conditions on preferences – stored in some repositories – to be specified within the policies' rules. As conditions within rules need to be expressed based on preferences' values, evaluating the policies' rules requires the PDP to obtain the value of the preferences during the decision making process. However, good practice requires separating the decision making from the data access. And in the considered case, preferences themselves are personal data- stored in some data repositories.

In the remainder of this paper, we propose an extension to the XACML architecture that solves this problem. Our solution uses some of the concepts of the Identity Governance Framework (IGF) [15] to allow access control decisions to be made based on preferences' values. This, without making any XACML component – i.e., neither the PDP nor the PEP – access the preferences and the personal data items. This guarantees that privacy preferences, as any other personal data, are accessed only by authorised principals.

4   Assumptions

In order to define our solution, we make assumptions that apply to the considered organisation and assumptions that are specific to the proposed approach. The former are realistic as they cover techniques that are already in place in most organisations. The latter have only a marginal impact on existing organisations' identity and access management solutions (IAM). as require new components to be added to existing IAM systems and which, we believe, can adapt to legacy systems: this because our solution is independent of the data access protocol used by the data repositories where are stored the personal data items (see Sections 5 for the details). Our assumptions are:

1. **The data collector is an organisation.** This, because most of the time, individuals are required to disclose some personal data when they request an organisation to provide them some services.
2. **A trusted third party (TTP) is available at the data controller.** This TTP manages cryptographic keys and issues certificates to principals at the data collector. Such TTP can be internal to the organisation. If we consider the employee scenario of Section 2, the TTP could be the organisation's human resources service as it has the means to verify employees' identities and therefore to vouch for these employees' identities to third parties.
3. **Principals have encryption and signing capabilities.** They are able to sign messages that they generate and encrypt/decrypt those that they send/receive. In many organisations solutions relying on encryption are deployed which provide employees remote access to these organisations' information systems. Therefore most organisations already have the capabilities to support encryption and signing.
4. **The proposed extended XACML architecture is initialised by some trusted administrators.** At the initialisation of the system, the data collector's system administrator specifies the set of preferences that should be taken into account by the system for each personal data item or group of personal data items to be collected. Subsequently, data subjects are free to specify the value that they wish for these preferences. The policy administrator specifies the policies. It also specifies, in a response formatting file signed with his private key, the format in which the AA should return personal data to requesting principals. As most organisations do have information systems managed by specialists, it is highly probable that the

management of policies as well as the initialisation of the system will be achieved by such specialists.

5. **A front-end application is available which allows the data subject to send their personal data items and privacy preferences to the data collector's AA.** The front-end application displays some forms containing fields to be filled in by the data subject with suitable personal data items. The forms also contain some privacy preferences fields permitting the data subject to specify how each personal data item or group of personal data items must be used by the data collector.

6. **A mechanism is in place that permits the data subject and the data collector's AA to negotiate an Attribute Authority Policy Markup Language (AAPML) contract specifying how the personal data items and the preferences should be used by the AA.** The AAPML contract can be consumed by a PEP [16]. It is important to note that we use AAPML for the purpose it has been defined for (see [17]). The definition of AAPML policies is out of the scope of this paper, however examples of AAPML policies can be found in [16, 17].

7. **The data subject discloses their personal data items and privacy preferences to an AA situated at the data collector.**

8. **An extension to the XACML language exists which allows policies' rules to contain conditions expressed on the value of preferences stored in some data repositories.** We do not discuss this extension.

9. **Components are trusted to behave as specified.** We assume that they cannot be tampered with.

5   Proposed Extended XACML Architecture

As discussed in Section 3, there is the need to define a solution relying on an open standard for access control which allows data collectors to enforce consent based on fine-grained preferences and which fulfil the requirements defined in Section 1. XACML is a standard that specify an access control architecture relying on the PEP/PDP model introduced in [18] and a rule-based access control language allowing fine-grained access control. Therefore, XACML is a promising candidate to solve our problem. However, as in its current form XACML does not allow access control to be made based on fine-grained privacy preferences used to express conditions within the policies, XACML needs to be extended. Different approaches are possible to achieve this. One of these is to modify the PDP to make it support preference-based access control. However, this would massively impact on existing IAM solutions as they also would have to be redeployed. Here, we propose a solution that is designed to allow access control to be made based on fine-grained preferences without having to heavily change existing IAM solutions. Only minor changes in the message flow are required. The proposed solution further transfers the complexity of providing preference-based access control to specific components located next to the data. Therefore, preference-based access control becomes a modular functionality that can easily be added and removed, as needed, from existing IAM solutions without degrading the security of the services provided by these IAM solutions.

The proposed extended XACML architecture is represented in Figure 1. The first part is the existing XACML architecture. Its role is to make authorisation decisions

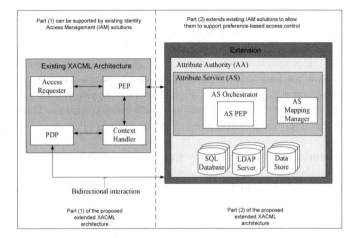

Fig. 1. Extended XACML architecture and the interactions between its components

and to return, when applicable, the requested data to authorised requesting principals. Our extension only impacts on the manner in which the core XACML components interact and on the definition of the access control policies' rules. Indeed, for our solution to be scalable, policies' rules should be expressed in a general enough manner to make them apply to all data subjects' personal data items and preferences. To achieve this, we do not hard code the preferences values within the policies' rules. We only specify the logic relationships that these preferences must verify. The second part is the proposed extension. It is the AA component which is trusted by the data subjects to manage their personal data as they specified. This component provides to the XACML components the minimum information they need to make authorisation decisions based on fine-grained privacy preferences and guarantees, at the same time, that personal data are never disclosed to them. When positive authorisation decisions are returned by the PDP to the AA, the AA extracts the personal data concerned by the response, encrypts them using the access requesters' keys and returns the obtained encrypted personal data to the XACML PEP. The XACML PEP then transmits these data to the access requesters. The AA is composed of two subcomponents: the data repositories and the attribute service (AS). The data repositories store the personal data items and the preferences sent by the data subjects to the data collector. It is important to note that data repositories can rely on different data access protocols [19, 20]. The AS is the component that evaluates how a request, from a component – e.g., XACML component, to access some personal data items or preferences must be dealt with. More specifically, the AS determines – based on the AAPML contract established with the data subject concerned by the request – whether the requested data can be returned to the requesting component. If the data can be returned, the AS identifies the protocols used by the repositories where are stored the data and accordingly formats some requests permitting data to be extracted from each of these repositories. After having obtained the data, the AS determines – using an authenticated response formatting file – the format under which these data must be returned to the requesting component. This is done based on the principle that no personal data must be accessible to any XACML component. Specific formatting of the response, such as additional filtering, may also be specified in the AAPML contract established with the data subject. If it is the case, the filtering is also performed by the AS before the response is returned. Such filtering can, for instance, be the removal of the data subject's Social Security Number from the data items to be returned. Controlling the format under which data have to be returned to a component ensures that components only know the minimum information needed to perform their tasks properly. It therefore permits our extended XACML architecture to run access authorisation processes without ever exposing personal data to unauthorised principals. Three subcomponents help the AA to provide the foregoing. The:

- **Authentication Service Policy Enforcement Point.** The AS PEP is a subcomponent of the AS Orchestrator. It stores the AAPML contracts established with the data subjects, based on which it determines whether some personal data items and privacy preferences, stored in the AA's data repositories, can be returned to the AS Orchestrator. Therefore, the AS PEP guarantees that the AA always manages the personal data that it stores as specified by the data subject.
- **Authentication Service Mapping Manager.** The AS Mapping Manager manages the different data representations that are used in the data repositories. It allows the AS PEP to properly format the data access requests to be sent to the data repositories. Therefore, it makes it possible for the proposed extended XACML architecture to be used with data repositories relying on different protocols and to adapt to any legacy system.
- **Authentication Service Orchestrator.** The AS Orchestrator orchestrates the mechanisms that make it possible to deal with access requests made to XACML components or authorisation responses received from XACML components. Its behaviour is constrained by its internal AS PEP that must first authorise an action to be performed on personal data, then access these personal data and return them to the AS orchestrator, for the AS orchestrator to perform the authorised action on the obtained personal data.

The AS Orchestrator relies on an authenticated response formatting file that defines the format of the responses that the AS Orchestrator must return, depending on the nature of the received request and on the requesting principal(s).

The AS Orchestrator receives two types of messages from the XACML components. It receives some property requests from the PDP to verify whether some preferences associated with some personal data items verify the conditions specified in the policies' access control rules. The response formatting file specifies that the AS orchestrator must respond to a property request by: *true* if the conditions are verified and *false* if the conditions are not verified. It also receives positive authorisation responses from the PDP. After receiving a positive response, the AS Orchestrator requests its AS PEP to send it the personal data whose access has just been authorised by the PDP. Once these data have been received, they are formatted as required by the AS Orchestrator before being sent to the XACML PEP.

6   Data Flow

The mechanism that allows the PDP to evaluate policies based on preferences is represented in Figure 2 and works as follows. An entity that wants to access some personal data sends an access request to the XACML PEP (cf. (1) in Figure 2).

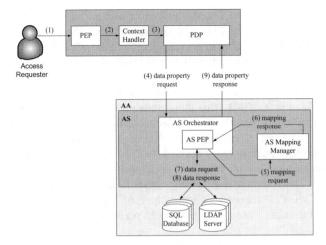

Fig. 2. Evaluation of access requests

The process is the same as defined in XACML (cf. (1) to (3) in Figure 2) until the PDP receives the request and evaluates the corresponding policy. As policies contain conditions depending on the value of preferences specified by the data subjects whose personal data need to be accessed (cf. Figure 3), the PDP needs to know whether these conditions are verified for the request being evaluated. For that, the PDP sends a data property request to the AS Orchestrator (cf. (4) in Figure 2) which then requests its AS PEP to return it the suitable preferences. The AS PEP verifies that the AAPML contract, established with the data subject whose preferences need to be accessed, authorises the access. If yes, the AS PEP sends a mapping request to the Mapping Manager (cf. (5)). After having received the AS Mapping Manager's response (cf. (6)), the AS PEP can send some properly formatted data requests to the suitable data repositories (cf. (7)). Once it has received the requested data, the AS PEP returns

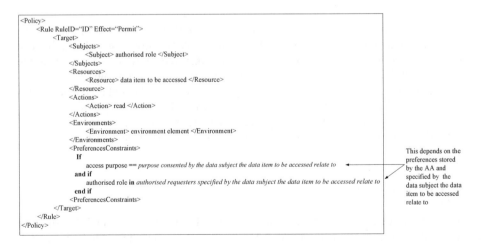

Fig. 3. A non-formal example of a policy

them to the AS Orchestrator. The AS orchestrator then identifies the format of the response it must return to the PDP and verifies whether the properties requested by the PDP are verified by the data items received from the AS PEP. If it is the case, the AS Orchestrator returns *true* to the PDP and *false* otherwise (cf. (9)). The PDP can then evaluate the policies.

After the PDP has rendered its authorisation decision, it sends it to the context handler, as defined in XACML, that then sends it to the XACML PEP (cf. (1) and (2) in Figure 4). Two types of authorisation decisions can be returned to the context handler: "*Deny*" if the access to the requested data has been denied, "*Permit*" if the access to the requested data have been authorised. In the later case, the message sent by the PDP to the context handler may further contain some obligations. When the XACML PEP receives a *Deny* response, it directly sends it to the access requester. However, when the XACML PEP receives a *Permit*, the XACML PEP waits for the AS Orchestrator to send it the data whose access has been permitted.

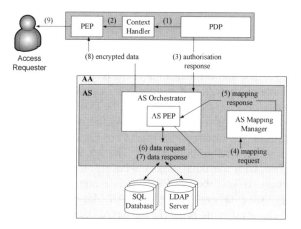

Fig. 4. Management of access authorisation response

After having sent the response to the context handler, the PDP sends the AS Orchestrator an authorisation response (cf. (3)) that contains information about: the data whose access has been authorised, the entity that requested the access and the XACML PEP to which the data item to be extracted must be returned. The AS Orchestrator uses a similar process to the one previously detailed to obtain the data items whose access has been permitted (cf. (4) to (7)). Once the AS Orchestrator does have these data, it encrypts them with the access requester's key and sends them to the XACML PEP (cf. (8)). The PEP then returns the requested data to the access requester (cf. (9)).

7 Current Status

Some of the components, including the XACML PEP and PDP on which our solution relies, have already been implemented. We are leveraging and extending the IGF framework to implement the other aspects of our solution and integrate it with the existing components. The solution proposed in this paper is in the process of being implemented in the context of the EnCoRe project. The final implementation will result in a prototype and a demonstrator which will be used as a basis for testing our approach and future extensions.

8 Conclusion

European data protection regulation mandate that organisations use personal data only as consented by data subjects. In this context, solutions have been proposed to deal with consent management matters, but by only providing generic opt in/out choice. In this paper, we have proposed a solution that extends the XACML architecture so that access control is driven by fine-grained preferences, which represent data subjects' consent. The proposed approach does not require major changes for existing identity access management (IAM) solutions. Only minor changes are required in the message flow. The proposed solution further transfers the complexity of providing preference-based access control to specific components located next to the protected data. Therefore, preference-based access control becomes a modular functionality that can easily be added and removed, as needed, from existing IAM solutions without degrading the security of the services provided by these solutions. The Future work will consist in managing requests to access personal data of a set of data subjects.

References

[1] UK Parliament: Data Protection Act 1998 (1998),
    http://www.opsi.gov.uk/acts/acts1998/ukpga19980029en1
    (accessed October 1, 2009)
[2] The European Parliament and the Council of 24 October 1995: Directive 95/46/EC of the European Parliament and of the Council of 24 October 1995 on the protection of individuals with regard to the processing of personal data and on the free movement of such data (1995), http://eur-lex.europa.eu/LexUriServ/LexUriServ.do?uri=CELEX:31995L0046:EN:HTML (accessed October 1, 2009)
[3] W3C: The Platform for Privacy Preferences 1.0 (P3P1.0) Specification (2002),
    http://www.w3.org/TR/P3P/ (accessed October 2, 2009)
[4] Karjoth, G., Schunter, M., Waidner, M.: Platform for enterprise privacy practices: Privacy-enabled management of customer data. In: Dingledine, R., Syverson, P.F. (eds.) PET 2002. LNCS, vol. 2482, pp. 69–84. Springer, Heidelberg (2003)
[5] OASIS: eXtensible Access Control Markup Language (XACML) Version 2.0 (February 2005),
    http://docs.oasis-open.org/xacml/2.0/accesscontrol-xacml-2.0-core-spec-os.pdf (accessed September 29, 2009)
[6] Prime project: Prime project website, https://www.prime-project.eu/ (accessed March 26, 2010)
[7] EnCoRe Project: EnCoRe project website, http://www.encore-project.info/ (accessed October 26, 2009)

[8] Agrawal, R., Kiernan, J., Srikant, R., Xu, Y.: Hippocratic Databases. In: Proceedings of the 28th VLDB Conference, Hong Kong, China, pp. 143–154 (2002), http://www.almaden.ibm.com/cs/projects/iis/hdb/Publications/papers/vldb02hippocratic.pdf (accessed October 2, 2009)

[9] Byun, J.W., Li, N.: Purpose based access control for privacy protection in relational database systems. The VLDB Journal 17(4), 603–619 (2008)

[10] IBM: The Enterprise Privacy Authorization Language (EPAL), EPAL 1.2 specification, http://www.zurich.ibm.com/security/enterprise-privacy/epal/Specification/index.html (accessed October 2, 2009)

[11] Anderson, A.H.: A comparison of two privacy policy languages: EPAL and XACML. In: SWS '06: Proceedings of the 3rd ACM Workshop on Secure Web Services, pp. 53–60. ACM, New York (2006)

[12] OASIS: Privacy policy profile of XACML v2.0 (February 2005), http://docs.oasis-open.org/xacml/2.0/accesscontrol-xacml-2.0-privacyprofile-spec-os.pdf (accessed September 29, 2009)

[13] Casassa Mont, M., Thyne, R., Bramhall, P.: Privacy Enforcement with HP Select Access for Regulatory Compliance (2005), http://www.hpl.hp.com/techreports/2005/HPL-2005-10.html (accessed October 2, 2009)

[14] Kolter, J., Schillinger, R., Pernul, G.: A privacy-enhanced attribute-based access control system. In: DBSec, pp. 129–143 (2007)

[15] Liberty Alliance Project: Identity Governance web page, http://www.projectliberty.org/strategic initiatives/identity_governance (accessed September 29, 2009)

[16] Hunt, P., Levinson, R.: AAPML: Attribute Authority Policy Markup Language (November 2006), http://www.oracle.com/technology/tech/standards/idm/igf/pdf/IGF-AAPML-spec-08.pdf (accessed September 30, 2009)

[17] Pohlman, M.B.: Oracle Identity Management Governance, Risk, and Compliance Architecture, 3rd edn. Auerbach Publications (2008)

[18] Yavatkar, R., Pendarakis, D., Guerin, R.: A Framework for Policy-based Admission Control. RFC 2753 (Informational), Internet Engineering Task Force (January 2000), http://tools.ietf.org/pdf/rfc2753.pdf (accessed September 29, 2009)

[19] Zeilenga, K.: Lightweight Directory Access Protocol version 3 (LDAPv3): All Operational Attributes. RFC 3673, http://www.ietf.org/rfc/rfc3673.txt (accessed February 1, 2010)

[20] Chamberlin, D.D., Boyce, R.F.: A structured English query language. In: FIDET '74: Proceedings of the 1974 ACM SIGFIDET (now SIGMOD) Workshop on Data Description, Access and Control, pp. 249–264. ACM, New York (1974)

An Agent Based Back-End RFID Tag Management System

Evangelos Rekleitis, Panagiotis Rizomiliotis, and Stefanos Gritzalis

Dep. of Inf. and Comm. Syst. Eng., University of the Aegean
Karlovassi, Samos, GR 83200, Greece
{erekl,prizomil,sgritz}@aegean.gr

Abstract. Motivated by the plethora of RFID security protocols and the interoperability problems that this diversity causes, we propose a software agent-based platform that allows an RFID back-end subsystem to integrate and manage heterogeneous tags that are based on non-standardized implementations. In addition, we introduce a new suite of lightweight tag management protocols that support tag authentication, time-based tag delegation and ownership transfer. The protocols can take advantage of the proposed agent-based platform and do satisfy all the standard security and privacy requirements.

Keywords: RFID, software agent, privacy, security, delegation, ownership.

1 Introduction

Radio Frequency Identification (*RFID*) is a sensor-based technology, used, primarily, to identify and track products or living organisms [12]. This is achieved by using devices, called transceivers or readers, to query embedded integrated circuits, called transponders or tags. RFID tags may, either be self-powered (active) or require power from an external source (passive), usually the reader, or a hybrid, using both internal and external power sources. The main goal, of such a system, is to replace and enhance the now ubiquitous barcode, as well as allow new tracking, access management and security services (e.g. e-passports, anti-counterfeiting mechanisms, etc.). To make RFID systems economically viable, strict restrictions have been placed, mainly, on the tag side, whose implementation has to be power, space and time efficient. However, these restrictions cause sever security and privacy problems, since well known and trusted solutions, like public-key cryptography, are no longer applicable, and efficient alternatives are required.

Going through the corpus of published research work on RFID security and privacy, one realizes that, the main focus is in the front-end system communication, i.e. the reader-tag interaction; while, only a limited number of published work studies the back-end part of the system (e.g. [14,10]). This can be partially justified by the general belief that the back-end system, usually, comprises of well known and understood server-based technologies ([4]). Thus, it comes at no

S. Katsikas, J. Lopez, and M. Soriano (Eds.): TrustBus 2010, LNCS 6264, pp. 165–176, 2010.

surprise that there exists a plethora of cryptographic algorithms, protocols and tag implementations, incompatible with each other, that satisfy different and, at times, contradicting requirements. This babel has caused grave interoperability problems.

Moreover, an even closer look of the published papers, reveals that, while tag authentication is covered by numerous protocols, the issue of tag delegation has not been sufficiently addressed yet. Tag delegation meaning the capability to allow a third party, tag authentication and read access to an owned tag, while maintaining the right to revoke this privilege, under some predefined conditions. Molnar et al. [11] proposed an authentication protocol using pseudonyms and secrets, organized in a tree structure, to offer secure ownership transfer and time-limited, recursive delegation; the tree scheme was compromised in [3]. Fouladgar et al. [5] also used pseudonyms to construct an authentication protocol, where delegation lasts for a predetermined number of queries. A similar protocol, supporting a limited kind of delegation, was proposed in [3]. Other research on ownership transfer include [15,9,13,8,16].

In this paper, motivated by the interoperability problems caused by the diversity of cryptographic protocols, we propose a software agent-based RFID back-end system that simplifies the integration and management of heterogeneous RFID tags. The new system is able to implement different security or communication protocols, by offloading part of the management and communication functions, from the back-end and the tag reader, to a, per tag dedicated, agent, residing in a repository. The concept of using software agents to complement RFID-based systems is not new. In [7] mobile software agents were employed to monitor the transport parameters of tagged items, and in [2] a multi agent-based back-end application subsystem, excluding tag management, is proposed, while Chen et. al. in [1] implement the whole back-end subsystem, including tag management, using a Multi Agent System. However, to the best of our knowledge, no previous work exists, that combines both RFID and agent technologies and specifically addresses security and privacy concerns. We fill this gap by making the agent based back-end security conscious. Due to space constraints we have chosen to focus on the tag managing portion of the data processing subsystem, not dwelling in technicalities.

At the second part of the paper, we complement this architecture with a novel suite of tag management protocols. The proposed suite of protocols covers all the standard, important security and privacy requirements (data confidentiality, backward & forward untraceability, etc) supporting, among other operations, tag authentication, tag ownership transfer and time-based tag delegation. It goes without saying that, while all the protocols fit nicely the proposed agent-based infrastructure, they, none the less, can also be used with a more conventional back-end system without any modifications.

The paper is organized as follows. In Section 2, the software agent-based platform is described and its main characteristics are analyzed. In Section 3, a new suite of lightweight protocols for tag management is introduced and its security is evaluated. Finally, in Section 4, we present some concluding remarks and provide some directions for future research work.

2   Agent-Based RFID Platform

In this section, we propose a software agent-based RFID platform that addresses security and privacy concerns. In the vast majority of the RFID security research papers, the abstract RFID system consists of 3 main components, namely the **RFID tags**, the **tag readers** and the **back-end subsystem** (Fig. 1).

The back-end subsystem is responsible for managing all information related to the tags. It can be thought as the combination of a *Back-end Database*, which associates tag identifiers to information related to the tagged objects, and a *Back-end Application subsystem* that performs business specific functions ([17]). It is assumed that communication between the back-end components as well as between the back-end subsystem and the readers is secured, by suitable means, while the reader-tag communication is not.

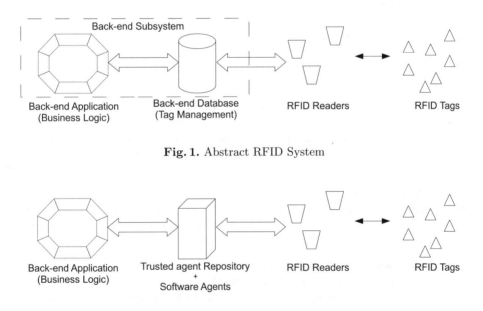

Fig. 1. Abstract RFID System

Fig. 2. RFID System with Software Agents

The proposed agent-based platform appears in Fig. 2. The Back-end Database and the tag-related records are replaced by an *Agent Repository* and *Tag Agents*, respectively.

The **Agent Repository** is a host platform that provides, to residing or visiting agents, necessary computational resources and services. From a security perspective, we distinguish between trusted and untrusted (alien) repositories. A trusted repository is one complying with our security and privacy (S&P) policy, and acts as a safe haven for the managed agents. That is, it enforces all necessary security means to protect them, prevent unauthorized access and tampering. To each entity that owns and wishes to manage a set of tags, corresponds a trusted repository, thus there is no need for a central 'trusted' agent repository.

A **Tag Agent** is an autonomous, software entity that manages one and only one RFID tag. Each tag agent stores relevant tag information, including all data required to interact with the rest of the back-end and to manage the RFID tag (including tag owner's credential, S&P policy, important business logic etc).

By default, it is assumed that the tag agents reside in the protected environment of a trusted repository and, for security reasons, are not allowed to travel outside of it. However, mobility is a desired characteristic, as there are cases where we would like to send an agent to an alien platform; e.g. when a tagged item changes owner, or when we wish to delegate tag access to an off-line reader or third party. For this, we allow the creation of partial **agent clones** that hold only a subset of the original agent's information. By using suitable security and privacy policies, we can control the amount of information exposed, while maintaining functionality.

2.1   Basic Tag Operations

We will now describe, in brevity, how the main tag-related operations are performed by the agent-based platform.

Tag Initialization: During a tag's initialization (e.g. assignment of a unique identifier (uID), secret key), an agent is created that has all the necessary information (credentials, policies, tag information, communication protocols, etc.) to communicate securely both with the rest of the back-end system, as well as, the tag.

Tag's Data Access: Agents enforce access control mechanisms, to allow authorized entities to access, append or modify tag's data, based on the entity's permissions. So, it is possible to regularly and in an automatic way update/modify information (e.g. location, status, etc.) related to a tagged item.

Tag Authentication/Secret Update: Any of the proposed authentication and secret update protocols can be applied. More specifically, the agent is able to instruct the reader on the correct protocol to use, when communicating with the tag, and provide the required information. So, with respect to security, the agent knows which authentication protocol the tag implements and has knowledge of the secret keys used and it is able to update and generate those keys, identifiers, pseudonyms etc., accordingly.

Tag Ownership Transfer: For tag implementations supporting secure ownership transfer, the agent-based back-end can facilitate the process and ease information management. To wit, the previous owner is able to decide the amount of information she wants to pass to the new owner. This is achieved by creating and forwarding, to the new owner, a suitably constructed *agent clone* that supports the tag secret update operation. For example, at a retailer's point-of-sale, the retailer would remove any sensitive data pertaining to the shop's logistics system, as well as, perform a secret update operation (to alter the secret, stored in the tag, to a temporary value). The agent clone would then be populated with the new temporary secret, along with any data required by law (e.g. expiration date, manufacturer, etc.) and data that would add value to the transaction and allow for better after sales services. As a final step, the new owner takes tag-ownership by performing the secret update operation, under a controlled environment (to avoid eavesdropping from the retailer).

Tag Delegation: This operation is supported through the use of clone agents. A suitable clone is created and forwarded to the delegated entity, allowing interaction with the corresponding tag, sans access to the tag owner's repository. For implementations not supporting revocable delegation rights, a tag owner would only use this trivial delegation for trusted entities under his control. On the contrary, when revocation is practicable and desirable, the tag's owner would provide a specially constructed agent clone, according to the protocol instructions. As soon as the delegation expires or is revoked, the clone would stop functioning and the delegated entity wouldn't be able to interact with the tag any longer, thus preserving backward security. The protocol, we present in Section 3, allows for temporal, revocable delegation.

2.2   Advantages

The perceived benefits of the agent-based platform include:

Support for heterogeneous tags: Since reader-tag interaction is supervised by agents, the back-end can be oblivious of the implementation details.

Simplified key management: Accordingly, all relevant actions are offloaded to the agent, minimizing the complexity of handling heterogeneous tags or tags having different security & privacy needs.

Facilitates ownership transfer and tag delegation: For implementations supporting such advanced features, the platform provides suitable agent clones, coupled with appropriate privacy policies, to manage information exposure. On the receiver's side, they offer the advantage of carrying the tag's implementation details; alleviating worries about introducing and integrating a foreign technology to his own platform. (Problems, such as code safety, must be dealt suitably before executing an alien agent.)

Support for fine grained S&P policies: In addition to any generic policies residing in the Repository, each agent carries his own, individual, S&P policy. Thus the owner can choose between enforcing a general one-for-all policy or applying specialized and elaborate policies on individual tags or tag groups. Such policies will also be able to govern reader devices and effectively restrain or permit access to important information.

Support for complex business logic: The proposed infrastructure, can be instructed to manipulate tags' data, according to the organization's needs, introducing automation in data gathering and data handling.

3   A Novel Suite of Lightweight RFID Management Protocols

In this section, we describe a suite of lightweight tag management protocols that can take advantage of the proposed agent-based infrastructure. The proposed protocols support tag operations, like authentication, delegation/revocation and ownership transfer, by satisfying at the same time important security and privacy requirements, such as data confidentiality and untraceability. While all the new protocols nicely fit the proposed agent-based infrastructure, they can, also, be used in more typical RFID systems, consisting of back-end databases, with trivial modifications.

3.1   Basic Protocols

The proposed suite supports tag delegation (by using time-based / temporal pseudonyms) and privacy preserving ownership transfer (with secret updating), while imposing limited hardware requirements. More specifically:

The tag must implement a secure one-way function $h(\cdot)$ and a pseudorandom number generator (random selection of an element from a finite set using a uniform probability distribution is denoted as $\in_\mathbb{R}$). In addition, the tag needs to store 3 values, namely an l-bit secret value *secret*, shared between the tag and the corresponding agent, a time-dependent tag identifier (TID) and a time value $(horizon)$, which designates a specific point in time and is publicly known. Time is an important concept in the delegation of the tag and it's representation, comforts to the ISO 8601 international standard [6].

Next, we describe the main suite protocols, namely *tag query, delegated tag query, secret updating* and *time horizon updating*. The delegated tag query protocol is of special significance, as it supports the delegation of a tag, by taking advantage of the new agent-based platform. In addition, this delegation is only temporal and it is automatically revoked after a given time period.

Tag Query

1. The reader sends to the tag: the ID of the reader's repository (Rep_ID), an l-bit random $nonce_A \in_\mathbb{R} \{0,1\}^l$ and the current time, c_time.
2. If c_time designates a point in time 'older than' $horizon$, then the tag replaces c_time with $horizon$. It generates a $nonce_B \in_\mathbb{R} \{0,1\}^l$ and computes a time-dependent identifier $TID_{c\_time} = h(Rep\_ID, secret, c\_time)$. Then it computes a pseudonym $Pseud = h(nonce_A, TID_{c\_time}, nonce_B)$, which is sent to the reader along with $nonce_B$.
3. The reader forwards the received values, along with $nonce_A$ and c_time to the Repository.
4. At the Repository, the freshness of the received c_time is checked against the clock; if a discrepancy is found, suitable actions, e.g. raising an alarm, take place. Further, each agent compares c_time to the stored $horizon$ value; and

if found older they replace it with *horizon*. Subsequently, every agent computes it's own time-depended ID ($TID'_{c\_time} = h(Rep\_ID, secret, c\_time)$) and then computes the pseudonym $Pseud' = h(nonce_A, TID'_{c\_time}, nonce_B)$ and compares it to the tag's (received) $Pseud$.

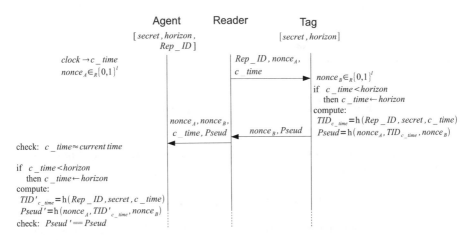

Fig. 3. Compact schematic of Tag Query

A match, signals the discovery of the correct agent. Having found the managing agent, the application can continue with its business process.

Delegated Tag Query: The protocol, depicted in Fig. 4, is identical to the Tag Query protocol, with one notable exception, a clone agent is used. The owner of the tag creates a delegation agent clone, *d_Agent*, and sends it to the 'temporary user' of the tag. The clone, does not store the secret value, but instead stores one fixed, time-dependent identifier $TID_{d\_time} = h(Rep\_ID, secret, d\_time)$ and the corresponding time value (*d_time*). The identifier is precomputed by the original managing agent, to be used by a specific Repository (*Rep_ID*), for the predetermined time period. The *d_Agent* can be used to track and locate the tag for as long as the horizon value, stored in the tag, is anterior or equal to *d_time*. Therefore, the tag owner can revoke the tag delegation, by updating the horizon with a posterior time value. As soon as the tag is updated with the Time Horizon Update protocol, the *d_Agent* clone becomes obsolete.

We deliberately have not enforced any additional checks on the freshness of the current time *c_time*. In the security analysis section the design choices will be justified in detail.

Tag Secret Update

1. Execute Tag Query protocol and if successful continue.

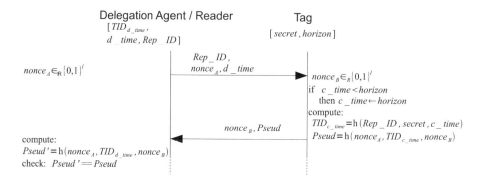

Fig. 4. Compact schematic of Delegated Tag Query

2. The agent chooses a new secret $(secret_{(new)})$, it generates a third $nonce_C \in_\mathbb{R}$ $\{0,1\}^l$ and computes a session key

$$session\_key = h(secret_{(old)} \oplus nonce_B, nonce_C).$$

It then XORs both $(NS = session\_key \oplus secret_{(new)})$ and calculates a checksum value $Scheck = h(secret_{(old)} \oplus nonce_C, secret_{(new)} \oplus nonce_B)$. It sends to the Reader all three values: $nonce_C, NS$ and $Scheck$.

3. The Reader forwards all three values to the Tag.

4. The Tag computes the session key

$$session\_key' = h(secret_{(old)} \oplus nonce_B, nonce_C),$$

extracts the new secret $(secret'_{(new)} = NS \oplus session\_key')$ and computes $Scheck' = h(secret_{(old)} \oplus nonce_C, secret'_{(new)} \oplus nonce_B)$. If the checksums match then it replaces the old secret with $secret'_{(new)}$.

5. The agent performs a Tag Query operations using $secret\_new$, if successful, the tag was updated and the agent's old secret is replaced with $secret\_new$.

Time Horizon Update

1. Execute Tag Query protocol and if successful continue.
2. The agent chooses the new horizon value, $horizon_{(new)}$, and computes a checksum value

$$NH = h(horizon_{(new)}, secret, nonce_B).$$

It sends both to the reader.

3. The Reader forwards both values to the Tag.
4. The Tag computes $NH' = h(horizon_{(new)}, secret, nonce_B)$ and checks if it is equal to the received NH. If yes, it replaces the existing $horizon_{(old)}$ value with $horizon_{(new)}$.

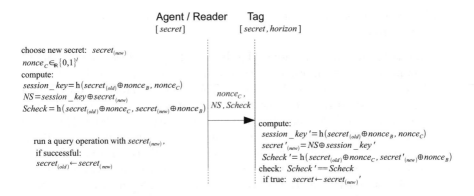

Fig. 5. Compact schematic of Tag's Secret Update

5. The agent performs a subsequent Tag Query operation, using a c_time value older than $horizon_{(new)}$. If the tag replies with a pseudonym generated using the value $TID_{horizon_{(new)}}$, we can be assured the horizon value was updated correctly.

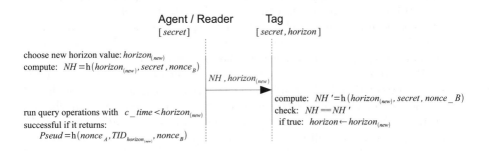

Fig. 6. Compact schematic of time Horizon Update

3.2 Security Analysis

Due to space constraints, we will concentrate on the delegated tag query protocol, since it is the one that mainly takes advantage of the new agent-based platform and, at the same time, is the most challenging one. The analysis of the other protocols is much easier and in most the cases the same arguments apply.

We have no illusions, about the security of the delegation agent. As soon as it leaves the trusted Repository, the new holder can manipulate it, in any way she wants, e.g. by stripping the d_Agent's logic and keeping only the data and TID_{d_time}. Therefore, implementing, in the clones' logic, freshness or any other kind of checks, beyond the one enforced by the TID, cannot increase security. The security of the protocol depends only on the security of the one-way function, the randomness of random generator and the size (l bits) of the secret values.

We enumerate some of the main privacy and security properties that the protocol satisfies, below:

1. **Tag Information Privacy:** The delegated agent clone contains only the minimum possible information concerning the tag, viz. all the information the temporary owner needs to know. The most crucial data concerning the tag, of course, is the secret key. However, by construction, only the values TID_{d_time} and d_time are stored in the delegated agent clone. Thus, even if the attacker acquires the clone, her gain (for instance by inverse engineering the clone agent's code) is limited to this values. Since the one-way function used is considered secure, the attacker cannot learn any extra information.

2. **Tag Location Privacy:** The responses of the tag are anonymous, since the tag emits, only, two messages, $nonce_B$ and $Pseud$, that differ, in a random way, every time a new query arrives. Thus, these messages cannot be linked to any particular tag.

3. **Tag Impersonation attack:** this attack is possible only if the tag is cloned. Otherwise, as analyzed above, the secret key can be computed only by inversing the hash function, which is computationally infeasible.

4. **Resilience to Replay attack:** The protocol is a typical challenge-response authentication protocol using random numbers to resist replay attacks.

5. **Resilience to locating a tag, using a revoked delegation agent clone:** this attack is considered successful when the attacker is able to locate a tag that has been previously delegated, even after the revocation of this delegation. There are two main concerns. The first has to do with the accuracy of the current time and the other with the temporary value TID_{d_time}.

   We have chosen to design the protocol in such a way that the accuracy of the current time is not critical. In other words, it is not expected that all entities will be truthful —to the extent of their clock accuracy— on what the current date and time is. To wit, lying about time doesn't affect the security of our protocol. We will now see why this holds:

   Assuming that the attacker has access to an old (revoked) agent clone. If she chooses to send any time value, older than the tag's *horizon*, the tag will reply with a random nonce and a pseudonym that depends on the *horizon* and the nonce. Given the security of the one-way function $h(\cdot)$, she won't be able to link it to the clone's TID_{d_time} value or distinguish it from a random value. If she sends a contemporary time value (equal or newer than *horizon*) the tag's reply will again appear random; even though now the pseudonym will depend on the nonce and the time value sent. Whats more, even if the attacker retrieves the value TID_{d_time} from the delegated agent, she won't be able to extract any further information concerning the tag.

4   Conclusions and Future Work

In this paper, we have briefly introduced an RFID system, based on software agents and agent cloning, in order to cope with interoperability problems, caused by the diversity of tag management protocols. In addition, we complemented, the said infrastructure, by describing a suite of novel lightweight tag management protocols that support, among others, secure and privacy preserving tag authentication, delegation and ownership transfer.

Future research work includes interesting issues, such as identifying suitable access control model and S&P policy language to enforce privacy on the agents and their clones. Since agents carry in their payload not only data, but also executable code, known solutions for safe code, such as signed code, code decoupling, runtime checking etc. need to be evaluated for suitability. Finally, the scalability of the proposed platform with increasing number of heterogeneous tags must be investigated.

References

1. Chen, R.S., Tu, M.A.: Development of an agent-based system for manufacturing control and coordination with ontology and rfid technology. Expert Syst. Appl. 36, 7581–7593 (2009), http://portal.acm.org/citation.cfm?id=1508324.1508647
2. Chow, H.K.H., Choy, K.L., Lee, W.B.: A dynamic logistics process knowledgebased system - an rfid multi-agent approach. Know.-Based Syst. 20(4), 357–372 (2007)
3. Dimitriou, T.: rfiddot: Rfid delegation and ownership transfer made simple. In: Proceedings of the 4th international conference on Security and privacy in communication networks, SecureComm '08, pp. 34:1–34:8. ACM, New York (2008) http://doi.acm.org/10.1145/1460877.1460921
4. Fischer-Hbner, S., Hedbom, H.: WP12: A holistic privacy framework for RFID applications: Future of IDentity in the information society. Deliverable D12.3, FIDIS consortium: Future of Identity in the Information Society (April 2008), http://www.fidis.net/resources/deliverables/hightechid/d123-a-holistic-privacy-framework-for-rfid-applications/doc/13/
5. Fouladgar, S., Afifi, H.: An efficient delegation and transfer of ownership protocol for RFID tags. In: First International EURASIP Workshop on RFID Technology, Vienna, Austria (September 2007)
6. ISO 8601:2004: Data elements and interchange formats – Information interchange – Representation of dates and times. ISO, Geneva, Switzerland (2004)
7. Jedermann, R., Behrens, C., Westphal, D., Lang, W.: Applying autonomous sensor systems in logistics–Combining sensor networks, RFIDs and software agents. Sensors and Actuators A: Physical 132(1), 370–375 (2006), http://www.sciencedirect.com/science/article/B6THG-4JG5FBT-4/2/2dd9c816f409137409e604c48b68db05
8. Koralalage, K.H., Reza, S.M., Miura, J., Goto, Y., Cheng, J.: POP method: An approach to enhance the security and privacy of RFID systems used in product lifecycle with an anonymous ownership transferring mechanism. In: Proceedings of the 2007 ACM symposium on Applied computing SAC'07, pp. 270–275. ACM, Seoul (2007), http://doi.acm.org/10.1145/1244002.1244069
9. Lim, C.H., Kwon, T.: Strong and robust RFID authentication enabling perfect ownership transfer. In: Ning, P., Qing, S., Li, N. (eds.) ICICS 2006. LNCS, vol. 4307, pp. 1–20. Springer, Heidelberg (2006)
10. Molnar, D., Soppera, A., Wagner, D.: Privacy for rfid through trusted computing. In: Proceedings of the 2005 ACM workshop on Privacy in the electronic society, WPES '05, pp. 31–34. ACM, New York (2005), http://doi.acm.org/10.1145/1102199.1102206

11. Molnar, D., Soppera, A., Wagner, D.: A scalable, delegatable pseudonym protocol enabling ownership transfer of RFID tags. In: Preneel, B., Tavares, S. (eds.) SAC 2005. LNCS, vol. 3897, pp. 276–290. Springer, Heidelberg (2006), http://www.springerlink.com/content/27344v3647u75803

12. OECD: Radio-Frequency identification (RFID): drivers, challenges and public policy considerations. Tech. Rep. DSTI/ICCP(2005)19/FINAL, Organisation for EconomicCo-operation and Development (OECD), Paris (March 2006), http://www.oecd.org/dataoecd/57/43/36323191.pdf

13. Osaka, K., Takagi, T., Yamazaki, K., Takahashi, O.: An efficient and secure RFID security method with ownership transfer. In: Wang, Y., Cheung, Y.-m., Liu, H. (eds.) CIS 2006. LNCS (LNAI), vol. 4456, pp. 778–787. Springer, Heidelberg (2007), http://portal.acm.org/citation.cfm?id=1417774&coll=&dl=

14. Rieback, M.R., Crispo, B., Tanenbaum, A.S.: Is your cat infected with a computer virus? In: PERCOM '06: Proceedings of the Fourth Annual IEEE International Conference on Pervasive Computing and Communications, March 2006, pp. 169–179. IEEE Computer Society Press, Pisa (2006)

15. Saito, J., Imamoto, K., Sakurai, K.: Reassignment scheme of an RFID tags key for owner transfer. In: Enokido, T., Yan, L., Xiao, B., Kim, D.Y., Dai, Y.-S., Yang, L.T. (eds.) EUC-WS 2005. LNCS, vol. 3823, pp. 1303–1312. Springer, Heidelberg (2005), http://dx.doi.org/10.1007/11596042_132

16. Song, B.: RFID tag ownership transfer. In: Conference on RFID Security. Budaperst, Hungary (July 2008)

17. Weis, S., Sarma, S., Rivest, R., Engels, D.: Security and privacy aspects of Low-Cost radio frequency identification systems. In: Hutter, D., Müller, G., Stephan, W., Ullmann, M. (eds.) Security in Pervasive Computing. LNCS, vol. 2802, pp. 454–469. Springer, Heidelberg (2004), http://www.springerlink.com/content/yvmfpkwc9nq6hqdw

Assessing the Usability of End-User Security Software

Tarik Ibrahim[1,2], Steven M. Furnell[1,3], Maria Papadaki[1], and Nathan L. Clarke[1,3]

[1] Centre for Security, Communications & Network Research, University of Plymouth, Plymouth, United Kingdom
[2] Department of Mathematics, Faculty of Science, Assiut University, Assiut, Egypt
[3] School of Computer and Security Science, Edith Cowan University, Perth, Western Australia
{tarik.ibrahim,steven.furnell,maria.papadaki,
nathan.clarke}@plymouth.ac.uk

Abstract. From a previous study we have determined that commercial security products can suffer from a usability perspective, lacking the necessary attention to design in relation to their alert interfaces. The aim of the paper is to assess the usability of alerts in some of the leading Internet security packages, based upon a related set of usability criteria. The findings reveal that the interface design combined with the user's relative lack of security knowledge are two major challenges that influence their decision making process. The analysis of the alert designs showed that four of the criteria are not addressed in any of the selected security measures and it would be desirable to consider the user's previous decisions on similar alerts, and modify alerts according to the user's previous behaviour.

Keywords: Security, Usability, Human Computer Interaction (HCI), Home Users, Intrusion Detection Systems, Security Software, Network Scanning.

1 Introduction

Until relatively recently, home users could rely upon basic anti-virus (AV) as a sufficient level of protection for their systems. However, with evidence suggesting that as much as 95% of Internet attacks are directed towards home users [1], AV alone is no longer enough to protect against the range of threats [2]. Therefore, the deployment of other advanced solutions such as Firewalls, Intrusion Detection Systems (IDS) and Intrusion Prevention Systems (IPS) becomes necessary. Meanwhile, the management and manipulation of these solutions may require a level of IT literacy and security knowledge that many home users may not possess. The findings of [3] validate the requirement for high skilled staff to mange IDS in organizations, and it can easily be recognized that home users will face more difficulty in this respect. In recent years, security vendors have moved towards integrated AV, firewall and IDS tools, which are commonly marketed as *Internet Security* solutions [4]. However, although the combination of tools can provide users with a convenient and comprehensive solution, this does not necessarily guarantee attention to improving the usability. Ibrahim et al. [5] proposed a set of novel Human Computer Interaction - Security (HCI-S) usability criteria and applied them to the evaluation of a typical alert raised by Norton 360. Even from a single example, this

S. Katsikas, J. Lopez, and M. Soriano (Eds.): TrustBus 2010, LNCS 6264, pp. 177–189, 2010.

served to highlight a number of potential usability issues, and was considered sufficient to justify a wider evaluation of other tools against the same criteria. The current paper therefore investigates and assesses the usability of alerts across a wider range of security software.

The rest of the paper is organized as follows: Section 2 provides a brief description of our pre-proposed HCI-S usability criteria for end-user security tools. Section 3 then describes the approach that was used to generate alerts within the different tools, in order to yield a basis for evaluation. Section 4 then analyses and assesses the usability of the resulting alerts according to the HCI-S usability criteria. Finally, Section 5 presents conclusions about the findings and future directions of the research.

2 Usability Criteria for End-User Security Tools

Many studies have considered criteria for Human Computer Interaction (HCI). For example, Nielsen [6], [7] proposed a set of usability heuristics that are widely accepted and adopted. However, while numerous studies have addressed the issues of HCI and IDS individually, relatively little has been done to combine HCI and security together, and there is still an opportunity to integrate and extend the research in both disciplines to better support end users. For instance, Johnston et al. [8] modified Nielson's criteria and proposed a new set of usability criteria for security interfaces designed for end-users, evaluated via an analysis of Windows XP's Internet Connection Firewall (ICF). From this basis and other related work, Ibrahim et al. [5] proposed a further set of HCI-S usability criteria addressing the interface design of security alerts issued to end-user. These criteria are listed and summarised as follows:

1. **Interfaces Design Matches User's Mental Model:** Alert designers should attempt to think as users to develop interfaces match their mental model.
2. **Aesthetic and Minimalist Design:** Irrelevant or rarely needed information should not be displayed in the security alert.
3. **Visibility of the Alert Detector Name:** The appearance of the security tool name, which triggers the alert, is useful, specially, with the existence of more than one installed security tool on the user's system.
4. **Establish Standard Colours to Attract User Attention:** In general, the use of red and yellow colours in security alert interfaces is fairly standard. The red indicates a high severity alert; while the (orange or yellow) indicates a low severity one.
5. **Use Icons as Visual Indicators:** Users are most often affected by the use of pictures and icons in the interfaces.
6. **Explicit Words to Classify the Security Risk Level:** The user requires written confirmation of the security risk level and that information must be obvious in the main alert interface, not hidden in a secondary interface.
7. **Consistent Meaningful Vocabulary and Terminology:** The alert sentence(s) should be simple, short and informative and the words used in these sentence(s) should be familiar to the user.
8. **Consistent Controls and Placement:** The *Allow* and *Block* buttons exists in some security alerts without providing the user with any insight about the impact

of this selection (e.g. the allowance or the blocking might be permanent or temporary).

9. **Learnability, Flexibility and Efficiency of Use:** The current criterion stresses the use of explanatory tooltips for concepts or security terms that appear in the alert to enhance the system flexibility, while providing links to a built-in library or/and an Internet web page, to increase the system efficiency.

10. **Take Advantage of Previous Security Decisions:** This criterion consists of two parts as follows: the user's own alert history (i.e. his previous responses to the alert) and community decisions (i.e. responses of other individuals to the alert).

11. **Online Security Policy Configuration:** Designers should develop an efficient default configuration for the security policy. The aim of the criterion is in guiding the user to adjust the security settings to avoid, if possible, any conflict between the intended primary tasks and the security configuration.

12. **Confirm / Recover the Impact of User Decision:** Sometimes, user errors are inevitable and vary from simple mistakes to dangerous errors. Therefore, the user should receive a confirmation message after performing any response, which will affect the security of the system.

13. **Awareness of System Status all the Time:** The user requires a simple report declaring the state of the system as a result of their response to the alert.

14. **Help Provision and Remote Technical Support:** The alert should be designed to let the users be self-sufficient; however, some novice users will still require further support. Tools should therefore provide built-in help and remote technical support.

15. **Offer Responses that Match User Expectations:** The actual impact of the available alert responses options does not always match the user's expectation. Therefore, good alert design is not only what is required to obtain a secure system but also to ensure the user's correct comprehension and understanding.

16. **Trust and Satisfaction:** Users' lack of understanding and/or inability to react correctly to alerts can strongly influence their resulting trust and/or satisfaction.

3 Assessing Security Tools Alerts

This section outlines the selection of the Internet Security tools against which the usability criteria were applied, along with the method by which the tools themselves were tested in order to generate the required security alerts. Having already identified Norton 360 during the earlier study, nine further Internet Security suites were selected to give a wider basis for evaluation. The selections were made on the basis of products recommended in a related review [9], plus the addition of products from F-Secure and Kaspersky (both popular options within the home and small business user communities). A further criterion was that each product should incorporate an intrusion detection or/and prevention capability (ensuring the ability to detect attacks against systems). The resulting list of tools was as follows (noting that free trial versions were used in some cases): BitDefender Internet Security 2009; CA Internet Security Suite Plus 2009; F-Secure Internet Security 2009; Kaspersky Internet Security 2009; McAfee Internet Security 2009; Norton 360 Version 2.0; Panda Internet Security 2009; Security Shield 2009; Trend Micro Internet Security Pro 2009; and Webroot Internet Security Essentials. The resulting set is considered to represent a representative sample of the available security tools. However, it should be noted that the aim of the evaluation (and indeed this paper) is not to identify the best product, but rather to determine the extent to which usability issues can be identified across a wider base of software.

Network scanning represents the initial step in many types of attacks [10]. Many tools can be used, for instance Nessus [11] and Nmap [12]. This study adopts the default profiles of Nmap command lines within Zenmap GUI [12] to investigate the design of the alert interfaces triggered as a consequence. The evaluation experiments were held in a closed test bed environment consisting of two computers running Windows XP. Scanning processes were performed from the attacker computer running Zenmap GUI against the victim computer running the candidate security products. Table 1 illustrates the Zenmap GUI profiles and the correspondence Nmap command lines that are tested.

Table 1. Zenmap GUI profiles and the associated Nmap command lines

	Zenmap GUI Profile	Nmap Command Line
1	Intense scan	nmap -PE -PA21,23,80,3389 -A -v -T4 192.168.x.x
2	Intense scan plus UDP	nmap -PE -v -PA21,23,80,3389 -sU -A -T4 192.168.x.x
3	Intense scan, all TCP ports	nmap -PE -v -p1-65535 -PA21,23,80,3389 -A -T4 192.168.x.x
4	Intense scan, no ping	nmap -A -v -PN -T4 192.168.x.x
5	Ping scan	nmap -PE -PA21,23,80,3389 -sP 192.168.x.x
6	Quick scan	nmap -T4 -F 192.168.x.x
7	Quick scan plus	nmap -T4 --version-light -sV -F -O 192.168.x.x
8	Quick traceroute	nmap -p22,23,25,80,3389 --traceroute -PN 192.168.x.x
9	Regular scan	nmap 192.168.x.x
10	Slow comprehensive scan	nmap -PE -v -PS21,22,23,25,80,113,31339 --script=all -PO -PA80,113,443,10042 -sU -PP -A -T4 192.168.x.x

4   Analysis of End-Users Security Alerts According to HCI-S Criteria

During the evaluation, alerts were generated by all of the tools apart from McAfee, which did not issue any visible responses to the scanning attempts (note: this is not to suggest that they were undetected, but rather that the user was not explicitly notified in real-time). However, the variety of alerts generated via the other products satisfies the aim of the study. The rest of the section focuses upon analyzing some key examples of these, according to the HCI-S usability criteria from [5]. Rather than commenting extensively against each tool, the discussion is structured according to the criteria headings, with examples being drawn from across the tools to illustrate significant issues.

4.1 Interfaces Design Matches User's Mental Model

Of the tools that explicitly notified the user of detecting a suspicious activity, all but Webroot's issued a response on behalf of the user. As shown in Fig. 1, Webroot's was the only alert that did not explicitly indicate whether the product had managed to handle the detected intrusion or not, nor give the user any further interaction options.

Fig. 1. Webroot's Internet Security Essentials alert interfaces

It is likely that alerts issued to users would be more usable through the occurrence of a user response sector in the bottom of the alert. For instance, Norton 360 (i.e. Fig. 2a) and Trend Micro are considered to be the only products that match the current criterion as they implicitly identified that the perceived intrusion access is blocked and present a user with *Allow* and *Block* options. Hence, the user has the benefit of both the automatic security response and the manual option to adjust and/or confirm the response. By contrast, Fig. 2b illustrates a different example of Norton's alert that does not match the current criterion because the alert does not include a description of the cause of the alert, or any links or tooltips to provide the user with more information.

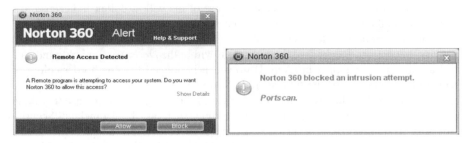

Fig. 2. Norton 360 intrusion alerts: (a) interactive (left) and (b) notification (right)

4.2 Aesthetic and Minimalist Design

In some cases alerts are too minimalist, with examples from Security Shield and BitDefender shown in Fig. 3. In these cases the source of the intrusion should be identified to the novice in a more meaningful manner (as they are unlikely to be greatly informed by the IP address), whereas more informed users may be interested in additional options (such as the opportunity to suppress further notifications).

Fig. 3. Security Shield & BitDefender alerts interfaces

4.3 Visibility of the Alert Detector Name

With the exception of Webroot, all of the security tools provide the name of the detector in the head of their alert interfaces. Instead of indicating the name of the product suite (i.e. the thing that the user may most likely recall installing or recognise that they are running), Webroot's alert is attributed to the firewall, as shown in Fig. 1. Of course, many of the Internet security suites consist of integrated security solutions based on underlying components such as anti-virus, anti-spyware and firewall, and so it is perhaps not surprising that alerts appear under the name of these components rather than that of the wider suite. However, it would still be useful for the vendor name to appear so that the user has a basis for making the association back to the product they recognise. The problem with the anonymous alerts shown in Fig. 1 is that the user may wonder if they were caused by something else (e.g. by the Windows firewall or faked by malware).

4.4 Establish Standard Colours to Attract User Attention

The use of standard colours to express information to users in a simple and rapid way should be considered and addressed better to improve the design of alerts. With the exception of the traffic light colours, there are almost no other standard colours to represent the alert severity. Therefore, most likely, the use of the green colour indicates that the system status is secure, the use of the yellow colour indicates a low risk level and the red colour indicates a high risk level. For instance, Norton 360 and F-Secure used yellow in the exclamation icon to indicate the risk level of the detected activity. In contrast, Panda used the red colour within the *No Entry* symbol to indicate that an intrusion attempt is blocked. However, it is noticed that the border colour of most of the studied alerts are blue apart of Norton and Webroot's that are yellow and green, respectively. The use of the blue border could be significant in case that these products are adapting a standard colour-coding such as the Homeland Security Advisory System (HSAS), where a wider range of colours are adopted (i.e. green, blue, yellow, orange, or red) to determine the severity of the threat level [13]. Finally, it is arguable that Webroot's use of the green colour provides a false secure impression to the user. Therefore, it is recommended to design alerts that have an appropriate border colour as an indicator to the threat level, and to avoid insignificant and misleading ones.

4.5 Use Icons as Visual Indicators

The use of icons as visual indicators should be essential, relevant and significant. Likely, users receive the primary alert message through the colours and icons. For instance, F-Secure and Norton 360 (i.e. Fig. 2a) use an exclamation mark icon as a visual indicator to indicate an intrusion attempt. Most likely, the yellow colour used within the icons indicates a low threat level. Unlike F-secure, Norton 360 alert confirms that indication explicitly through assigning *Risk Level: Low* within a complementary interface. Meanwhile, Panda uses the *No Entry* symbol aligned with a padlock icon, as shown in Fig. 4, to indicate that an intrusion attempt is detected and blocked. However, it is suggested to deploy appropriate icons that does not contradict criterion 4, *Establish Standard Colours to Attract User Attention*. Furthermore, Panda is the only product that uses two methods for deploying icons in the alert as an information mark icon is placed next to the technical term *Denial of Service* to indicate that there is more information available if required. The use of this icon is relevant and it would be more usable if the icon colour was more visible.

Fig. 4. Panda Internet Security 2009 alert interfaces and tooltips

4.6 Explicit Words to Classify the Security Risk Level

This criterion identifies one of the remarkable limitations within the design of the studied alerts. With the exception of Norton and Trend Micro, none of the evaluated products explicitly classify the security risk level. Norton 360 (i.e. Fig. 2a) determined the security risk level as *Risk Level: Low* in a complementary interface through clicking *Show Details*. In contrast, Trend Micro is more explicit by determining the security risk level in the main alert as *Risk: Safe*. However, assigning the risk to be *Safe* raises a question of the benefit of issuing the alert in the first place. From the usability perspective, addressing the optimal location for assigning the security risk level is required. Therefore, it is recommended to present the risk level explicitly in the alert main interface, and then offer the associated reason for assigning this classification within a secondary interface.

4.7 Consistent Meaningful Vocabulary and Terminology

In general, the sentence(s) in most of the security alerts are simple and short, but there is no guarantee that these words are familiar to the user. For instance, Panda used the term *Denial of Service* aligned with a tooltip, but the provided information is neither a description nor a definition for the technical term. As most of the products make security decisions on behalf of the user, the user's main concern is likely to be whether the product has managed to deal with the problem or not. For instance, the words *denied* and *protected* are used to describe the product's response, but the most dominant word is *blocked* (as in *Intrusion attempt blocked!*). However, locating this sentence at the top, as shown in Fig. 4 , would satisfy some novice users who might decide not to run through the rest of the alert. In contrast, BitDefender and Security Shield use the sentence *Your computer has been protected!* to emphasize that the product had successfully protected the user from a threat, but the location of the sentence is at the bottom. Finally, it was found that the terminology within the alerts that requires user interaction such as Trend Micro's and Norton 360 (i.e.Fig. 2a), does not impede the user from making a security decision.

4.8 Consistent Controls and Placement

Most of the alerts do not supply users with explicit control features. Meanwhile, F-Secure provides buttons that enable the user to investigate the alert. In contrast, Norton 360 (i.e.Fig. 2a) and Trend Micro alerts consist of (*Allow* and *Block*) buttons located at the bottom of the alert interface. Most likely, this location is appropriate as the user reaches the buttons after running out through the alert. The main limitation of these buttons is that there is no indication of whether the impact of the user action is temporary or permanent. One solution could be appending another two buttons and explicitly defining the impact on the buttons such as *Allow Once* and *Allow Always.*

4.9   Learnability, Flexibility and Efficiency of Use

The use of explanatory tooltips for concepts that appears in the alert and/or the adoption of links to Internet web pages are rare among the evaluated alerts. For instance, Panda interfaces from Fig. 4 include the terms *Port scan* and *Denial of Service*, both of them are linked with explanatory tooltips but neither of them provides detailed information of the nature of the attack. instead, they determine the protocol, the remote IP address and the ports used in the attack. Furthermore, Kaspersky includes a *View report* link, but the report does not provide the user with extra information and only includes the same information of the main alert in a more organized style. The alerts of Kaspersky and Panda share the same feature of having a drop list in the title bar at the top-right of the alert, Panda's list consist of two elements, *Help* and *Non-serious message settings,* with the *Help* option guiding the user to access a general built-in help and its introductory interface explains that the intrusion attempt is blocked via the built-in firewall. Therefore, relocating these features from the drop list to a better location within the alert interface (such as the bottom of the alert) would be more visible and useful.

4.10   Take Advantage of Previous Security Decisions

While all of the previous criteria were addressed by at least some of the evaluated security alerts, none of the products explicitly enabled users to leverage previous decisions to help them cope with the current alert. Therefore, the focus is upon assessing the alerts that required the user interaction such as Trend Micro's and Norton 360 (i.e. Fig. 2a). These products do not impede the user from making a security decision as the products already perform a blocking decision, identify the security risk level and provide response buttons. The novice user who does not have an experience with the cause of the present alert and does not have any further advice to call upon might find it more secure to implement the alert default response as these products did not specify any explicit recommendation to follow, such as accompanying the *Block* button with the word (recommended).Therefore, it is worth establishing an alert history that stores the user's previous decisions, to provide a source of reference if a similar alert arises in the future. Furthermore, it is suggested that the use of the social navigation method [14], would enrich the alert and to some extent support the user. Social navigation is considered to be a promising method in guiding novice users to make security decisions based on relevant individual decisions from those who have previously encountered similar alerts in their own environments.

4.11   Online Security Policy Configuration

This criterion is interested with integrating security policy features within the design of the alert itself. There are some attempts to provide this feature within some of the evaluated security products. For instance, CA and F-Secure provide a check box alongside text; *Don't show this alert dialog again.* Meanwhile, Trend Micro is more specific and uses a check box alongside the text; *Stop warning about this program,* and. since the program name occurs in the main alert, it would be clear that the user's decision affects only future events involving this program whatever the source IP address is, while in the previous instance it is not clear whether the decision would affect the program, the IP address, the port, or all the alerts. Another advantage of Trend Micro is that the check box is ticked by default as an explicit recommendation to the novice user. In contrast, Panda and Kaspersky adopt a different type of online configuration by providing a drop list. Panda list contains the *Non-serious message settings* option which allows adjustment of alerts. While, Kaspersky provides the options *Disable this notification, Disable all notifications* and *Settings...,* the impact of the first option is unexplained to the user. As such, they may be unclear about whether the impact of selecting this option is to disable the future similar alerts (i.e. with the same details), to disable all alerts associated with the same type of attack regardless of the source, or to perform some other action. The previous examples are not the expected level of online security policy configuration and need to be enhanced as the exact impact of some options were not completely clear and some other options were irrelevant (i.e. related to configuring other types of notifications that are not linked to the current alert) which overloads the user with unnecessary secondary security issues at an inappropriate time. However, they are the only available examples in this study and one suggestion to satisfy this criterion is to provide an option to avoid frequent triggering of low-level alerts.

4.12   Confirm / Recover the Impact of User Decision

Confirming and recovering the impact of users' decisions is the second HCI-S usability criterion that is not addressed amongst the evaluated products. The absence of this criterion is illustrated by assessing Norton 360 (i.e. Fig. 2a) and Trend Micro, which provide control buttons that implement user's responses immediately without warning or reminding the user of the response impact, neither before nor after making the decision. Furthermore, there is no obvious method that informs the user of how to recover from wrong or inappropriate decisions. It is suggested that the security product should request additional confirmation, if the user overrides the recommended option. The objective of the message is to display the user's current decision and the perceived impact, and whether the user prefers to proceed accomplishing the decision or return back to the main alert interface to alter the response. However, the current suggestion combines both the benefit of confirming the user decision and a primary recovery method. Moreover, in some cases the user might perform inappropriate decision that affects the functionality of their intended tasks. Therefore, developing usable methods to recover from undesired decisions is a requirement. A suggested solution is to make benefit of criterion 10, *Take Advantage of Previous Security Decisions*, where all the previous user decisions are stored and then recalled when required. Hence, the user could access the recently issued alerts and the corresponding decisions, and attempt to change a previous decision if possible (e.g. if the user subsequently wishes to allow a program that was previously blocked by mistake). Finally, the product can make use from criterion 4, *Establish Standard Colours to Attract User Attention*, and decrease the possibility of the recovery situations by appending a green border around the recommended response button.

4.13 Awareness of System Status All the Time

This is the third criterion that is not fully addressed through the evaluated products. Most likely, users who installed security measures within their personal computers presume that the security situation is under control and there is no need to worry until they receive a security alert. When that happens, most of the evaluated security alerts declare that an intrusion attempt is detected and blocked. Hence, this is the type of awareness of the system status that these products provide to the user who will subsequently believe that he is protected. Meanwhile, as mentioned earlier, the McAfee product did not issue any alert during the evaluation, even though that the logs confirmed that it managed to detect the incoming traffic from the attacker computer. Hence, the user is not aware of the system status based on McAfee security policy. Furthermore, it is noticed that some products, such as Security Shield and BitDefender, display alerts that disappear quickly without the user's permission. Hence, there is a high possibility that the users would not notice the occurrence of the threat, especially if they were not looking at the screen at the time. If it is considered acceptable for users to miss them, then it questions the necessity of displaying the alerts in the first place. In contrast, Norton 360 (i.e. Fig. 2a) and Trend Micro, which provide a response capability, do not inform the user with the impact of the response issued by the user. The user ought to receive a message informing him about the real impact and the consequences of his response. Therefore, the awareness of the system status all the time is not available. For instance, if the user decided to use criterion 11, *Online Security Policy Configuration*, and disabled the appearance of all alerts, it would be useful to get the product icon in the notification area to produce yellow, orange, red pulses as the occurrence of low, medium, red security risk levels, respectively.

4.14 Help Provision and Remote Technical Support

The alerts generated by most of the tools do not need help or remote technical support; not because of their completeness, but because of the lack of user decision responsibility. Meanwhile, Panda and F-Secure provide a built-in help which might be useful to enhance user knowledge but it does not support the user response since there are not any response controls in the alert interface. In addition, as mentioned earlier, the location of Panda *Help* is not appropriate since it is embedded in a drop-down list. CA's product uses the question mark icon as a visual indicator aligned with a *Help* link to attract the user but the link provides no specific information relevant to the present alert. The assessment of Norton 360 (i.e. Fig. 2a) and Trend Micro - the two products that provide control features - reveals that no help or remote support is provided within Trend Micro apart from *Risk: Safe*. In contrast, Norton 360 is considered to be the only product that satisfies the criterion, as it provides a variety of help provision and remote support to the user. From a usability perspective, the main limitation is in the location of the options. For further details, an extensive discussion of Norton 360 is available within [5].

4.15   Offer Responses That Match User Expectations

This is the final criterion that is not fully addressed through the evaluated products. Firstly, most tools in the evaluation do not provide a user response component in the alert interface. Arguably, a portion of users would find it appropriate to have response options within the alert design. Secondly, Norton 360 (i.e. Fig. 2a) and Trend Micro are the only products that satisfy this feature and the assessment of the generated alerts reveals that there is no obvious method provided for the user to assess whether the response matches their expectation or not. Those users who have the privilege to respond to the alert perform their actions based upon their individual understanding. It is suggested to raise an explicit message after the user response to identify the real impact of the response. Hence, the user will be able to determine whether the response has achieved what they expected.

4.16   Trust and Satisfaction

In all likelihood, security products that managed to address most of the former HCI-S usability criteria are also able to satisfy and obtain the trust of users. Looking at specific factors that may improve this potential, we can consider whether the user is likely to feel they are getting the extent of information and feedback that seems convincing. For example, the design of the security alerts of Norton 360 and F-secure provide users with a level of satisfaction because of the amount of relevant information they attempt to provide. For instance, the main interface of F-Secure provides a *Details* button that lets the user access more information about the cause of the alert, and then onwards to access the alert logs via a *Show Alert Log* option.

4.17   Summary Results

Table 2 summarizes the findings across the full set of tools and criteria (note that because Norton 360 generated two types of alerts the associated results column sometimes presents differing results, with the first relating to the alert represented in Fig. 2a and the other relating to Fig. 2b). The findings reveal a remarkable limitation is that choosing the *High* setting of the firewall alerts within the CA product bombards the user with hundreds of alerts (up to a maximum of 500). Most likely, the user will dismiss these alerts instead of suspending the intended task to investigate the massive amount of alerts. From a usability perspective, it is impractical to overwhelm the user, in one second, with this amount of alerts specially that they only vary in detailed information of hundreds of local and remote ports used during the penetration. From the usability perspective, although the use of the *Show Details* link within Norton 360 (i.e. Fig. 2a) is usable, it would be preferable to avoid using the vertical scroll bar within the interface. Finally, the paper demonstrated to what extent the HCI-S usability criteria are addressed through the evaluation of collection of users security products. The findings reveal the strength and the weakness within the design of the issued alerts and some primary solutions are suggested as an attempt to resolve these weakness. It is anticipated that integrating the adequate features of the evaluated alerts, avoiding their limitations, and implementing the unaddressed HCI-S usability criteria, will enhance the design and make it more usable.

Table 2. The usability aspects of end-user security software

No	Novel Criteria	BitDefender	CA	F-Secure	Kaspersky	Norton	Panda	Security Shield	Trend Micro	Webroot
1	Design Interfaces Match User Mental Model	✗	✗	✗	✗	✓✗	✗	✗	✓	✗
2	Aesthetic and Minimalist Design	✗	✓	✓	✗	✓✗	✓	✗	✓	✗
3	Visibility of the Alert Detector Name	✓	✓	✓	✓	✓	✓	✓	✓	✗
4	Establish Standard Colours to Attract User Attention	✗	✗	✓	✗	✓	✓	✗	✗	✗
5	Use Icons as Visual Indicators	✓	✗	✓	✗	✓	✓	✓	✗	✗
6	Explicit Words to Classify the Security Risk Level	✗	✗	✗	✗	✓✗	✗	✗	✓	✗
7	Consistent Meaningful Vocabulary and Terminology*	✓	✗	✓	✓	✓	✓	✓	✓	✓
8	Consistent Controls and Placement	✗	✗	✗	✗	✓✗	✗	✗	✓	✗
9	Learnability, Flexibility and Efficiency of Use	✗	✗	✓	✓	✓✗	✓	✗	✓	✗
10	Take Advantage of Previous Security Decisions	✗	✗	✗	✗	✗	✗	✗	✗	✗
11	Online Security Policy Configuration	✗	✓	✓	✓	✗	✓	✗	✓	✗
12	Confirm / Recover the Impact of User Decision	✗	✗	✗	✗	✗	✗	✗	✗	✗
13	Awareness of System Status all the Time	✗	✗	✗	✗	✗	✗	✗	✗	✗
14	Help Provision and Remote Technical Support	✗	✗	✗	✗	✓✗	✗	✗	✗	✗
15	Offer Responses Match Expectations	✗	✗	✗	✗	✗	✗	✗	✗	✗
16	Trust and Satisfaction	✗	✗	✓	✗	✓	✗	✗	✗	✗

* With the exception of the terminology that requires the assistant and the adoption of criterion 9 in some instances, the current criterion is rated according to the meaningful vocabulary to the end-user.

5 Conclusions

This paper investigated the usability of security alerts issued via a range of security products. The analysis showed that four of the HCI-S usability criteria (10, 12, 13, 15) are not addressed in any of the selected security measures. Specifically, none of the evaluated tools address criterion 10, to Take Advantage of Previous Security Decisions. Therefore, it would be desirable to leverage previous decisions on similar alerts, and modify alerts accordingly to account for the user's previous behaviour. For example, if the user has consistently overridden the recommended option in a particular alert, the system can change the default option to their previous choice, or offer them the option to repeat their decision in future without the need for an alert. In order to give this level of flexibility, it is important to enable users to make informed decisions and recover from them if needed. Therefore, it is important to address criteria 12, 13, 15 as well (namely Confirm / Recover the Impact of User Decision, Awareness of System Status all the Time, and Offer Responses Match Expectations). Future work will focus on addressing these missing criteria and increasing the end-user's opportunity to customize the security measure.

References

1. Symantec: Symantec Internet Security Threat Report. Trends for January 07 – June 07, Symantec Enterprise Security, vol. XII (September 2007)
2. House of Lords. Science and Technology Committee. 5th Report of Session 2006–07. Personal Internet Security. United Kingdom Parliament. HL Paper 165–I. London: The Stationery Limited,
   `http://www.parliament.the-stationery-office.co.uk/pa/` `ld200607/ldselect/ldsctech/165/165i.pdf` (accessed: 15/11/2009)
3. Ibrahim, T., Furnell, S.M., Papadaki, M., Clarke, N.L.: Assessing the Challenges of Intrusion Detection Systems. In: Proceedings of the 7th Annual Security Conference. Las Vegas, USA (June 2-3, 2008)
4. Lai, K., Wren, D.: Antivirus, Internet Security and Total Security Performance Benchmarking,
   `http://www.passmark.com/ftp/antivirus_09-` `performance-testing-ed1.pdf`
5. Ibrahim, T., Furnell, S.M., Papadaki, M., Clarke, N.L.: Assessing the Usability of Personal Internet Security Tools. In: Proceedings of the 8th European Conference on Information Warfare and Security (ECIW 2009), Military Academy, Lisbon & the University of Minho, Braga, Portugal (July 6-7, 2009)
6. Nielsen, J.: Enhancing the explanatory power of usability heuristics. In: Proceedings of ACM CHI'94 Conference, Boston, Massachusetts, USA, April 24-28, pp. 152–158 (1994)
7. Nielsen, J.: Ten usability heuristics,
   `http://www.useit.com/papers/heuristic/` `heuristic_list.html` (accessed: 14/12/2008)
8. Johnston, J., Eloff, J.H.P., Labuschagne, L.: Security and human computer interfaces. Computers & Security 22(8), 675–684 (2003)
9. Top Security Software, `http://www.2009securitysoftwarereviews.com` (accessed: 26/01/2009)
10. Barnett, R.J., Irwin, B.: Towards a Taxonomy of Network Scanning Techniques. In: Proceedings of the 2008 Annual Research Conference of the South African Institute of Computer Scientists and Information Technologists on IT Research in Developing Countries: Riding the Wave of technology (SAICSIT '08), Wilderness, South Africa, October 6-8, pp. 1–7 (2008)
11. Nessus. The Network Vulnerability Scanner, `http://www.nessus.org` (accessed: 26/01/2009)
12. Nmap. Nmap Security Scanner,
    `http://insecure.org/nmap` (accessed: 26/01/2009)
13. Siraj, A., Vaughn, R.: A Dynamic Fusion Approach for Security Situation Assessment. In: Proceedings of the Fourth IASTED International Conference on Communication, Network, and Information Security (CNIS 2007), Berkeley, California (September 24-26, 2007)
14. Chiasson, S., van Oorschot, P.C., Biddle, R.: Even experts deserve usable security: Design guidelines for security management systems. In: Proceedings of Symposium on Usable Privacy and Security (SOUPS '07), Pittsburgh, PA, July 18-20 (2007)

Building ISMS through the Reuse of Knowledge

Luis Enrique Sánchez[1], Antonio Santos-Olmo[1],
Eduardo Fernández-Medina[2], and Mario Piattini[3]

[1] Departament R&D, Sicaman Nuevas Tecnologias, Juan José Rodrigo 4,
13700 Tomelloso, Spain
[2] Rearch GSyA Group, University of Castilla-La Mancha, Paseo de la Universidad 4,
13071 Ciudad Real, Spain
[3] Rearch Alarcos Group, University of Castilla-La Mancha, Paseo de la Universidad 4,
13071 Ciudad Real, Spain
{Lesanchez,Asolmo}@sicaman-nt.com,
Eduardo.FdezMedina@uclm.es,
Mario.Piattini@uclm.es

Abstract. The information society is increasingly more dependent upon Information Security Management Systems (ISMSs), and the availability of these systems has become crucial to the evolution of Small and Medium-size Enterprises (SMEs). However, this type of companies requires ISMSs which have been adapted to their specific characteristics. In this paper we show the strategy that we have designed for the management and reuse of security information in the information system security management process. This strategy is set within the framework of a methodology that we have designed for the integral management of information system security and maturity, denominated as "Methodology for Security Management and Maturity in Small and Medium-sized Enterprises (MSM2-SME)". This model is currently being applied in real cases, and is thus constantly improving.

Keywords: ISMS, ISO27001, Security Knowledge Reuse, Pattern, SME.

1 Introduction

It is extremely important for enterprises to introduce security controls which will allow them to discover and to control the risks that they may be confronted with [1-3]. However, the introduction of these controls is not sufficient, and systems which manage security in the long term, thus permitting a swift reaction to new risks, vulnerabilities and threats are also necessary [4, 5]. Unfortunately, the current companies often do not have security management systems, or those which do exist have been created without the appropriate guidelines or documentation, and with insufficient resources [6, 7].

Therefore, in spite of the fact that real-life has shown that for a business to be able to use information technology and communication with guarantees it needs to have at its disposal guidelines, measures and tools which will allow it to know at all times both the level of its security and those vulnerabilities which have not been covered

S. Katsikas, J. Lopez, and M. Soriano (Eds.): TrustBus 2010, LNCS 6264, pp. 190–201, 2010.

[8], the level of successful deployment of these systems is, in reality, very low. This problem is particularly accentuated in the case of SMEs, which have the additional limitation of not having sufficient human and economic resources to be able to carry out an appropriate management [7].

Therefore, and taking into consideration the fact that SMEs represent the vast majority of enterprises, both at a national and at an international level, and are extremely important to business as a whole, we believe that advances in knowledge reuse oriented research to improve security management for this type of enterprises, may make important contributions in this area, and may contribute not only towards improving the security in SMEs, but also towards improving their level of competitiveness. In recent years we have, therefore, created a methodology (MSM2-SME) for security management and for the establishment of a security maturity level in SMEs' information systems [9-12]. We have also developed a tool that completely automates this methodology [13], which has been applied in real cases [14], and which has allowed us to evaluate the methodology, the tool, and the improvement effects produced by knowledge reuse provided by this tool.

We have paid particular attention to the methodology's capacity for knowledge reuse through the definition of reusable patterns, which are a complete parametrizable configuration that permit the immediate implantation of ISMSs in businesses, taking advantage of the knowledge obtained in the previous implantation of other ISMSs in companies that share similar structural characteristics (business sector and size). In order to validate this methodology we have recently created a single pattern denominated as "Root Pattern" with the intention of it being as generic as possible in order for it to serve as a basis from which to create new more specific patterns. Our objective is to create a pattern for each business sector, which will be obtained from the NACE code (The European standard of industry classification), and the experience of applying this methodology will, therefore, increase with each pattern. This signifies that the implementation of the ISMSs (in each business sector) will be progressively more precise, more economic and faster. We can therefore conclude that the principal contribution of this paper centres on presenting the elements of which the GSMP (Generation of Security Management Patterns) process in the MSM2-SME methodology is composed [14-16]. This process is entrusted with the generation of patterns, and a first pattern, denominated as the "Root Pattern", will serve as a basis for the generation of other patterns.

The paper continues in Section 2, which briefly describes the existing security management methodologies and models and their current tendencies. In Section 3 a brief introduction to our proposal for a security management methodology oriented towards SMEs is provided. In Section 4 we concentrate on knowledge reuse patterns and the activities which permit them to be generated. Finally, in Section 5 we present our conclusions and future work.

2   Related Work

Attempts to reduce the lacks that ISMSs have been shown to have in businesses, and the losses that they cause, have led to the appearance of a large number of processes [17] and information security frameworks and methods [18], whose need for implantation is being increasingly recognised and considered by organizations but, as has been shown, are inefficient in the case of SMEs [19] and do not take into consideration aspects which are, from our point of view, fundamental, such as knowledge reuse.

With regard to the most prominent standards, it is possible to state that the majority of security management models have taken the ISO/IEC17799 and ISO/IEC27002 international standards as their basis, and that the security management models which are most successful in large companies are ISO/IEC27001, COBIT and ISM3, but that they are very difficult to implement and require too high an investment for the majority of SMEs [20]. This is owing to the fact that they are oriented towards large companies, and aspects such as knowledge reuse, which are fundamental to SMEs in that they reduce the cost of instalment and maintenance in these types of systems, take second place.

Numerous bibliographic sources detect and highlight the difficulty that SMEs confront with the use of traditional security management methodologies and maturity models which were conceived for use in large enterprises [21-24]. It is repeatedly justified that the application of this type of methodology and maturity models to SMEs is difficult and costly. Moreover, organisations, including those which are large, have a greater tendency towards adopting groups of processes which are related as a set rather than dealing with processes independently [25].

The aforementioned methodologies and security management models have not proved to be valid in SMEs for three reasons:

- They tackle only part of the security management system and almost none of them tackle the deployment of these systems from a global perspective, which thus obliges companies to acquire, implement, manage and maintain various methodologies, models and tools to manage their security.
- We can conclude that although various standards, regulations, guides to good practices, methodologies, and security management and risk analysis models exist, they are not integrated into a global model which can be applied to small and medium-sized enterprises with a guarantee of success.
- And what is most important, none of them centre on knowledge reuse which, according to our research, is fundamental if viability is to be guaranteed not only during the ISMS installation phase but also during its lifecycle.

Therefore, and to conclude this sub-section, it could be said that it is pertinent and opportune to tackle the problem of developing a new methodology for the management of security and its maturity for information systems in SMEs. This methodology must be capable of reusing the knowledge acquired in previous instalments, and have the objective of making large reductions in costs which would make the installation of ISMSs in SMEs viable.

3 MSM2-SME Overview

The methodology for the management of security and its maturity in SMEs that we have developed will allow any organisation to manage, evaluate and measure the security of its information systems, but is oriented mainly towards SMEs, since it is these organisations which have the highest level of failure in the deployment of existing security management methodologies.

One of the desired objectives of the MSM2-SME methodology was that it will be easy to apply, and that the model developed on it will permit the greatest possible level of automation and reusability to be obtained with a minimum amount of information collected in a greatly reduced time. To do this, during the development of this methodology priority has been given to the search for solutions that will permit a high resolution of the reuse of knowledge acquired in previous installations, with the objective of making significant reductions in costs and obtaining better results in general, at the expense of a slight reduction in the precision obtained, but always ensuring that the results will be of a sufficiently high quality.

Knowledge reuse is achieved through a structure of matrices which allow us to relate the various ISMS components (controls, actives, threats, vulnerabilities and risk criteria) that the model will use to generate a considerable part of the necessary information, thus notably reducing the time needed to deploy and develop the ISMS.

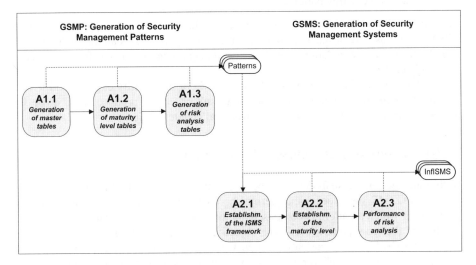

Fig. 1. The sub-processes of the methodology

The entire weight of the knowledge reuse process falls on the first of the two sub-processes of which the MSM2-SME methodology is composed. Figure 1 shows details of these sub-processes and the activities of which they are composed. Each of these sub-processes will be briefly analysed below:

- GSMP – Generation of Security Management Patterns: The principal objective of this sub-process is to create the structures that are necessary to store the knowledge obtained from different instalments with the objective of being able to reuse it in future instalments, thus obtaining great advantages. These structures will contain reusable patterns, and will permit both the time needed to create the ISMS and the maintenance costs to be reduced, signifying that they are suitable for the dimensions of an SME. The use of patterns is of special interest in the case of SMEs since their special characteristics tend to mean that they have simple information systems which are very similar to each other.

Each pattern will contain the knowledge obtained during the installation of an ISMS in a company, and will be suitable for reuse by companies with similar structural characteristics.

When tackling the construction of an ISMS, the company must determine whether it can reuse any of its existing patterns. If the situation arises that it is not possible to totally adapt a pattern to another company because it has certain specific characteristics, this pattern can be reused and later refined to adapt it to its special casuistry. And if a pattern exists which can be totally adapted to its characteristics it will not be necessary to use this methodology process, which will suppose an enormous reduction in costs for the SME when generating the ISMS.

- GSMS – Generation of Security Management Systems: The main objective of this sub-process is to create a suitable ISMS for a company by using an already existing pattern.

The methodology's most complex sub-process is the generation of a pattern (GSMP), which is why as part of our research we have developed a first pattern, denominated rRPSM (root Reusable Pattern for Security Management) from which new patterns can be developed.

The generation of new patterns will be carried out by security experts, and it will create enormous reductions in cost that other sub-processes produce since it can be reused by other companies with similar structural characteristics.

4   Generation of Patterns and Root Pattern

In this sub-section we shall describe the different activities in the MSM2-SME methodology's GSMP sub-process that permit the creation of new patterns, analysing the elements of which a pattern is composed and the standards and regulations used in the creation of the "root pattern", with the objective of guaranteeing good quality results. Finally we shall show three sub-sections with some of the most characteristic elements of the "root pattern" in relation to their maturity levels, procedures and profiles.

During our research, in which we used the research in action method [26, 27], we obtained a first pattern by using the knowledge acquired in various installations. In this first pattern, denominated rRPSM, we introduced the common characteristics detected principally in SMEs in which we had made installations using our methodology. We therefore consider that rRPSM contains a first valid pattern from which new refined patterns can be derived, with the objective of applying them in groups of companies with common structural characteristics, in order to successively obtain more precision without incrementing the cost of process generation and installation of the ISMS. The rRPSM was obtained by using the knowledge of a group of domain experts. It was later refined through the application of the methodology with various clients from the SNT2[1] company.

As Figure 2 shows, a pattern contains all the elements that are necessary to generate an ISMS and the relationships that can be established between them. One fundamental aspect for which the results of the methodology are suitable is that the root

---

[1] SNT is a technology company specializing in security consulting for ICT.

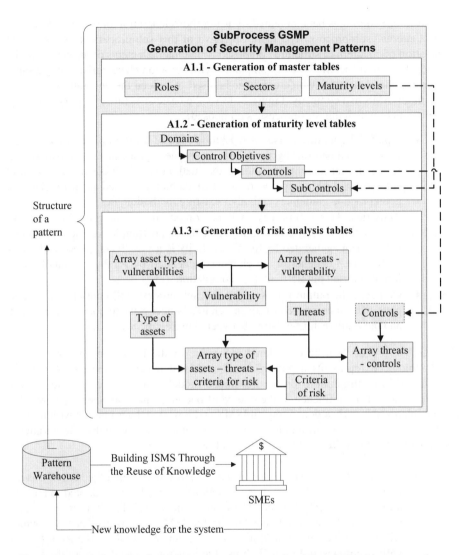

Fig. 2. Principal elements of which a pattern is composed and the relationships among them

pattern or origin pattern from which the remaining patterns are derived has been created from a solid base. To do this, the creation of the root pattern in the MSM2-SME methodology has always been based on internationally recognized standards and regulations which will guarantee its validity.

The main objective of this pattern is that it will serve as a starting point to create new more specific patterns (for concrete sectors and company-sizes) in such a way that the generation of new patterns can be carried out by taking the Root Pattern as a reference, cloning it (copying the structure of pattern A onto pattern B) and then carrying out the appropriate modifications to adapt it to a specific type of company.

The Root Pattern has been obtained by using the "Generation of Security Management Patterns" sub-process. The main objective of this sub-process is to permit the generation of a pattern (a structure composed of the main elements of an ISMS and its relationships for a specific type of companies with common characteristics – the same sector and the same size) which can later be used to reduce the generation time and costs of an ISMS in a company. Figure 2 shows the basic structure of inputs, activities and outputs of which this sub-process is composed:

- Inputs: The input consists of the knowledge of a group of security domain experts obtained during the ISMS deployment process. This knowledge is recurrent and incremental during the methodology's lifecycle. The second entrance will be composed of a set of elements derived from regulations, good practice guidelines and other existing methodologies.
- Activities: This sub-process will be composed of four activities. Activity A1.2 cannot be carried out until A1.1 has been completed since it requires the elements generated by the first activity if it is to function correctly. Activities A1.3 depend on the elements generated by A1.2 and cannot therefore be carried out until after its completion.
- Outputs: The output produced by this sub-process will consist of the complete pattern composed of all the elements necessary to construct an ISMS and the relationships existing between those elements.

The GSMP process can be considered to be one of the main contributions of this methodology. It represents a powerful test bank which permits the analysis of the various ISMS configurations on the developed models since it allows us to make a detailed study of the influence of the choice of one element or another, or of the different relationships when generating an ISMS and how they later interact with it.

Each of the activities carried out to obtain the elements of which the "Root Pattern" is composed will now be briefly described below:

- *Activity A1.1. – Generation of Master Tables:* The main objective of this activity is to determine which general elements can be best adapted to the pattern which is being created. The input is the knowledge of a group of security domain experts obtained during the ISMS deployment process, which will permit the selection of a subset of elements of which the Root Pattern will be composed. Figure 3 shows the structure created to store the knowledge from this activity and the values load in the root pattern. Thus, for example, we have initially introduced six profiles and some subprofiles for the element created to contain the roles and profiles. The principal sources from which the elements that fill the different components in this zone of the root pattern have been extracted are analysed below:

  o Roles: The Root Pattern is composed of the roles proposed by the ISACA[2] Company for the members of its systems department, and it has been completed with the principal profiles defined in the methodology.

---

[2] ISACA: Information Systems Audit and Control Association.

- o Maturity Levels: The Root Pattern is a variation of the Eloff proposal [28] and has 3 maturity levels, although other models with 5 maturity levels were also studied.
- o Business sectors: This Root Pattern has been composed of the proposals of the NACE code (The European standard of industry classification).

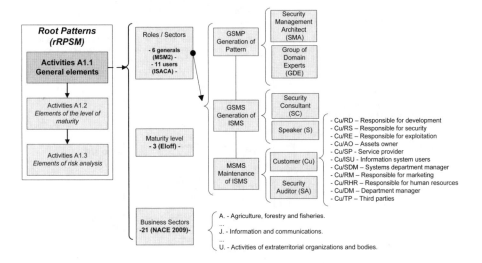

Fig. 3. Root Pattern elements for Activity A1.1

- *Activity A1.2. – Generation of maturity level tables:* The main objective of this activity is to determine the controls and maturity rules that can be best adapted to the pattern that is being created, and which will later be used to determine the company's present security maturity level, and the maturity level to which it would be advisable to evolve. The inputs are the knowledge of a Group of Security Domain Experts obtained during the ISMS deployment process, the maturity levels obtained from the "Establishing the maturity levels" task and a set of elements from which the final elements that will form this part of the Root Pattern will be selected. Figure 4 shows the structure created to store the knowledge from this activity and the values load in the root pattern. Thus, for example, we have introduced 133 controls for the element created to contain the controls, initially taking ISO/IEC27002 as our basis since it is an internationally recognized standard. One of the principal advantages of this pattern structure is that it can easily be adapted to other international regulations. The principal sources from which the elements with which the different components in this zone of the root pattern have been extracted are analysed below:

  - o Maturity rules: These are used to define the level of security that it is desirable for the company to attain, i.e., the maximum maturity level that it should be able to attain based on its structural characteristics.

    o   Security controls: The ISO/IEC27002 [29] proposals for good practice guidelines have been used in the Root Pattern, and the controls have been decomposed into a set of sub-controls, which has allowed the company's current security management level to be obtained with greater precision.

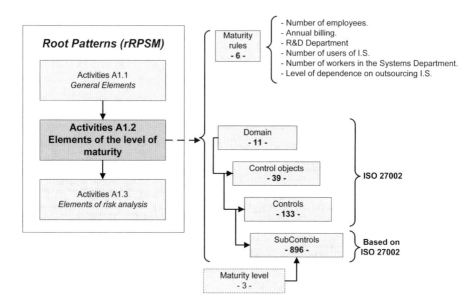

Fig. 4. Root Pattern elements for Activity A1.2

- *Activity A1.3. – Generation of risk analysis tables:* The main objective of this activity is to select those elements which are necessary to be able to carry out a low cost basic risk analysis of the activities of which the company's information system is composed which can be adapted to the requirements of SMEs, in activities subsequent to the methodology. The inputs are the knowledge of the group of security domain experts which was obtained during the ISMS deployment process, the controls selected in the Establishing Controls task, which are stored in the patterns repository, and a set of elements (types of activities, threats, vulnerabilities and risk criteria) which are necessary for the creation of the risk analysis.

    Figure 5 shows the structure created to store the knowledge from this activity and the values load in the root pattern. The selection of elements for this zone of the root pattern is based on the contents of Magerit's risk analysis methodology [30] and on the ISO/IEC27005 standard [31], from which a set of elements is obtained. For example, in the case of threat types we have considered the six most important threat types derived from Magerit and have established 1040 relationships between these and the controls selected in the previous activity.

The patterns are under constant evaluation and are up-dated with the knowledge obtained from the Group of Domain Experts in each new deployment.

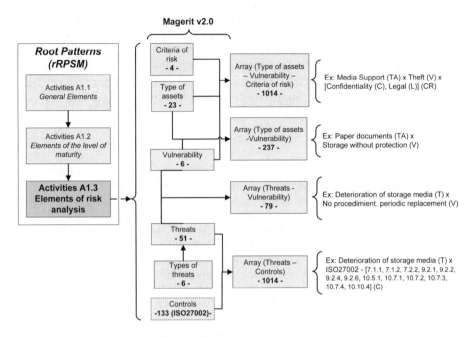

Fig. 5. Root Pattern elements for Activity A1.3

5 Conclusions

This paper shows the mechanisms defined in the MSM2-SME methodology that make it possible to reuse knowledge acquired in different instalments, thus obtaining enormous benefits (cost reductions, robust results, etc.). We have also analysed the root pattern, which was developed from the starting point of all the knowledge obtained in order to create new more refined patterns for other companies.

We have shown how the root pattern has been developed from internationally renowned standards to guarantee a high quality in the results obtained when implementing ISMSs, and how the structure of the patterns allows them to be adapted to any type of regulation. This will even make it possible to take only parts of the patterns, which supposes an enormous potential when applying our methodology.

We have defined how this model can be used and the improvements that it offers in comparison to other models which tackle the problem only partially or in a manner which is too costly for SMES.

All future improvements to the methodology and the model are oriented towards improving its precision, whilst always respecting the principal of the cost of resources, i.e., we seek to improve the model without incurring higher generation and maintenance costs of the ISMS.

Acknowledgments

This research is part of the following projects: BUSINESS (PET2008-0136) granted by the "Ministerio de Ciencia e Innovación" (Spain), SEGMENT (HITO-09-138) project financed by the "Consejería de Educación y Ciencia de la Junta de Comunidades de Castilla-La Mancha", SISTEMAS (PII2I09-0150-3135) project financed by the "Consejería de Educación y Ciencia de la Junta de Comunidades de Castilla-La Mancha" and MEDUSAS (IDI-20090557) project financed by the "Centro para el Desarrollo Tecnológico Industrial. Ministerio de Ciencia e Innovación" (CDTI).

References

1. Fernández-Medina, E., et al.: Model-Driven Development for secure information systems. Information and Software Technology Journal 51(5), 809–814 (2009)
2. Kluge, D.: Formal Information Security Standards in German Medium Enterprises. In: CONISAR: The Conference on Information Systems Applied Research (2008)
3. Dhillon, G., Backhouse, J.: Information System Security Management in the New Millennium. Communications of the ACM 43(7), 125–128 (2000)
4. De Capitani, S., Foresti, S., Jajodia, S.: Preserving Confidentiality of Security Policies in Data Outsourcing. In: WPES'08. ACM, Alexandria (2008)
5. Barlette, Y., Vladislav, V.: Exploring the Suitability of IS Security Management Standards for SMEs. In: Hawaii International Conference on System Sciences, Proceedings of the 41st Annual, Waikoloa, HI, USA (2008)
6. Vries, H., et al.: SME access to European standardization. Enabling small and medium-sized enterprises to achieve greater benefit from standards and from involvement in standardization. In: E.U. Rotterdam School of Management (ed.) Rotterdam, the Netherlands, pp. 1–95 (2009)
7. Wiander, T., Holappa, J.: Theoretical Framework of ISO 17799 Compliant. Information Security Management System Using Novel ASD Method in Technical Report, V.T.R.C.o. Finland, Editor (2006)
8. Wiander, T.: Implementing the ISO/IEC 17799 standard in practice – experiences on audit phases. In: AISC '08: Proceedings of the Sixth Australasian Conference on Information Security, Wollongong, Australia (2008)
9. Sánchez, L.E., et al.: Security Management in corporative IT systems using maturity models, taking as base ISO/IEC 17799. In: International Symposium on Frontiers in Availability, Reliability and Security (FARES'06) in Conjunction with ARES, Viena, Austria (2006)
10. Sánchez, L.E., et al.: MMISS-SME Practical Development: Maturity Model for Information Systems Security Management in SMEs. In: 9th International Conference on Enterprise Information Systems (WOSIS'07), Funchal, Madeira (Portugal) (June 2007b)
11. Sánchez, L.E., et al.: Developing a model and a tool to manage the information security in Small and Medium Enterprises. In: International Conference on Security and Cryptography (SECRYPT'07), Barcelona, Junio, Spain (2007a)
12. Sánchez, L.E., et al.: Developing a maturity model for information system security management within small and medium size enterprises. In: 8th International Conference on Enterprise Information Systems (WOSIS'06), Paphos, Chipre (March 2006)

13. Sánchez, L.E., et al.: SCMM-TOOL: Tool for computer automation of the Information Security Management Systems. In: 2nd International Conference on Software and Data Technologies (ICSOFT'07), Barcelona-España Septiembre (2007c)

14. Sánchez, L.E., et al.: Practical Application of a Security Management Maturity Model for SMEs Based on Predefined Schemas. In: International Conference on Security and Cryptography (SECRYPT'08), Porto–Portugal (2008)

15. Sánchez, L.E., et al.: Managing Security and its Maturity in Small and Medium-Sized Enterprises. Journal of Universal Computer Science (J.UCS) 15(15), 3038–3058 (2009)

16. Sánchez, L.E., et al.: MMSM-SME: Methodology for the management of security and its maturity in Small and Medium-sized Enterprises. In: 11th International Conference on Enterprise Information Systems (WOSIS09), Milan, Italy, pp. 67–78 (2009)

17. Kostina, A., Miloslavskaya, N., Tolstoy, A.: Information Security Incident Management Process. In: SIN'09, North Cyprus, Turkey (2009) ACM 978-1-60558-412-6/09/10

18. Ohki, E., et al.: Information Security Governance Framework. In: WISG'09, Chicago, Illinois, USA (2009) ACM 978-1-60558-787-5/09/11

19. Siponen, M., Willison, R.: Information security management standards: Problems and solutions. Information & Management 46, 267–270 (2009)

20. Gupta, A., Hammond, R.: Information systems security issues and decisions for small businesses. Information Management & Computer Security 13(4), 297–310 (2005)

21. Batista, J., Figueiredo, A.: SPI in very small team: a case with CMM. Software Process Improvement and Practice 5(4), 243–250 (2000)

22. Hareton, L., Terence, Y.: A Process Framework for Small Projects. Software Process Improvement and Practice 6, 67–83 (2001)

23. Tuffley, A., Grove, B.,, M.: SPICE For Small Organisations. Software Process Improvement and Practice 9, 23–31 (2004)

24. Calvo-Manzano, J.A., et al.: Experiences in the Application of Software Process Improvement in SMES. Software Quality Journal 10(3), 261–273 (2004)

25. Mekelburg, D.: Sustaining Best Practices: How Real-World Software Organizations Improve Quality Processes. Software Quality Professional 7(3), 4–13 (2005)

26. Dick, B.: Applications. Sessions of Areol. Action research and evaluation (2000)

27. Kock, N.: The threee threats of action research: a discussion of methodological antidotes in the context of an information systems study. Decision Support Systems, 265–286 (2004)

28. Eloff, J., Eloff, M.: Information Security Management - A New Paradigm. In: Annual research conference of the South African Institute of Computer Scientists and Information Technologists on Enablement Through Technology SAICSIT'03, pp. 130–136 (2003)

29. ISO/IEC27002, ISO/IEC 27002, Information Technology - Security Techniques - The international standard Code of Practice for Information Security Management (2007)

30. MageritV2, Methodology for Information Systems Risk Analysis and Management (MAGERIT version 2), Ministerio de Administraciones Públicas, Spain (2006)

31. ISO/IEC27005, ISO/IEC 27005, Information Technology - Security Techniques - Information Security Risk Management Standard (under development) (2008)

Mechanizing Social Trust-Aware Recommenders with T-Index Augmented Trustworthiness

Soude Fazeli[1], Alireza Zarghami[2], Nima Dokoohaki[1], and Mihhail Matskin[1,3]

[1] Royal Institute of Technology (KTH)
[2] University of Twente (UT)
[3] Norwegian University of Science and Technology (NTNU)
{soude,nimad}@kth.se a.zarghami@utwente.nl misha@imit.kth.se

Abstract. Social Networks have dominated growth and popularity of the Web to an extent which has never been witnessed before. Such popularity puts forward issue of trust to the participants of Social Networks. Collaborative Filtering Recommenders have been among many systems which have begun taking full advantage of Social Trust phenomena for generating more accurate predictions. For analyzing the evolution of constructed networks of trust, we utilize Collaborative Filtering enhanced with T-index as an estimate of a user's trustworthiness to identify and select neighbors in an effective manner. Our empirical evaluation demonstrates how T-index improves the Trust Network structure by generating connections to more trustworthy users. We also show that exploiting T-index results in better prediction accuracy and coverage of recommendations collected along few edges that connect users on a network.

Keywords: Social Networks, Social Trust, Recommendation, Collaborative Filtering, Trust networks, Ontological modeling, Performance.

1 Introduction

Semantic Web vision noted trust as one of the most crucial technologies enabling a future Web of openness and collaboration, collectively referred to as "'Web of Trust'" [1]. Emergence of Social Networks and most importantly Web-Based Social Networks (WBSN)[2] from one side, and research into trust from the other side, combined with Semantic Web technologies created an exclusive opportunity to merge existing efforts and create means for Social Network Analysis (SNA) at the top of Semantic Web [3]. Among many systems which have realized the impact of so called "Social Trust", Recommender Systems have been the most influential ones. Recommenders are software systems which retrieve data items on users behalf, by taking into account similarity between users interests (social or collaborative based), or just by considering similarity between items (content-based), or by considering both item and user similarity (hybrid). Social Recommender Systems which are extended with trust phenomena have proven to provide users with more reliable recommendations.

In this paper, we propose a measure called T-index inspired by H-index[4] for enhancing a Social Recommender System. We employ T-index to keep a list of the most trustworthy users who already rated an item. We refer to this list as *TopTrustee* list

S. Katsikas, J. Lopez, and M. Soriano (Eds.): TrustBus 2010, LNCS 6264, pp. 202–213, 2010.
© Springer-Verlag Berlin Heidelberg 2010

which is attached to each item. As a result, when a user rates an item, she/he is able to find users who might not be accessible within an upper bound of traversal path length, although they can be trustworthy users who share similar interests in the respective item. We demonstrate how utilizing T-index improves the structure of generated trust networks in the context of movie recommendations.

The rest of the work is documented as follows: Section 2 provides the background and related works. Section 3 describes our approach and then, Section 4 shows our experimental results and discussions. Finally, we conclude and present an overview of the future work in Section 5 .

2 Background

As Social Networks has become increasingly popular, there is a growing need to model their structure on Semantic Web. FOAF (Friend-of-a-Friend) vocabulary [5] describes users' information and their social connections through concepts and properties in the form of an ontology using Semantic Web technologies [6], [7]. Golbeck[7] proposes an ontology for extending FOAF vocabulary to model trust relationship between users. Although Golbeck's ontology provides an efficient structure, every relationship describes only one subject. Dokoohaki et al. [8] introduces an ontology for modeling structure of trust relations between users that is more efficient in terms of the size of the generated networks using ontology. We extend this ontology to model trust between users with an extra element for measuring T-index-based trustworthiness of a user.

Massa and Avesani present an architecture for a trust-aware recommender in which the "web of trust" is explicitly expressed by users[9]. There exists some efforts to formalize the trust where it can not be explicitly expressed by users. Two computational models of trust are proposed by O'Donovan and Smyth[10] as profile-level and profile-item-level based on the past behavior of user profiles. Lathia et al.[11] introduce a "value" which is based on difference between a user's and its recommenders' ratings. This value is used to update the trust between the user and its recommenders. Their presented method is similar to the models presented by O'Donovan and Smyth in [10]. The trust-based collaborative filtering algorithm used in their method requires a centralized user-item matrix which might lead to scalability problem as the number of users increases. Weng et al.[12] assume each user as a peer connected to other users in a decentralized trust network of users. In this paper, we adapt the formalization presented by Lathia et al.[11] to derive the trust value between users. We propose an agent-setting in which every user is considered to be an agent connected to other users to form a trust network. Such a setting should provide better scalability since the distributed allocation of trust-related data is supported.

3 A Semantic Trust-Ware Recommendation Framework

Our goal is to create trust relationships among all types of users with respect to different types of items, accessible through unique URI across heterogeneous networks and environments. To achieve this, we have developed an ontological framework, shown in

Fig. 1, composed of three main modules: Semantic Profile Manager, Trust Engine and Recommendation System.

Upon rating an item by a user, the Semantic Profile Manager module either creates or updates an ontology-based profile for both user and item.

The Trust Engine module generates a so-called *trust network* of users based on the profile information of users and items in a distributed manner. To do so, a user profile extends the trust ontology to keep top-n neighbors and its mutual trust values with them. Note that there is no global view of a trust network for users and they are only provided with information regarding their neighbors and rating history. Therefore, it is possible to maintain users in different groups on several servers to achieve better scalability. To cope with privacy requirements, these servers can be located in different organizations while profiles of users and items are accessible only through their URI.

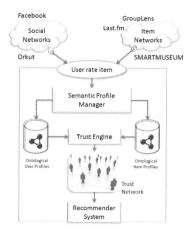

Fig. 1. Ontological Framework

The Recommendation System module enables traversals through the trust network to collect recommendations for a target user and finally makes a predicted rating for the user.

The whole model is built on top of a knowledge acquisition system to improve manipulation of ontological data. The presented ontological framework provides us with high interoperability and openness to deal with heterogeneous networks.

3.1   TopTrustee and T-Index

In order to build trust relationships among users, we enhance Collaborative Filtering with two novel concepts: T-index and TopTrustee.

T-index. The H-index [4] was defined by Jorge E. Hirsch, a physicist, "'as the number of papers with a citation number higher or equal to H, as a useful index to characterize the scientific output of a researcher'''. Extending this idea, we propose an estimate of a user's trustworthiness called T-index, similar to the H-index in showing the number of trust relationships between a user and its trusters with trust value higher than or equal to T. T-index can be introduced as Indegree of nodes in a trust network which provides not only number of incoming edges as a regular Indegree, but it also considers the weight of incoming trust relationships. For a node on a network, Indegree represents the number of head endpoints adjacent to a node while Outdegree is the number of tail endpoints.

Algorithm 1. Computing T-index

1: **procedure ComputeT-index** $\langle user, TrusterList \rangle$
2:     $TrusterValueList \leftarrow TrusterList.\text{sort}(trustValue, descending)$
3:     **for all** $trustValue$ **in** $TrusterValueList$ **do**
4:         $trustValue \leftarrow \text{multiply}(trustValue, Max_{T-index}).\text{rounded}$
5:     **end for**
6:     $Counter \leftarrow 1$
7:     **for all** $trustValue$ **in** $TrusterValueList$ **do**
8:         **if** $Counter < trustValue$ **then**
9:             $Counter \leftarrow Counter + 1$
10:         **else**
11:             **break**
12:         **end if**
13:     **end for**
14:     $T\text{-}index \leftarrow Counter - 1$
15:     **return** $T\text{-}index$
16: **end procedure**

The algorithm 1 describes how T-index is computed for a user. First, we introduce the maximum value of T-index as a global variable which defines the precision of T-index computation. Thus, we multiply all trust values (shown as label of arrows in Fig. 2) which are in the the range of 0 to 1, by this maximum value. In the example presented by Fig. 2, we assume the maximum value of T-index as 10, for the sake of simplicity. Then, we start to count the number of trusters until the counter becomes greater than the trust values.

In this work, we define cluster as a group of users who all trust a common user, called Centric User as the most trustworthy one within the cluster. Fig. 2 shows u_a and u_f as centric users of two clusters.

Item's TopTrustee. An item's *TopTrustee* is a user who has already rated the item and can join item's *TopTrustee* list if its T-index value is higher than a certain threshold. In fact, *TopTrustee* list introduces trustworthy users to the user who has just rated the item. The users in *TopTrustee* list may have no trust relationship with the user yet as they can not be reached through the maximum path length of L. However, They might be a source of useful information for the item's rater. We form *TopTrustee* lists by exploiting T-index.

As shown in Fig. 2, when u_b rates item i_a, its mutual trust values with all users in two sets are computed and updated. The first set is its *top-n neighbors* as the first n users

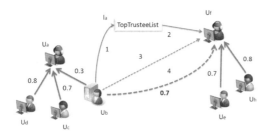

Fig. 2. A scenario of utilizing TopTrustee List

who are not only directly connected to the user but also provide the highest mutual trust values with the user. The other set is the item's *TopTrustee* list. The arrows between the users and the *TopTrustee* list show that the users rated i_a. u_f has rated i_a and is already located in i_a's *TopTrustee* list. After computing the trust value between u_b and u_f based on the trust formula presented by [11], u_b finds u_f more trustworthy than u_a as one of its current top-n neighbors even though u_f is not accessible to u_b within path length of L. Eventually, u_b adds u_f to its top-n neighbors. As a result, u_b can be provided by u_f with more reliable recommendations in comparison with u_a's recommendations.

3.2   Semantic Profiling Manager

Semantic Profile Manager module is responsible for creating and updating ontology-based profiles for both user and item.

Ontological User Profile. We take advantage of the trust model presented by Dokoohaki et al. [8] to define the trust between users who are expressed using the *FOAF Agent* concept. Dokoohaki's trust ontology has three concepts. *Relationship* is the main element which expresses the trust relations on top of the Social Network of FOAF user profiles. *MainProperties* and *AuxiliaryProperties* are the other main components of aforementioned ontology, which respectively define essential and optional attributes for relations which exist in between users on the network. Two associations connect both *MainProperties* and *AuxiliaryProperties* to the *Relationship* concept. *Relationship* always has a sink and a source, which is described by a *Truster* and a *Trustee*. Reader is refered to [8] for more information about the complete structure of trust ontology. In our model, a trust value is computed based on users' ratings to different items, possibly in different contexts. To compute the trust value between users, we follow the approach proposed in [11] based on the difference of a user's rating and its recommender's rating to their common item(s). As a result, as the distance between their rating values increases, trust decreases linearly.

As shown in Fig. 3, we create an instance of *Relationship* concept between two users for whom a trust value is computed. The users are specified as *Truster* and *Trustee* and their trust value and subject is assigned as *MainProperties* [8] to the instance defined earlier. In addition, we assign T-index as a *MainProperty* of the *Relationship* instance. We also define the *RankRelation* concept for associating a user to an item by a rank

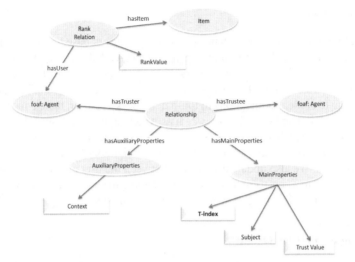

Fig. 3. User Ontology Model

value. This concept is used to keep track of rated items by a user that we refer to as *user profile*.

Ontological Item Profile. We have developed an ontology for item's knowledge domain which can be extended by all other ontologies in the same domain. We introduce a new concept called *TopTrustee*, which is derived from the notion of item's *TopTrustee* described in section 3.1, and we assign it to an individual item to create a list of users who rate the item. The list of raters is ordered by their T-index. In a real world scenario, these *TopTrustee* lists can be implemented by Distributed Hash Tables (DHT) [13] with unique URI as their keys.

3.3   Trust Engine

We adapt the formalization of trust presented by Lathia et al.[11] based on difference of a user's rating and its recommender's rating to their common item(s). As the difference of their rating values decreases, trust value between them increases linearly. Suppose we have two users u_a and u_b. Trust between them is formalized as follows [11]:

$$T(u_a, u_b) = 1 - \frac{\sum_{i=1}^{n}(r_{u_a,i_i} - r_{u_b,i_i})}{r_{max} * n} \tag{1}$$

This formula computes the total differences between a user's rating values and its recommender's rating values over n historical ratings of u_a multiplied by the maximum value in each rating scale (i.e., 5). This trust value is used to update the trust between the user and its respective recommenders.

3.4 Trust Network

We gradually build up the trust relationships between users based on the rating information of user profile and item profile to generate a so-called *trust network* of users.

As mentioned, we keep top-n neighbors of a user in an ontological structure based on their mutual trust values. The list is updated on "'rating a new item'" event. If the event leads up to some modifications in top-n neighbors of a user, then T-index value is recalculated and updated in all *TopTrustee* lists which contain the user. The scenario is described as follows: when a user rates a new item, we compute its trust with all item's *TopTrustees* who do not exist in its current top-n neighbors but might be potentially trustworthy users. We also update trust values between the user and its top-n neighbors. Eventually, we form a new top-n neighbors by selecting the most trustworthy users from the union of its preceding neighbors and the potential trustees.

3.5 Recommendation System

There is no central view of similar users' ratings in distributed recommender systems. Thus, in order to generate a recommendation, we need to find a solution for gathering neighbors' opinions. Traversals through neighbors would be an appropriate solution for collecting an item's ratings. In addition, length of connected edges between users through the trust network should be limited to an upper bound (L). However, defining a suitable value for L is challenging as it leads to a trade off between accuracy and performance. Therefore, as the number of parallel traversals and L increase, we can achieve better prediction accuracy and coverage for recommendations, while we require more resources of bandwidth and computations. On the other hand, a user is allowed to traverse through its either direct or indirect neighbors as long as its mutual trust value does not fall down a predefined minimum threshold (v).

After collecting all the information from a user's neighborhood by traversals, we aim to minimize the risk of recommending irrelevant items to a user [11]. Therefore, predicted rating value provides us with the fact that whether the user is interested in an item or not. Prediction value is taken as a weighted average of user a's neighbors ratings[14]. Reader is advised to refer to Zarghami et al.[15] for more information regarding collecting the recommendations and making predictions.

4 Evaluation

4.1 Setup

We evaluate above presented method based on *MovieLens*[1] dataset which consists of 943 user profiles. Ratings are based on five point scale. The profiles are divided into training and test sets including 80% and 20% of ratings, respectively. To design ontological profiles for user and item, we use Protégé[16]. We take advantage of Protégé API in Java for implementing the recommendation system. First, we build up trust-aware social networks as described before, based on the training data and we visualize

---

[1] http://www.cs.umn.edu/research/GroupLens/data/

the constructed networks by Welkin[17] to study effect of T-index on structure of the networks. Then, we use a traversal mechanism for collecting recommendations through the trust networks. In fact, evaluating the trust computation is not our concern. As we explained in Section 3.3, we have adapted a light-weight trust formalization to conduct our experiments for investigating the impact of T-index on the performance of our recommendation system.

In this work, we aim to show how the network structure based on trust relationships in a social setting, can be affected by T-index. To do so, we first compare Indegree distribution of top-10 trustworthy users with different values for T-index. Then, we build trust networks with and without T-index to observe the difference. The differences includes both inferred and trimmed edges made when T-index is employed. We study the effect of T-index variation on the prediction coverage and accuracy of recommendations collected based on rating values of neighbors who provide mutual trust value higher than the minimum threshold(v) as 0.1 and can be reached within the upper bound for path length of traversals (L) as 3.

We run our experiment in different settings for various sizes of top-n neighbors for each user as n and *TopTrustee* list for each item as m. Although utilizing T-index we achieved more improved results, we have gained the most significant improvement when experimenting with $m=5$ and $n=5$ in previous work. Therefore, we choose the values of both n and m to be 5 for studying the Indegree distribution and trust networks structure in an effective manner. We also consider different values for T-index which range from 0 meaning no T-index is used to other values 25, 50, 100, 200, 500, 1000. To study coverage and accuracy, the values of n are tuned to be $\in 2, 3, 5, 10, 20, 50$ while m stays the same as 5.

4.2 Results and Discussions

In the first step, we study the Indegree distribution of the top-10 trustworthy users for various values of T-index while n and m are both equal to 5. As mentioned earlier, Indegree represents incoming edges to a node as a user who is trusted by others. As shown in Fig. 4, when T-index is employed (T-index$<>$ 0), the top-10 trustworthy users' weights in terms of incoming trust relationships are more balanced. This means that users have on average more opportunities to find the most similar centric nodes as their main clusters. As a result, the load of incoming trust relationships imposed on the most trustworthy user, is distributed among other trustworthy users which makes our recommendation system more resistant against node failures or bottlenecks on the trust networks. Thus, the results significantly change when T-index is used, regardless of its non-zero values (25, 50, 100, 200, 500, 1000).

To study the effect of T-index on trust networks structure, we generate two trust networks with and without T-index while n and m are the same as 5. Fig. 4 shows that the Indegree distribution dramatically declines for the first top-5 trustworthy users without using T-index and the first top-10 trustworthy users with applying T-index. However, for the most trustworthy users placed after the first ten, the Indegree distribution has a steady decrease continuously. For the sake of simplicity, we only study the trust networks structure of the users who are directly connected to at least one of the top-10 trustworthy users.

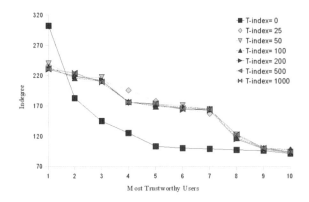

Fig. 4. The Top-10 trustworthy users Indegree

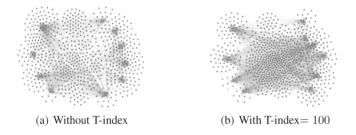

(a) Without T-index   (b) With T-index= 100

Fig. 5. Generated Trust Networks for Top-10 Trustworthy Users ($n= 5$, $m= 5$)

Fig. 5(a) and Fig. 5(b) depict the trust networks structure with and without T-index, (T-index=100) and (T-index=0), respectively. Figs. 5(a) and 5(b) show the trust networks' structure with and without T-index, for T-index=100 and T-index=0, respectively. For the sake of simplicity, we display only users(displayed as nodes) and their connections (trust relationships) to top-10 trustworthy users. As mentioned, each cluster is described as a group of like-minded users in terms of trust. It is shown that the number of common users between clusters increases which enables users of different clusters to find each other easier. In our case, more users form divergent areas of users' interests, presented as clusters, can be accessible.

To justify the results, we compare the formed trust networks with and without T-index to show the inferred and trimmed edges individually. Fig. 6(a) indicates that inferred edges are mostly located between centric nodes. Therefore, the number of users which belong to different clusters, grows in the centric area of the figure. In contrast, 6(b) reveals that most of the trimmed edges are located in just one cluster.

Finally, we study coverage and MAE of the generated recommendations for several n with different T-index values while the value for m is the same and equal to 5. As shown in Fig. 7(a), the minimum coverage for $n= 2$ without T-index is more than 85% which is improved in camparison with the result of similar work[12] with coverage$< 60\%$ at

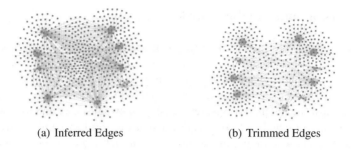

(a) Inferred Edges   (b) Trimmed Edges

Fig. 6. Alignment of Trust Networks for Top-10 Trustworthy Users ($n= 5$, $m= 5$)

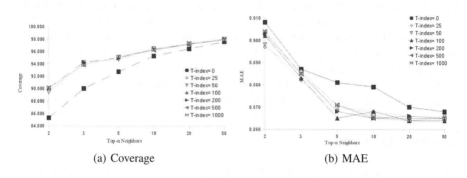

(a) Coverage   (b) MAE

Fig. 7. Comparing the results based on different T-index values

the same path length ($L= 3$) and even for larger sizes of n. Fig. 7(a) shows that coverage has improved at all values of n when T-index is employed. We also demonstrate that the coverage improvement is almost the same for all non-zero values of T-index. Nevertheless, we achieve better results for coverage as the size of neighbors list (n) decreases. As shown in Fig. 7(b), the maximum MAE value for $n= 2$ without T-index is less than 0.91 which outperforms a similar work[12] with MAE> 0.96 considering the same threshold for path length of traversals ($L= 3$). It shows that including items' *Top-TrusteeList* in "top-n neighbors" can improve the results. On the other hand, it reveals that utilizing T-index achieves better results. As with coverage, we observe in Fig. 7(b) that T-index improves MAE for all values of n. However, the extent of improvement of MAE changes with a constant value of T-index and different values of n. For instance, although MAE has the most effective result with T-index$= 100$ and $n= 5$, it has its worst value with the same T-index when $n= 10$. Despite coverage, T-index does not always make MAE better as the size of neighborhood list decreases. Fig. 7(b) shows that MAE is improved significantly with T-index when $n= 5$ and 10 whereas MAE result is trivial when $n= 3$ and 50. In conclusion, while using T-index results in better prediction accuracy and coverage of recommendations, accuracy is more affected by different values of T-index and the size of neighborhood list (n).

5   Conclusion and Further Work

In this work, we have formed trust networks of users on which recommendations are collected by neighbors either directly connected or indirectly connected. The indirect relationships between users are established through trust propagation mechanism. We have proposed an estimate of a user's trustworthiness called T-index, similar to H-index [4] to show the number of trust relationships between a user and its trusters with trust value higher or equal to T. We employ T-index to form an item's *TopTrustee* list which include users who might not be reachable through a predefined maximum path length of traversals. We have shown that by utilizing items' *TopTrustee* list, traversals length for finding users who rate a desired item, decreases which results in high performance. To justify the results, we have analyzed and visualized the effect of T-index on the structure of generated trust networks based on the experimental data. We have demonstrated that T-index boosts the number of common users between different clusters. It results in better prediction coverage and accuracy of recommendations collected within few edges that connect users on trust networks.

We plan to assess T-index value for each user in a distributed manner like gossip based aggregation[18] for alleviating the problem of malicious nodes on trust networks.

Acknowledgment

This work has been done within the FP7-216923 EU IST funded SMARTMUSEUM project and is part of the IOP GenCom U-Care project which is sponsored by the Dutch government under contract IGC0816.

References

1. Berners-Lee, T., Hendler, J., Lassila, O.: The semantic web. Scientific American (May 2001)
2. Golbeck, J.: Computing and applying trust in web-based social networks (2005)
3. Golbeck, J., Hendler, J.: Accuracy of metrics for inferring trust and reputation in semantic web-based social network. LNCS, pp. 116–131. Springer, Heidelberg (2004)
4. Hirsch, J.E.: An index to quantify an individual's scientific research output. PNAS 102(46), 16569–16572 (2005)
5. (FOAF) Last modified Feb-2009, http://www.foaf-project.org/
6. Dokoohaki, N., Matskin, M.: Structural determination of ontology-driven trust networks in semantic social institutions and ecosystems. In: International Conference on Mobile Ubiquitous Computing, Systems, Services and Technologies (UBICOMM '07) and the International Conference on Advances in Semantic Processing (SEMAPRO 2007), pp. 263–268. IEEE Computer Society, Los Alamitos (2007)
7. Golbeck, J.A.: Computing and applying trust in web-based social networks. PhD thesis, University of Maryland at College Park, College Park, MD, USA, Chair-Hendler, James (2005)
8. Dokoohaki, N., Matskin, M.: Effective design of trust ontologies for improvement in the structure of socio-semantic trust networks. International Journal on Advances in Intelligent Systems 1st(1942-2679), 23–42 (2008)
9. Massa, P., Avesani, P.: Trust-aware collaborative filtering for recommender systems. In: Meersman, R., Tari, Z. (eds.) OTM 2004. LNCS, vol. 3290, pp. 492–508. Springer, Heidelberg (2004)

10. O'Donovan, J., Smyth, B.: Trust in recommender systems. In: IUI '05: Proceedings of the 10th International Conference on Intelligent User Interfaces, pp. 167–174. ACM, New York (2005)
11. Lathia, N., Hailes, S., Capra, L.: Trust-based collaborative filtering. In: IFIPTM 2008: Joint iTrust and PST Conferences on Privacy, Trust Management and Security, Department of Computer Science, p. 14. University College London, London (2008)
12. Weng, J., Miao, C., Goh, A.: Improving collaborative filtering with trust-based metrics. In: SAC '06: Proceedings of the 2006 ACM Symposium on Applied Computing, pp. 1860–1864. ACM, New York (2006)
13. DHT: Last modified March-2009,
    `http://en.wikipedia.org/wiki/Distributed_hash_table`
14. Bell, R., Koren, Y.: Scalable collaborative filtering with jointly derived neighborhood interpolation weights. In: International Conference on Data Mining (ICDM'07), pp. 175–186. IEEE, Los Alamitos (2007)
15. Zarghami, A., Fazeli, S., Dokoohaki, N., Matskin, M.: Social trust-aware recommendation system: A t-index approach. In: Proceedings of the IEEE/WIC/ACM International Joint Conferences on Web Intelligence and Intelligent Agent Technologies, WI-IAT 2009 (2009)
16. Protégé: Copyright, Stanford Center for Biomedical Informatics Research (2009),
    `http://protege.stanford.edu/`
17. Welkin: Copyright 2004-2008 Massachusetts Institute of Technology,
    `http://simile.mit.edu/welkin/`
18. Jelasity, M., Montresor, A., Babaoglu, O.: Gossip-based aggregation in large dynamic networks. ACM Trans. Comput. Syst. 23(3), 219–252 (2005)

Security for Dynamic Service-Oriented eCollaboration*
Architectural Alternatives and Proposed Solution

Christoph Fritsch and Günther Pernul

Department of Information Systems,
University of Regensburg, 93053 Regensburg, Germany
{christoph.fritsch,guenther.pernul}@wiwi.uni-regensburg.de
http://www-ifs.uni-regensburg.de

Abstract. Current challenges on the markets cause companies to interact with one another and strive after becoming members of virtual organizations assuming that in doing so they can achieve sustainable competitiveness and remain successful despite increased competition. This new openness has strong implications and poses intense demands on organizations' security systems. In this paper we present architectural considerations and our concept of a security infrastructure to cope with these challenges. The presented approach aims at minimizing the lead-time before usage of external services can start by employing a security intermediary for mediation purposes.

Keywords: SOA Security, ESB Access Control, Virtual Organizations.

1   Introduction and Motivation

Today's companies are facing strong challenges and pressure in the markets: the economic crisis demanded maximum flexibility to survive and increased competition due to the globalization requires shorter innovation cycles and continuous improvement of products and value creation processes. More and more companies are realizing that their ways of doing business have to be advanced as they can no longer solely trade as fully self-contained actors. Many of them are beginning to reconsider their entrenched business structures and aim for collaborative value chains and flexible cross company business network structures to perform future business with anybody, anywhere, anytime regardless of underlying information technology infrastructures [13]. Surveys by [3] or [10] back this trend and predict a significant increase of virtual organizations (VOs) and eCollaboration in the forthcoming years.

---

* The research leading to these results is receiving funding from the European Community's Seventh Framework Programme under grant agreement no. 217098. The content of this publication is the sole responsibility of the authors and in no way represents the view of the European Commission or its services.

S. Katsikas, J. Lopez, and M. Soriano (Eds.): TrustBus 2010, LNCS 6264, pp. 214–226, 2010.

Especially information and communication technology (ICT) has repeatedly been identified as the most critical success factor for efficiently running collaborative projects [7], [16]. The need for tight integration of cross-organizational value chains is still rapidly increasing and organizations' boundaries are becoming more fluid and permeable.

This new openness to speedily establish VOs and the associated rapid but tight integration of IT systems with partnering organizations has strong implications and poses intense demands on organizations' security systems. Flexible security measures and infrastructures to enforce them have to be in place. Security of the company's IT properties has to be guaranteed at all times even if the number and the identities of people authorized to access single services vary frequently and swiftly. The more flexible and rapid an organization wants to join a virtual business network, the more effective and powerful its security infrastructure in general and its access control schemes in particular must be. In this paper we therefore present our fundamental considerations regarding several architectural alternatives for developing a flexible access control infrastructure for networked enterprises, particularly tailored to rapid but still reliable and trustworthy linkage of single services from a pool of service candidates. We assume the following cooperation model: A VO is composed of a set of partnering organizations each offering a set of services that contribute to a single goal common to all collaboration partners. The goal is defined through a business process model in which each task either refers to a service or a human task performed by a collaboration partner. Services are either statically defined (i.e. pre-assigned at collaboration design time) which requires non-negligible start-up efforts such as searching and opting for appropriate service providers out of a pool of several candidates and establish relationships with him by some means or other. Or services are dynamically selected at the latest possible time, i.e. at service invocation time which is roughly sketched in Fig. 1.

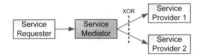

Fig. 1. Ideal service-oriented eCollaboration

For that reason we consider a service broker reasonable and essential. In contrast to previous pure service registry approaches, our service broker is not limited to service registration functionality but introduces an additional layer of indirection and mediation. The service broker can provide standardized interfaces for different kinds of services (e.g. a travel booking services) and service providers (e.g. travel companies) register their service instance for a given type of service. Several authors such as [8], [9] and our initial prototype proved the feasibility of this approach.

The remainder of this paper is organized as follows: In Chapter 2 we present the fundamental security functions for flexible service-oriented VOs from different perspectives. Subsequently, Chapter 3 introduces our approach to tackle the particular security requirements in short-term business networks in more detail and lay out some preliminary implementation considerations in Chapter 4. Chapter 5 provides information on related work and similar approaches before we draw some conclusions and identify future work in the concluding Chapter 6.

2   Security Functions and Implications

We first want to exemplify the basic security requirements our approach is governed by. As a basic non-security principle for our proposed security infrastructure we try to get along with as little need for adaption as possible at both client and service provider side. We aim at relieving both from performing extensive efforts before they can benefit from the newly gained flexibility to rapidly offer existing services to new customers and embed these into their applications.

2.1   Fundamental Security Functions

The flexibility gained from our understanding of VOs strengthens the need for a security infrastructure that is highly reliable and adaptive at the same time. Appropriate security and access control mechanisms in particular are required to ensure that only authorized actors can invoke supporting service while the business process flows from one activity to the next.

In more detail, the following security functions are essential for secure VOs: Usually users first name their claimed identity, termed *identification*. Closely connected is *authentication* during which the system validates the user's claimed identity. Typically both steps precede *access control* which aims at preventing unauthorized use of a resource as well as use of resources in an unauthorized manner. To perform reasonable access control, resource owners first have to specify and allocate access rights to potential users, termed *authorization*. In many cases access rights are directly assigned to user identities but further more elaborate approaches for specifying access rights based on different criteria such as role membership or various attributes of users are well-engineered[18]. These more powerful approaches partially permit *anonymization* or *pseudonymization*, i.e. service usage without disclosing the user's authentic identity. During the interaction of users with resources and services, different *communication security functions* such as encryption and digital signature arise to ensure security aims such as confidentiality and integrity. Last but not least *auditing* allows for recording and reviewing all security-related events.

2.2   Different Perspectives: End User, Service Provider, Broker

Different stakeholders in VOs have different demands concerning security functions. We therefore briefly sketch the perspectives of the most important actors.

End users are usually mainly interested in uncomplicated utilization of required services. If confidential data is transfered communication security functions are inquired, whereas identification is only considered important if it bears advantages such as enhanced or eased functionality due to personalization. Anonymization or pseudonymization might be of interest if users do not want to disclose their authentic identity to access a particular resource.

Service providers mainly focus on authorization, access control and auditing to govern access to their resources and track potential violations. They might be interested in validated identities of their users for accounting purposes and in communication security functions in case they offer confidential information. User anonymization/pseudonymization is usually rather irrelevant.

Service Brokers are trying to please both, users and SPs. Depending on the degree of trust both parties put in one another, service brokers may mediate for example between user's demand for anonymization and service providers' request for authentic user identities for billing purposes.

2.3   Interim Implications

From our definition of dynamic service-oriented eCollaboration can easily be deduced that identity-based authorization and access control does not fit our needs as they imply service providers to know all potential service requesters in advance. If service requesters are permitted access to single services if they can prove their identity – as it is common nowadays – the results are users holding separate accounts at each service provider. Indeed, single-Sign-On (SSO) solutions such as for example Shibboleth[1], OpenID[2] or Cardspace[3] alleviate the problem, still they do not represent fully applicable solutions mainly due to their limitation to services requiring a web browsers as user interface. If services are considered in a broader sense, including modern (SOAP-based) web services as well as legacy applications made available either way, other access control approaches such as role- (RBAC) and attribute-based access control (ABAC)[18] in particular are far more eligible. These approaches introduce an additional layer of indirection between individual users and their access rights and thereby allow for more flexible and dynamic definition of access control policies. More generally spoken, identification becomes less important for the benefit of identity-independent authorization and access control.

3   Approaching Flexible Access Control for VOs

This chapter introduces the system architecture of the SPIKE[4] access control infrastructure and the conceptual model behind in more detail. Our approach allows for dynamic service selection at collaboration run-time and particularly

---

[1] http://shibboleth.internet2.edu/

[2] http://openid.net/

[3] http://www.microsoft.com/windows/products/winfamily/cardspace

[4] http://www.spike-project.eu/

considers access control as the most relevant security function in dynamic service-oriented VOs.

3.1 Architectural Alternatives

The most popular approaches to embed security modules into distributed systems are depicted in Fig. 2 and briefly outlined below. Typically, security modules have to be implemented on both client- and server-side, yet both parties do not necessarily have to decide on the same architectural alternative.

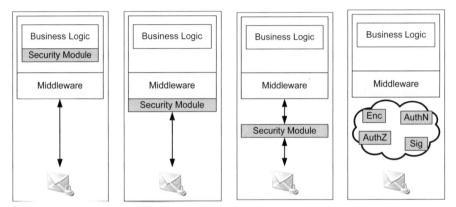

(a) Embedded into the Application   (b) Security in the Middleware   (c) Security as Infrastructure   (d) Security as a Service

Fig. 2. Architectural Alternatives for Implementing Security

Security embedded into the Application. Fig. 2(a) depicts the concept of security components integrated into each and every application. Developers of services and clients have to extend the business logic of service and client respectively by additional security functionality which has to be invoked explicitly. As a result, security functionality is strongly interlinked with the business logic making both potentially more complex, hard to maintain and hard to test for correctness. In addition, interlinkage of business and security functionality might complicate service usage for potential customers. Developers at client- and service-side have to be expert in both, business logic of the service and security issues. If qualified developers are available this approach can provide superior performance due to the direct API communication between business and security logic.

This architectural alternative imposes further disadvantages such as poor scalability and reusability of both, business and security functionality which applies to service providers as well as to service requesters. Most notably, the security modules of service clients have to be particularly tailored to a single service instance rendering this approach cumbersome for the kind of dynamic eCollaboration we aim for.

Security in the Middleware. In contrast to the embedded security approach, security components as part of the middleware (Fig. 2(b)) allow for clear separation of business and security logic. Considering that in most cases services are not operated stand-alone but are deployed into some runtime environment or middleware, this approach seems plausible without causing additional complexity. The approach enables business experts to take care of new business logic without considering security while security can be added in a second step by security experts, which in turn do not have to crasp every detail of the business logic. Thus the security in the middleware approach enables implicit and configurable integration of security.

While this approach apparently meets the situation at service provider side, it might be different for potential service requesters. Security components in the middleware are only feasible for them if the service client is running within some middleware which might be the case for example if the service interface at client side is integrated into some web application deployed to some application server. Still in many cases external services are integrated into stand-alone applications rendering the security in the middleware approach mainly feasible for service providers, not necessarily for service requesters.

Security as Infrastructure. The Security as infrastructure approach (Fig. 2(c)) is quite similar to security in the middleware. While both allow for separation of business and security logic, this approach goes one step further regarding positioning of the security modules. Instead of providing the security modules as part of the middleware, security nodes are freely deployed between service implementation and service client. Usage of the external security nodes is typically configured at the network routing layer. In comparison to other alternatives, this approach does not only decouple security from the business logic but both purely communicate by means of message exchanges, i.e. the security components intercepts messages from and to particular services and clients. Usually neither service nor client notice the existence of the security modules in between implying that security functions are utilized implicitly making it suitable for both service providers and service requesters.

It must be mentioned that this approach imposes severe security implications if applied faulty. While it might be reasonable to provide services without any security functionality within the own company's frontiers for example for simplicity and performance reasons, it has to be guaranteed that all service communication with external organizations implicitly passes the security node. However, if applied correctly, this approach provides maximum flexibility and great reusability and extensibility. In contrast to security in the middleware it is even applicable to stand-alone services and allows defining appropriate security configurations and security credentials depending on sources and targets of messages.

Security as a Service (SaaS). Security as a Service (Fig. 2(d)) is regularly proposed as the most promising approach for realizing security functions especially in SOAs. The common promise is that neither service client nor service provider have to pay attention to security components but can solely focus on business logic. Security functionality is provided by distributed security components operated by various providers in the 'cloud' and is implicitly integrated into communication between service requester and service provider. Only rarely a clear usage scenario that includes integration and allocation of distributed security components is explained. In our opinion issues such as sequence of and orchestration control over different security services are not yet considered satisfactory and certain security functions such as encryption or signature can not be provided by external parties in a reasonable way.

As a result we do not consider security as a service – at least in its currently prevalent denotation – a well-engineered and mature architectural alternative. Rather its reasonable and practicable sub-concepts are already known from and implemented in security in the middleware and security as infrastructure approaches.

3.2   Conceptual Model

The SPIKE approach clearly separates between communication security on the one hand and identification, authentication, authorization and access control on the other hand. This work clearly focuses on the latter. To meet the general requirements of minimum initial adjustment efforts shortly addressed in Chapter 2, we aim at establishing as much functionality as possible neither at the client nor at the service but as part of the infrastructure in between. The conceptual model of our proposed flexible access control infrastructure for service-oriented VOs can be derived from Fig. 3 and is based on the security as infrastructure approach. The main actors are users, service providers (SPs), identity providers (IdPs) and the service broker acting as a security intermediary at the same time.

A *user* does not invoke services directly but needs some client application to do so. For the sake of simplicity and because the client application only provides technical means to employ given services, we do no distinguish between both. In our scenario, a user demands a given business functionality and does neither pay attention to the technical realization nor does she pay attention to the chosen service provider as long as it performs reliably.

Service providers aim at attracting as many service users as possible. Therefore, their rationale is not on shielding their services from unknown users but rather on ensuring that the unknown users confirm to their conditions for service usage. As a result, service providers are not primarily interested in the identity of service requesters but in further attributes e.g. for billing purposes. For that reason they may define the access policy for their services based on security tokens or attributes potential users have to hold and exhibit to gain access.

We assume that service users manage their profile at some *identity provider*. The profile or 'digital identity' consists of all attributes, security and access tokens the user holds. This is an established concept proven by several implementations such as Shibboleth, OpenID or Cardspace.

Furthermore, we assume that service requesters try to access new services of previously unacquainted service providers frequently and rapidly which is why an intermediate *service broker* seems reasonable. In addition to its service selection and mediation functionality, we employ it as a security intermediary. Otherwise dynamic selection of appropriate service instances by a service broker was only possible if all service candidates had the same security policy and therefore required the same security credentials for successful access control. On the contrary, our security intermediary may complement service requests by additional security tokens and mediate between several formats.

The overall service invocation procedure is as follows: For any kind of available service the security broker provides a generic interface for which service providers register their particular implementation. Client applications are built against the service broker interfaces. For invoking a particular service capability, a user dispatches a service request message to the broker. The service broker selects an appropriate service instance from the pool of registered services before the security and access policy of the chosen service is analyzed to extract required 'access tokens' for that service. These tokens are requested from the user's IdP, are attached to the service request which is finally dispatched to the selected service instance. The service instance checks the obtained security token and, based on the result, access is approved or denied.

3.3   Proposed System Architecture

Fig. 3 sketches the proposed SPIKE security architecture which focuses on enabling flexible access control in particular. We positioned security components at five locations distributed across the different parties. Required preparatory work that has to be completed before the access control infrastructure can be employed is narrowed down to basically three preconditions: (1) service users hold their attributes and access tokens at some freely chosen IdP (2) a service broker publishes an interface description for the inquired service (3) one or several service providers registere their service implementation at the service broker.

A service request, constructed in a way to match the service interface offered by the service broker, originates from the user's client application. The outbound security component (No. 1 in Fig. 3) complements the message by information on the user's IdP, i.e its address and an access token to gain access to the user's profile. Potentially further communication security mechanisms as defined in

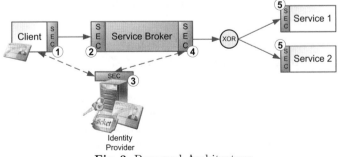

Fig. 3. Proposed Architecture

the service's interface description can likewise be considered by the outbound security module at client side.

The inbound security module at the service broker (No. 2 in Fig. 3), i.e. SPIKE platform side, extracts the information on the user's IdP and the access token from the service request. As a next step, an appropriate service instance for the inquired service functionality is selected from the pool of registered services.

The outbound security module (No. 4 in Fig. 3) retrieves and analyzes the security and access control policy of that service to find out about alternative access tokens or attribute sets that are required to gain access to the selected service instance. It tries to fetch required credentials from the user's IdP leveraging the access token transferred by the user. In case of the user not holding one of the access tokens defined in the security policy of the service, the process is aborted. No. 3 in Fig. 3 depicts the security module at IdP side that protects the user's profile from illegitimate access. As a final step the outbound security module at service broker side enriches the service request by the security tokens received from the user's IdP and forwards the request to the selected service provider. Further security mechanisms such as encryption can likewise be applied here.

Finally, the inbound security module at service provider side (No. 5 in Fig. 3) checks the incoming request for existence and validity of requested security tokens. If the check is successfully, access to the service is granted.

As can be seen from the descriptions above, we built the SPIKE approach regarding separation and distribution of individual security components within the architecture in conformance with the XACML [19] and ISO10181-3 [1] standards. The client represents the access requester or initiator while the service instance represents the target or resource. The IdP conforms to the functions of the policy information point (PIP). The policy enforcement point (PEP) or access control enforcement function (AEF) is provided by the service instance inbound security module. Our current design assumes that the access control decision purely depends on the availability of some security token in the service request. However, depending on the implementation of the SPIKE security infrastructure, the policy decision point (PDP)/access control decision function (ADF) can be performed by the outbound security module of the service broker or the inbound security module of the service instance, respectively. Finally, the policy administration point (PAP) does not exist as a single component but, following the idea of the WS-Security standards, rather each service instance is capable of providing its security policy in a machine-readable form as part of its interface description.

4 Implementation Considerations

For the evaluation of our security and access control infrastructure we are currently in the process of detailing all individual components and building a prototype which is going to be tested within the SPIKE project. A lively open source community provides numerous individual software components we can reuse and base our implementation upon.

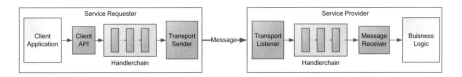

Fig. 4. Client and Service Security Handlers

An Enterprise Service Bus (ESB) offers many message transformation and mediation functionalities required by our service broker component. The JBI specification [22] marked an important step towards a common understanding of the term ESB and currently several rather mature open-source implementations of that standard such as Apache Service Mix[5] or Sun's OpenESB[6] are available. To put the outbound security module at client side and the inbound security module at service side into practice, implementations of the WS-Security standards provide appropriate ground work. Fig. 4 depicts the concept of a chain of security handlers as it is implemented by WS-Security implementations such as Axis2[7] or WSIT[8]. These handlers are configured to intercept the information flow at client and service side and configurably take care of security functionality transparent to the business logic. Last but not least, the concept of in- and out-interceptors in ESBs as depicted in Fig. 5 provides an applicable starting point for implementing required functionality for security components No. 2 and No. 4 in Fig. 3. The Apache CXF binding componentfor JBI-based ESBs employs this concept currently only for SOAP-based web services. From our current point of view, propagation of this concept to other kinds of services should be possible.

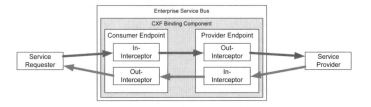

Fig. 5. ESB In- and Out-Interceptors

5   Related Work

VOs and enterprise networks as a dynamic, inter-enterprise configuration for sharing resources and competencies have been identified as a promising alter-

---

[5] http://servicemix.apache.org/
[6] https://open-esb.dev.java.net/
[7] http://ws.apache.org/axis2/
[8] https://wsit.dev.java.net/

native by several authors such as [13], [10] and [3]. [15] stressed the issue of a flexible software and service selection and sourcing strategy while [17] particularly emphasized the short-term nature of virtual enterprises which conflicts with time being the most important factor in the development of trust between collaboration partners. As a result, novel ideas such as the trust negotiation and authorization approach for VOs by [23] have been developed.

OASIS published several standards such as WS-Security[9], WS-SecurityPolicy[10], WS-Federation[11] and WS-Trust[12]. However, all of them only define how to apply security mechanisms to individual SOAP messages, rendering their application to companies interested in opening their business processes – holding hundreds of individual services, resulting in thousands of different SOAP messages – a well-engineered but too low-level technical basis for unreflected deployment.

Bertino et al. [6] discuss three essential classes of security services – identity management, authentication and access control – in more detail and propose a service-oriented approach to security. The service-oriented security architecture presented by [20] considers the same services and bears a prototype based on an ESB like our approach.

The FedWare federated identity management middleware service by [14] employs an external IdP as we do but instead of open standards they base their approach on the Sun Java System Identity Manager. In contrast, the distributed access control infrastructure by [5] does not employ an IdP and does not permit user participation regarding transfer and usage of the access tokens. The web service architecture for decentralized identity- and attribute-based access control by [12] considers many of these issues but is particularly tailored to web services while our approach is open for all kinds of services due to mediation capabilities of ESBs. The security credential mapping approach by [2] introduces a concept to mediate between different credential formats such as X.509 certificates, SAML and username tokens and Kerberos tickets, rendering this work an oportune starting point for extending our IdP. Still this work is currently determined to GRID services, only.

Several further authors such as [21] or [4] tackle usage and access control in SOAs and VOs in particular mainly from a conceptual perspective, focusing access control models and policy languages. Still inadequate understanding of the security issues and potential solutions together with the false belief that companies have to do costly investments into security infrastructures [11] impede broad spreading.

6   Conclusion and Future Work

In this paper we have presented the architectural concept of a security infrastructure for dynamic service-oriented VOs. The presented approach aims at min-

---

[9] http://www.oasis-open.org/specs/#wssv1.1
[10] http://docs.oasis-open.org/ws-sx/ws-securitypolicy
[11] http://docs.oasis-open.org/wsfed/federation
[12] http://docs.oasis-open.org/ws-sx/ws-trust

imizing the leadtime before usage of external services can start by employing a
security intermediary for mediation purposes. We primarily focus on access control
but the overall architecture permits implementing further security functions
as well. We presented several architectural alternatives and the conceptual model
and architecture of our approach in detail and completed this work by preliminary
technical considerations towards the implementation of a first prototype.
This prototype is then going to be evaluated within the SPIKE project.

Beyond that tentative prototype, current and future work covers detailing and
refining several aspects of our approach. Access control to users' security tokens
and attributes hosted at the IdP is not yet fully sorted out but an adapted
OAuth[13] protocol seems to provide a promising approach. Furthermore, availability
and absence of required access tokens might even be considered during
the selection phase of an adequate service instance just as other user defined
service selection criteria such as service availability, price range, load or other
quality of service criteria. Last but not least even users' 'privacy attitude', i.e.
which access tokens or which set of attributes are they willing to disclose for a
particular type of service, might be considered during the service selection phase
and necessitates further research.

References

1. International Organization for Standardization (ISO): Information Technology -
   Open Systems Interconnection - Security Frameworks in Open Systems - Part 3:
   Access Control. ISO/IEC 10181-3 (1996)
2. Ahsant, M., Gonzalez, E.T., Basney, J.: Security Credential Mapping in Grids. In:
   Proc. of the 4th International Conference on Availability, Reliability and Security
   (ARES'09), pp. 481–486 (2009)
3. AT&T: Collaboration across borders: An AT&T survey and white paper in co-
   operation with the Economist Intelligence Unit (2008)
4. Aziz, B., Arenas, A., Martinelli, F., Matteucci, I., Mori, P.: Controlling Usage in
   Business Process Workflows through Fine-Grained Security Policies. In: Furnell,
   S.M., Katsikas, S.K., Lioy, A. (eds.) TrustBus 2008. LNCS, vol. 5185, pp. 100–117.
   Springer, Heidelberg (2008)
5. Belsis, P., Gritzalis, S., Skourlas, C., Tsoukalas, V.: Design and Implementation
   of Distributed Access Control Infrastructures for Federations of Autonomous Domains. In: Lambrinoudakis, C., Pernul, G., Tjoa, A.M. (eds.) TrustBus 2007. LNCS,
   vol. 4657, pp. 125–134. Springer, Heidelberg (2007)
6. Bertino, E., Martino, L.D.: A Service-oriented Approach to Security - Concepts and
   Issues. In: Proc. of the 8th International Symposium on Autonomous Decentralized
   Systems (ISADS'07), pp. 7–16 (2007)
7. Broser, C., Fritsch, C., Gmelch, O., Pernul, G., Schillinger, R., Wiesbeck, S.: Analyzing Requirements for Virtual Business Alliances - the Case of SPIKE. In: Proc.
   of the International ICST Conference on Digital Business, DigiBiz 2009 (2009)
8. Chang, S.H., La, H.J., Bae, J.S., Jeon, W.Y., Kim, S.D.: Design of a Dynamic
   Composition Handler for ESB-based Services. In: Proc. of the IEEE International
   Conference on e-Business Engineering (ICEBE '07), pp. 287–294 (2007)

---

[13] http://oauth.net/core/1.0a/

9. D'Mello, D.A., Ananthanarayana, V.S.: Quality Driven Web Service Selection and Ranking. In: Proc. of the 5th International Conference on Information Technology: New Generations (ITNG '08), pp. 1175–1176 (2008)

10. Eid, T.: Gartner Research: Gartner Says Worldwide Web Conference and Team Collaboration Software Markets Will Reach \$2.8 Billon in 2010 (2007)

11. Gutiérrez, C., Fernández-Medina, E., Piattini, M.: Web Services Security: Is the Problem Solved? In: Proc. of the 2nd International Workshop on Security In Information Systems (WOSIS 2004), pp. 293–304 (2004)

12. Hebig, R.N., Meinel, C., Menzel, M., Thomas, I., Warschofsky, R.: A Web Service Architecture for Decentralised Identity- and Attribute-based Access Control. In: Proc. of the 7th IEEE International Conference on Web Services (ICWS'09), pp. 551–558 (2009)

13. van Heck, E., Vervest, P.: Smart Business Networks: How the Network Wins. Communications of the ACM 50(6), 28–37 (2007)

14. Hoellrigl, T., Dinger, J., Hartenstein, H.: FedWare: Middleware Services to Cope with Information Consistency in Federated Identity Management. In: Proc. of the 5th International Conference on Availability, Reliability and Security (ARES '10), pp. 228–235 (2010)

15. Iyer, B., Freedman, J., Gaynor, M., Wyner, G.: Web Services: Enabling Dynamic Business Networks. Communications of the AIS 11, 525–554 (2003)

16. Kasper-Fuehrer, E., Ashkanasy, N.: The Interorganisational Virtual Organisation: Defining a Weberian Ideal. International Studies of Management & Organisation 33, 34–64 (2003)

17. Lawson, R., Hol, A., Hall, T.: Challenges of eCollaboration among SMEs. In: Proc. of the 20th Bled eConference: eMergence (2007)

18. Lopez, J., Oppliger, R., Pernul, G.: Authentication and Authorization Infrastructures (AAIs): A Comparative Survey. Computers & Security 23, 578–590 (2004)

19. Moses, T.: eXtensible Access Control Markup Language (XACML) Version 2.0. OASIS Standard (2005)

20. Opincaru, C., Gheorghe, G.: Service Oriented Security Architecture. Enterprise Modelling and Information Systems Architectures Journal 4(1), 39–48 (2009)

21. Pretschner, A., Massacci, F., Hilty, M.: Usage Control in Service-Oriented Architectures. In: Lambrinoudakis, C., Pernul, G., Tjoa, A.M. (eds.) TrustBus 2007. LNCS, vol. 4657, pp. 83–93. Springer, Heidelberg (2007)

22. Ten-Hove, R., Walker, P.: Java Business Integration (JBI) 1.0. Java Specification Request 208 (2005)

23. Winslett, M., Lee, A.J., Perano, K.J.: Trust Negotiation: Authorization for Virtual Organizations. In: Proc. of the 5th Annual Workshop on Cyber Security and Information Intelligence Research (CSIIRW '09). pp. 1–4 (2009)

Analyzing Information Security Awareness through Networks of Association

Aggeliki Tsohou[1], Maria Karyda[1], Spyros Kokolakis[1], and Evangelos Kiountouzis[2]

[1] University of the Aegean, Dept. of Information and Communication Systems Engineering,
Samos GR-83200, Greece
{agt,mka,sak}@aegean.gr
[2] Athens University of Economics and Business, Dept. of Informatics, 76 Patission Str.,
Athens GR-10434, Greece
eak@aueb.gr

Abstract. Information security awareness is a continuous effort to raise attention to information security and its importance, in order to stimulate security-oriented behaviors. Despite the increasing interest of researchers on the topic and the continuous notifications of global security surveys for its significance, awareness remains a critical issue of information security. Related approaches propose techniques and methods for promoting security without theoretical grounding and separately from the overall information security management framework. The aim of this paper is to suggest a theoretical and methodological framework which facilitates the analysis and understanding of the issues that are intertwined with awareness activities, in order to support the organization's security management.

Keywords: Security awareness, due process, actor network theory, security management.

1 Introduction

Information systems are a primary asset of organizations; organizations rely on them for collecting and processing information, supporting decision making and enhancing distance communication. This fact, in conjunction with the increasing flow and accumulation of information as a result of information and communication technologies advancements, has led to a continuous and increasing interest for security. However, while the scientific and practical breakthroughs towards protecting information systems grow, the threats against information security proliferate as well. In this race, humans and their interaction with information and communication technologies play a fundamental role and is frequently regarded as the weakest link of security [3], [5]. One of the main practices that are applied in order to enable people act as an ally for information security endeavor, is information security awareness.

There are several different approaches to the definition of security awareness; it is commonly agreed, however, that the information security awareness focuses on a continuous effort to raise wide audiences' attention to information security and its importance, in order to stimulate security-oriented behaviors [11], [16] ,[24], [30].

S. Katsikas, J. Lopez, and M. Soriano (Eds.): TrustBus 2010, LNCS 6264, pp. 227–237, 2010.
© Springer-Verlag Berlin Heidelberg 2010

Information security awareness methods to communicate security messages are categorized [13] into *promotional* (events, posters, games, etc.), *educational/interactive* (presentations, brief sessions, workshops, etc.), *informational* (i.e. leaflets, newsletters, web site postings, e-mails), and *enforcing* (confidentiality agreements, required awareness exam or test, etc.). Security topics include [29] password usage and management, protection from malicious code, security policies, web usage, spam, data backup, social engineering etc. The significance of security awareness initiatives has been highlighted lately by global security surveys which indicate that in practice a) most security losses were caused due to non-malicious, merely careless behavior of insiders [9], and that b) information security awareness is critical for organizations to achieve a strategic view of information security [4], [12]. Researchers have also emphasized the need for security awareness initiatives in order to enhance information security [8], [15], [16], [31], [36], [39].

Despite all this, awareness remains a critical issue of information security. Awareness research investigates related challenges and proposes techniques and methods for addressing the fact that security awareness programs lack theoretical grounding [38], [31], and that they are implemented separately from the overall information security management framework [37]. This paper addresses the following research question *"How is an information security awareness initiative incorporated in an organizational environment?"* The paper proposes a framework for analyzing and understanding the events related with the implementation of security awareness activities, in order to facilitate their incorporation into the organization's security management. This framework is the outcome of theoretical analysis which has been grounded on actor network theory and the due process model.

The paper is structured in six sections. Current section has presented the research area and question. In section 2 we present the theoretical approaches that have been applied in the literature for the exploration of information security awareness. Next, we present the connection between information security awareness and information security management processes. In section 4, the proposed theoretical and methodological framework is described, while in section 5 we justify its applicability on information security awareness. The final section presents our conclusion and issues for further research.

2   Current Approaches on Information Security Awareness

In general, most proposed information security awareness frameworks suggest or implement awareness methods and techniques, such as methods to convey security messages, artificial intelligence tools, computer games etc., without justifying their choices and specifying their theoretical foundations [38], [31]. Moreover, those research approaches that are theoretically grounded and examine the security awareness challenges and problems are based solely on psychological or behavioral theories.

Thomson and von Solms [36] propose social psychology theories and utilize psychological principles for improving the effectiveness of security awareness programs. They develop an attitude system according to which users attitudes are affected by behavior intentions, behavior cognitions, and affective responses. According to this system, three methods can be applied in order to affect individuals' attitudes through persuasion: 1) directly changing their behavior, 2) using a change in behavior to influence a person's attitude; and 3) changing a person's attitude through persuasion. Finally, authors suggest a set of psychological principles and techniques for changing a person's attitude, including instrumental learning, social learning, conformity, reciprocity, self-persuasion and retention. Siponen [35] proposes a set of practical approaches and principles with respect to motivation, including logic, emotions, morals and ethics, well-being, feeling of security and rationality. His conceptual foundation for security awareness is based on the theory of reasoned action, the theory of planned behavior, intrinsic motivation and the technology acceptance model. Qing et al. [32] utilize the elaboration likelihood model as a framework for understanding the effectiveness of persuasive communications. Authors apply the elaboration likelihood model to explore the effectiveness of security messages and the change of recipient's behavior, by studying the effects of security message characteristics on users. Similarly, Puhakainen [31] aims at achieving behavioural changes towards IS users' compliance with IS security policies and instructions. To do so, the author employs attitudinal and instructional theories. Conclusively, conceptual foundations of information security awareness can be traced to psychological and behavioral streams. This paper advocates the need to apply approaches that take into consideration also the social and organizational aspects of security awareness.

3 Associating Security Awareness with Information Security Management

Since information systems, and their security, affect people in their various areas or roles or activities, different dimensions of information security awareness can be identified [34]: i.e. organizational dimension, general public dimension, socio-political dimension, computer ethical dimension, and institutional education dimension. The focus of this paper is on the *organizational dimension* of security awareness, meaning the organized and ongoing initiatives of awareness that aim at guiding the behavior and culture of an organization in regard to security issues [24]. Such a systematic and organized effort should be an inextricable part of an organization's information security management framework. Most relative studies, however, examine security awareness out of the context of security management. In the following we describe in brief the different awareness activities involved in the process of security management and the way these activities are intertwined with security management.

Information security management is a structured process for the implementation and ongoing management of information security in an organization [40]. It includes activities that aim at protecting information and information facilities so as to secure business continuity. It is therefore important that information security management is treated like any vital business function, with all its activities based upon business needs. Several security management frameworks have been proposed, including the following:

- Vermeulen and von Solms [40] organize security management activities into a) *preparation* elements (e.g. gain top management commitment, describe security vision and strategy), b) *implementation* elements (e.g. determine security requirements, formulate security policy, perform risk management, implement safeguards and procedures), and c) *maintenance* or *continuation* elements (e.g. monitor security situation, ensure proper incident handling). In this framework,, awareness activities are placed in the implementation phase.

- Wilson et al. [42] organize security management activities in four phases: *planning, organizing, directing* and *controlling. Planning* refers to the formulation of a security plan based on a systematic study of the organization's IS assets, and a listing of potential threats and proposed countermeasures. Security requirements are identified through a risk analysis and management process. *Organizing* includes activities for the implementation of the security plan, such as development of procedures and standards, implementation of security products and techniques, training of administrators. The *directing* phase involves leading and managing security administrators, and conducting user and management awareness programs. During this phase, the responsibility of managers to protect assets allocated to them and to ensure that subordinates are aware of the security policy and procedures is established. The final phase, *controlling*, involves, among others, monitoring the effectiveness of safeguards, internal and external auditing, and investigation of security breaches. In this framework, security awareness is placed in the directing phase.

- Finally, a widely accepted security management framework, described as an Information Security Management System (ISMS), is proposed in ISO/IEC 27001 (2005) [18] and is structured in four phases: a) establishment, b) implementation and operation, c) monitoring and review, and d) maintenance and improvement. In the *establishment* phase, the scope and boundaries of the ISMS are defined, an ISMS policy is described and risk management is performed in order to develop a risk treatment plan. The *implementation* phase involves the risk treatment plan implementation and operation of all security safeguards. Monitoring and reviewing activities include documentation of procedures that promptly identify attempted and successful security breaches, incidents, and errors, and also, performing regular reviews of the ISMS effectiveness. The final phase includes activities to maintain and improve the risk management process, and also, to take the appropriate corrective and preventive actions, to communicate the actions and improvements to all interested parties and to ensure that the improvements achieve their intended objectives. Within the ISO/IEC 27001 (2005) framework, awareness is an activity of the implementation phase.

This analysis indicates that information security awareness is strongly associated with the overall information security management process and should therefore not be performed or studied, separately from other security management activities. Current security management and security awareness initiatives, however, ignore this association. To effectively incorporate awareness activities into the security management process, the organizational, social and technical context needs to be taken into consideration. To fill this gap, this paper proposes a theoretical and methodological framework that has its grounds in Actor Network Theory, a theory that despite the fact that it has provided information systems researchers with interesting insights with regard to the role of technology in the organizational context, it remains unknown to the information security management field. The framework proposed can facilitate both the implementation and the study of security awareness as a managerial and social process, by providing insights in the context of information security management.

4 Actor Network Theory and the due Process Model

4.1 Actor Network Theory in Information Systems Research

Actor network theory (ANT) has been developed by the Science and Technology Studies (STS) researchers Bruno Latour [20], [22] and Michel Callon [6], [7], and further extended by the sociologist John Law [23]. The main purpose of the theory is to address the role of technology in a social setting and explore the processes by which technology affects and is affected by the social elements of a context over time [25]. Actor network theory postulates that technology is not a static artifact that can be introduced in a social setting without conflicts. On the contrary, artifacts incorporate the action designed by their constructor that restrains their usage; therefore artifacts are an entity with inscribed agency. ANT outlines how actors form alliances and enroll other actors, by using non-human actors, to strengthen such associations and their interests. This way, heterogeneous actor-networks are created which include human and non-human actors.

Furthermore, ANT studies the relationship between human and non-human actors; thus, the incentives and actions of people that align their interests around technological elements [14]. The study of the process by which the interests of different actors are aligned, enables the examination of the way stability of the network emerges and evolves. According to the ANT view, a stabilized network refers to an association of a capable amount of allies that have aligned their interests and thus they are willing to participate in a particular way of thinking and action in order to preserve the network. Stability means that the actor-network and its underlying ideas have become institutionalized and are no longer seen as controversial. During this motivation of other actors, human actors inscribe scenarios of usage in the non-human actors. This way they delegate roles and requirements by the potential allies. Therefore, stability is a product of ongoing negotiation and interest alignment, while its preservation depends on the ability to translate interests of actors into the interest of the network. Alignment and stabilization cannot be the result of a top-down plan of decision; it is the achievement of a process of bottom-up mobilization of actors [27]. ANT can be used in studies that explore and explain the processes by which networks of aligned interests are created and preserved or alternatively to explain the reasons why such networks fail to be stabilized [25], [41]. To do so, ANT enables the unpacking of the dynamic socio-technical process that led to the network creation.

ANT has been widely applied in information systems research as an analyzing tool for the understanding of the way social systems change with the involvement of technology. The target of ANT application in these studies is not to criticize the right or wrong directions or enrolment, but to explore the reasons why the process developed in a certain way. ANT adheres to the acknowledgment that every person has different perceptions of the information systems, and thus, its final translation is not influenced only by technological factors but social interaction as well. ANT has been applied for studying and explaining information systems project escalation [25], Enterprise

Resource Planning implementation [33], development and evaluation of information systems proposals [43], strategy formulation of telecommunication market [14] or the enrolment strategies of the personal digital assistants (PDAs) industry [2], while [17] have used ANT for the examination of standardization processes of information infrastructure. Conclusively, ANT has been widely used by information systems researchers for studying transformations or changes that are caused by technology in organizations or other social systems.

4.2 Translation and Inscription

As [25] state, Callon [7] has defined translation or the creation of an actor-network as "the methods by which an actor enrolls others" in a four-stage process: a) problematization, b) interessement, c) enrollment, and d) mobilization. During the *problematization* stage an initiating or focal actor identifies other actors with consistent interests. In this initial stage in building an actor-network certain actors position themselves as indispensable resources in the solution of the problems they have defined; this way they establish themselves as an "obligatory passage point" for the problems' solution. The *interessement* stage aims at convincing other actors whose interests are in line with the initiators' interests, by creating, if necessary, incentives to make them willing to overcome obstacles participating to the network. If this stage is successful, enrollment occurs. *Enrollment* involves the allocation of roles to the actors, and the attempt to extend the network by seeking more actors. In case an actor behaves differently from the role she was supposes to, then the actors *betrays* the network. Finally, during *mobilization* the focal actor examines whether the allies act according to the agreement and do not betray the initial interests. With the creation of an actor-network the focal actor intends to secure continued support to her interest from the enrolled actors and achieve network stability.

As already mentioned, during the translation phase, artifacts are used in order to stimulate other actors to participate and adopt a specific role in the network. To do so, a pattern or scenario of use is embodied in the artifact in order to describe anticipations and restrictions of future use [27]. When a pattern of actions is *inscribed* into an artifact, then the artifact becomes an actor imposing its inscribed pattern on its users. The flexibility of following the pattern varies according to the strength of the inscription. The strength of an inscription relies on three aspects [17]: the size and complexity of the surrounding actor-network which is linked to the inscription, the degree to which it is aligned with this surrounding network, and the strength of the inscription on its own. It is, however, impossible to know exactly what inscriptions are needed to achieve a given action; knowledge is gained by studying the sequence of attempted inscriptions.

4.3 The due Process Model

According to ANT, an actor-network can be studied with regard to the process of translation and the inscriptions that are embodied in artifacts. However, it is not possible to determine the stability (or not) of an actor-network in short-term. As [26] and [28] state, facts are not diffused in the classical sense. Instead, claims are translated and strengthened (or weakened) through the enrollment and inscriptions of additional human and non-human alliances. They are thereby constantly transformed as the network lengthens across time and space. Therefore, the final factuality of a particular claim will be decided in the long-term through a trajectory of transformations. (Figure 1). Actor-networks should not be analyzed regarding their static freeze frames (single moments or time); instead they should be analyzed based on the very different and dynamic picture that emerges when we view the transformations over time.

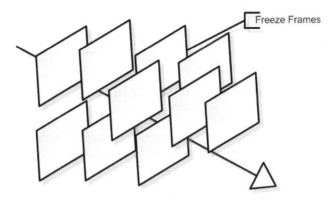

Fig. 1. The Trajectory of Transformations [21]

To follow the process of decision-making the Due Process Model [21] can be used. Whenever new candidates for existence (facts, claims, and technologies) are introduced, they bring a degree of perplexity in the network (Figure 2). A consultation/debate process concerning the legitimacy of the candidacy by the others follows that result in the establishment of the candidate's position in the network. Only through this process that candidate becomes accepted through institutionalization and after the candidate has been imbued with values through consultation and hierarchy. Alternatively she may be rejected and excluded. In case that an attempt is made to shortcut the process and move the candidate directly from moment 1 (perplexity) to moment 4 (institution) the likelihood of failure may be greatly increased.

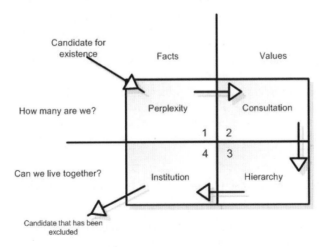

Fig. 2. The Due Process Model [21]

Applying the due process model in order to monitor the inclusion and exclusion of candidates can provide us with a dynamic view of the network's transformations over time. It should be, however, clarified that the due process phases do not coincide with the four phases of translation. Instead, the due process provides us with a tool to zoom in a particular moment in time and analyze the inclusion of exclusion of candidates.

5   Raising Information Security Awareness through the Dynamic due Process

In this paper we argue that through the lens of ANT and the due process model researchers and practitioners can more effectively analyze, understand and manage security awareness activities, as they interact with information security management with a specific organizational context. Information security awareness activities entail the participation of both human (e.g. awareness program's designers and the security messages recipients) and as non-human actors (e.g. awareness promotion tools or means such as leaflets, posters, etc.). The aim of any awareness initiative is to make its recipients behave in a security-oriented manner; therefore the whole set of actors (human and non-human actors) should exhibit the behavior of a *stabilized network* in order to pursue information security. To this end, non-human actors are involved by human actors – typically the designers of the awareness program – that have inscribed specific security-related roles and behaviors. For example, security awareness games embody several scenarios of users' security related behavior, and reward the ones which are aligned with information security best practices or policies. In addition, different interests are involved in security awareness efforts. Different security awareness groups of stakeholders (actors) – e.g. managers, administrators, security officers, end-users – have different interests that should be aligned in order to commit users in a specific way of acting and thinking so as to achieve security.

Conclusively, we can view information security awareness as a process of translating security goals in order to create a stabilized network of actors whose behavior is security-oriented. ANT-based analysis takes into account actors' different interests, roles and goals, and also the events and conditions that may affect the organizational and security management context. In addition, this analysis can provide insights with regard to the motives provided to information systems users and the strength of the applied inscriptions in order to contribute to network's stability. This framework can also enhance our understanding of the network's formation through time, highlighting the way security awareness actors align their interests and the way awareness actor-network transform over time. Finally, this analysis enables actors manage the transformations of the awareness actor-network and provide them with the ability to guide towards certain directions, instead of considering it an uncontrolled process with random outcome [28].

5.1   Applying the ANT-Based Framework in Information Security Awareness Activities

Information security managers are often faced with the challenge to obtain support for the development and implementation of an information security awareness program.

These programs are notorious for involving and committing to security numerous and diverse stakeholders from many parts of the organization (e.g. personnel department, information technology department, training officer, etc.). To achieve this aim they would need to form alliances, or in ANT terms, to form an actor-network. Although there is no recipe for the formation of an actor-network, it would be useful to have a list of candidate actors - human and non-human actors. Non-human actors may include, for instance, the information security policy or the information security plan/programme, relevant standards (e.g. [11], [29]) presentations of speakers in information security events, leaflets, software tools etc. Human actors, on the other hand, may include top managers, administrators, security officers, users, programmers, perpetrators (e.g. hackers). At this point we should note that the formation of an actor-network is a social process and it is rarely controlled by one of the actors (i.e. the "focal-actor"). As a result, a hacker would most probably not get invited, but her coincidental presence could be an opportunity for achieving stability in the network. Next, different interests of human actors and inscriptions in non-human need to be identified and management effort should focus on their alignment, in order to achieve security goals. Finally, by studying the related trajectories of transformation in retrospect, valuable lessons can be learned, so as to enhance the on-going process of raising security awareness.

6 Conclusions and Further Research

This paper illustrates the need to adopt an organizational perspective on the study and implementation of security awareness activities. We propose a theoretical and methodological framework based on Actor Network Theory ,which can facilitate both understanding and management of security awareness initiatives, due to the fact that different stakeholders (both human and non-human) and their possibly conflicting interests are considered. Our future research entails the application of this framework on a real-life case, so as to verify its explanatory and exploratory value in the organizational setting.

References

1. Albrechtsen, E.: A qualitative study of users' view on information security. Computers & Security 26(4), 276–289 (2007)
2. Allen, J.P.: Redefining the network: enrollment strategies in the PDA industry. IT & People 17(2), 171–185 (2004)
3. Barrett, N.: Penetration testing and social engineering: Hacking the weakest link. Information Security Technical Report 8(4), 56–64 (2003)
4. BERR, Information Security Breaches Survey, technical report, PriceWaterHouseCoopers, in association with Symantec, HP and The Security Company (2008),
   http://www.pwc.co.uk/pdf/BERR_ISBS_2008sml.pdf
   (accessed 10.1.2010)
5. Bresz, F.P.: People—often the weakest link in security, but one of the best places to start. Journal of Health Care Compliance 6(4), 57–60 (2004)
6. Callon, M.: Techno-Economic Networks and Irreversibility. In: Law, J. (ed.) A Sociology of Monsters? Essays on Power, Technology and Domination, pp. 132–161. Routledge, London (1991)

7. Callon, M.: Some Elements of a Sociology of Translation: Domestication of the Scallops and the Fishermen oφ St Brieuc Bay'. In: Law, J. (ed.) Power, Action and Belief: A New Sociology of Knowledge, pp. 196–233. Routledge and Kegan Paul, London (1986)
8. Chen, C.C., Shaw, R.S., Yang, S.C.: Mitigating Information Security Risks by Increasing User Security Awareness: A Case Study of an Information Security Awareness System. Information Technology Learning and Performance Journal 24(1), 1–14 (2006)
9. CSI, Computer crime and security survey 2009. Computer Security Institute (2009), `http://i.cmpnet.com/v2.gocsi.com/pdf/CSISurvey09_Executive-Summary.pdf` (accessed 31.3.2010)
10. Drevin, L., Kruger, H.A., Steyn, T.: Value-focused assessment of ICT security awareness in an academic environment. Computers & Security 26(1), 36–43 (2007)
11. ENISA , A new Users' Guide: How to Raise Information Security Awareness. European Network and Information Security Agency (2008), `http://www.enisa.europa.eu/doc/pdf/deliverables/new_ar_users_guide.pdf` (accessed 31.3.2010)
12. Ernst, Young: Annual global information security survey 2008 (2008), `http://www.ey.com/NZ/en/Services/Assurance/Technology-and-Security-Risk-Services/Global-Information-Security-Survey-2008` (Accessed at 10.1.2010)
13. Everett, C.J.: Security Awareness: switch to a better programme. Network Security 2006(2), 15–18 (2006)
14. Gao, P.: Using actor-network theory to analyse strategy formulation. Information Systems Journal 15(3), 255–275 (2005)
15. Goucher, W.: Getting the most from training sessions: the art of raising security awareness without curing insomnia. Computer Fraud & Security 2008(4), 15 (2008)
16. Hansche, S.: Designing a Security Awareness Program: Part I. Information Systems Security 9(6), 14–23 (2001)
17. Hanseth, O., Monteiro, E.: Inscribing behaviour in information infrastructure. Accounting, Management and Information Technologies 7(4), 183–211 (1997)
18. ISO/IEC 27001, Information technology - Security techniques – Information security management systems – requirements. International Standards Association (2005)
19. Kruger, H.A., Kearney, W.D.: A prototype for assessing information security awareness. Computers & Security 25(1), 289–296 (2006)
20. Latour, B.: Science in Action: How to Follow Scientists and Engineers Through Society. Harvard University Press, Cambridge (1987)
21. Latour, B.: Seminar series, Information Systems or Networks of Transformation? and The Politics of Nature. London School of Economics and Political Science, London (1998)
22. Latour, B.: Where Are the Missing Masses? Sociology of a Few Mundane Artefacts. In: Bijker, W., Law, J. (eds.) Shaping Technology, Building Society: Studies in Sociotechnical Change. MIT Press, Cambridge (1992)
23. Law, J.: Notes on the Theory of the Actor-Network: Ordering, Strategy and Heterogeneity. Systems Practice 5, 379–393 (1992)
24. Maeyer, D.D.: Setting up an Effective Information Security Awareness Programme. In: ISSE/SECURE, Securing Electronic Business Processes Highlights of the Information Security Solutions Europe/SECURE, Conference (part 1), Vieweg, pp. 49–58 (2007)
25. Mähring, M., Holmström, J., Keil, M., Montealegre, R.: Trojan actor-networks and swift translation: Bringing actor-network theory to IT project escalation studies. Information Technology & People 17(2), 210–238 (2004)

26. McMaster, T., Vidgen, R.T., Wastell, D.G.: Networks of association and due process in IS development. In: Larsen, T.J., Levine, L., DeGross, J.I. (eds.) Information Systems: Current Issues and Future Changes, pp. 341–357. IFIP, Laxenburg (1999)
27. Monteiro, E.: Actor-network theory and information infrastructure. In: Ciborra, C. (ed.) From control to drift. The dynamics of corportate information infrastructure, pp. 71–83. Oxford Univ. Press, Oxford (2000)
28. Nandhakumar, J., Vidgen, R.: Due process and the introduction of new technology: The institution of video – teleconferencing. In: Russo, N.L., Fitzgerald, B., DeGross, J.I. (eds.) Realigning Research and Practice in Information Systems Development: The social and organizational perspective, Proceedings of the International Federation for Information Processing (IFIP Working Group 8. 2), Boise, Idaho, USA, pp. 127–148. Chapman & Hall, London (2001)
29. NIST, Building an Information Technology Security Awareness and Training Program. NIST Special Publication 800-50, edited by Wilson M.: National Institute of Standards and Technology, csrc.nist.gov (2003) (accessed 10.1.2010)
30. Peltier, T.R.: Implementing an Information Security Awareness Program. Information Systems Security 14(2), 37–48 (2005)
31. Puhakainen, P.: A design theory for information security awareness. Doctoral Dissertation, Department of information processing science, University of Oulu (2006), http://herkules.oulu.fi/isbn9514281144/ (accessed 10.1.2010)
32. Qing, T., Ng, B., Kankanhalli, A.: Individual's Response to Security Messages: A Decision-Making Perspective, Decision Support for Global Enterprises. Annals of Information Systems, pp. 177–191. Springer, US (2007)
33. Scott, S.V., Wagner, E.L.: Networks, negotiations, and new times: the implementation of enterprise resource planning into an academic administration. Information and Organization 13(4), 285–313 (2003)
34. Siponen, M.: Five dimensions of Information Security Awareness. Computers and Society 32(2), 24–29 (2001)
35. Siponen, M.T.: A conceptual foundation for organizational information security awareness. Information Management & Computer Security 8(1), 31–41 (2000)
36. Thomson, M.E., von Solms, R.: Information security awareness: educating your users effectively. Information Management & Computer Security 6(4), 167–173 (1998)
37. Tsohou, A., Karyda, M., Kokolakis, S., Kiountouzis, E.: Aligning Security Awareness with Information Systems Security Management. Journal of Information System Security 6(1), 36–54 (2010)
38. Tsohou, A., Kokolakis, S., Karyda, M., Kiountouzis, E.: Investigating information security awareness: research and practice gaps. Information Security Journal: A Global Perspective 17(5&6), 207–227 (2008)
39. Valentine, J.A.: Enhancing the employee security awareness model. Computer Fraud & Security (6), 17–19 (2006)
40. Vermeulen, C., Von Solms, R.: The information security management toolbox – taking the pain out of security management. Information Management & Computer Security 10(3), 119–125 (2002)
41. Walsham, G.: Actor-Network Theory and IS research: Current status and future prospects. In: Lee, A.S., Liebenau, J., DeGross, J.I. (eds.) Information systems and qualitative research, pp. 466–480. Chapman and Hall, London (1997)
42. Wilson, J., Turban, E., Zviran, M.: Information Systems Security: A Managerial Perspective. International Journal of Information Management 12, 105–119 (1992)
43. Cecez-Kecmanovic, D., Nagm, F.: Understanding IS Projects Evaluation in Practice through an ANT Inquiry. In: Proceedings of the 19th Australasian Conference on Information Systems (ACIS), Christchurch, New Zealand (2008)

Efficiency Improvement of Homomorphic E-Auction

Kun Peng and Feng Bao

Institute for Infocomm Research
dr.kun.peng@gmail.com

Abstract. A design is proposed in this paper to apply a special membership proof technique and a range test technique to homomorphic e-auction. It answers three open questions. On one hand, the special membership proof technique has some limitations such that so far few appropriate applications have been found for it. Moreover, although only needing a constant cost and achieving very high efficiency the range test technique is so new that no appropriate application has been proposed for it. On the other hand, so far no efficient and secure solution has been found for homomorphic e-auction, especially in bid validity check and range test of sum of bids. In this paper, the special membership proof technique and the range test technique are applied to homomorphic e-auction such that all of them benefit from our new design. On one hand, the membership proof technique and the range test technique find an appropriate application and become practical technologies. On the other hand, homomorphic e-auction overcomes its bottlenecks in efficiency and achieves great improvement in performance.

1 Introduction

In a sealed-bid auction scheme, each bidder chooses his evaluation from a number of biddable prices and submits it to some auctioneers, who then open the bids and determine the winning price and winner(s) according to a pre-defined auction rule. The commonly applied auction rules include first bid auction (the bidder with the highest bid wins and pays the highest bid), Vickrey auction (the bidder with the highest bid wins and pays the second highest bid) and the κth bid auction (the bidders with the κ highest bids win, pay the κth or the $\kappa + 1^{th}$ highest bid and each gets an identical item). The first-bid auction and Vickrey auction can be regarded as special cases of the κth bid auction, which is a general solution. An auction must be correct, namely the auction result is strictly determined according to the auction rule. Fairness is necessary in any auction such that no bidder can take advantage over other bidders. A general e-auction scheme should be flexible enough to support various auction rules. Usually, bid privacy must be kept in an auction scheme, which means in the course of bid opening no information about any losing bid is revealed.

When bid privacy must be kept in a non-interactive auction, an efficient bid opening function is homomorphic bid opening [13,15,8,14,1,5,16,17]. To adopt

S. Katsikas, J. Lopez, and M. Soriano (Eds.): TrustBus 2010, LNCS 6264, pp. 238–249, 2010.
© Springer-Verlag Berlin Heidelberg 2010

this bid opening function, one-selection-per-price principle and homomorphic bid sealing must be employed. Each bidder has to submit a bidding selection at every biddable price to indicate whether he is willing to pay that price (e.g. 1 for "YES" or 0 for "NO"). Every selection is sealed with an additive homomorphic secret sharing or encryption algorithm (as will be explained in details in Section 2.3), so that the auctioneers can test at a price whether the sum of the bidding selections (and thus the number of bidders willing to pay the price) is smaller than κ without revealing any bidding selection. With this homomorphic bid opening mechanism, the winning bid can be determined without opening the separate bidding selections.

In homomorphic e-auction, each bidding selection must be in some special format (the certain values standing for "YES" or "NO") to guarantee correctness and fairness of the auction. So validity of the bids must be proved by the bidders and then publicly verified. However, proof and verification of bid validity is highly inefficient in the existing homomorphic e-auction schemes. Moreover, although binary search for the winning price only tests the sum of bidding selections at a small number of prices, each test is a range test (as will be explained in details in Section 2.2), which is not efficient in the existing homomorphic e-auction schemes when no privacy is compromised. Some methods [18,19,20,23] are proposed to improve efficiency of homomorphic e-auction. The methods in [18,19] strictly limit the auction rule and thus lose generality and flexibility. Short exponents are employed in [20,23] to improve efficiency, but this method has two drawbacks. Firstly, it weakens soundness of e-auction. Secondly, its advantage in efficiency is not very fair as other homomorphic e-auction schemes can improve their efficiency by employing shorter exponents and weakening soundness too. In this paper, we are interested in general and flexible e-auction with the same level of soundness as the existing homomorphic e-auction schemes [13,15,8,14,1,5,16,17]. So these improvements [18,19,20,23] are uncomparable with our new technique.

In this paper, an efficient homomorphic e-auction scheme is proposed. Its main idea is inspired by three observations. Firstly, although the membership proof technique in [6] is strictly limited in application area, it can efficiently implement bid validity proof in homomorphic e-auction. Secondly, although the range test technique in [21,22,24,25] has no other practical application but an inefficient e-auction design in [25], it is efficient and applicable to range test of sum of bidding selections in homomorphic e-auction. Thirdly, after these two techniques are employed in homomorphic e-auction, most exponentiations in computation are combined into some products of multiple powers, which are more efficient than the same number of separate exponentiations according to [3,2]. The new e-auction scheme employs these three optimisations and greatly improves efficiency of homomorphic e-auction.

2   Background

Application background and necessary preliminary knowledge are recalled and commented in this section.

2.1   The Membership Proof by Camenisch *et al* [6]

Camenisch *et al.* [6] propose a range proof scheme, which proves that a secret committed integer is in an interval range. A membership proof protocol is designed in [6] as a building block of the range proof scheme. In membership proof, a prover commits to a secret message s, publishes the commitment and then proves that s is in a finite set $S = \{s_1, s_2, \ldots, s_n\}$ without revealing it. The membership proof protocol in [6] employs a simple idea: the digital signature algorithm in [4] is employed and a verifier signs every message in S using his own private key and sends all the signatures to the prover, who then proves that he knows the signature on the message in the commitment.

In [6], an appropriate application is proposed for the range proof scheme, but no practical application is mentioned for the underlying membership proof protocol except for employing it as a building block in the range proof scheme, as it has the following limitations and concerns in application. Firstly, it is not universally verifiable. Secondly, it is compulsorily interactive. Thirdly, although the computational cost of a prover becomes constant (independent of n) and low, communicational cost and the computational cost on the verifier's side are both $O(n)$ and thus costly. So Camenisch *et al* do not recommend their membership proof technique as a general solution to membership proof due to the following reasons. Therefore, in most applications, the naive membership proof through zero knowledge proof of partial knowledge [9] must be employed, which proves that the committed message may be each message in the set one by one and then link the multiple proofs with OR logic. It is the only general membership proof technique although there are some other special membership proof techniques for very special environments like [7], which strictly limits the set S. However, the naive membership proof is too costly as it costs the prover and a verifier each $O(n)$ exponentiations and transfers $O(n)$ integers.

2.2   The Range Test by Peng et al [21,22,24,25]

Range test is a cryptographic operation to test whether a secret message is in an interval range without revealing any other information about it. Peng *et al* [24] propose an efficient range test protocol, which enables two parties to cooperate to test whether a secret integer is in an interval range or not. It only needs a constant cost independent of the size of the range, so is very efficient. Especially, when the range size is not very small, its advantage in efficiency is great over the previous range test schemes. However, its application to publicly verifiable multiparty computation systems like e-auction is limited. Peng and Bao [25] optimise applicability of the range test protocol in [24] and propose a practical way to employ it in e-auction with multiple auctioneers. However, the way to apply range test to e-auction in [25] is not based on homomorphic bid sealing and bid opening and thus is quite inefficient although its multiparty model is a useful improvement.

2.3   Homomorphic E-Auction

In homomorphic e-auction [13,15,8,14,1,5,16,17], Each bidder has to submit a bidding selection at every biddable price to indicate whether he is willing to pay the price. Every selection is sealed with a homomorphic bid-sealing function, so that the auctioneers can recover the sum of the selections of all the bidders at any price to detect whether enough bidders are willing to pay the price without revealing any bidding selection or their distribution. Correctness of homomorphic bid opening depends on validity of the bids. An invalid bid can compromise correctness of a homomorphic e-auction scheme, so must be detected and deleted before the bid opening phase. Homomorphic bid-sealing can employ secret sharing or additive homomorphic encryption, while the unsealing power is shared among the auctioneers. An encryption algorithm with decryption function $D()$ is additive homomorphic if $D(c_1) + D(c_2) = D(c_1c_2)$ for any ciphertexts c_1 and c_2. A typical additive homomorphic encryption algorithm with a distributed decryption function is Paillier encryption with distributed decryption proposed by Fouque $et\ al$ [10], which employs a multiplicative modulus N^2 and encryption algorithm $E(s) = g^s r^N$ where $N = pq$ and p, q are large secret primes. The decryption function is denoted as $D()$. With this encryption algorithm to seal the bids, homomorphic e-auction can be abstracted into the following protocol.

1. Suppose there are n bidders $V_1, V_2, \ldots, V_n$ and w biddable prices $p_1, p_2, \ldots, p_w$. It is required that $w < n$ and $n < N$, which is easily satisfied in any practical auction application.
2. Each bidder V_i chooses his bid p_ρ and generates his bidding vector $(s_{i,1}, s_{i,2}, \ldots, s_{i,w})$ where $s_{i,l} = 1$ for $l = \rho$ and $s_{i,l} = 0$ otherwise.
3. Paillier encryption with distributed decryption is employed to encrypt the bids where the private key is shared among the auctioneers $A_1, A_2, \ldots, A_m$. Each bidding vector $(s_{i,1}, s_{i,2}, \ldots, s_{i,w})$ is encrypted into $(c_{i,1}, c_{i,2}, \ldots, c_{i,w})$ where $c_{i,l} = g^{s_{i,l}} r_{i,l}^N$ and $r_{i,l}$ is randomly chosen from Z_N^* for $l = 1, 2, \ldots, w$.
4. Each V_i illustrates validity of his bid through proof of

$$KN\ [\ c_{i,l}^{1/N}\ ]\ \vee\ KN\ [\ (c_{i,l}/g)^{1/N}\ ]\ \text{for } l = 1, 2, \ldots, w \quad (1)$$

and
$$KN\ [\ ((\textstyle\prod_{l=1}^{w} c_{i,l})/g)^{1/N}\ ] \quad\quad\quad (2)$$

where $KN(X)$ denotes knowledge of X, (1) is proved by running the proof protocol in Figure 1 for $l = 1, 2, \ldots, w$ and (2) is a proof of knowledge of Nth root [12].

5. The sealed bids are adjusted: $c'_{i,l} = \prod_{j=l}^{w} c_{i,j}$ for $i = 1, 2, \ldots, n$ and $l = 1, 2, \ldots, w$. The final sealing result $c'_{i,l}$ contains 1 iff V_i is willing to pay p_l.
6. The auctioneers cooperate to search for the winning bids. Usually there are two searching strategies: downward search and binary search. The former starts from the highest biddable price and goes downwards, testing whether there are enough bidding selections of "1" at each price on its route until they are found at a price, which becomes the winning price. The latter follows the binary searching route among all the biddable prices, doing the same test at

each price on its route until just enough bidding selections of "1" are met at the winning price. No matter which search strategy is employed, at each price on the searching route, p_l, the auctioneers cooperate to compare $D(\prod_{i=1}^{n} c'_{i,l})$ and κ where κ is the number of items on sale and thus the number of winners. This comparison is usually implemented through a range test and its detailed implementation are different in the existing homomorphic e-auction schemes. Due to space limit, the details are not recalled here and interested readers are referred to the homomorphic e-auction papers. Note that some existing homomorphic e-auction schemes ignore the possibility $\kappa > 1$ and few of them completely maintain privacy in the range test. A detailed and completely private test will be designed in our new homomorphic e-auction scheme in Section 3. Both searching strategies can find the winning price.

- In a downward search, if $D(\prod_{i=1}^{n} c'_{i,l}) = \kappa$ is met p_l is the winning price; otherwise the search goes to the next lower price.
- In a binary search, if $D(\prod_{i=1}^{n} c'_{i,l}) < \kappa$ the search goes to the lower price; otherwise the search goes to the higher price.

The search goes on until it stops at the winning price.

7. The bidding selections at the winning price are decrypted to identify the winners. Note that the number of winners may be larger than κ and a tie may occur. Most existing homomorphic e-auction schemes do not provide detailed solution to a tie. A detailed winner identification mechanism able to handle a tie will be designed in our new homomorphic e-auction scheme in Section 3.

There are two efficiency bottlenecks in the existing homomorphic e-auction schemes. Firstly, bid validity check is too inefficient: repeating the proof and

---

1. V_i publishes
$$a_{s_{i,l}} = r^N$$

$$a_{1-s_{i,l}} = u_{1-s_{i,l}}^N / (c_{i,l}/g^{1-s_{i,l}})^{\lambda_{1-s_{i,l}}}$$

where $r \in Z_N^*$, $\lambda_{1-s_{i,l}} \in Z_N$, and $u_{1-s_{i,l}} \in Z_N^*$ are randomly chosen.

2. A verifier or a (pseudo)random function publicly generates a random integer λ in Z_N.

3. V_i publishes u_0, u_1, λ_0 and λ_1 where

$$u_{s_{i,l}} = r s_{i,l}^{\lambda_{s_{i,l}}}$$
$$\lambda_{s_{i,l}} = \lambda - \lambda_{1-s_{i,l}} \bmod Z_N$$

Public verification:

$$u_0^N = a_0 c_{i,l}^{\lambda_0}$$
$$u_1^N = a_1 (c_{i,l}/g)^{\lambda_1}$$
$$\lambda = \lambda_0 + \lambda_1 \bmod Z_N$$

Fig. 1. Repeated w times to implement proof and verification of (1)

verification protocol in Figure 1 to prove and verify (1) brings each bidder much higher a cost than bid encryption and a verifier at least $O(wn)$ exponentiations. Secondly, although binary search only goes through $\log_2 w$ prices, at each price on its route a range test in a range with a size κ is needed. So the search for the winning price is still not efficient enough, especially when privacy must be maintained or κ is large.

3   Efficient Homomorphic E-Auction

Several special characters of public proof and verification of bid validity in homomorphic e-auction are noticed as follows.

- In bid validity check in homomorphic e-auction, verifiers can be classified into two types: auctioneers and independent observers. The auctioneers are key players in e-auction and have contradictory interest against the bidders. They want to reach a dealing price as high as possible, while each bidder wants to beat the other bidders at a price as low as possible. So the auctioneers are keen to verify validity of the bids. The other verifiers are not involved in the auction application and are only independent observers, who have no interest in the e-auction. So usually they assume that the auctioneers (or at least some of them) try their best to challenge the bidders and they only act as witnesses, who do not input anything and only passively verify whether the bidders' responses match the auctioneers' challenges. Therefore, the auctioneers act as a main verifier and the other verifiers are their witnesses.
- In e-auction, usually only the bidders want to be non-interactive in bid validity check. On the other hand, the auctioneers as managers of the e-auction system should be able to interactively publish their initial challenges (in the form of signatures on the biddable prices). Actually they do not need to interact with each bidder. Instead they only need a bulletin board to publish the initial challenges.
- In e-auction, usually the auctioneers have powerful servers and high-speed communication channels, while the bidders may have low computing capability or low communication bandwidth. Moreover, there are many bidders, each of which must prove validity of his bid. So bid validity check (based on membership proof) must be repeated many times where the biddable prices are the same and the auctioneers are always the main verifier no matter which bidder is the prover. The other verifiers are only independent witnesses.

As these characters meet the application conditions of the special membership proof technique in [6], it can be employed in bid validity check in homomorphic e-auction. In our design, each bidder's bidding selections are combined into an integer, which is then proved to be in a set using the membership proof technique in [6]. The combination operation calculates a product of w powers, whose computation is more efficient than w separate exponentiations according to [3,2]. For high efficiency, binary search is adopted in the bid opening phase. The efficient range test technique in [21,22,24,25] is employed in the range test of the sum of bidding selections at the prices on the binary searching route. Therefore, the efficiency bottlenecks in homomorphic e-auction can be overcome. The homomorphic e-auction protocol with such improvements is as follows where κ same items are on sale.

1. Initial setting
   (a) Paillier encryption with distributed decryption is set up and the private key is shared among the auctioneers $A_1, A_2, \ldots, A_m$ where the parameters are the same as in Section 2.3, the message space is Z_N and the multiplicative modulus is N^2.
   (b) It is required that $n < N$, which is always satisfied with any practical n and secure N.
   (c) The digital signature algorithm in [4] is set up for the auctioneers.
   (d) A bulletin board is set up for the auctioneers and bidders to publish information.
2. Bidding phase (including bid validity check)
   (a) Each bidder V_i chooses his bid p_ρ and generates his bidding vector $(s_{i,1}, s_{i,2}, \ldots, s_{i,w})$ where $s_{i,l} = 1$ for $l = \rho$ and $s_{i,l} = 0$ otherwise. Each bidding vector $(s_{i,1}, s_{i,2}, \ldots, s_{i,w})$ is encrypted into $(c_{i,1}, c_{i,2}, \ldots, c_{i,w})$ where $c_{i,l} = g^{s_{i,l}} r_{i,l}^N$ and $r_{i,l}$ is randomly chosen from Z_N^* for $l = 1, 2, \ldots, w$.
   (b) The auctioneers cooperate to generate a set $S = \{S_1, S_2, \ldots, S_w\}$, where each S_i is a random integer in Z_N corporately chosen by all the auctioneers. S is published on the bulletin board.
   (c) The auctioneers cooperate to sign all the integers in S one by one using the digital signature algorithm in [4]. They publish the signatures $\gamma_1, \gamma_2, \ldots, \gamma_w$ on the bulletin board such that anyone can verify validity of the signatures.
   (d) The auctioneers calculate $C_i = \prod_{l=1}^{w} c_{i,l}^{S_l}$ for $i = 1, 2, \ldots, n$ and each bidder V_i proves that he knows the signature on the message in C_i by the auctioneers using the proof protocol in Figure 2 where $e()$ stands for bilinear mapping and more details can be found in [6].
3. Bid opening phase
   (a) The sealed bids are adjusted: $c'_{i,l} = \prod_{j=l}^{w} c_{i,j}$ for $i = 1, 2, \ldots, n$ and $l = 1, 2, \ldots, w - 1$ such that $c'_{i,l}$ contains 1 iff V_i is willing to pay p_l.
   (b) The auctioneers cooperate to search for the winning bid. To achieve high efficiency, binary search is employed. At each price on the searching route, p_l, the auctioneers cooperate to test whether $D(\prod_{i=1}^{n} c'_{i,l}) < \kappa$ as detailed in Figure 3. If $D(\prod_{i=1}^{n} c'_{i,l}) < \kappa$ the search goes to the lower prices; otherwise the search goes to the higher prices. The search goes along the binary searching route until it stops at the winning price.
4. Winner identification phase
   Suppose the binary search stops at price p_K. The auctioneers cooperate to decrypt all the bidding selections at p_K.

- If the number of selections of "1" at p_K is κ, no tie occurs. The bidders with selection "1" at p_K are the winners.
- If the number of selections of "1" at p_K is smaller than κ, the auctioneers cooperate to decrypt all the bidding selections at p_{K+1}. Suppose the number of selections of "1" at p_K is δ. The bidders with selection "1" at p_K and the first $\kappa - \delta$ bidders with selection "1" at p_{K+1} are the winners.
- If the number of selections of "1" at p_K is larger than κ the first κ bidders with selection "1" at p_K are the winners.

Suppose $C_i = g^\alpha \beta^N$ and $\alpha = S_\sigma$. Bidder V_i proves that α is in S as follows where $\gamma_l = g^{1/(x+S_l)}$.

1. V_i randomly picks ν in Z_N and publishes $\mu = \gamma_\sigma^\nu$. He proves that he knows $\alpha, \nu, S_\sigma, \beta$ such that $C_i = g^\alpha \beta^N$ and $\mu = g^{\nu/(x+S_\sigma)}$ as detailed in [6].
2. V_i randomly picks ϵ, τ, ω in Z_N and publishes $a = e(\mu, g)^{-\epsilon} e(g, g)^\tau$ and $d = g^\epsilon \omega^N$.
3. $c = H(\mu, C_i, a, d)$ where H is a hash function to generate (pseudo)random challenges.
4. V_i publishes $z_1 = \epsilon - cS_\sigma$, $z_2 = \tau - c\nu$ and $z_3 = \omega/\beta^c$.

Public verification:

$$d = C_i^c z_3^N g^{z_1}$$
$$a = e(\mu, y)^c e(\mu, g)^{z_1} e(g, g)^{z_2}$$

Fig. 2. Membership Proof to implement bid validity check

4   Analysis and Comparison

Security of the new homomorphic e-auction scheme is illustrated in the following.

- The new homomorphic e-auction scheme employs the same main strategy as the existing homomorphic e-auction schemes: bid sealing through additive homomorphic encryption, homomorphic bid opening, binary search for the winning bid and test of the sum of the bidding selections at each searched price. As security of such a homomorphism-exploiting strategy has been formally proved in the existing homomorphic e-auction schemes, applying it to the new homomorphic e-auction scheme is secure as well.
- The new bid validity check mechanism in the new homomorphic e-auction scheme is based on the membership proof technique by Camenisch et al [6] and a new combination mechanism to combine the bidding selections of a bidder into an integer in the set of the membership proof. The already-formally-proved security of the membership proof technique [6] and Theorem 1 guarantee that bid validity check in the new homomorphic e-auction scheme is secure.

1. $C'_l = \prod_{i=1}^{n} c'_{i,l}$.
2. – If κ is small (e.g. ≤ 3), the auctioneers runs the basic test as follows.
   (a) The auctioneers calculate

$$B_k = C'_l/g^{k-1} \text{ for } k = 1, 2, \ldots, \kappa.$$

   (b) All of them take turns to shuffle $B_1, B_2, \ldots, B_\kappa$ using a shuffling protocol (e.g. [11]), which re-encrypts and re-orders the input ciphertexts. The output of the last shuffling is $B'_1, B'_2, \ldots, B'_\kappa$.
   (c) The auctioneers test whether a zero is encrypted in $B'_1, B'_2, \ldots, B'_\kappa$ as follows.
      i. $k = 1$
      ii. For $j = 1, 2, \ldots, m$, each A_j randomly selects a non-zero integer t_j in Z_N and calculates $B'_{k,j} = B'^{t_j}_{k,j-1}$ where $B'_{k,0} = B'_k$. Each A_j publicly proves validity of his operation by proving knowledge of $\log_{B'_{k,j-1}} B'_{k,j}$ using zero knowledge proof of knowledge of discrete logarithm [26].
      iii. The auctioneers cooperate to decrypt $B'_{k,m}$. If the decryption result is zero, return $TURE$ and jump out of the loop.
      iv. If $k = \kappa$, return $FALSE$ and jump out of the loop; otherwise $k \leftarrow k + 1$ and goto Step 2(c)i to continue the loop.
      If $TURE$ is returned, a zero is encrypted in $B'_1, B'_2, \ldots, B'_\kappa$.
      If a zero is encrypted in $B'_1, B'_2, \ldots, B'_\kappa$, the basic test shows that $D(\prod_{i=1}^{n} c'_{i,l}) < \kappa$.
   – If κ is not small and the cost is high with the basic test, the range test technique (called advanced test in this paper) in [21,22,24,25] is employed to test whether $D(\prod_{i=1}^{n} c'_{i,l})$ is in $\{0, 1, \ldots, \kappa - 1\}$ more efficiently. The detailed implementation can be found in [21,22,24,25].

Fig. 3. Range test of the sum of the bidding selections at a price p_l

– The basic test of sum of bidding selections is straightforward and its security is obvious. The advanced test of sum of bidding selections in the new homomorphic e-auction scheme is based on the range test technique by Peng *et al* [21,22,24,25], whose security has been formally proved. So range test of sum of bidding selections in the new homomorphic e-auction scheme is secure.

Theorem 1. *If the bidding vector in* $(c_{i,1}, c_{i,2}, \ldots, c_{i,w})$ *is invalid, the probability that the message encrypted in* C_i *lies in* S *is negligible.*

Proof: As $(c_{i,1}, c_{i,2}, \ldots, c_{i,w})$ is invalid, there are the following two possibilities where $(s_{i,1}, s_{i,2}, \ldots, s_{i,w})$ is the bidding vector encrypted into $(c_{i,1}, c_{i,2}, \ldots, c_{i,w})$.

– There is only one non-zero integer in $s_{i,1}, s_{i,2}, \ldots, s_{i,w}$.
– There are more than one non-zero integers in $s_{i,1}, s_{i,2}, \ldots, s_{i,w}$.

In the first case, suppose $s_{i,L} \neq 0$. As $(c_{i,1}, c_{i,2}, \ldots, c_{i,w})$ is invalid, $s_{i,L} \neq 1 \bmod N$. So

$$D(C_i) = D(\prod_{l=1}^{w} c_{i,l}^{S_l}) = \sum_{l=1}^{w} s_{i,l} S_l = s_{i,L} S_L \neq S_L \bmod N$$

and the probability that

$$D(C_i) = D(\prod_{l=1}^{w} c_{i,l}^{S_l}) = \sum_{l=1}^{w} s_{i,l} S_l = s_{i,L} S_L = S_{L'} \bmod N$$
$$\text{and } L' \neq L$$
$$\text{and } 1 \leq L' \leq w$$

is $(w-1)/N$ as $S_1, S_2, \ldots, S_w$ are randomly chosen in Z_N. Therefore, the probability that

$$D(C_i) = S_{L'} \bmod N$$
$$\text{and } 1 \leq L' \leq w$$

is negligible.

In the second case, suppose only $s_{i,T_1}, s_{i,T_2}, \ldots, s_{i,T_\pi}$ are non-zero integers in $s_{i,1}, s_{i,2}, \ldots, s_{i,w}$ where $1 \leq T_1, T_2, \ldots, T_\pi \leq w$ and $\pi > 1$. Then

$$D(C_i) = D(\prod_{l=1}^{w} c_{i,l}^{S_l}) = \sum_{l=1}^{w} s_{i,l} S_l = \sum_{l=1}^{\pi} s_{i,T_l} S_{T_l} \bmod N.$$

So, as $S_1, S_2, \ldots, S_w$ are randomly chosen in Z_N the probability that

$$D(C_i) = S_{L'} \bmod N$$
$$\text{and } 1 \leq L' \leq w$$

is w/N and thus negligible.

Therefore, in both cases the probability that the message encrypted in C_i lies in S is negligible.   □

Due to space limit no further detail is given to illustrate security of the new homomorphic e-auction scheme. Interested readers can find more details in the references [13,15,8,14,1,5,16,17,6,24,25]. Our analysis focuses on efficiency comparison with the existing homomorphic e-auction schemes. The number of exponentiations needed for a bidder and an auctioneer are estimated in Table 1 to compare efficiency between the new homomorphic e-auction scheme and the existing homomorphic e-auction schemes. Suppose general e-auction application is supported and multiple identical items may be on sale. For simplicity, suppose $\kappa = 6$ and no tie occurs. For fairness of comparison, suppose Paillier encryption with distributed decryption and binary search are employed in all the schemes. Range test of the sum of bidding selections at any price should be completely private, so the basic test in Figure 3 is supposed to be employed in the existing homomorphic e-auction schemes. In the new homomorphic e-auction scheme, the most costly computation is $C_i = \prod_{l=1}^{w} c_{i,l}^{S_l}$ for $i = 1, 2, \ldots, n$, which requires an auctioneer to calculate n products of w powers. In the current security standard, N is 1024 bits long, so according to [2], each such product costs $2^{3-1}w + 1024 + 1024w/(3+1) = 260w + 1024$ multiplications, while an exponentiation with an exponent in Z_N cost $2^{3-1} + 1024 + 1024/(3+1) = 1284$ multiplications. So, cost of the n products of w powers is equivalent to $n(260w+1024)/1284$

exponentiations. It is illustrated in Table 1 that the new homomorphic e-auction scheme is more efficient for both the bidders and the auctioneers. An example is given in the table to more clearly and convincingly show the advantage of the new scheme in efficiency, where $n = 1000$ and $w = 1024$.

Table 1. Efficiency Comparison of Homomorphic E-Auction Schemes

scheme	bidder		auctioneer	
	cost	example	cost	example
secure existing	$6w$	6144	$4nw + 7\kappa \log_2 w + 3n$	4051420
new	$2w + 8$	2056	$\approx 0.2nw + 20 \log_2 w + 16n$	221000

5 Conclusion

The new homomorphic e-auction scheme is an appropriate application of the membership proof technique in [6] and the range test technique in [21,22,24,25]. Its efficiency is much higher than the existing homomorphic e-auction schemes.

References

1. Abe, M., Ohkubo, M., Suzuki, K.: 1-out-of-n signatures from a variety of keys. In: Zheng, Y. (ed.) ASIACRYPT 2002. LNCS, vol. 2501, pp. 415–432. Springer, Heidelberg (2002)
2. Avanzi, R., Cohen, H., Doche, C., Frey, G., Lange, T., Nguyen, K., Vercauteren, F.: Handbook of Elliptic and Hyperelliptic Curve Cryptography, HEHCC (2005)
3. Bellare, M., Garay, J.A., Rabin, T.: Fast batch verification for modular exponentiation and digital signatures. In: Nyberg, K. (ed.) EUROCRYPT 1998. LNCS, vol. 1403, pp. 236–250. Springer, Heidelberg (1998)
4. Boneh, D., Boyen, X.: Short signatures without random oracles. In: Cachin, C., Camenisch, J.L. (eds.) EUROCRYPT 2004. LNCS, vol. 3027, pp. 56–73. Springer, Heidelberg (2004)
5. Brandt, F.: Cryptographic protocols for secure second-price auctions (2001), http://www.brauer.in.tum.de/~brandtf/papers/cia2001.pdf
6. Camenisch, J.L., Chaabouni, R., Shelat, A.: Efficient protocols for set membership and range proofs. In: Pieprzyk, J. (ed.) ASIACRYPT 2008. LNCS, vol. 5350, pp. 234–252. Springer, Heidelberg (2008)
7. Camenisch, J., Lysyanskaya, A.: Dynamic accumulators and application to efficient revocation of anonymous credentials. In: Yung, M. (ed.) CRYPTO 2002. LNCS, vol. 2442, pp. 61–76. Springer, Heidelberg (2002)
8. Chida, K., Kobayashi, K., Morita, H.: Efficient sealed-bid auctions for massive numbers of bidders with lump comparison. In: Davida, G.I., Frankel, Y. (eds.) ISC 2001. LNCS, vol. 2200, pp. 408–419. Springer, Heidelberg (2001)
9. Cramer, R., Damgård, I., Schoenmakers, B.: Proofs of partial knowledge and simplified design of witness hiding protocols. In: Desmedt, Y.G. (ed.) CRYPTO 1994. LNCS, vol. 839, pp. 174–187. Springer, Heidelberg (1994)

10. Fouque, P., Poupard, G., Stern, J.: Sharing decryption in the context of voting or lotteries. In: Frankel, Y. (ed.) FC 2000. LNCS, vol. 1962, pp. 90–104. Springer, Heidelberg (2001)
11. Groth, J., Lu, S.: Verifiable shuffle of large size ciphertexts. In: Okamoto, T., Wang, X. (eds.) PKC 2007. LNCS, vol. 4450, pp. 377–392. Springer, Heidelberg (2007)
12. Guillou, L., Quisquater, J.: A "paradoxical" identity-based signature scheme resulting from zero-knowledge. In: Goldwasser, S. (ed.) CRYPTO 1988. LNCS, vol. 403, pp. 216–231. Springer, Heidelberg (1990)
13. Kikuchi, H., Harkavy, M., Tygar, J.: Multi-round anonymous auction. In: IEEE Workshop on Dependable and Real-Time E-Commerce Systems '98, pp. 62–69 (1998)
14. Kikuchi, H. (m+1)st-price auction. In: Syverson, P.F. (ed.) FC 2001. LNCS, vol. 2339, pp. 291–298. Springer, Heidelberg (2002)
15. Kikuchi, H., Hotta, S., Abe, K., Nakanishi, S.: Distributed auction servers resolving winner and winning bid without revealing privacy of bids. In: NGITA '00, pp. 307–312 (2000)
16. Omote, K., Miyaji, A.: A second-price sealed-bid auction with the discriminant of the p-th root. In: Blaze, M. (ed.) FC 2002. LNCS, vol. 2357, pp. 57–71. Springer, Heidelberg (2003)
17. Peng, K., Boyd, C., Dawson, E., Viswanathan, K.: Robust, privacy protecting and publicly verifiable sealed-bid auction. In: Deng, R.H., Qing, S., Bao, F., Zhou, J. (eds.) ICICS 2002. LNCS, vol. 2513, pp. 147–159. Springer, Heidelberg (2002)
18. Peng, K., Boyd, C., Dawson, E.: A multiplicative homomorphic sealed-bid auction based on Goldwasser-Micali encryption. In: Zhou, J., López, J., Deng, R.H., Bao, F. (eds.) ISC 2005. LNCS, vol. 3650, pp. 374–388. Springer, Heidelberg (2005)
19. Peng, K., Boyd, C., Dawson, E.: Optimization of electronic first-bid sealed-bid auction based on homomorphic secret sharing. In: Dawson, E., Vaudenay, S. (eds.) Mycrypt 2005. LNCS, vol. 3715, pp. 84–98. Springer, Heidelberg (2005)
20. Peng, K., Boyd, C., Dawson, E.: Batch verification of validity of bids in homomorphic e-auction. Computer Communications 29, 2798–2805 (2006)
21. Peng, K., Boyd, C., Dawson, E., Okamoto, E.: A novel range test. In: Batten, L.M., Safavi-Naini, R. (eds.) ACISP 2006. LNCS, vol. 4058, pp. 247–258. Springer, Heidelberg (2006)
22. Peng, K., Dawson, E.: Range test secure in the active adversary model. In: ACM International Conference Proceeding Series, AISW2007, vol. 249, pp. 159–162 (2007)
23. Peng, K., Dawson, E.: Efficient bid validity check in elGamal-based sealed-bid E-auction. In: Dawson, E., Wong, D.S. (eds.) ISPEC 2007. LNCS, vol. 4464, pp. 209–224. Springer, Heidelberg (2007)
24. Peng, K., Bao, F., Dawson, E.: Correct, private, flexible and efficient range test. Journal of Researchand Practice in Information Technology 40(4), 275–291 (2008)
25. Peng, K., Bao, F.: Practicalization of a range test and its application to e-auction. In: EuroPKI '09 (2009)
26. Schnorr, C.: Efficient signature generation by smart cards. Journal of Cryptology 4, 161–174 (1991)

Author Index

Printing: Mercedes-Druck, Berlin
Binding: Stein + Lehmann, Berlin